Capitalism
and
Human Obsolescence

Capitalism
and
Human Obsolescence

Corporate Control versus
Individual Survival
in Rural America

by JOHN A. YOUNG and JAN M. NEWTON

LandMark Studies
ALLANHELD, OSMUN **Montclair** **UNIVERSE BOOKS** **New York**

ALLANHELD, OSMUN & CO. PUBLISHERS, INC.
19 Brunswick Road, Montclair, New Jersey 07042

Published in the United States of America in 1980
by Allanheld, Osmun & Co. and by Universe Books
381 Park Avenue South, New York, New York 10016
Distribution: Universe Books

Library of Congress Cataloging in Publication Data

Young, John, 1941 (Mar. 16)-
  Capitalism and human obsolescence.

  Bibliography: p.
  1. Plant shutdowns—United States.   2. United
States—Rural conditions.   3. Capitalism.
I. Newton, Jan, 1941-   joint author.   II. Title.
HD5853.2.U5Y68   330.9'73   78-71099
ISBN 0-916672-22-0

Printed in the United States of America

Contents

TABLES

Foreword

The economic domination of the large-scale capitalist enterprise in the United States is based as much on what Antonio Gramsci called "ideological hegemony" as on the cold discipline of the labor market and outright physical coercion. Ideological hegemony consists of beliefs and cultural traditions inculcated by schools, churches, family, state, and community which cultivate working class submission to capitalist rule. In Gramscian terms, popular consensus or voluntary acquiescence is the *sine qua non* of ideological hegemony. Marxists who take Gramsci's theory seriously oblige themselves to engage in ideological struggle against capitalist hegemony, as well as in traditional economic and political struggles. Ideological struggles range from straightforward "critiques of everyday life," such as those which the women's movement has advanced with some success, to theoretical critiques of bourgeois legitimation systems which, when successful, "explode bourgeois truths" (to use Claus Offe's expression). In the last analysis however ideological hegemony is overcome through political practice. The idea that there can be a good society based on slave labor cannot be destroyed theoretically until the slaveowning class itself is destroyed practically. But first it is required that the slaves themselves have no illusion that slavery can exist in a good society. Marxists argue that more or less the same idea applies to wage slavery in the capitalist mode of production. In the course of economic and political struggle the working class disabuses itself of illusions about the real character of capitalist social relationships. Marxist intellectuals are believed to play an important part in this process of undermining capitalist ideology, but its central illusions—those of individualism and the sanctity of private property—disappear when the capitalist class itself disappears, not before.

In *Capitalism and Human Obsolescence*, John Young and Jan Newton in many ways adhere to a Gramscian standard of theoretical critique. In this series of case studies of economic underdevelopment, where the communities investigated depend on one industry and suffer displacement of workers and small producers, the reader will find two distinct yet related levels of argumentation. The first level is straightforward economic analysis of technology, production, employment, profits, etc. in the Oregon lumber industry, Hawaiian plantation agriculture, copper mining industry in Arizona, small farming in California, and small business in a declining region of Washington State. These studies document the ruthless exploitation of land, timber, mineral resources, and last but not least, human beings. Drawing on official statistics, interviews, and other sources, the authors demonstrate that economic hardship generally and unemployment, small business bankruptcy, etc. in particular are explicable only in terms of the profit hunger and economic and political power of the large-scale capitalist enterprise and the capitalist system generally. These studies document the fact that large corporations are not satisfied merely to organize profitable operations in the primary producing sector; big capital always seeks the highest profits possible and if these can be found elsewhere mines, land, and people will be abandoned. Natural resources and people will be sacrificed to capital's obsession with maximum profits and "accumulation without limit." Owing primarily to the "frontier" character of the industries and regions studied— that is, thanks to the absence of a strong organized working class the corporations more or less get their own way. Weak union locals, col- laborationist International unions, and powerless local governments are no match for large-scale capital. Nor are the small farmers and businessmen who exemplify classic "self-exploitation" in their struggle for economic survival, especially when confronted by large-scale capitalist power and state agencies dominated or influenced by the big corporations. In short, the authors convincingly demonstrate that economic insecurity, unemployment, poverty, etc. are systemically produced by capitalism—the corporations' bottom line allows no room for human development and human freedom.

The importance of these studies, however, goes beyond the economic analyses of supply, demand, and profitability conditions in the industries and regions chosen for investigation. These studies are "Gramscian" in the sense that there is a second and deeper level of argumentation pertaining to capitalist ideology. The authors show that in almost every case along with economic hardship and poverty, the corporations, abetted by state agencies, systemically generate false explanations of business failure, unemployment, and so on. The discrepancy between the economic reality and the conscious- ness of this reality by the victimized workers and small producers is expecially poignant in "frontier" economies where ideologies of hard work, individual initiative, self-help, and the like have been hegemonic from the beginning. Nativism and frontier extremism are seen as defenses against rural pro- letarianization defined as being displaced and feeling unneeded. The authors show that the false beliefs that working people adopt, which derive from idealized visions of the past, are in fact necessary for their own emotional survival and well-being. The range of deceptions and self-deceptions runs from a strong sense of selfhood and faith in the efficacy of hard work and initiative to rather grotesque images of "supercowboy" and "superlogger" which function to conceal the powerlessness of ordinary people without a sense of collective solidarity and power. Although permitting workers and small producers to retain some shred of dignity, these beliefs and the almost angry persistence with which they are held totally obscure the real causes of economic and social misfortune. This is especially true of the various "blame the victim" ideologies which function with particular viciousness in the cases the authors describe.

It needs to be stressed that the false beliefs concerning economic hardship do not merely turn reality upside down. They also reflect reality; they are reality's mirror-image as well. This proposition can be demonstrated by citing two of the authors' case studies. The first describes the closing of a copper mine in Arizona; the second describes the long-term decline of a small county in Washington. In both cases the authors state or imply that the working class itself had an important albeit unconscious and perhaps unseen role in the decisions of capitalist enterprises to abandon the regions and make the people living there "obsolete." The main motive for closing the copper mine and expanding operations elsewhere was to purge the work force both of younger workers with relatively high voluntary turnover rates and older workers who were effectively "burned out." The company claimed that the real reason for the mine closure was that the mine itself was played-out. But the authors document with first-hand evidence that this was a gross fabrication. In a roughly similar case, in the farming region in Washington State, worker resistance in the form of strike action "forced" capital to abandon the region for a more congenial location. Careful readers will find analogous situations in nearly all the case studies. The only conclusion which can be plausibly drawn from these studies is that when workers become too "uppity" or old and tired or well-paid they become useless for capitalist exploitation. Hence, in fact collective action and struggle constitute living critiques of the individualist ideologies essential for capitalism's smooth operation and survival. At the same time, collective action and even individual resistence in the form of absenteeism constitute negative symbols for capitalist corporations which in many cases subsequently abandon the workers and force them back in fact on their individual resources. This is an example of capitalism's ultimate mystification which reflects and distorts (or refracts) reality simultaneously.

I confess to some excitement with the conclusions which the authors draw from their exemplary synthesis of economic and critical theoretical analysis. Again and again we are reminded that the real issue everywhere is economic but especially political power. These studies document many cases of direct corporate power over governments and state agencies as well as the indirect power which big capital exercises through its ability to refuse to invest in new equipment, employ workers, cooperate with government agencies seeking environmental balance, and so on. The authors argue that the real solution to the problems capitalism engenders lies in the political realm, in their words, the transformation of "dependency" relationships into "adversary" relationships. Workers, small producers, and ordinary people must have political power; otherwise victimization and self-victimization appear by all accounts to be inevitable. No Marxist could possibly disagree with this conclusion, and especially with the authors' judgment, with which I concur, that "Americans are saying that they are ready for a life which is more democratic." For this reader, the exciting ideas concern the authors' emphasis on not only the need for economic alternatives but also on the need to acquire popular control over non-elective, appointed state agencies (such as those regulating lumbering in

Oregon; organizing manpower retraining and community planning in Hawaii; and Federal agencies dealing with agriculture and small business regulation and loans). I heartily agree with their view that "if democratization of appointed bodies, bureaucracies, and officials of the state is combined with the demands of grassroots political organizations for accountability of elected officials to their constituencies, we can bring about a decline in the influence of monied special interests." However, I would like to have seen it emphasized that the struggle for a democratic state must extend democracy into hitherto-fore undemocratic, bureaucratically organized everyday "working activities" of the state.

The great strength of these studies is the authors' documentation of workers' and small businessmen's deeply held and grossly idealized views of what the frontier was really like and how these views affect their lives. The human beings described in this book apparently at heart want their own businesses and to be left alone. For many, a subsistence way of life and a social and psychological "turning inward" are preferable to collective organization and political struggle. Yet the yearning for democracy remains; the desire for "really free enterprise" is not empty emotional rhetoric. Far be it for someone like myself, an outsider, to judge the political and social realities of these regions which in reality have long ago ceased to be frontiers in any real sense of the word. Perhaps it is true that the word "socialism" is anathema to most of the workers interviewed and studied; perhaps the authors have hit on at once a realistic and progressive strategy with their emphasis on the promotion of the development of "really free enterprise" alternative to the corporate economy in the frontier regions and small towns. From my point of view, however, it is open to question whether their recommendations are related to any feature inherent in capitalism as such or merely to special features of the rural political economies which they chose to investigate. The authors imply that the ideological legacy of the frontier might be expected to affect the reactions of urban workers and small producers in similar fashion. Whatever the case, the answers the authors supply to the big question they raise at the beginning of the book, "why don't workers and small producers fight back when they are displaced and abandoned by big capital?" are clear and lucid and politically very helpful.

James O'Connor
November, 1979

University of California
Santa Cruz, Cal.

Preface

This book originated from a five-state regional research project sponsored by the Western Rural Development Center at Oregon State University. Those most familiar with the project refer to it by its descriptive title, the "Social Marginalization Project." The organization of the project was unique in its reliance upon cooperation across geographical, disciplinary, and administrative boundaries. The responsibility for research design, data collection, and analysis was shared by the authors with agricultural economists, sociologists, and anthropologists at five land-grant institutions in the western United States. Harland I. Padfield, director of the Western Rural Development Center from July 1972 through June 1977, acted as the administrator of the project, although some administrative prerogatives were exercised locally by the directors of agricultural experiment stations at participating universities. The authors, as members of the Western Rural Development Center staff, were given the special charge of coordinating the scientific aspects of the work, synthesizing the results, and writing a final report. This book serves as the final report. From the authors' standpoint, however, it represents much more, for it is based on our own analysis of the data, our own theoretical interests, and our insights into the workings of the American social and economic system.

We benefited greatly from our association with other scientists and field workers with whom we exchanged views frequently and from whom we received valuable comments on the work. Four of five state project leaders spent six months or more in close association with us at the Western Rural Development Center, and the authors made a number of site visits to each state during the course of the research. In addition, several regional project meetings were held for the purpose of comparing notes and standardizing procedures. Although the diversity of types of people studied and different data available made complete uniformity of method impossible, the topical focus of the research on the consequences of economic decline and loss of employment in rural communities was maintained fairly well intact. Because of some understandably divergent interests among state project leaders, however, not all of the work that was done is summarized or mentioned in this book. Neither are its interpretations intended to represent those of other scientists, field workers, and reviewers who helped us in our work. The authors take full responsibility for the views expressed here.

A variety of funding sources made the Social Marginalization Project possible. Funds administered directly through the Western Rural Development Center were provided by Grant Nos. 216-15-98, 416-15-75, 316-15-95,

516-15-44, 616-15-58, and 701-15-77 from the Cooperative State Research Service, USDA. A small amount of supplemental funding was provided by Grant No. GA SS 7404 from the Rockefeller Foundation. Supplemental funds were also obtained from the Agricultural Experiment Station at the University of Arizona, the University of California Agricultural Experiment Station (Project H–3110), the Hawaii Agricultural Experiment Station (Project No. 449), the Oregon Agricultural Experiment Station (Project No. 54), and the Washington State Agricultural Experiment Station (Project No. 1974).

Our most heartfelt thanks go to Harland I. Padfield, former director of the Western Rural Development Center, for his unwavering commitment to and support of the effort that went into research and writing. It was not always certain that funding would be continued, and it was largely because of his persistence that the project was allowed to run its course. We are equally appreciative of his role as a scholar and scientist in helping to initiate the research, allowing us to draw upon his experience, and providing us with intellectual stimulation as the project progressed. We also thank Russell Youmans, who became director of the Western Rural Development Center in July 1977 and continued to give us necessary support through the last three months of the project. State project leaders whom we thank for their cooperation are Robert N. Anderson, University of Hawaii; Paul W. Barkley, Washington State University; William E. Martin, University of Arizona; Jerry A. Moles, University of California at Davis; and Joe B. Stevens, Oregon State University. Harry Ayer and Edwin Carpenter of the University of Arizona also participated in the project as social scientists. We are very grateful to Sheila Forman, who not only acted as a special consultant to the project but also was gracious enough to share part of her own research on Molokai. Field workers were assigned a difficult task and are to be commended for their willingness and dedication. It is they who made it possible for us to see the world through the eyes of our respondents. Field workers include Dana Deeds in Arizona; Jeanette A. Blomberg, Thomas F. Love, and Judith Thompson in California; Rebecca Pestaño in Hawaii; William W. Pierson in Oregon; and Joanne Buteau in Washington. We owe Richard F. Rankin a special debt of gratitude for his very professional and competent handling of computer data-processing chores. His task was made especially burdensome because we were continually working back and forth between a number of divergent sets of data.

Valuable comments on a preliminary version of this book were received from several persons who were not formally associated with the project. In this regard, we thank Robert R. Alvarez, James W. Angresano, Seth Schein, Courtland L. Smith, and David Wellman.

Our deep appreciation goes to Jonathan Walker, who took time off from running a recall campaign and organizing cooperatives and a union of forestry workers to help us write several key parts of the final chapter. His first-hand knowledge proved invaluable.

Capitalism
and
Human Obsolescence

1 Bearing the Capitalists' Burden

Conflict over Natural Resources in the West

On 24 May 1977 a convoy of 300 log trucks rolled into our nation's capital. The loggers had driven their big rigs from the Pacific to the Atlantic, arriving in Washington, D.C., with a set of demands and a present for President Jimmy Carter. They carried with them a three-ton peanut carved from a giant redwood tree. The peanut, the loggers, and their big trucks were indeed a traffic stopper on the streets of the capital. The delegation included participants from another demonstration, involving more than 800 trucks that had rumbled, honked, and snaked their way through Eugene, Oregon, ten days earlier. The Oregon delegation was joined by a group of California loggers who had recently staged their own boisterous rally in San Francisco. It was the omnibus wilderness-area acts, at that time under consideration by Congress, that brought the loggers out of the woods and into the streets of Washington. The demonstrating loggers displayed a striking degree of solidarity and grit against unwanted legislation that threatened to take vast numbers of trees forever out of saw's reach by consigning them to new wilderness areas.

Eugene and San Francisco provided preliminary staging areas for the battle that is shaping up, between environmentalists and "commercial interests," over timber resources in the West. Both cities were the site of House subcommittee hearings on HR 3454, the Endangered Wilderness Act. The hearings brought out vocal and well-organized partisans on both sides of the issue. In Oregon the loggers even held their own "hearings" at a county fairgrounds ten blocks away from where the subcommittee and its audience gathered. Many loggers, mill workers, and timber company representatives exhibited mutual support at both meetings; a large green and white button identified them and their rallying call: "Jobs First." Meanwhile, outside the building where the official hearings were in progress, the families of wood-products workers carried placards and joined in a noisy but orderly demonstration. In their midst was a large wooden bin filled with metal lunch pails and hard hats. "Out to lunch . . . permanently," a sign announced.

The message contained an unintended irony, for it seemed to some observers that the demonstrators were indeed "out to lunch." Why else would they so enthusiastically support a position that was in the timber companies' interests, but not so clearly in their own? Many of the stands of timber at issue in the struggle over wilderness acreage are located on land so steep and inaccessible that they will have to be logged by helicopter, a technique requiring relatively little labor. Even the industry's estimate of the number of jobs at stake is surprisingly small: 75 wood-products jobs a year would be

1

provided by the logging of French Pete Creek Valley, one of the four areas in Oregon targeted for wilderness classification in the congressional bills.

In fact, several factors affect the number of wood-products jobs far more than the number of trees available for harvest. For example, economic analysts for the International Woodworkers of America calculate that the export of logs, from the Pacific Northwest and northern California to Japan, cost the area 11,400 sawmill and planer-mill jobs in 1976. The effect of log exports combined with the effect of mechanization enabled one Weyerhaeuser mill in North Bend, Oregon, to reduce its work force from more than 400 in 1972 to fewer than 200 in 1977. Finally, according to State Forestry Department figures, 2 million acres of Oregon forest land presently need to be replanted (Eugene *Register-Guard*, July 11, 1977: 11A). Reforestation of this land—a labor-intensive activity—could provide more jobs than harvesting the 658,359 acres of timberland proposed for wilderness.

Why aren't loggers and their families out demonstrating for increased reforestation, a slower rate of mechanization, and curtailed log exports? How can this apparent irony be explained? Moreover, why do ordinary people often seem to act in a way that serves not their own interests but rather those of large corporations? That, in part, is what this book is about. But it is important to know how we came to ask ourselves these questions, for they are not the ones with which we began our research. To explain how we arrived here requires that we go back to the beginning and retrace a five-year odyssey.[1]

Declining Rural Communities

The social marginalization research project began with a theory that economic deterioration in rural[2] communities was contributing to urban poverty and unemployment in America. One goal of the project was to document and explain the nature of this relationship between rural and urban areas by monitoring adaptations to economic decline in selected rural communities. It was expected that one adaptation would be the migration of unemployed rural people to more populous areas. The research design included methods for following such émigrés and observing their fate in urban communities.

In many places in the western United States it is possible to observe both individual and community adaptations to economic decline. The primary criteria used in choosing five sites for the present study were community dependence upon one industry and the imminent displacement of workers and small producers from their jobs. The people and settings selected include wood-products workers in several counties in Oregon; miners in Bisbee, Arizona; pineapple workers in Molokai, Hawaii; small farmers in Colusa County, California; and shopkeepers in Lincoln County, Washington.

Several reasons exist for believing that many rural people who migrate to urban areas will end up among the ranks of the unemployed and poor. First, rural residents have historically responded to declining opportunities in the countryside by "voting with their feet," i.e., moving to more populous areas where jobs are thought to be abundant. Migration from country to city does not necessarily produce jobs, however. While urban labor markets may be more robust in many ways than rural ones, this does not necessarily mean that rural men and women will readily find employment. In fact, they are likely to experience considerable difficulty. The economies of rural communities are typically dominated by one industry, usually agriculture, mining, lumbering, fishing, or sometimes light manufacturing. Thus rural people commonly experience a very limited work setting. For example, men sometimes spend their lives at the same job with the same company, as have their fathers and grandfathers before them. Such workers may be quite skilled, as is the case with the copper miners in Arizona; but their skills (rock blasting, drilling, mucking) are not readily transferred to industrial jobs in an urban setting.

Working in a rural setting is unique in still other ways. It is not uncommon for co-workers also to be neighbors and relatives, a circumstance that blurs the distinction between public (work) life and private (home) life. The two domains overlap constantly, as when eggs, milk, or other home-produced goods are brought to work to sell or exchange among co-workers. A sense of community in the work place results from such activities. This is not to argue that a sense of community among urban workers does not exist, but rather that it is a different sort in the rural context. The difference is shaped both by the relationship between home life and work life and by the fact that the life of the community is dominated by the presence of a single important industry. A worker socialized in a rural setting may therefore find compartmentalization of his work life in an urban setting extremely disorienting and distasteful.

Rural people who move to the city often find themselves decidedly worse off. If urban labor markets prove difficult to penetrate for rural loggers, miners, or mill workers, they are left with few familiar resources upon which to rely. Resources previously used to combat hard times will have been left behind: gardens, livestock, reciprocal arrangements for sharing labor, knowledge, skills, and commodities, and the assistance and support of friends and relatives. Failure to find work in the city may lead ultimately to financial dependence on the state rather than on the local community, including one's friends and relatives. Hence we viewed the growing urban problems of poverty, welfare dependence, and unemployment as at least partly related to the continuing stagnation of rural communities and the resulting migration to cities.

This initial goal of the study—to describe and analyze the nature of the relationship between rural economic decline and urban poverty and unemployment—was thwarted. Despite the fact that all five research sites underwent the anticipated economic decline, involving extreme hardship for residents, few of the affected families left their communities. During the several years of field research in each site, there was no significant exodus to be monitored.

Another historic but less common response to rural economic decline is to "stay put" and develop a way of life that allows for a lower standard of living and provides ways of coping with economic insecurity. For example, some coal miners and their families stayed in Southern Appalachia during the

1950s, even though the demand for their labor fell by about 45 percent. The grim, hard times that followed have been amply documented in many books, including Harry Caudill's *Night Comes to the Cumberlands* (1963) and Kathy Kahn's *Hillbilly Women* (1973). What is clear from these accounts is that it is sometimes virtually impossible to force people to leave a dying community against their will, since human resourcefulness provides the means to survive, even in the absence of income from employment.

What has not been analyzed in these types of situations is the longer-term adaptation that grows out of immediate survival strategies. This became the subsequent focus of our research. One finding was that adult workers in families that remained in declining rural communities and subsisted through prolonged unemployment became *increasingly* unemployable. This may be either a labor demand or labor supply problem, or both. On the demand side, employers appear to discriminate against people who have "unstable" work histories or a long, recent period of unemployment (Young and Stevens, 1976). It is not clear whether this discrimination is based on the assumption that enforced leisure dulls the work ethic or that skills become rusty with disuse. In any case, it is demonstrable that workers' chances of employment decline when or if they experience repeated or prolonged unemployment.

On the supply side, we found that, with time, people who are unemployed begin to feel less confident about their ability to find work and question whether jobs actually exist for them. This is the essence of what economists call the "discouraged worker" phenomenon: As people lose hope of finding a job, they stop looking and drop out of the labor force. When significant numbers of people stop looking for work, economists note that the rate of labor-force participation declines. These rates tend to be relatively lower in rural areas than in urban ones, and it is easy to imagine why rural workers are easily discouraged: In a typically stagnant community there are precious few jobs to be had.

The ongoing process of field research continued to alter our perceptions and to modify the research questions. Each site produced some unexpected situation (for example, the unions involved did nothing to delay or challenge corporate decisions to move production elsewhere). We were also forced to see the research problem in much broader terms. Three new questions emerged: (1) If people, individually and in communities, were experiencing and adapting to a deterioration of their way of life, what had caused the decline? (2) If a cause could be identified, what were people doing about it? (3) If communities were not mobilizing to counter the threat to their economic existence, why not? Simply put, these are the questions this book addresses and attempts to answer.

American Frontier Extremism: A Response to Economic Decline

We found that each community's economic deterioration had been set in motion by the actions or decisions of large economic units (usually, but not always, large corporations) that operated in or near the community. In some cases, like Molokai and Bisbee, the decision was precipitous: Dole and Phelps-Dodge, respectively, shut down their production facilities and moved to new locations where there was assurance of higher profits. In Oregon the decline in logging and mill jobs has been more gradual, beginning in the early 1960s and continuing to the present. But here, too, the decline has been caused by corporate decisions designed to increase profits; for example, shipping unprocessed logs to Japan, where higher prices can be obtained, or mechanizing various aspects of production in the woods and mills. In Colusa County, California, and Lincoln County, Washington, large farms are the units that have undermined the basic economic health of the community. The increasing complexity and scale of farming is driving both small family farms and local shopkeepers out of business. In this regard, the basic commonality existing between all five sites is the exploitative relationship between the corporation or large producer that dominates the local economy and a disaffected group of laborers, small-scale farmers, or shopkeepers. By "exploitation" we mean a circumstance in which one group is systematically benefited at the expense of the other. Obviously such a relationship is not possible unless one party is more powerful than the other. A central theme of the following chapters is to describe and analyze the exploitation of people and resources in the communities studied.

The answer to the second question is more complex. There were two apparently contradictory elements in people's responses to the economic decline of their communities. On one hand, there was a generally expressed level of ideological support for the prevailing economic order. On the other, there was an expressed hostility toward large corporations and particular financial institutions. Further elaboration will show that these simultaneously held views are, in fact, not contradictory. It will first be necessary to document more concretely the content of these views. We will begin by describing the nature of expressed ideological support for the American economic system.

The field notes in all sites were developed independently of one another, and yet all contain instances of people making supportive or sympathetic statements about a company, or a group of producers, whose actions were the source of their own economic malaise. In one instance, an unemployed Oregon mill worker who had been caught in plant-wide layoffs by Georgia Pacific said that he felt the company was "justified in laying men off." As he explained it, "Georgia Pacific is a growth company and even though they may put men out of work in one area they are always hiring men in another area." When the worker was asked about the company's practice of replacing senior employees with inexperienced, younger men, he felt that was also justified: "If a company is going to grow and make money, it has to save money wherever it can. This is a lot like my own family. We have to try to save money by cutting costs. It is smart management." This worker maintained support for the company even though he had been laid off several times and had been without work for many months following the last layoff; and he continually expressed frustration and anxiety about his job insecurity.

Such statements were often made as a more general affirmation of the

"American way" of doing things, as in another mill worker's observation that "the free-enterprise system is good because it makes you really work harder." Working harder was indeed what he was doing: He often worked seven days a week to hold down two jobs—working swing shift at a plywood mill and working part-time at a cemetery. However, his family was barely making ends meet, and debts were accumulating at a rapid rate. The circumstances of his own life make his statement seem fundamentally misguided.

In the survey responses and field notes, there were many instances of expressed empathy with or approval of the very economic institutions that seemed to be illegitimately exploiting human and natural resources in these rural communities. We came to the conclusion that all such views represent a profile of beliefs that we chose to call a "frontier ideology." To understand this ideology is to understand the seemingly contradictory statements that were recorded in the field. How then are we to define frontier ideology? Basically this concept refers to traditional and somewhat anachronistic values of hard work, being close to the land, personal independence, and individual initiative. In the very midst of resource depletion and economic decay, there is also an intense dedication to free enterprise, i.e., economic growth and what economists call laissez-faire capitalism. As Padfield (in press) has noted, this ideological position constitutes a refusal to recognize destructive forces impinging upon the community—like the denial of death in a dying patient. Hence, the irony exists that community residents, in feeling that their welfare is somehow dependent on the welfare of capitalist benefactors, affirm the necessity and propriety of the very actions taken by large corporations and economic units that are destructive to themselves and their communities.

This contradiction between belief and reality (commonly referred to as cognitive dissonance by psychologists) has two consequences. On one hand, rigid belief in the *symbols* of a now decaying economic order impairs realistic adjustment to a deteriorating situation. On the other hand, such rigid belief has high utility in serving to suppress psychological tensions that develop in the face of economic insecurity and to preserve pride in one's occupational and social identity (Padfield, in press).

Rural communities, such as those described in this book, regale the passerby with many flamboyant displays of the potency and affluence of their ancestors and predecessors. "Heldorado Days," a community celebration in Tombstone, Arizona, for example, re-creates the glory of an 1880 silver-mining community. Bumper stickers, letters to the editor, and tavern conversations contain many depictions of rural archetypes: the super-cowboy ("You're Damn Right I'm a Cowboy!), the super-logger ("Sierra Club, Kiss My Axe," or "Hike to Hell"), the super country patriot ("Register Communists, Not Firearms"). Evocation of the latter hero-type sometimes takes other than symbolic form. For example, local political action may be directed against intrusive, threatening elements. Informal as well as formal vigilante groups, such as the "Minute Men" and the "Posse Comitatus," sometimes take direct action against individuals and institutions that symbolize ideological deviance. They also take action against what they frequently call "conspiracies" which are reported almost weekly in rural newspapers. It seemed to us that these phenomena, and the frontier ideology from which they arise, could be interpreted as manifestations of a quest for the power and identity of a bygone era—a kind of American frontier extremism—a version of what anthropologists call "nativism," or, alternatively, a contemporary expression of what political observers identified in the past as rural populism.

Padfield (in press) has suggested that both the symbolism and the direct political action constitute an impulse to what might be called modern rural proletarianism.

The true hallmark of the proletarian, Toynbee warns us, is neither poverty nor humble birth, but a consciousness—and the resentment which this consciousness inspires—of being disinherited from his ancestral place in society and being unwanted in a community which is his rightful home; and this subjective proletarianism is not incompatible with the possession of material assets. (Nisbet, 1969 : 21, in Padfield, in press)

The awareness of being disinherited and unwanted is more than a subjective state, however. It has a material basis in these people's status as obsolete workers and entrepreneurs: They are no longer needed, no matter how useful they may still feel themselves to be.

Whether they are small-scale farmers, shopkeepers, or workers, rural people are becoming proletarianized in at least one of two ways. First, as the following chapters demonstrate, they are extremely vulnerable to the increasing concentration of capital and the movement of large companies. As one consequence rural people find that they have been made obsolete in the process of production. Perhaps equally important, they are culturally out of date—a phenomenon made more threatening by the new wave of urban immigrants to rural communities.[3] The political ideology of the newcomers invalidates the frontier ethic of rural inhabitants and puts them on the defensive. For example, the ecologically conscious posture of ex-urbanites often conflicts with the desire of loggers or miners to permit further resource exploitation, which they see as necessary for renewed economic growth; and hard-working Filipinos on Molokai resent a recent invasion of "lazy hippies" into their community. Older residents may be opposed to change for sentimental reasons. In one Lincoln County town, for example, older citizens successfully opposed civic-improvement projects and downtown renovation, saying: "If we tore those old buildings down, the wind would blow through town." Value conflict in agricultural settings may develop because rural people wish to preserve existing agricultural land or oppose pollution of the land with chemicals and fertilizers. Whatever the specific terms of the conflict, it is clear that rural people, living in and adapting to economic decline, perceive newcomers as competitors for the economic opportunities that still exist or which may develop as a result of increased population. In addition, urban to rural migration implies competition for the personal use of the land, space, air, and water for recreational and other purposes.

Accounts of symbolic bravura, vigilantism, and apparent support for the prevailing economic order capture only one aspect of the complex dialectic that we found in the course of field study. As noted earlier, there was also a strong and pervasive expression of sentiment that in some respects seemed incompatible with frontier ideology. It was typified by statements of resentment against large corporations and large farms, accompanied by cynicism about their motives. For example, shopkeepers in faltering Lincoln County, Washington, expressed general approval of small towns and rural schools as an ideal type, but they registered disillusionment and bitterness about the future of their *own* communities. They identified large farms and "big business" as the executioners in the slow death of the county's three small towns. As will be seen shortly, copper miners and townspeople in Bisbee, Arizona, were so cynical about the mine closure that city officials could not arouse any citizen interest in alternative economic development plans: "Phelps-Dodge will be back, they're just closing down temporarily for a tax break." In some instances, the communities even organized to fight back. The Filipino community of plantation workers in Molokai, Hawaii, organized an effective resistance to the plans by their corporate landlord to evict several families.

In our more aggregate data, too, there were indications of disaffection with some basic aspects of corporate power. When we surveyed a group of Oregon mill workers who were laid off in the 1974 recession, 60 percent disagreed with the statement that "a mill is justified in having periodic layoffs in order to make a better profit." Many of these same workers subverted their employer's interests, using direct yet subtle means. Their job turnover, for example, was very high, with some of the younger workers moving among as many as five mills in a year. In management's view, such behavior constitutes a "poor attitude toward work" or an indication of unreliability or instability. However, it is also possible to view high quit rates as a concrete reaction to the alienation from work under monopoly capitalism, wherein large, powerful, and self-serving corporations control the conditions of work and rob workers of their individual autonomy. James O'Connor (1975:328) suggests that both absenteeism and quitting are forms of worker struggle.

Absenteeism requires individualist self-organization in the form of breaking an implicit agreement with the boss to remain on the job for a particular time and using laborpower for something else (or resting it). Quitting also requires individual self-organization because normally workers work less hard or well once they have decided to quit (their mind is on their new job). . . . When workers quit or absent themselves from work during the production period, the normal result is a reduction in production and in profits.

The Manpower Administration of the U.S. Department of Labor notes that absenteeism and job turnover are "costly to employers in loss of production, forced substitution of untrained workers, increased insurance rates, replacement training of standby employees, and record keeping. . . . Some employers, in estimating their costs, equate every one percent of absenteeism to one percent of lost profits" (1972:19). We take the view that quitting and other forms of "work instability," such as absenteeism, are self-organized acts of resistance to employers and to the nature of everyday work under capitalism.

Another form of such resistance revealed itself in this study, in its most recognizable form, as a yearning to be one's "own boss," i.e., an independent producer or craft worker. Among many small farmers in Colusa County and shopkeepers in Lincoln County, independence was maintained despite severe economic hardship. In some instances, these persons had been independent producers all of their lives and were resisting prevailing trends that were making it more difficult to be self-employed. (In other instances they were seeking to realize for the first time a lifelong dream of being their own boss.) In the Oregon wood-products communities this dream (of working for oneself) was voiced by virtually every worker under 40 years of age that we interviewed. Many of the Bisbee copper miners expressed the same goal. It is not, as one miner told us, that they wished to be "big capitalists," or "to be the boss of other people and get rich." Such people have "little dreams—to be one's own boss; to earn enough for small pleasures, like a boat, camper, icebox, and a new car."

As O'Connor (1975:331) suggests, it is actually anticapitalist (although not necessarily progressive or radical) to strive for a mode of production that is based on craft work, autonomy from a boss, and self-control of production knowledge. These workers sought to extend to their work lives the same independence and individualism that they believe they have as consumers. Historically, the reaction of workers to the development of capitalist production has had this very same thrust: "Anarchist labor[4] develops first among newly-proletarianized artisans, peasants, etc. . . . In essence, anarchist labor seeks to stop the development of capitalism. It consists of the resistance of the old mode of production to the new mode. (O'Connor, 1975:331). We found that this kind of historically documented reaction to capitalist production is occurring in contemporary rural communities.

At this point, perhaps a short summary of this discussion should be offered. The rural communities described here are faced with declining economic opportunity and an influx of culturally different people. On both counts, material and ideological, they are becoming proletarianized—"disinherited from [their] ancestral place in society and . . . unwanted in a community which is their rightful home." It is this process that calls forth the range of symbols, ideologies, and actions described above. These elements seem not only unrelated but contradictory; for example, a frontier ideology is expressed that affirms the *ideals* of a free-enterprise economy at the same time that newcomers, large firms, and particular financial institutions are viewed with hostility, distrust, and cynicism. In addition, rural workers undermine the *practice* of laissez-faire capitalism when they quit jobs frequently or leave in order to remove their labor from production for others and become their own bosses.

In practice the coexistence of both these views is understandable. A frontier ideology, which includes support for free enterprise, economic growth, and individual initiative, has important survival value. Although anachronistic, it enables individuals and communities to invoke the resilience, potency, and identity of a bygone era. By affirming the efficacy of the past, some pride is preserved in the present. Besides, it would be foolhardy to expect rural Americans to disavow the prevailing economic system when there is no alternative offered to which they might give their support. However, this same emphasis on independence, individual initiative, and the value of hard work prompts a range of reactions to the present hardships. Loss of jobs and shabby treatment by large corporations is seen as unfair, and the residents fight back. While "the system" is affirmed, individual companies, financial institutions, public officials, and politicians are the object of local hostility and cynicism.

Rural communities are no longer frontiers, but they act as though they were, for reasons of self-preservation. In fact, most were long ago invaded by large-scale corporate and monopoly capitalism—the likes of Weyerhaeuser, Dole Pineapple, Phelps-Dodge, and many others. One response to this intrusion, and to the community powerlessness and human obsolescence that has inevitably accompanied it, is an impulse to frontier extremism which, in symbolic and behavioral form, expresses a disinherited or proletarianized status. This seems to us to be an unexplored and crucial part of rural community life in America. It suggests the third and final question: Why hasn't this rural proletarianization led to greater social awareness and political mobilization? We cannot claim to have more than a tentative answer, but we find it intriguing. It is introduced in the next section and then examined in the context of concrete examples in the chapters that follow.

Social Change as the Prerogative of Capitalists

One basic factor limiting political mobilization and meaningful social change in America is the dominance of economic interpretations of and solutions for political imbalances. Even the prescriptions and programs of activist groups and radical movements have an economic cast to them. Strategies such as strikes, boycotts, and sit-ins imply the centrality of economic redress for problems of a fundamentally political nature. The New Deal, the War on Poverty, and other liberal policies all demonstrate, in their ideology and programmatic content, the insistence on converting political problems into economic ones. In this way, direct political confrontation, whether with ideologies or institutions, is avoided, and dependence on those who have established themselves (by hook or crook) in positions of power is strongly reinforced.

What might a real political confrontation look like? There is a simple concrete example at hand. Recently an unemployed mill worker in Oregon circulated petitions to put a referendum on the state ballot. This initiative would add to the list of all candidates for each public office an additional alternative—"None of the above." Then, in order to be elected, a candidate would have to receive a simple majority of all votes cast, including the votes for "None of the above." If no candidate obtained a majority, there would be no winner. An appointee would fill the vacancy for ninety days, and a second election would be held. The second slate would exclude by law any of the previous candidates, along with the temporary appointee. Nervous citizens in Oregon were afraid that under such a revision of state electoral law anarchy would reign. Their concern reflects an implicit understanding of just how undemocratic our democratic electoral process has become. Given a real choice, citizens might well turn out to vote in large numbers and reject all candidates. Such a referendum challenges both the ideology and the institutions of representative government in America; it is a direct political confrontation.

A second kind of direct political challenge is to struggle for complete democracy within appointed branches of government that formulate and implement most of the important policies of the state.[5] Appointed agencies of executive and legislative branches of government include such diverse entities as the U.S. Departments of Labor and Defense; the regulatory agencies (such as the Food and Drug Administration); and state welfare, educational, zoning, and law-enforcement bureaucracies. It is unconstitutional for the people to elect representatives to such agencies except perhaps at the county or city level. Consequently, the part of the government where the actual day-to-day work is carried out is not only organized in a bureaucratic way but also is profoundly undemocratic. If government is to be organized to serve the interest of the people as opposed to the interests of wealthy and powerful capitalists, it is imperative that laws be changed to replace appointed agencies with directly elected, representative bodies.

The following example illustrates the potential impact if state government were to be completely democratized. The State Board of Forestry in Oregon develops and recommends plans for the utilization of timber resources in the state. Of the thirteen-member board, all of whom are appointed, six are forest industry representatives, while only two are specifically charged to "represent the public interest." In a report to the governor this year, the Board recommended a large increase in tree harvest from federal timberlands from now until the year 2000—"to fill the void left by the cutting of most of the mature timber on private timberlands in Oregon." The level of harvest on federal lands is a matter of vital concern to Oregonians. It affects not only the beauty of the state but also the basic ecological balance of entire zones. The common practice of clear-cutting whole stands of timber can lead to serious soil erosion, damage to the watershed, destruction of fish and wildlife, and serious fire hazards. Some clear-cut areas are so parched and barren that successful replanting (or reforestation) is virtually impossible. It has long been known that the State Board of Forestry represents the interests of the timber industry, which diverge increasingly from those of the people of Oregon, the overwhelming majority of whom have identified *conservation of the state's natural resources* as their first priority. (This has been the case now in several annual statewide surveys conducted by the Oregon Agricultural Experiment Station.)

There was a statewide public reaction to the Forestry Board's report, and a citizens' group developed and sent a counterproposal to the governor. This proposal called for reforestation of fallow forest lands, labor-intensive rather than energy-intensive forest management, the formation of cooperative forest worker groups, and a change in the composition of the State Board of Forestry to end its domination by timber corporations. However, what if the members of the thirteen-member board were not appointed, but were *elected* by citizens? Given the public mood in Oregon, a set of recommendations for timber management very different from those released by the appointed board would surely result.

Imagine this example of democratic representation multiplied countless times for the whole range of government agencies. Citizens would begin to gain control over important decisions. It is precisely this type of collective political response that both the capitalist state and large corporations fear the most. Thus direct political confrontation is rejected, subverted, or recast as an economic struggle. This subversion of political challenge and the defining of problems exclusively in economic terms is a dominant reality in America. We think it is a critical element in the maintenance of the ideological status quo. Because this economic reductionism is so pervasive, it is difficult for Americans even to recognize how qualitatively different and potent a political solution could be.

It is in this regard that contemporary rural communities are particularly instructive. Rural communities are acutely powerless: Economic devastation can come under the guise of things as mundane as a new highway or a more advanced harvesting machine. The daily lives of rural residents are affected by powerful people who are truly remote from them, such as the boards of directors of the multinational corporations that extract oil, coal, timber, natural gas, ore, and metals from rural areas. People's livelihoods and collective existence as a community can be sharply circumscribed by corporate banking institutions that place the community off-limits for commercial credit and make it extremely difficult for small family businesses and farms to raise the money to continue their operations or to initiate new enterprises. A whole community can be effectively doomed to slow death in this way. With the possible exception of a handful of cities, this vulnerability to the profit aspirations of credit and lending institutions is not nearly so acute in urban America. Even cities such as New York, however, can be severely crippled by policies of monetary institutions.

Rural communities are deeply affected, too, by bureaucratic state institutions such as zoning commissions, highway departments, forest services, agricultural-experiment stations, and land trusts. The economic fragility of rural communities has a basic political cause: They are powerless to deal with the large corporations and government agencies that control their lives. However, the political content of their situation—their powerlessness—is either not publicly stated or is denied. This denial is, in part, what the frontier symbolism is fashioned to enhance. The super-logger, super-cowboy, and super-patriot are all potent, proud individuals. As long as the community is economically stable, or growing, the reality of powerlessness can be avoided. However, in circumstances where the economy is not working—in decaying inner cities and stagnating rural communities—a concrete understanding of the inconsistency between the existence of political problems and narrowly economic solutions could push a rural proletarianism toward political mobilization. This potential for an increased political awareness must therefore be managed or subverted by those in power. The management of ideology and the conversion of political crises into economic debates are two important tactics used to protect the favored position of monopoly capitalism in the United States.

What is Monopoly Capitalism?

The problems of rural workers, farmers, and shopkeepers described in this book are inextricably tied to the workings of a social system dominated and controlled by giant corporations. As pointed out by O'Connor (1973), monopoly over technical advances allows such firms to maintain prices while costs are reduced in order to extract higher profits. Smaller competitive firms have a slower rate of capital accumulation because technological changes widely introduced through competition in the marketplace make it necessary for them to lower prices. Monopolistic firms have a greater influence on the economy as a whole because they have more capital to reinvest. They determine through their investment policies which changes to make in the technology of production, the types of jobs available, and what markets to operate in. A higher intake of profits also allows monopolistic firms to expand into competitive industries to further increase their power and reduce the number of smaller, competitive firms.

The control of big corporations is further consolidated through financial institutions, such as banks and insurance companies. David M. Katz (1978) points out that these institutions control the use of great amounts of financial assets—stocks, bonds, mortgages—and that in many instances these assets give the financial institution controlling leverage or at least a great deal of influence over corporate policy. As a result of the interest of a financial institution in a number of different corporations, there is increased pressure created toward cooperation and merger, both to reduce competition and to integrate suppliers, producers, and marketing outlets. Through the diverse holdings of a financial institution, such as the Chase Manhattan Bank, the influence of just a few capitalists (the Rockefellers, for example) extends to a host of unrelated industries throughout the world capitalist economy. In the context of such a financial empire, emphasis is placed on maximizing the overall profits to be derived from many unrelated industries without concern for the well-being of any particular industry, community, or country. Corporate managers are paid high salaries to insure that social responsibility is not exercised at the expense of profits. Meanwhile real control is exercised by a few powerful capitalists through the banking system. Ironically, their power derives not only from exercising control over the trust funds and accounts of the wealthy but also from the large pension funds and vast numbers of small checking and savings accounts held by working people.

The profit imperative, which is inherent in monopoly capitalism, largely determines the choices made throughout the American social system. First, it has created what Harry Braverman (1974) calls "abstract labor," i.e., workers are regarded abstractly, not as individuals with valuable skills but as interchangeable parts or mere factors of production. The labor process is planned ahead of time, the tasks performed by workers are trivialized, and workers understand less and less about the production process in which they function. As workers become more alienated from their work, management expands and refines the techniques used to control and manipulate the labor force.

Second, the profit imperative has made it more difficult for the independent producer to exist, thereby increasing the dependence of the total work force on the corporate mode of production. In agriculture the overuse of technology in pursuit of profits has led to chronic food surpluses in domestic markets and expansion into foreign markets to counteract trade deficits created by corporate investments in goods that are manufactured overseas and sold back to domestic markets. Small farm operators, whose suppliers, buyers, and creditors are all under the control of monopoly capital, have largely disappeared, along with many small retailers, in dying rural communities.

An increase in monopoly power has also meant an increase in the amount of involvement by the government to stabilize a system that is found dissatisfying and even oppressive by large numbers of people. Compensatory features are introduced to remedy the ills of the system—social security, welfare, and police protection. At the same time, government is required to increase its intervention in the economy with various fiscal programs and subsidies to insure that its imbalances enhance the amount of capital accumulating in the hands of monopoly capitalists. In order to guarantee that government protects corporate interests, democratic processes are subverted through well-financed lobbying efforts, the formation of organizations to influence the policy-making process (e.g., the Trilateral Commission), and large donations to finance political candidates, most of whom come from higher socioeconomic backgrounds and are willing to do the bidding of their financial backers. Monopoly capitalists also exercise ideological control over public beliefs and opinions through media advertising focused on consumerism, through narrowly limited debate on "critical" economic and social (not political) problems, and through various forms of intimidation and threats about what might happen if the system were to be significantly changed. Although the process of ideological control remains obscured, it is perhaps the most important element in the maintenance of corporate power.

Declining Communities as the Ideological Achilles Heel of Laissez-Faire Capitalism

The following accounts of five communities that are experiencing economic decline are essentially case studies in corporate control and the management of ideology.[6] A clear scenario can be gleaned from our study of these apparently divergent places. We summarize it here, as a kind of model of what is now occurring in boom/bust communities all over the West. The appropriate place to begin is with the end of a phase of economic growth or boom.

Prerogatives exercised by the monopoly sector of the U.S. economy are directly responsible for the economic decline (and boom) of rural (and urban) areas. Decline often begins with the decision by a large firm to establish a new production site. The reasons behind such decisions are typically quite straightforward. First, a firm may seek inexpensive land in order to build an expanded or more modern production facility. Everyday business terms, such as *mechanization* (replacing human labor in production with machines, which may require a different kind of physical plant); *diversification* (adding new products or services to one's production line, which may require an expanded plant); and *integration* (bringing geographically diffused production sites together in closer proximity) are the shorthand expressions for reasons to move. A need for more or cheaper land, for any of the above reasons, may bring formerly urban-based companies to rural sites, or prompt firms located in rural America to move overseas.

Labor supply considerations are equally important in the decision to move. Historically, the epochal and massive movements of large firms in this country have been away from unionized and relatively better paid labor and toward places where they can take advantage of unorganized and cheaper labor. Examples are the well-known migration of the American textile industry from the Northeast to the Southeast, and the movement to the West of automative assembly and light manufacturing plants. Workers organized into unions are workers who have increased control over the conditions and remuneration of work. In both ways, they can wage a struggle with employers and potentially affect the firm's profits, i.e., win a relatively larger or at least stable *share* of the revenues. Part of the motivation for companies to move to rural areas or to sites overseas is that in both places there may be a higher rate of unemployment and a lower rate of labor-force participation than in urban America. Hence, there is a larger potential pool of workers and, with excess labor supply, a downward pressure on wages.

Still other considerations fall under the euphemistic rubric "a better business climate." These include a minimal amount of government regulation, such as lack of pollution controls and low local tax rates on property and on corporate income. Overseas, the favorable climate sometimes consists of laws against unions or strikes.

In addition, a firm may consider a move to the site of a new, unexploited resource in order to leave behind one that has been depleted. Timber companies, for example, moved to the Pacific Northwest after they had exhausted the vast stands of trees in the Northeast and the Great Lakes region. Such companies as Weyerhaeuser, Georgia-Pacific, Boise Cascade, and International Paper do not intend to be caught with their trees down. Since the late 1960s they have bought large areas of timberland in Indonesia, Malaysia, South Korea, and the Philippines. When the forests of the Northwest are depleted, they will have somewhere else to go.

Finally, firms may consider closing down a plant in order to move to a location that is more suitable, in still other ways, to the implementation of a new technology. For example, the newest copper-mining technology requires certain geological conditions that are not present in the older mines in Bisbee, Arizona. Employing the new technology required (sooner or later) that Phelps-Dodge move its operations to new sites where the necessary rock mechanics were present. In each of these cases, the basic consideration by the firm is one of profitability. As one Bisbee miner put it, "It's not that Phelps-Dodge can't make a profit here, it's that they can make a bigger one somewhere else." Such is often the case. Once this decision has been made, a set of secondary, individual decisions is set in motion as mobile individuals and households attempt to leave the doomed community and perhaps move to a capital-created opportunity elsewhere.

Herein lies the instructive difference between growing and dying communities. It is in growing communities where economic viability most effectively perpetuates the illusion of political autonomy. Economic growth provides an environment wherein economic solutions appear to work and conventional definitions of social reality are reinforced. When these solutions cease to work, the most natural thing for economically viable people to do is to depart for areas that are currently growing. If they are successful,

. . . their instrumental strategies are rewarded and their ideological constructs of reality maintained. *Solutions* to the problems of the declining community, especially solutions to the predicament of those who remain or of the economically frustrated who return, are vastly more difficult. In contrast to growing communities, dying rural communities (and dying urban neighborhoods) are sore spots. [The visible festering of these sores] constitutes the ideological Achilles' heel of laissez-faire capitalism. (Padfield, in press)

Policymakers and politicians wish it would go away.

It is at the end of growth or the beginning of decline that conflict in public ideology begins. "The conflict is subtle because it presents itself largely in terms of private versus public strategies. Despite individual doubts and the private search for individual options, public hope in conventional economic solutions is steadfastly maintained by local officials and businessmen" (Padfield, in press). For example, in Oregon there is a growing surplus of wood-products workers relative to jobs in this industry, and this is a circumstance that will become steadily worse over the next twenty-five years. The publicly circulated solution to this employment problem has been to seek an increased harvest of trees from federal lands in Oregon—it is "trees or jobs," as the public slogans put it—but this ignores the "tree famine" that has been caused by substantial overcutting and a paucity of replanting on corporate-owned timberlands. Other solutions are more appropriate. These include bringing about a slower rate of mechanization in the industry and a faster rate of reforestation, especially on private lands. However, both of these solutions would require that control over certain aspects of private production be in the hands of the people of Oregon, i.e., that the excesses of corporate power be curbed by political means.

Another example in which inappropriate solutions are publicly sanctioned comes from Molokai, Hawaii. The announced closure of Dole's pineapple plantation brought a timid but earnest reaction from the community of Filipino workers. They circulated a petition asking Dole to reconsider and delay the closure for at least two years. Local union officials instructed members not to sign and successfully squelched the community's initiative to ask that *their needs* be considered. Instead, union officials, local community action program bureaucrats and politicians all pointed to the development of a new resort on Molokai as the solution to the pending joblessness. It should come as no surprise that when the resort opened only a very few Molokai residents were employed there.

As community decline continues, ideological conflict centers around the issue of achieving local autonomy, which is necessary as a means of rejecting inappropriate (economic) solutions publicized by those in positions of authority. This issue crystalizes around the fear of "political interference," which has, in fact, been made necessary by increased reliance on federal dollars to support social services, which are in greater demand because of high levels of unemployment and an eroded local tax base. Local concern over dependence on the government is ironic, for true local autonomy never existed in the first place. New awareness of dependence arises as people are severed from their dependence on private companies and are left for the government to care for (Padfield, in press).

The "administered community" represents the cumulative end result of economic (as opposed to political) problem-solving and points to the inevitable conclusion that power in American society lies with monopoly capital and the agencies of government. With respect to the position of weakness in which communities and local institutions, such as families and schools, find themselves, encouragement is given to respond individually with economic rather than (threatening) political solutions. How communities and individuals are expected to behave is also culturally compatible with frontier ideology, which emphasizes the sanctity of capitalist enterprise and the perception of political problems in economic terms.

The consequences attached to economic responses are familiar. Shopkeepers and small farmers sell out, die out, or declare bankruptcy; professional classes take their services to better markets; and skilled workers "vote with their feet," against the declining community and for a growing one, or, to use another cliché from social science, they suddenly become aware of a "preference" for a new location. Local schools increase their vocational curriculum (now more fashionably known as "career education") in the belief that the community's future workers will find themselves more saleable if they have a different or increased configuration of vocational skills. Families reconsider their work roles, typically resulting in an increase in female labor-force participation, which otherwise has been historically low for rural women. It is perhaps surprising that most people choose not to move from declining communitites, at least not within the first few years. But it is not so surprising that the incidence of staying is highest among unskilled, low-wage workers, the young, and the aged, all of whom may find themselves better off using their limited resources to survive where they are.

Since individual economic solutions, although resourceful in many ways, are not always sufficient, the government is left with the task of compensating for the hardships and inequalities arising from the unchallenged exercise of capitalist prerogatives. It not only provides financial compensation for the unemployed and welfare benefits for nonparticipants in the labor force, but it also employs welfare workers to manage poor people and law-enforcement apparatus to control those who are deviant or alienated enough to become criminals.

Conclusion: The Inevitability of Human Obsolescence Under Capitalism

"Economic obsolescence" is a term usually reserved for describing physical capital (i.e., machinery or buildings) that is no longer useful in production. As new technology develops, machinery becomes outmoded and obsolete because, while it may still have years of productive life left, it is not efficient in combination with the new methods. Obsolete machines are looked upon as replicas of extinct species, oddities to be regarded with nostalgia in Fourth of July parades and public museums. As Americans, we take pride in seeing visible evidence of progress. A new closed-cab air-conditioned tractor, which allows one person to plow 50 acres per day, juxtaposed with a hand-held plow, which allows a person to plow only two acres a day, provides an undeniable measure of progress, because progress is equated with technological development in American culture. Although the old plow is a curiosity symbolic of the past, it is also a discarded object and somewhat ludicrous in a present-day context.

The fact that human beings are made to become obsolete is not so widely recognized or is not conceived in these terms. Nonetheless, like natural resources and machines, human labor is also what economists call a "factor of production" and therefore comparable in economic terms to machines in the cost-benefit calculations of large-scale capitalist enterprises. The comparability of machines and human beings extends also to their tendency to become obsolete because they are no longer useful in a modernized or "better mechanized" production process. New machines not only replace obsolete machines, they also replace human beings whose labor is no longer needed. One fully modern tractor has replaced 24 of the 25 persons needed as farmers when all that was available was a hand-held plow. Moreover, the farmer who remains to use the tractor, along with many other sophisticated or expensive machines, is a new breed of farmer-businessman who has evolved a style of life to replace that of previous generations. Replicas of obsolete farmers and obsolete lifestyles also appear in our Fourth of July parades and public museums. In a present-day context they appear as oddities and seem perhaps as ludicrous as obsolete machines.

The argument here is not that technology itself causes problems or that it is not desirable to provide people with useful skills. *The difficulty is that usefulness is determined on the basis of industrial profits, which can be raised by exploiting both physical and human capital.* The worthy goal of producing self-sufficient persons who have basic economic and social skills to provide for their own welfare has been subordinated to the goal of procuring inputs useful to large-scale capitalist enterprise. The problem of human obsolescence is then compounded by a lack of individual self-sufficiency and a dependence on society for support. People become obsolete when they are no longer useful to capitalists and when they are left without a self-sufficient means to earn a living.

People without desired characteristics (e.g., youthful, attractive, dutiful) remain unemployed and become obsolete. Many of them become discouraged of ever finding a job and drop out of the labor force. Nonparticipation in the labor force is a measurable phenomenon, but little public attention is given to it because not working is seen as a voluntary act on the part of the nonparticipants. Meanwhile, the level of unemployment among people in the labor force is closely monitored and regarded as an important issue, because it indicates how well or how poorly capitalist industry is using the human resources at its disposal. In fact, the rate of male labor-force participation has steadily fallen since the early 1950s—from 87 percent to 79 percent in 1974. We reject one interpretation of this trend, ascribing it to "an increased demand for leisure time" on the part of male workers and their families. Although an increased number of workers are choosing to retire at an earlier age, thus contributing to the falling rate of participation, we argue that this "voluntary retirement" must not be seen as an alternative initiated by labor in labor's interests. The persons whose lives this book describes were *thrown out* of work and *pushed out* of the labor force. And it is a mockery when their former employers, union officials, and elected representatives pronounce this one-way, dead-end street "a rational decision to take early retirement."

Human obsolescence is an inevitable part of capitalism; and it represents an enormous waste of human potential, whatever the euphemistic name given to it by social scientists, employers, or politicans. This book depicts the suffering attendant upon companies' decisions to discard people. It also documents the means by which the true cause of the suffering—the unrestrained exercise of capitalist prerogatives—is obscured, or labeled and advertised as being in the public interest. Human obsolescence poses *the basic dilemma* to those who run a capitalist economy. The way out of the dilemma is not more growth, more capitalism, nor more control of our lives by the government; rather, it is to organize our lives, for ourselves, around human needs rather than corporate profit. It does not matter what name is given to such a system. The crucial point is that regardless of what we are led to believe by those who control our lives, work is not now organized either to meet or to achieve human fulfillment.

Notes

1. While it is not customary (and hence probably unwise) for researchers to be so candid about the nature and process of their work, we must confess that no word could more aptly describe our research project.

2. By rural communities we mean *those places outside of urbanized areas with a population of fewer than 10,000 residents*. This is a more liberal criterion than that used in the U.S. Census classification of population, but we think it is justified. First of all, in the last census 21.3 percent of all Americans lived in "the country," as we traditionally conceive it. That is, they did not live in an identifiable "place" or community. If we add to this group those people who live in unurbanized places with a population of up to 2,500 persons (i.e., 5.2 percent), we have 26.5 percent of all Americans in 1970. This combined group is what the census classifies as "rural." This is, of course, quite arbitrary. While a larger "place" (e.g., one with 2,500 to 10,000 residents) may be classified as an "urbanized area" in census enumeration, many of these communities are rural in terms of the economic characteristics in which we are currently interested. That is, there is a relatively high proportion of farms in the nearby, surrounding area; the kinds of jobs available are very limited; and per capita income and female labor-force participation is low and unemployment high *relative to the U.S. as a whole*. All of these phenomena are related to the problems of economic dependence and decline that we address in this book. Therefore, we have added an additional category of persons to the census's count of rural Americans—those living outside urbanized areas, in places of 2,500 to 10,000 population. In so doing, we add only 7 percent more to the previous total of 26.5 percent; but this new group, comprising all Americans who live in unurbanized places of 10,000 or less and totaling 33.5 percent of the population, is a more meaningful "rural" category for our purposes.

3. Population growth is now occurring in previously declining rural communities. This does not mean that every county in the United States is now growing, but in the thirteen Western states, the average percentage gain in rural counties between 1970 and 1974 was more than 10 percent. In Western metropolitan counties population also increased, but by a lesser amount.

4. In political usage, anarchy can be simply defined as the absence of a government or ruler. Anarchist labor is labor in the absence of a boss or employer—each worker is his or her own boss.

5. This example is essentially paraphrased from James O'Connor's letter to the editor, *Progressive*, vol. 41, no. 8 (August 1977), p. 46.

6. The conceptual framework of this section is largely drawn from a paper by Padfield (in press).

2 Taming The "Timber Beast"

A Woodlot for the United States

This chapter focuses on the interrelated problems of dependence on one industry, declining employment, and conflict over the use of natural resources in Oregon. The relevance of this discussion extends even further to the lushly forested regions of northern California, Washington, and Idaho. However, the issues with which we are concerned are more prevalent and sharply defined in Oregon. Wood products is unquestionably Oregon's most important industry, and the "timber beast"[1] is the industry's most important factor.

Indeed, there are a few regions in the nation whose continued economic viability is so closely linked with the success or failure of just one major economic sector. More than 33 percent of the employment in all manufacturing for the total Pacific Northwest in 1971 was accounted for by direct employment in forest products manufacturing. In Oregon that share was about 44 percent. (Stanford Research Institute, 1974, Phase II:2; in Lembcke, 1976:8)

Lumber and wood-products manufacturing occurs in all but two of Oregon's thirty-six counties and accounts for the economic base in many of the state's communities. Since it has the largest remaining stands of timber of any state, Oregon serves as a woodlot for the rest of the country. The diversity in kinds of wood is also astonishing; every kind of softwood in the West can be found in Oregon. The fortunes of the work force and thus the state's economic health are closely tied to the demand for the various kinds of wood and wood products.

The wood-products industry is a notoriously unstable one because it depends on the construction industry, particularly home building, for a large proportion of its sales. In turn, the demand for housing is very sensitive to interest rates and to the availability of mortgage loans. Because these factors are highly cyclical, so, too, are people's decisions to buy new homes. A national recession, such as occurred in 1973–74, has disastrous consequences for people's willingness and ability to finance new homes, and it may cause construction to come to a near standstill. Sagging orders for lumber and other building materials are followed closely by layoffs and mill closures. Thus it was that the national recession of 1973–74 had an impact on the Oregon wood-products industry in 1975. Official unemployment in the industry reached 25 percent. County-wide rates of unemployment, i.e., unemployment in all sectors, ranged from 10 to 25 percent. More than 100 mills closed in a three-year period from 1974 through 76 (Lembcke, 1976:8).

Oregonians have long understood the very close relationship between the health of the national economy and local jobs in the wood-products industry. In recent years editorial writers, public officials, and timber company representatives have talked anxiously about an additional and important relationship—that between wood-products jobs and level of tree harvest. "Trees mean jobs" is one way that this relationship is expressed. Although this statement is not totally untrue, it is not the total truth. The fact is that the number of jobs in Oregon's wood-products industry is related more to practices within the industry than to levels of harvest. For example, the mechanization of logging and mill work has had and will have a more significant impact on employment than the level of harvest. Some people call it "technological change," and economists refer to it as "the substitution of one factor of production for another." In either case, it means the loss of jobs; and despite the fact that mechanization will be the primary factor causing a projected future decline in wood-products jobs, it is never mentioned in the public debate over this issue. Part of the problem in clarifying the public debate is that large timber companies control sufficient wealth and possess sufficient power to define the issues to suit their own interests.

The existence of a large pool of surplus labor also has gone undetected and hence unameliorated, in part because unemployed wood-products workers sometimes become discouraged about finding work, drop out of the labor force, and become invisible. While nonparticipation in the labor force is a measurable phenomenon, little public attention is given to it, because labor-force withdrawal is seen as a voluntary act on the part of the nonpartici-pants. Our analysis suggests otherwise: The wood-products workers in this study were thrown out of work and pushed out of the labor force because their skills were no longer needed by industry.

Many people think of Oregon as part of the last American frontier. It is true that a motorist might still be forced to stop on a major highway as kerchieved cowboys drive a large herd of cattle across and down the road. A frontier ideology prevails in many communities too. Among the wood-products workers in this study, for example, there is a strong emphasis on individual initiative and self-reliance. Family resourcefulness includes such things as home building, barn raising, auto and appliance repair, extensive gardening and canning, and swapping a variety of foodstuffs, tools, skills, and knowledge. To capitulate to a "store bought" product or service is to admit incompetence: "I couldn't make it myself."

Another aspect of these workers' impulse to independence and autonomy is their frequently expressed desire to "be my own boss", i.e., to start a small business or earn an income from inventions. They have heard about the projected decline in wood-products jobs, and their most preferred escape from potential unemployment rests with their dreams of becoming small entrepreneurs. Unaware of the deteriorating plight (described elsewhere in this book) of small farmers and shopkeepers in other rural communities, they believe in the possibility of permanent and meaningful work outside the arena of corporate capitalism. In other words, they believe that the future can be like the frontier past.

The Great Land Grab

The first sawmill in Oregon was established in the 1830s, and lumber export had begun at a time when the Oregon Territory was being watched by the acquisitive eyes of the English and American governments. The central role of wood in the region's economy even then is illustrated by the fact that sawlogs and lumber were often used for barter. By 1846 Oregon had become a state, and there existed seventeen flour and sawmills, which increased to thirty just four years later. Trade lanes were opened up to London, Liverpool, Australia, and the Sandwich Islands (the Hawaiian Islands). Before 1880 the list of foreign ports included some in India, South Africa, the South Sea Islands, and the west coast of South Africa. Substantial lumber trade with China began in the 1880s, and log exports to Japan soon followed.

Transporting logs from the forest to local mills, domestic markets, and ports was the biggest problem in these early decades. Before the use of the crosscut saw, logs were dragged in long lengths and dumped into the nearest river to be floated down to their first destination. These were the days of oxen teams and skid roads.

The skid road was made by placing skids [small logs] at right angles to the line of haul about eight feet apart. The skids were then greased to make the logs slide along easier. The grease [dogfish oil] had to be applied hot ahead of the team, and after [the team] . . . had trudged and slipped and slid down the road much of the effectiveness was lost by the time the logs got there.

The number of oxen in a team [varied] from six to sixteen. . . . [They] wore heavy yokes which varied in weight from two hundred and twenty-five to four hundred pounds. . . . It required no little skill and courage to drive an ox team, because they were temperamental as movie stars and have bequeathed to us the old saying as "strong as an ox." They did not even like to have strangers watch them work. The ox teamster was the king of the logging camp. (Sherman, 1934: 16–17)

The wood-products industry seems to have developed steadily but rather slowly up to the 1880s, hampered as it was by a lack of adequate transportation to potential inland markets. The logs and lumber products that were not used in the local economy were transported to the West Coast and foreign markets by boat. Other parts of the United States still relied upon the lumber-producing centers of New England and the Great Lakes. The rapid depletion of forest resources in these areas caused some eyes to turn toward the lush, long-log forests of the Pacific Northwest, but getting the logs from forests in the West to markets in the populous East was a problem.

The coming of the railroad opened up vast opportunities for the marketing of Oregon timber. Rails "connected the region to the Midwest and, indeed, to the whole rapidly expanding market that the United States was becoming" (Tyler, 1967:5). From 1880 to 1890, 122 mills were built, or approximately one-third of the total plants in operation by 1890 (Sherman, 1934:28). During the same period U.S. Census figures show a fivefold increase in capital investment in Oregon's mills, from 1.57 to 8.1 million dollars. Portland, the undisputed capital in the region in 1880, grew from 3,533 residents to 207,426 in the thirty years ending in 1910! The region was expanded and changed under the new conditions of industrial capitalism.

Small-scale agriculture and lumbering that had previously exported modest surpluses by freight wagon, river boat or windjammer became the new commercial agriculture and the complex lumber industry of the twentieth century. The population of Washington and Oregon swelled, increasing faster than the population of the nation as a whole. . . . Strangers, whom the old settlers would never have encountered on the Oregon Trail—Scandinavians, Finns, Germans by the thousands—poured into the region. Business units and organizations increased in size and complexity. . . .
As one might expect, the changing society clung to its values of hardy enterprise, agrarian simplicity and equality, self-reliance and individualism. . . . [However] the older values . . . became, in fact, less and less appropriate. (Tyler, 1967:2)

These sweeping changes contain one passing item that is of particular interest to us: the increasing size of business units and organizations. By 1913, the degree of concentration in timber-resource ownership was of such concern that the Federal Bureau of Corporations made an extensive national study of it. The bureau's report contained these conclusions:

1. The concentration of a dominating control of our standing timber in a comparatively few enormous holdings is steadily tending toward a central control of the lumber industry.
2. There is a vast speculative purchase and holding of timberland far in advance of any use thereof.
3. There is an enormous increase in the value of this diminishing natural resource, with great profits to its owners. This value, by the very nature of standing timber, the holder neither created nor substantially enhances. (Bureau of Corporations, 1913:97)

By 1914 nearly half of all the privately owned American timberland was in the Pacific Northwest. One-fourth of this land was held by the Northern Pacific Railroad, the Southern Pacific Railroad, and the Weyerhaeuser Corporation. As the Bureau of Corporations noted, the principal business interest of these early landlords was not logs, but rather speculation in timber values. Since there were such huge profits to be made in just holding the land, none of the large owners made any attempt to cut and process timber until at least 1915. In some sections of the region, "the value of timberland, virtually worthless in 1900, rose fifty-fold, the increment exceeding comfortably the estimated six percent cost of taxes, fire protection, and office expense in merely holding the land" (Tyler, 1967:7). Some tracts in Oregon increased in value by a factor of 20 (2,000 percent!) in the space of 15 years, greatly enhancing the wealth of the owners.
What the bureau's report omits is discussion of the central role played by the federal government in facilitating this concentration of timber resources. "The bounty of the federal government," wrote one commentator, "had holes in its land laws through which six logging teams could be driven abreast" (Meany, 1935:179). That land policy was shaped by congressional legislation of two types. First, there was a class of laws designed to promote the settling

and clearing of land for agricultural purposes by private citizens. Examples of such legislation were the Preemption and Homestead laws and the Timber and Stone Act. Explicit limits were placed on the amount of public land a settler could acquire for his own use through each of these acts. The second class of laws included special grants for railroads and general grants for state education and local improvements. For these, federal law set no specific limit to the amount of public land that could pass into private hands through the grants. Each of these two classes of laws was vulnerable to grand manipulation by land speculators.[2]

Before 1891 timbermen made most use of the first class of laws for purposes of land consolidation (Meany, 1935:195). In general, these laws provided that an actual settler on the soil had the right to enter claim on a 160- to 320-acre tract of land after a specified period of residence (for example, five years under the Homestead acts). However, a clause provided that the settler might purchase the land outright, for $1.25 to $2.50 an acre, after a much shorter period of residence (12 to 14 months). These prices were substantially below the actual value of the land at that time. "The applicant for homestead privilege had to swear that he took the land in 'good faith for the purpose of making a home for himself,' and not for sale or speculation, but if he changed his plans he could spend the minimum residency, buy his lands, and dispose of them as he saw fit" (Meany, 1935:195–96). The land settlement laws were easily and flagrantly abused. A "dummy" homesteader or "entryman" was hired to file for and purchase claims. These were then immediately turned over to the timber company, which had advanced the $1.25 per acre for the tract.

The "entryman" did not always take the trouble to clear even an acre of his homestead to make it [look inhabited]. While waiting for final ownership papers he would set up his home in a shake shanty . . . which was totally unfit for human habitation except during a few months of summer. Frequently, ostensible quarters were established in the fire-gutted stump of a giant cedar, where "residence" was maintained to the satisfaction of government officials. Prominent among the evidence at the Oregon land fraud trials were photographs of virgin and heavily wooded mountain sides, the reputed sites of [settlers'] dwellings and cabbage patches, the existence of which corrupt government agents had affirmed upon personal "investigation." (Meany, 1935:199)

One C. A. Smith of Minneapolis developed a particularly clever method of land piracy. He arranged tours to Oregon for vacationing Midwestern school teachers. The group traveled at his expense and then repaid his generosity by entering claims to Oregon homestead land and transferring the title to its host. They got a pleasant trip and Smith got untold acres of Oregon forest land (Meany, 1935:203). Although it was not at all what Congress had intended, the Preemption and Homestead acts, and the Timber and Stone Act, which superseded them, "had the practical effect of assembling large tracts to suit the speculative interests of the timberman. . . . The [Timber and Stone Act] remained in force during the period of greatest concentration of timber ownership in the Pacific Northwest." (Meany, 1935:205)

However, direct federal land grants to railroad companies and individual states provided the means for amassing the most spectacular private holdings of forest land. Oregon provides a prototypical case. The state received altogether 4,345,230 acres of land through federal grants (Meany, 1935:207). These gifts of land were for various purposes, such as "internal improvements," construction and support of universities and an agricultural college, construction of a capitol, and creation of a common school fund in each township. Meany (1935:207) notes that Oregon "was especially prodigal in the disposal of her federal land gifts." By 1930 the state had sold or given away title to 3,733,303 acres, or 86 percent of the original grants, leaving a meager balance of 612,928 acres.

To whom did state lands go and by what means? First of all, Oregon put the land that was to have been used for support of state universities and common schools on a preemption basis. This meant that Oregon settlers had the opportunity to purchase up to 320 acres of state-owned land, typically at $1.25 per acre. This provision was subject to the same abuse as were the federal lands made available by the Preemption and Homestead acts. The 320 acres acquired for settling could be—and often were—immediately resold to speculators. By 1930 two of the largest and richest private timber holdings in the state consisted almost entirely of the land once granted to the state for the common-school fund in each township. Meanwhile, only 240 acres remained of the state university grant. Today, the state owns less than one percent of the timberland within its borders.

The direct land grants to railroad corporations had a similar, enabling effect on the rapid concentration of Pacific Northwest timberlands in private hands. In the state of Washington the railroad's grants "were equivalent to the combined area of Maryland, New Jersey and Massachusetts," and in Oregon Southern Pacific was granted 1,934,580 acres (Meany, 1935:218). These grants of land to the railroad corporations had specific conditions attached to them. Congressional intention was that, after the completion of railroad construction, much of the land would be sold to settlers in 160-acre lots at $2.50 per acre. The purpose was to encourage migrants to the new frontier to settle along a route of transportation and to allow the railroad to receive revenues from the land sales as compensation for having built the lines. Such was the spirit of the law. In practice, an altogether different outcome ensued. Southern Pacific sold part of its land in large blocks to other corporations, notably Weyerhaeuser. "By 1910, the Weyerhaeuser Timber Company held 1,230,000 acres of timberland in western Washington and 380,599 acres in western Oregon" (Meany, 1935:222). All of the company's Washington land and half of that in Oregon came from the railroad grants. The corporation's Oregon timber reserves were at least double the above figure, however, because it was affiliated with other timber companies that held substantial acreage. Large companies based in Minneapolis and Pennsylvania became the third and fourth largest owners of Oregon timberland, while Weyerhaeuser was second.

The parcels of land that were not sold to other corporations were held by

Southern Pacific for speculative purposes: ". . . the railroad contended that inasmuch as the land was timbered, there could be no bona fide settlement upon it, and therefore the company determined to obtain the increment itself. . . . The company was accused of waiting until its $25,000,000 land grant was worth $50,000,000 before selling it." (Meany, 1935:216). This tactic is called land speculation, and it was so obviously contrary to the original intent of the railroad grants that the federal government sued Southern Pacific. Eventually, the railroad was forced to forfeit all lands not sold by 1913. In this way, 2,200,000 acres were returned to the U. S. government, and this resulted in the government's holding a great deal more timberland in Oregon than does the state itself.

The U.S. Bureau of Corporations noted in its 1913 report on concentration of timber holdings that the 68 largest landowners held 70.7 percent of western Oregon's timberland in 1910. Even at that early date, it was clear that such concentrated control of this valuable natural resource would have future implications for consumers and citizens. With control over the source of raw materials came the power to set prices. Companies also had the power to influence local government. "Timbermen took active pride in the election of their fellows to office, and many local and national representatives were selected from their ranks" (Meany, 1935:234). Thus owners of large mills and timber holdings became mayors, city councilmen, governors, and congressmen.

One consequence of the timbermen's influence in political matters was a substantial underassessment of the value of their holdings. This resulted in lower taxes on their property. Since the major cost incurred in holding land for speculative purposes is the taxes that must be paid, it was very advantageous to have the land value, and hence the taxes, underestimated. When the land was eventually sold, the profit was even greater than it would have been if the land had been taxed at full value.

In 1860 settlers in Oregon were still fighting Indian wars. Just 50 years later they were involved in battles to save "their" land. They did not recognize that the battles were futile, that the race to accumulate and control Oregon's timber wealth was over and apparently irreversible by 1910. Nonetheless, social tensions were created from a residue of resentment that continued to fester in the wake of the land grab. In the pain and confusion, it is not surprising that pioneer settlers "clung to [the older] values of hardy enterprise, agrarian simplicity and equality, self-reliance and individualism" (Tyler, 1967:3). There was, for instance, a deep agrarian distrust of "nonproducers," e.g. speculators, and of "Eastern money and exploitation." These sentiments at times erupted into the populism that still characterizes Oregon politics. Yet the strong frontier ethic of individualism and egalitarianism was not turned to violence against the lumber barons or the corrupt officials who permitted their plunder of the area's resources. It seems instead to have found its release in violent resistance to the attempts of ordinary working men to join together in their own behalf. It was against unions, and most especially against the Industrial Workers of the World, or "Wobblies," that local communities in

Oregon reacted most violently. A vigorous struggle ensued, while the real menace to Oregon's agrarian populism—large-scale corporate capitalism—went unidentified and uncontested.

Lumberjacks and Timber Barons

The full effects of monopoly timber ownership have been recognized only in the last decade. They are an important cause of the economic failure of small mills, the owners of which do not own timberland and increasingly cannot afford to buy timber. Another part of the contemporary picture is the nature of the relationship between employers and the wood-products labor force. The industry is characterized by high rates of job turnover, layoffs, closures, and accidents. Employer complaints that mill workers "don't give a damn" are matched by worker observations that they are expendable to the firms. One employer put it explicitly: "You guys [chip-truck drivers] are a dime a dozen. I could fire any one of you and have a replacement in five minutes." The rather distrustful relationship between employers and workers in the industry also has historical antecedents.

As was noted earlier, the demand for various forest-related products is highly changeable. An industry that must adapt to a highly unstable demand for its product will, if left to its own devices, also exhibit an unstable demand for the labor it employs. Historically,

. . . labor had to be supplied as cheaply as possible, and with the least fuss. The last thing any large or small lumber company wanted was to be tied to a labor contract or wage rates, seniority rights or job security. The ideal labor force was in fact the labor force that obtained in the industry before World War I, an army of transients without residential roots that could be hired cheaply when needed and discharged just as easily when not needed. (Tyler, 1967:8)

Organized labor was always an anathema to the lumber companies. One author characterizes the pre-World War I lumber work force as one made up in large part of "bums," "hoboes," and "skid road characters." Since these types were thought to be disreputable anyway, the employers felt no "responsibility or paternalism" toward them (Tyler, 1967:8). This statement puts the situation rather mildly. In fact, the conditions under which men were asked to work in the logging camps and sawmills were appalling.

. . . life in the camps was primitive indeed. The typical camp lay at the end of a railroad spur or dirt road. . . . A half-dozen or more rough shacks served as bunkhouses for the working crews. Outside the huddled ring of shacks stood the foreman's office, the camp store, the "cookie's" shack with its garbage piles and swarms of flies, and the latrine. About two dozen men—oftentimes more—slept in each bunkhouse in fetid congestion. Because logging camps of necessity were impermanent establishments, having to move every year or two with the progress of the cut, they represented an overhead burden which the companies wished to keep to a minimum.

Loggers worked in all kinds of weather and frequently returned to camp in wet and muddy clothes. Most camps had no facilities for bathing or for drying clothes, and the men ate their leaden supper of cheap starches and grease while sitting in their wet clothes. After supper the men gathered in the yard in sullen groups to wait for darkness to drift up from the valley below before they squeezed into the crowded bunkhouses. Inside these shacks, as one investigator discovered, "the sweaty, steamy odors . . . would asphyxiate the uninitiated." As the odors thickened from pipes, tobacco juice, sweat and drying clothes, the men relaxed as best they could and exchanged gossip about recent binges and favorite prostitutes in the nearest town, or aired their grievances against the foreman. . . .

In one camp investigated in 1917, eighty men crammed into one crude barrack built to accommodate fewer than half that number. The building had no windows, and the doors at either end furnished the only ventilation. When the men pressed into their bunks for the night, they closed the doors against the cold, stoked up the stoves, and went to sleep under "groundhog conditions." In another study of logging camps made during the winter of 1917–1918, the investigators discovered that half the camps had only crude wooden bunks, half had no bathing facilities, and half were infested with bedbugs. (Tyler, 1967:89–90)

Coupled with the neglect and greed that produced such conditions was an intransigent attitude on the part of employers.

Most of them espoused a primitive philosophy of economic individualism and adhered religiously to their convenient versions of laissez-faire liberalism, a constellation of beliefs that made them antagonistic to even the most conservative forms of trade unionism. . . . [For the employers, the degrading work conditions] were merely a part of the game and the inevitable products of the sacrosanct free market. Efforts by workers to improve conditions through collective effort were seen as impertinent tamperings with economic law and the prerogatives of property ownership. (Tyler, 1967:86)

Even those few employers who were sympathetic to worker grievances about camp conditions were still rigidly opposed to any kind of union. This can be understood, in part, as a reaction to the competitive and highly unstable position in which the lumber manufacturers found themselves. Profits in manufacturing wood products were not large. Even during the lucrative years of World War I, "three-fourths of the region's sawmills brought in yearly gross receipts of less than $50,000" (Tyler, 1967:88). As we have seen, it was instead the ownership of timberland that was a highly profitable business. In view of the competition, many small manufacturing plants maintained that they could not afford to "regularize" the conditions of work. From their perspective it was necessary to "cut and clear out," or to stop and start production with a suddenness that matched volatile changes in lumber prices. From the employers' point of view the best work force was thus an itinerant one—easily hired and fired. This point of view continues to be held even at present.

The attitude among employers had predictable results. For example, labor turnover in the industry was, and still is, substantial. In 1918 the average length of a lumber-camp job was estimated at between 15 and 30 days (Meany, 1934:331). Turnover was also high in the mills. "Four Oregon mills with an average crew of 343 per mill kept records of the number of separations in 1919, 1920, 1921, and found the rate of turnover to be about 205 percent a year"

(Sherman, 1934:45). This rate of turnover meant that in a year's time, an average of 703 men left their jobs in each of the mills.

We ordinarily think of rapid turnover as involving an economic cost to employers. However, since it was within the power of the companies to reduce the turnover by improving the work conditions, the situation must have worked to their ultimate benefit. One way in which it did benefit employers was in enabling more intense exploitation of workers currently on the job. A universal 10-hour day prevailed in the industry, and 16 hours in the woods was not uncommon. Since the men were paid by the day, there was no extra pay for any extra work. A crew of lumberjacks that quit because of exhaustion from the long hours and disagreement over the pay could always be replaced with a fresh contingent. In fact, many unscrupulous employers benefited even more directly from high turnover. It was common for them to enter into an arrangement with a local employment agency whereby all their available jobs would be filled through the agency. The agency charged the workers a one-dollar fee for each job. In some instances, the agency split the fees with the employer, who would fire the workers almost as quickly as they were hired. For example, the Somers Lumber Company in Spokane, Washington, hired 3,000 men during one winter in order to maintain a crew of 50 (Tyler, 1967:34). The elimination of such exploitative practices was often a demand of striking workers. Another demand frequently made by strikers was for a uniform wage scale. Wage scales for the same work fluctuated widely from job to job; and the pay was sometimes sharply reduced, without advance notice. Work in the woods and mills was also very hazardous, a factor that contributed to many spontaneous walkouts and strikes.

The Industrial Workers of the World began organizing loggers and sawmill workers in 1905 and continued over the next decade. It has been estimated that a majority of loggers joined the IWW at one time or another during this period; and by 1917 a considerable reservoir of sympathizers existed. Support for the IWW was tested in a call for a general strike on 20 June 1917. Within a month the Pacific Northwest's lumber industry "creaked to a dead stop," with 90 percent of the area's logging and milling operations closed down. The Wobblies found themselves in control of a major strike—one that they would later recall as "the high-water mark" of their influence (Tyler, 1967:85).

Oregon and Washington mill owners were united in their unyielding opposition to negotiation. They raised a half-million-dollar "fighting fund" to break the strike and refused all offers of mediation by federal and state officials. The strike became a deadlock, and this was made a more serious problem because of the wartime need for Pacific Northwest lumber. In particular, military aircraft could not be built without a large and continuing supply of Sitka spruce, a variety found only in this region. For reasons of "national security," the federal government intervened in the strike by sending a special division of 25,000 soldiers to work as strikebreakers in the woods and mills. A corps of 2,000 officers was deployed to organize strikers into a "company union" known as the 4–L's. The strike was broken.

One observer summed up the industry's chronic antagonism between employer and worker:

The Pacific Northwest is the last place to which one would look for the promise of permanent industrial peace. . . . It was not only the filthy bunk-houses of the lumber camps, the desolation of the soggy woods, and the constant peril from crashing trees and flashing ropes that made the lumber industry so anarchic; even more, it was the tough pertinacity and rugged individualism of the employers, the sullen lonesome hatred of the lumberjacks and the timid stolidity of the mill workers. . . . The Northwest is inevitably associated . . . with a violence of labor disputes as bitter as civil war. (Boas, 1918:226)

Consolidating the Gains . . . But for Whom?

In sharp contrast to the turbulent history of strikes and violence that characterized the industry from 1890 through World War I, the following period, to the present, has been surprisingly placid. Yet the technological and organizational structure of the industry has changed greatly and has had a significant effect on workers. The evolution of Oregon's wood-products industry since World War II has been particularly dramatic. These changes can be summarized in three categories: concentration and mergers, diversification and capital flight, and mechanization. Each type of change has an accompanying impact on the wood-products labor force and on the regional, timber-dependent economy. The changes and their effects are described below.

As is true with most industries in the United States, the forest-products industry is dominated by a small number of corporations, in this case "The Big Six." In 1977 Georgia-Pacific, International Paper, Weyerhaeuser, and Champion International each reported more than three billion dollars in sales. Boise Cascade and Crown Zellerbach each exceeded the two-billion-dollar sales mark. An additional seven forest-products corporations posted sales of over one billion dollars.

Forest-products corporations exhibit the same tendencies toward concentration as do U.S. corporations in general. The trend toward fewer and larger firms is evident in the industry and has largely been carried by a strategy of merger and elimination of smaller competitors. Since World War II merger activity has been greater within the forest-products industry than within the U.S. industrial sector as a whole, and it accelerated during the late 1960s. Many mergers were with smaller firms that had timber holdings. This strategy was intended to increase the timber supply available to the larger firms. The merger activity of the Big Six from 1950–70 is shown below. Total number of mergers are listed first (the second figure indicates the number of mergers that included acquisition of timberlands):

Mergers of the Big Six Forest-Products Corporations, 1950–70
Georgia-Pacific 86:43
International Paper 13:4

Weyerhaeuser 24:7
Champion International 46:16
Boise Cascade 83:15
Crown Zellerbach 6:3

(Source: LeMaster, 1977)

Land acquisitions for all the corporations took place primarily in the Pacific Northwest and the South. One major effect of the 1950–70 mergers, then, was to increase the already vast timber holdings of the large companies. By 1977 these six companies owned more than 68 percent of all private commercial timberland in Oregon.

Another effect of the mergers was a decline in smaller competitors. Between 1948 and 1962, for example, the number of small sawmills was reduced by 85 percent (Table 2.1). Closures, as well as mergers, appear to have affected this figure. The total number of mills has continued to decline to the present.

Table 2.1.   Changes in the Number of Lumber-Producing Mills in the Pacific Northwest, 1948-62.

		Number of Sawmills in Operation		
	Class of Mill[a]	1948	1962	Percent Change
D	(less than 40,000[b] board feet)	1,328	202	-85
C	(40,000-80,000 board feet)	191	128	-33
B	(80,000-120,000 board feet)	53	77	+45
A	(more than 120,000 board feet)	103	86	-71
	TOTAL	1,675	493	-71

[a]Mill size or "class" is determined by the level of production in board feet per eight-hour shift.
[b]Board foot is the customary unit of measure in lumber. A board foot is the equivalent of an inch-thick plank twelve inches long and wide.

Source: Mead, 1966.

Another consequence of concentration has been a loss of community control, which might otherwise compel companies to exercise responsibility. Large producers operate in many states and foreign countries. Decisions about layoffs or closures are made without apparent regard for the consequences to workers or to timber dependent communities. With increasing scale comes an increasing physical distance from and a lack of sensitivity to the communities in which these firms have plants.

Concentration and merger activity in the timber industry have been accompanied by diversification of production. Oregon is still the nation's largest producer of such basic products as softwood lumber, softwood plywood, and red-cedar shakes and shingles. Added to these, however, is a growing variety of newer products, such as pulp, paper, paperboard, insulation board, and particle board.[3] Secondary industries concerned with furniture and mobile-home manufacture, wood preservation, and mill work have also appeared on the scene. At the same time there is a growing market for by-products: adhesives, preservatives, hardwood overlays, paper chemicals, and plastic.

The manufacture of a greater variety of wood products and by-products has been caused, at least in part, by the depletion of old-growth timber. Only the old-growth stands produce the large cuts of lumber that have traditionally been used in building construction. Since they have overcut and depleted the larger trees on their private holdings, industry has found it necessary to develop products and markets that can effectively utilize younger, smaller trees. Thus the increased use of paperboard and particle board in new homes does not owe to the changing tastes of homeowners, but to the economics of lumber production. A related trend since World War II has been the growth of the mobile-home industry. Mobile homes now offer a housing alternative to an increasing number of families who find themselves priced out of the conventional housing market. Manufactured fiberboard and plywood are the most common materials used in mobile homes. Neither requires much wood, and, in fact, some fiberboard has no wood content at all! Modern pulp and paper plants can also accommodate small logs that come from younger trees.

Privately owned, old-growth timber is fast becoming scarce in Oregon because of overcutting by the timber companies. The industry has turned to publicly owned lands for their old-growth supply. In addition, they have developed the technology and markets to utilize younger and/or second-growth trees. Since second-growth timber on industry lands in Oregon is not yet "ripe" for harvesting, corporations have increasingly moved their operations out of the Northwest to the Southeast. Such a strategy is not without precedent. Historically, timber corporations have exhausted the timber supply in one region at a time and then moved to new sources of supply. The climate of the Southeast produces a high yield of small-diameter, softwood trees, and it has now become an attractive location for the newer pulp and paper plants that can process these trees. Also, the trees in this area are closer to markets in the East and Midwest, so transportation costs are lower. The availability of cheap labor further enhances the attractiveness of the Southeast. In 1971 the five largest lumber-producing states in the Southeast paid an average hourly wage of $2.36 to wood-products workers. The comparable wage in Oregon and Washington was $4.31.

While the economic reasons for diversification are clear enough, there is at least one negative consequence that is never publicly mentioned. Newer production processes in chip, pulp, and paper manufacture rely more on machines than on human labor, and as such they are capital intensive. This is shown in the relatively high value of "capital assets per employee" in the pulp and paper sector. The 1968 Census of Manufacturers reports that "assets per employee" were $25,872 per worker in the paper and allied-products sector, and only $9,063 in the lumber and wood-products sector. Thus, as timber corporations diversify into pulp and paper production, they can eliminate jobs while expanding the value of total output. Since 1958 value added (i.e., the value of the product minus the cost of raw materials) has increased more than three times as rapidly in the Southeast as in the Northwest. This factor increases the attractiveness of the Southeast as an area for new investment and forebodes a continued drain of investment monies and jobs away from Oregon and Washington.

Although concentration, merger, diversification, and capital flight have had the effect of reducing the number of mills and jobs available to Oregon workers, mechanization has had even greater consequences. A specific example of the effect of mechanization on employment is provided by Weyerhaeuser's recent large investments in its Washington plants. According to a company news release, "The $400 million program will bring about major shifts in job location and content, and in skills which will be required in the new manufacturing processes." (Lembcke, 1976: 13). The new manufacturing processes mean, among other things, that Weyerhaeuser Mills B and C near Everett, Washington, have been able to make labor-force reductions from a previous level of 900 workers down to 500 workers. Further reductions are scheduled.

The total magnitude of the problem is indicated by the fact that capital expenditures per year by companies in the Pacific Northwest have more than tripled, from $126 million in 1947 to $435 million in 1971. At the same time, the total number of plants and mills in the region has steadily declined, from 9,320 in 1954 to 5,490 in 1972, a reduction of 41 percent. Thus increasing capital expenditures have been used to enlarge and further mechanize the plants of a decreasing number of existing firms.

Data on employment tell the same story. The number of workers employed in the Oregon wood-products industry decreased by 10.7 percent between 1960 and 1970 (Table 2.2), so the steady increase in capital expenditures since 1954 has occurred alongside a decline in employment.

Table 2.2. Experienced Civilian Labor Force[a], Wood-Products Industry in Oregon.

	1960	1970	Percent Change
Lumber and wood products	79,559	68,279	-14.2
Paper and allied products	7,083	9,101	+28.5
TOTAL	86,642	77,380	-10.7

[a]Fourteen years and older.

Source: U.S. Census of Population, 1960 and 1970.

Another way to examine the extent of mechanization—or the substitution of machines (capital) for labor—is to look at changes in labor intensity over a given period. This can be done by measuring the ratio of wages to value added, a ratio that indicates the relative importance of labor's input to the value of production. Table 2.3 shows the value added and labor intensity of the Northwest timber industry from 1937 to 1976. According to these figures, the value added rose by almost four times from 1954 to 1976—from about $1.18 billion to $4.66 billion. Since national lumber prices only doubled during the same period, the increase in value added was not solely because of inflation.

The figures for labor intensity show a steady decline, with significant reductions occurring between 1937 and 1954 and again between 1967 and 1971. The shift to capital intensity, which these figures represent implicitly, was greater in lumber and wood products than in paper and allied products. Note, however, that the paper and allied-products sector has always been substantially less labor intensive than the lumber and wood-products sector.

Table 2.3. Labor Intensity and Value Added in the Pacific Northwest Forest-Products Industry, 1937-1976, with Separate Consideration for the Lumber and Paper Sectors Within the Industry.

Year	Forest Products Value Added ($Million)	Paper Value Added as Percent of Forest Products	Labor Intensity		
			All Forest Products	Lumber	Paper
1937	210.1	12.8	.54	-	-
1947	815.3	21.1	.34	-	-
1954	1,178.9	24.2	.45	-	-
1958	1,205.8	29.5	.46	-	-
1963	1,508.4	29.6	.44	.50	.29
1967	1,737.0	30.6	.45	.52	.30
1971	2,843.7	40.6	.34	.45	.18
1972	3,202.5	24.0	.37	.39	.30
1973	4,083.2	27.0	.32	.33	.27
1974	3,937.1	28.0	.33	.37	.24
1975	3,584.0	30.0	.37	.42	.25
1976	4,663.1	26.0	.34	.37	.27

Source: Northwest Bulletin, Pacific Northwest Research Center, vol. 2, nos. 8, 9, 10 (May, June, July 1978), p.4.

These data illustrate a secular, or long-term, trend toward capital intensiveness in the wood-products industry. The substitution of capital for labor in production means the loss of jobs; it also means increasing profits for wood-products corporations.

All of these structural changes—concentration and merger, diversification and capital flight, and mechanization—have had significant effects on workers and on the timber-dependent economy of Oregon. Yet, as noted earlier, these changes have not been accompanied by significant labor disturbances, and the historical antagonism between employer and worker has noticeably diminished. Why has this been so? The answer lies primarily in corporate manipulation of information given to the public and an intensive industry campaign designed to blame job losses on declining levels of harvest. The purpose of this campaign is not only to disguise the real causes of unemployment but also to convince citizens of the need to support a larger harvest of trees from public forestlands and to stop further preservation of public lands in expanded wilderness areas. This strategy of manipulation and propaganda is described next.

It Is Hard to Know the Facts

A provocative, full-page ad appeared on Thanksgiving day, 1977, in several Oregon newspapers. The ad pictured a young family with downcast faces, and bold type proclaimed: "Dan Brammer, husband and father, lost his job due to the timber shortage. How many more must suffer?" The text of the ad explained that passage of a wilderness-area proposal currently being considered in a Senate/House Conference Committee would mean the loss of 956 jobs and $15 million in income to affected Oregon communities. "Don't jobs count?" asked the 30 signatories to the ad. One week later a small news item on the back pages of several of the same papers noted that an investigation of the situation by Rep. Jim Weaver (D-Ore.) turned up the surprising information that Dan Brammer was laid off by a log exporter based in California. In an interview the manager of the mill for which the young man worked said that the layoff "was not related to a shortage of timber." Weaver, who has differed sharply with lumber industry officials, charged that Brammer "is being exploited by some members of the timber industry who want to divert attention from the log export issue. They are blackmailing Oregon workers with threats of unemployment." The ad, it turns out, was initiated and paid for not by a group of concerned citizens but by the Northwest Timber Association, an organization of timber producers. Other, similar full-page ads have appeared in Oregon papers on a regular basis.

Another item in several Oregon papers revealed that news articles on the controversy surrounding the use of herbicides in forests had been reprinted and circulated in a pamphlet, with the headlines and contents of the articles altered. The alterations made the "reprinted" articles, and the newspapers from which they came, appear wholly supportive of the use of herbicides. In fact, this was not the case. The reprints were prepared and circulated by the Managed Forest Council—also a timber industry organization.

These are only two examples of a pervasive and influential campaign now being waged in the Pacific Northwest by the timber industry. The purpose is to convince residents of the area that it is in their interests to support such things as the harvest of more trees from public land and the use of herbicides and to oppose the expansion of wilderness areas. Fraud, deception, and manipulation of the public interest characterize this campaign, but it has been so successful that even local newspaper editorials now echo it. They inform the reader that a "tree famine" is imminent and that timber companies must be allowed to cut down more trees from national forestlands or layoffs, unemployment, and mill closures will result. It is not surprising that the ordinary citizen is concerned and misled. What are the "facts?"

One basic fact is that the projected tree famine is actually a result of the timber industry's rapid liquidation of timber from its land. The industry no longer has a stable source of private timber, and its representatives now seek increases in the annual harvest from federal timberlands in Oregon to make up for declining harvests on private forestlands (Wyant, 1977:130). They warn that the choice is between trees or jobs.

This alleged trade-off seems credible enough; the level of harvest does affect the availability of job opportunities in wood products. However, the harvest/employment relationship is overshadowed by more important factors. For instance, an industry practice of exporting unprocessed logs to Japan has greatly diminished the levels of employment in Oregon and Washington. In 1970 softwood log exports from western Washington and Oregon were about 2.9 billion board feet. This figure is projected to reach 3.8 billion board feet by the year 2000 (Wall 1973:5). Economic analysts for the International Woodworkers of America calculate that the export of logs, from the softwood region of the Pacific Northwest and northern California to Japan, cost the area 11,400 sawmill and planer-mill jobs in 1976. No wonder timber industry representatives would like to divert attention away from the log export issue: Not only is this practice highly profitable to the large corporations, but the job loss because of log exports dwarfs the projected unemployment that would result from the most expansive wilderness proposal.

Another basic fact is that wood-products jobs are declining, and this trend will continue. The U.S. Forest Service has projected a 45-percent decline in Pacific Northwest wood-products employment from 1970 to 2000 (Wall, 1973). The report that contains these projections has been widely circulated in Oregon and has caused a great deal of alarm. However, the most potentially controversial section of the document has never received public comment and remains obscured by the dramatic projections of job loss. In this section the employment projections were tested to see how they might change if alternate assumptions about the future were made. For instance, what if log exports dropped to zero and all timber was domestically processed? (Legislation to this effect has been under consideration in the Congress.) It turns out that the net effect of stopping all log exports from Oregon and Washington would be a 19-point *improvement* in the projected employment decline of 45 percent. Next, the effect of harvest levels on employment was tested by assuming that timber output was held constant at the 1970 level. This assumption approximates the situation that industry says will bring instability to the Oregon economy, yet under the "test" of unchanged harvest levels, there was little change in the employment projection; it improved by 9 percentage points. The most important factor affecting future employment levels was technological change, including "the substitution of one factor of production for another." When this was held constant, the result was that "forest employment in the year 2000 would be 47 percent greater" than now projected (Wall, 1973:6).

If timber corporations really want "Jobs First," as they claim, they are in the best position to promote such a goal. The two factors most affecting future job decline—technological change/mechanization and the export of logs—are controlled and can be varied by the firms themselves. Instead, they have chosen to mislead and deceive the public about the real cases of past, present, and future job decline, meanwhile continuing to mechanize their operations, export more logs, and move production to sites in the Southeast and abroad.

How Many Wood-Products Workers Are There?

If jobs in the wood-products sector have been declining since 1954, what has been happening to the workers? Have they been absorbed into other sectors, or have unemployment, underemployment, and declining labor-force participation been the consequences of secular job decline? Our examination of these questions was based on results of a 1974 statewide survey by Joe Stevens that describes the size and characteristics of the entire wood-products labor force. Analysis of worker perceptions and coping strategies makes use of data from a smaller and more detailed survey of mill workers laid off in the recession of 1974. These sources of information are supplemented by field notes and taped interviews with a smaller sample of unemployed mill workers. The three data sets are described more precisely below.

The 1970 Census of Population for Oregon indicates that there were a total of 68,279 persons in the wood-products labor force in 1969, or about 8 percent of total employment in the state. (This figure includes only timber and wood-products workers and excludes the 8,843 workers in paper and allied products. The following discussion excludes the latter group.) There has been a relative and absolute decline in the importance of wood-products employment since the early 1950s, when the industry employed more than 80,000 people—13 percent of the state's total employment. While it is undeniable that wood-products jobs are declining, the usefulness of the census count must be questioned.

For purposes of the census, a "wood-products worker" is someone whose primary work activity, *in the week prior to census enumeration,* was in the wood-products industry. Although accurate in this specific sense, the census count misses certain kinds of people. The least important omission, from our perspective, is that of students who may work in the woods or mills during the summer but remain out of the labor force while in school. A second, more important group is composed of people who work in wood products when jobs are available, but who intermittently find work in other occupational areas. Workers with high job turnover or frequent periods of unemployment are also likely to be missed by the census.

The highly cyclical nature of work in wood products means that there may well be many workers in precisely these categories—people who work in wood products but who will not be counted as such. It was partly in response to this suspected inadequacy in the census count that the 1974 statewide survey of mill workers and loggers was carried out. Sampling for the survey was based on Oregon Employment Division records for 1972.[4] A random sample of 189 workers, each of whom had worked in the lumber and wood-products sector at some time during 1972, was drawn from this file. Sampling was done in such a way that it is possible to make inferences to the total labor force in the state's lumber and wood-products sector.

Survey results revealed a much larger wood-products work force than that indicated by the census or by any other previously published data. "Whereas Census data indicated that there were about 68,279 persons in the experienced wood products labor force in 1969, the state-wide survey revealed that a total of 110,581 workers had received some wage or salary payment in the industry during 1972" (Stevens 1976:32). The fact that the census data were for 1969, while the figures from the statewide survey were for 1972, does not explain the 62-percent difference between these two results. State employment records for 1969 revealed a monthly wood-products employment average (i.e., the number of people actually working in any given month, averaged over the year) of 70,959. This differs little from the comparable monthly average figure of 75,200 in 1972.

What is apparent from the statewide survey is that a large number of workers who received some earnings from the wood-products industry did not maintain continuous employment in it and hence eluded the census count. Combining a total of 110,581 people working in the industry at some point during the year with an average monthly employment of 75,200, it is clear that a large number of workers were without wood-products jobs at any given time. To put it another way, there were about *three* workers for every two available wood-products jobs in 1972, amounting to a sizeable labor surplus. What did these surplus workers do when they could not find jobs in the woods or mills? There are a limited number of possibilities. They may have been among the substantial ranks of the unemployed in the industry (i.e., in the labor force and actively seeking work). They may have dropped out of the work force and ceased looking for work, in which case they were not officially counted as unemployed. Alternatively, they may have sought and found employment outside the wood-products sector.

The statewide survey contained extensive data on individual, lifetime work histories. These data were examined to obtain specific information about the unemployment, underemployment, job changing, and labor-force participation of wood-products workers. An initial result of our analysis of work histories was the discovery of two distinct groups in this labor force. The first group, numbering 99 respondents in the survey and an estimated 67,080 in the total wood-products work force, reported all their jobs during 1972 as being in one sector of the industry (for example, in logging). In addition, their overall work histories showed few or no instances of unemployment, self-employment, or withdrawal from the labor force. This group, which Stevens (1976) called nonmobile workers, represents a stable and steadily employed work force with relatively little job changing. It is interesting that the estimated number of nonmobile workers—67,080—is quite close to the 1970 census count of 68,279 workers. This further suggests that the census may be counting primarily the stable, fully employed workers in the industry.

The second group, numbering 90 in the survey and an estimated 43,501 in the total industry work force, was occupationally mobile in 1972. They either left or entered the wood-products industry during that year, or they did both. They also evidenced more periods of unemployment and labor-force withdrawal than the first group. Stevens called this group of workers "mobile."

In addition to these differences in labor-force participation, there were marked demographic variations between the two groups. Nonmobile workers, for example, were on the average 14 years older than mobile workers. Of the nonmobile group 60 percent were over the age of 40, while two-thirds of the mobile workers were 28 years old or less. As might be expected, age differences were reflected in other characteristics, such as marital status and extent of formal education. Thus far more of the nonmobile group (88 percent versus 60 percent) were married. With regard to education, nearly 80 percent of the mobile workers had completed high school, as compared to 60 percent of the nonmobile workers. Mobile workers were also the most urban. The population of their communities averaged 8,000, and 30 percent lived in towns with a population of more than 20,000. In contrast, the average community size for the nonmobile group was 2,050.

Given the age difference between the two groups, it is not surprising that there was a large difference between them in the total number of years worked. Both groups had averaged about six jobs to this point in their lifetime, but for the mobile workers these six had occurred within a span of 6.2 years as compared to an 18-year work history for the nonmobile group. Thus the average length of job for the mobile workers was about one year, while the older, nonmobile workers averaged about four years per job.

As suggested earlier, those wood-products workers with histories of job turnover and labor-force withdrawal may include students. In this case, an "interrupted" work history does not carry the same meaning as it does when involuntary unemployment or labor-force withdrawal is involved. Detailed data on labor-force participation were used to separate students from nonstudents within the mobile group, and student-workers were omitted from our further analysis of worker adaptation.

Table 2.4 provides a summary of several work-history characteristics for nonmobile and mobile workers, with the latter group subdivided by labor-force participation. As might be expected, substantial differences exist between the groups. Median earnings for the two types of mobile workers were markedly different, but both were much lower than the $10,262 median for nonmobile workers. Those mobile workers who were in the labor force throughout the year had the higher average earnings—$7,704—a figure still lower than the average $8,850 reported for all Oregon manufacturing workers in 1972.[5] The other group of mobile workers reported average earnings of only $5,049. It is not unreasonable to assume that these low earnings are related to interrupted labor-force participation and hence to declining employment opportunities in wood products. Work histories indicate that some in the group were injured and could not work; others retired or volunteered for military service during the period covered by the interview; and still others simply stopped looking for work.

Table 2.4.   Characteristics and Size of Different Groups of Wood-Products Workers, 1972.

Worker Group	Number in Survey Sample	Estimated Number in Statewide Population	Percent of Unemployment Rate	Median Earnings
Nonmobile and in labor market throughout 1972	99	67,080	2.4	$10,262
Mobile and in labor market throughout 1972	51	24,652	10.0	$7,875
Mobile and out of labor market for part of 1972	11	5,316	10.5	$4,950

Several factors may account for the relatively low earnings of these two mobile groups. First, their work histories showed on the average that they had been unemployed more than 10 percent of the time. In comparsion, the historic unemployment rate for nonmobile workers was 2.4 percent. Second, more than half the jobs listed by mobile workers in both groups were lower-paying jobs outside the wood-products industry. In contrast, non-mobile workers reported relatively few jobs outside the wood-products sector. We also know that mobile workers changed jobs frequently, averaging one and a half years per job; and they averaged less time per job in wood products than in jobs outside the industry. Finally, even when these workers were able to find logging or mill jobs, their average hourly wage of $4.04 was about 25 percent less than the $5.16 average paid to nonmobile workers.

These data on unemployment, job turnover, and labor-force participation suggest that for a sizeable group of Oregon wood-products workers, a declining number of jobs in the industry means they cannot find work even when they try and that they often resort to lower-paying jobs in other sectors, change jobs frequently, and sometimes give up looking for work altogether. The combination of these labor-market strategies results in very marginal earnings, with the lowest earnings reported by workers who are out of the labor force the most. It seems reasonable to conclude that these strategies represent an adaptation to the lack of jobs in the wood-products sector.

Getting Along Without a Steady Job

The recession of 1974–75 provided the chance to gather further information on how wood-products workers were adapting to an evolving job shortage. Many mills shut down, and layoffs pushed the unemployment rate to 25 percent in those counties whose economies are particularly dependent upon the timber industry. We interviewed 70 workers from three mills that had closed during this period. (This group is hereafter referred to as the "three-mills sample.") Extensive information on work histories was collected, using questionnaire items comparable to those on the statewide survey. In addition, we obtained behavioral and attitudinal data on job search, family life, future plans, and orientation toward the industry.

A third set of data was also compiled during this period—case studies of twelve wood-products workers and their families. These respondents were selected because they had recently experienced a layoff and resembled either mobile or nonmobile workers in several key respects, i.e., age, job stability, historic rate of unemployment, number of jobs outside the wood-products industry, and earnings. Data from these case studies are used below to illustrate the findings from the three-mills survey.

A preliminary analysis of the work histories and demographic characteristics of the three-mills sample revealed that within this group of 70 workers there were two distinct subgroups. As shown in Table 2.5, their respective characteristics matched closely those of the mobile and nonmobile worker groups identified earlier. (Selected mean values from the statewide sample are shown in parenthesis.) For instance, one grouping of workers was

Table 2.5.   Characteristics of Two Groups of Workers in the Three-Mills Sample.
(mean values given[a], unless otherwise stated)

	Nonmobile Group N=55		Mobile Group N=15	
Age, in years	43.9	(43.0)[b]	25.9	(28.6)[b]
Education, in years[c]	11.2	(10.6)	11.9	(12.5)
Total years worked	16.85	(18.1)	5.67	(6.2)
Number of jobs in last 5 years	1.14		3.67	
Average length of job, in years	4.3	(3.8)	1.3	(1.3)
Times quit job, in last 5 years	.16		1.67	
Months of unemployment in last 5 years	.04		.50	

[a]Unless otherwise noted, the differences between means for the two groups were all significant at (at least) the .05 level, using a two-tailed t-test.
[b]Numbers in parentheses are mean value from the 1972 statewide sample.
[c]The difference between means for this variable is significant at (at least) the .10 level.

relatively young, better educated, and more often unemployed. Their work histories showed frequent job changes and an average job length of just over one year. Several other variables that cannot be directly compared also reinforce the conclusion that the three-mills sample contains two distinct groups analogous to mobile and nonmobile workers in the statewide sample. This finding enabled us to use the three-mills sample to extend the initial analysis of difference between mobile and nonmobile workers by examining the extensive behavioral and attitudinal data from this later survey.

In an open-ended survey item, respondents mentioned a number of adjustments made necessary by the loss of jobs and income. For one thing, a good deal of "belt-tightening" was required. This included such things as "taking in boarders," "skipping mortgage payments," "baking bread," "cutting our own hair," "selling the car and buying a bike," and "having garage sales." In all, 78 percent of the 70 workers in the three-mills sample reported that they had initiated specific changes in their lives in order to save money. Respondents also reported that their families produced goods for home consumption as a means of saving money and combating financial insecurity. Of the men, 33 percent remodeled or rebuilt houses in their spare time. A full 89 percent did repairs around the house rather than hiring someone to do them, and about the same number repaired their own cars or trucks. Since being laid off, half the men had been spending more time doing house and vehicle repairs, as a result of both their increased efforts to save money and to cope with their extra time. Two-thirds of the households had vegetable gardens, and 40 percent were doing more gardening since the layoffs. To provide food for their families, 70 percent of the men hunted or fished. Nearly half of the total group were spending more time in these activities since being laid off.

None of the families that we interviewed was relying on public assistance, such as food stamps or welfare. This was true despite the fact that they generally favored the *idea* of giving economic relief to the poor; for example, three-fourths of the men said they approved of unemployed people receiving welfare, and one-fourth agreed with the statement that, "If someone is really down and out he is justified in getting money however he can." Evidently, they felt that what was permissible for others was not necessarily good for themselves. Many of the men explained that people lose dignity when they accept "handouts." They were convinced that their children would not be able to respect them if they became welfare recipients. Some also claimed that their families had been brought closer together and were now better prepared to weather bad times by relying on their own resourcefulness.

What was especially evident with these families was a spirit of independence, cooperation, and neighborliness. There were many instances of sharing and exchanging between families. For example, 70 percent of the people interviewed said that they were either sharing or exchanging food, housing, clothing, or other resources with other households, while a quarter of the men indicated that they exchanged labor and tools for home and auto repairs with other men. Often, what a family could not grow, raise, build or fix itself could be acquired in trade with other families.

The Rex Tuttle family was one of the most resourceful that we encountered. Even though Tuttle[6] had found a mill job soon after being laid off, he was adding two additional rooms onto his house, using lumber that he had salvaged from a neighbor's burned-out barn. The Tuttles had milk cows, chickens, three or four pigs, two horses, and a large garden. Tuttle took milk and eggs to work, where he sold about 30 gallons of milk and 16 dozen eggs each week to his co-workers. Milk and eggs were sometimes traded for vehicle repairs and other things needed by the family. The family estimated that their livestock yielded about 500 pounds of meat a year, while canning and freezing produced about 136 quarts of food from the garden. (Another family that outdid the Tuttles produced an average of 760 quarts of food each summer in a major effort that involved all of the family for most of the summer months.)

For a time Tuttle held down a second part-time job at a cemetery in addition to working swing shift at the mill. He sold produce during his breaks and sometimes "did the bills or balanced the checkbook." This routine was exhausting, however: "I was getting hardly any sleep and I made a $250 mistake in the checkbook. We were in big trouble that month!" Tuttle pointed out that some of the younger guys at the mill "knock off a day and just work four." But as he said of himself: "I work seven days a week whenever they'll let me, 'cause I need the money. If you have a family and want your kids to have any kind of decent life, you gotta figure all the angles all the time and have a lot of deals going, just to make ends meet. . . . A free enterprise system is good because it makes you really work harder!"

Two significant differences emerged in the immediate adaptation by nonmobile and mobile workers. First, mobile workers appeared to be harder hit and were forced to take more severe measures to cope with financial hardship. On the average, mobile workers mentioned five or six kinds of things done to save money and meet expenses, whereas nonmobile workers seldom mentioned more than three. Second, mobile workers showed more initiative and interest in making it on their own. Virtually everyone in the mobile group, compared to only 40 percent in the three-mills sample as a whole, stated that they would like to start their own business. All of the case-study families were engaged in some attempt to do so, including making terrariums, building wood-burning stoves, running a mobile truck-repair service, cutting up and selling scrap iron, and marketing inventions.

These men did not plan to be working in wood products if they could figure a way out. To become one's own boss is not a realistic alternative for all mobile workers who are either unemployed or are dissatisfied with their present jobs. Small businesses suffer a very high rate of failure; more than half do not make it through the first year of operation. However, many things still seem possible in Oregon, with its populism, abundant resources, and lingering frontier ideology.

The Relentless Search for "A Better Job"

The more active adaptation of mobile workers carried over to their search for jobs. Workers in the mobile group of the 3-mills sample, for example, made five times as many contacts with friends about jobs as those in the nonmobile group (Table 2.6). The number of relatives contacted was roughly eight times greater for mobile workers, who also inquired more about jobs outside the wood-products sector. Apparently these contacts produced some results, for a much smaller proportion of the mobile group was still unemployed at the time the interviews began.

Table 2.6. Comparison of Job Search among Mobile and Nonmobile Workers in the Three-Mills Sample.
(mean values given[a], unless otherwise stated)

Job Search	Nonmobile Group N=55	Mobile Group N=15
Times contacted friends about a job, per week	.435	2.20
Times contacted relatives about a job, per week	.111	.933
Times inquired about nonmill[b] work, per week	1.59	3.13
Percentage of group still unemployed	43.6	20.0

[a]The differences between means were significant at the 0.1 level (using a two-tailed t-test), unless otherwise noted.
[b]The difference between these two means was significant at (at least) the .15 level (two-tailed probability).

The search for jobs, however, is frustrating and does not easily lead to success. After being laid off permanently in October 1974, Dick Roper decided to pursue the possibility of job retraining through the county's CETA program.

I was the fifth person accepted when they opened for business. Then I kept checking back and they told me that several things were "in the works" for me. But the weeks kept rolling by and nothing happened. Finally, I just got so fed up with the promises that I went to their office and demanded "what were they doing with my case." The guy that's been handling my case said there was nothing new to tell me and then he asked me to leave.

At one time, the CETA office informed Roper that he was scheduled into a training class at the local community college. After waiting several days for confirmation from either CETA or the college, Roper called the school to find out if his name was on the enrollment list. It was not, and the college told him that they had never heard from CETA regarding his case.

Roper was also disgruntled by other attempts to find work through institutional channels. Repeated contacts with the Human Resources officer at the county's employment office yielded nothing. He followed up any and all leads in the "Help Wanted" section of the paper and beat on many doors, asking for work. In December Roper finally found a job as a service-station attendant. His monthly take-home pay was $700—a very small amount with which to feed and clothe five children. The family was forced to rely on their church for extra food and a total of $800–900 in monetary assistance to meet monthly mortgage payments. As the months went by, Roper became increasingly frustrated. He complained that he had done everything he could think of to find a decent job, and yet at 35 he was still searching: "It seems like I can't rely on my type of employment anymore, and I feel like I haven't been able to make much progress in getting job security and advancement"

Most mobile workers appeared to keep a watchful eye out for other jobs even while employed. The truck drivers were able to do this every day while waiting for other men to load or unload. One of our respondents worked for a company that hauled wood chips and dimensional lumber from the mills to lumberyards and other places. The first chance to talk to other drivers came when he checked in at 6:00 A.M. and got his beginning delivery for the day.

Loading takes about an hour, but it may take three to four hours if there are several trucks loading ahead of you. During the wait you catch up on your paperwork, check out the truck and talk to other drivers. We talk about politics, the economy, news. But mostly we exchange information about the market for lumber and about jobs.

I'd say about 45 percent of the drivers here have their eyes open for other jobs. But you only talk about it with drivers you trust; other guys go run to the boss. If he knew you were looking for other work he'd fire you on the spot!

This man worked 56 to 70 hours a week. He ate his lunch in the truck. "You get paid for every hour you work and I can make extra bucks that way." He often worked 12-hour days, and he disliked the job intensely.

I hated to take this job, but economics forced me into it because I'd been unemployed for two and a half months. Almost every night after work some of the guys get together at a coffee shop to discuss the pressure the boss puts on them and how to cope. I don't go very often though; I can't see that they're going to do anything about the problem. Now if they'd get together in a body and all go see the owner to do something about it, that'd be fine. But they don't; it's all just "mouth action."

All twelve men interviewed for the case studies kept a log of their time during a one-week period in March 1974. Kenny Pack's log contained a particularly detailed account of routine job-hunting activities during that week. Pack was a millwright who had been unemployed since October 1973.

Monday: Left home at approximately 7:30 A.M. enroute to Cascade (small nearby town) to look for work. Stopped by the sawmill to see friends who work there. Talked about job prospects in and around the Cascade area. . . .

Left the mill and stopped by a friend's house in town. Had lunch together and traded information about job openings we heard of.

Pack noted that because of lumber market fluctuations and the common management practice of laying off whole shifts of workers, nearly everyone who works in a small sawmill tries to keep up with the latest job information. Thus it is in the interest of currently employed mill workers to collect and trade ongoing information about jobs.

Tuesday: Left home at approximately 8:30 A.M. enroute to Weyerhaeuser mill in Lakeside. Went to update my application form and talk to the personnel manager.

In the evening a friend called and told me that there may be some job openings at the Weyerhaeuser plant in Springfield.

Wednesday: Left home at 8:00 A.M. for Eugene to inquire about work at Boggs Lumber Company. Talked to the maintenance/construction foreman at the plant for about an hour. Went from Eugene to the Springfield Weyerhaeuser plant to update application and talk to personnel manager. Checked out the job lead from last night. The personnel manager and millwright superintendent were both out, so I talked to a friend of mine in the office—an insurance representative. He didn't really know about any job prospects at the mill.

Later conversations with Pack revealed that he "blew up" during the visit with his friend. It seems he had been "checking in" at the Springfield Weyerhaeuser plant every month for five months. The personnel manager kept telling him, "We're not hiring, Check back." Pack took that to mean that there would be a job for him in time. This particular Wednesday when he checked in, he told his friend that he was tired of "checking back"; that he wanted to know if Weyerhaeuser was seriously interested in hiring him; and that he wanted to know before he left—today!" As his friend was not in any position to give him concrete information about openings at the mill, Pack got very mad and left.

Thursday: Left home at 8:00 A.M. to go to the veneer plant at Alpine. Picked up a time card and filled out insurance papers. Supposed to start work next Monday. . . . Left at 10:00 A.M. and drove to Lakeside to the Kimble manufacturing plant. Asked if they were hiring and left my name. After checking with them, I drove to a friend's house and we talked about jobs around Lakeside. About 1:00 P.M. I went to Firply—a small plywood mill—to see if they were hiring. Had heard that the millwright job was open, so talked to the plant manager about the job. They had already filled it.

Pack went back to work on April 18, six months after being laid off. During those intervening months, he often made three or four contacts about work each day, talking with mill foremen, personnel managers, and friends. He even wrote letters of inquiry to several mills in Canada. Pack was very bitter about his contacts with the local employment office.

Why did mobile workers so relentlessly engage in such a frustrating and time-consuming search for work? It is not that they had a low level of commitment to wood-products work, or that they preferred changing jobs every year. Actually, the opposite was true. Rather, their restlessness was caused by disappointment with their employers. Respondents frequently complained about speed-up, low-quality products and the cavalier attitude of the companies. The following statements are typical:

The work is not challenging, and is not really "work" at all: It doesn't take much brains to pull short pieces of wood off a chain and sort them. Part of the problem is that mills are no longer after quality. When you know how poor the product is you're making, you just don't feel satisfied, and there is no sense of accomplishment. I actually think I'm overpaid for my present job. I should demand a pay cut! That might make me feel more dignity.

I won't take a job unless I can do it thoroughly and with the knowledge that my work will be excellent. There was this really good commercial on TV last week that sorta pictures how I feel about it. People are shown doing various kinds of jobs and then they sign or initial what they've done. That's how it should be. More than anything else I gotta have pride in my work. I'd like to find a job like that, you know, where I could sign my name to the stuff.

The problem is that millwork is very boring. There's a better way they could do it. Even if we just traded jobs once in a while. Rather than have all these different wages, just pay everybody the same and give 'em all a chance to try everything. "Cause now it gets damn monotonous. Everyone I know is looking for a way to get out of the mill."

We're conscientious men. I just wish once in a while they'd tell us, "Hey, you did a good job."

The matter of job safety was raised time and again. The sawmills were described as dusty, smokey, and noisy.

I started having trouble with my hearing, you know, so I went to the doctor and he tested me and they found I had a 40-percent hearing loss. I'd only been working at the mill for a year. Not too long ago the "feds" came in and made the company lower the noise level in the plant. Which the company could've done all along, but they just don't give a damn.

This same man cleared his throat constantly and seemed to have a perpetual cough. Although he did not directly blame the dust and smoke at the mill for these problems, he said that his throat was "constantly itchy" at work.

The men who drove trucks between the mills and lumberyards reported other kinds of hazards:

Safety factors are a real bearcat! The main thing is the bunkers. They got plugged up sometimes and you're supposed to go up in the "crawl hole" and unplug it. The suction is terrific on those things when they break loose. You hang onto anything you can to keep from getting sucked down and suffocated with the chips, sawdust, whatever you're loading. You ever try to get a grip on a piece of slick flat metal?!

They're supposed to have lights up in the bunkers and safety straps for the guys to hang onto, but 90 percent of 'em don't. It wouldn't be nothing for them to rig those things up, but they don't.

The truck is 14 feet high and you're up another 12–15 feet above that when you're trying to unplug one. I'll tell you it really gets to ya.

A good friend of mine—another driver—was killed on the railroad tracks last month. See, the trains come in around midnight and switch without their lights. When you're leaving that mill you gotta cross the tracks to get to the highway, but you have to practically drive onto the tracks to see if they're clear because your view is blocked. It's just like the bunkers: you go in there late at night, no lights, nobody is around. You fall in and nobody's gonna find you until 6 or 7 hours later. The small mills don't even have a watchman around to see if things go OK. It shakes you up a little bit.

The safety conditions are horrible! The taxpayers' money is going to guys who are supposed to be checking on this stuff, and they're not doing their job. I have never seen a safety man around in all the years I've worked these jobs. See, what happens is that they walk into a mill and all the foremen hate them. So, it's just easier for them to spend two minutes in the mill and then go get some coffee, to get away from the tension.

These personal accounts about the hazards of wood-products work are supported by other evidence. The wood-products industry was the leading contributor to Oregon's 1976 death statistics, accounting for nearly 40 percent of all industrial fatalities. Logging accidents alone accounted for three-fourths of the casualties within the wood-products sector. Despite technological progress, which could conceivably make work safer, the industry has the worst accident and injury record in the nation. In 1969 injuries per one million employee hours averaged 14.8 for all manufacturing jobs, compared to 34.6 for wood-products jobs (Bureau of Labor Statistics). In addition to the fact that wood-products work causes many fatal injuries, it is also extremely unpleasant and generally unhealthy. Not only are noise levels too high to permit conversation with co-workers but also evidence exists to show that excessive noise is a contributing factor in nervous disorders, vascular deterioration, and cardiac problems. Since loggers and mill workers work in places that are cold and damp most months of the year, another occupational hazard is a higher-than-normal incidence of arthritis (Scott, 1973).

What mobile workers wanted was a job that is satisfying, has good benefits and security, is safe, and provides them with a sense of dignity and accomplishment. The problem is that these characteristics, while not at all unreasonable to expect, are not typical of wood-products work. In a way, the continual search for a better job indicates that these men were not willing to accept this fact. They were searching for a place of work that would be different. It seems clear that their higher job turnover does not mean they are less committed to work than the nonmobile workers, who stay where they are and wait things out.

Workers Who Wait it Out: Why Do They Appear So Loyal to the Industry?

It is apparent from the low level of activity exhibited by nonmobile workers that they have chosen a wait-and-see approach. For the most part, they have been content to hope that their former company will reopen or that another company will come looking for an experienced worker. This general posture is reflected in the fact that one-third of the nonmobile workers disagreed with the statement: "I would like to leave the wood-products sector and find another line of work" (Table 2.7).[7]

Why should workers who have recently been laid off express such a strong

Table 2.7. Reactions to Statement of Preference about Leaving the Wood-Products Sector.

Response	Nonmobile Workers[a] Percent N=55	Mobile Workers[b] Percent N=15
Strongly disagree	3.8	0.0
Disagree	30.2	6.7
Neither agree nor disagree	20.8	26.7
Agree	35.8	53.3
Strongly agree	9.4	13.3
TOTAL	100.0	100.0

[a]Mean response for nonmobile workers: 3.17.
[b]Mean response for mobile workers: 3.73.
Note: The two-tailed t-test is significant at the .035 level.

orientation toward an industry in which employment opportunities are declining? At first we thought their perceptions about availability of work in the future might be a factor. However, more than half the men in both groups agreed with a survey item which stated that opportunities in mill work would decrease in the future. Only 9 percent in either group disagreed with this assessment. Thus we could not attribute a difference in desire to stay in the wood-products sector to a difference in perceptions regarding future opportunities. Next, we examined workers' attitudes about their previous employer. Did some workers experience worse treatment than others? The answer is no. There were no differences between nonmobile and mobile

Table 2.8. What Nonmobile and Mobile Workers Expect to be Doing in Five Years[a].

Response	Nonmobile Workers Percent N=55	Mobile Workers Percent N=15
Working, in a mill	50.0	6.7
Working, not in a mill	20.4	46.6
Whatever I have to do to survive	16.7	40.0
Going to school	9.2	0.0
Other (e.g. farming)	3.7	6.7
TOTAL	100.0	100.0

[a]The distribution of responses between groups is significantly different at the .009 level (two-tailed t-test).

workers in how they felt they had been treated and paid. Although respondents as a whole tended to disagree with the statement that "A company is justified in laying people off in order to protect its profits," again there was no significant difference between nonmobile and mobile workers.

The question of industry orientation was further explored in answers to this open-ended question: "What do you expect to be doing in five years?" The coded responses in this case revealed a sharp difference between the two groups (Table 2.8). Half the nonmobile workers saw themselves working in a mill, whereas only 7 percent of the mobile workers thought they would be doing this.

Interestingly, half the mobile workers answered this question about expectations for the future by mentioning some type of non-wood-products work, while an additional 40 percent replied to the effect that they would be doing whatever they had to do to survive. The responses of the mobile workers are consistent with their perceptions about declining future opportunities in wood products and the relative lack of substantial work alternatives in Oregon, i.e., most of these workers predict a decline in mill work, and only a few see themselves working in a mill in five years. However, this perception of declining work opportunities is one shared by nonmobile workers. Why then do at least half of this group expect to be working in a mill in five years? Perhaps this prediction has some relationship to the senior status of these workers, and perhaps it is wishful thinking.

Workers in the nonmobile group have seniority and very stable work histories. If the layoffs they experience are because of temporary mill closures, they can realistically expect to be among the first workers rehired when production resumes. In fact, 22 percent of the nonmobile workers in the three-mills sample had been rehired by their former employer within seven months after being laid off. In contrast, the number of mobile workers hired again by the same firm during this time period was less than 7 percent. However, 80 percent of the mobile workers found jobs elsewhere (usually outside the wood-products sector), compared with 54 percent of the nonmobile group. Clearly, the older wood-products workers do not find themselves as employable if they are thrust into the general job market along with other, younger workers. Seniority helps primarily if the mill where they have worked reopens. Hence, workers with seniority must count on two things. First, they will have an advantage over younger workers when it comes to the order in which layoffs and rehirings occur. Second, a permanent closure will not hit their particular mill. Nothing is so predictable in this industry, however; and in holding to this strategy these workers make themselves extremely vulnerable to being abandoned. Even so, this may be the most realistic strategy, insofar as specific alternatives do not exist for men in their positions.

A strong feeling of resignation existed among nonmobile workers. For example, more than half the men in the nonmobile group agreed with the statement: "I have found that things will usually happen regardless of what I think or do about it"; whereas 83 percent of the mobile group disagreed (Table

2.9). The pattern of response in this case was dramatically different, and it was more so than for any other question asked.

Here are some possible reasons for these differences. Men in the nonmobile group have spent nearly all their adult work lives in an industry that is characterized by a highly cyclical demand for labor. With an average work history of 17 years, most of these workers first found jobs in wood products at a time when the labor surplus was not yet a serious problem. They stuck with their jobs, built seniority, and developed some degree of protection from the industry's cyclical blows. However, their adaptation ultimately became a passive one. Its nature is evident in their wait-and-see posture taken during the 1974 layoffs. They made few, if any, contacts about other jobs and

Table 2.9. Reactions of Nonmobile and Mobile Workers to the Statement: "Things Usually Happen Regardless..."

Reaction	Nonmobile Workers[a] Percent N=55	Mobile Workers[b] Percent N=15
Strongly disagree	0.0	8.3
Disagree	26.5	75.0
Neither	22.4	0.0
Agree	49.0	16.7
Strongly agree	2.0	0.0

[a]Mean response for nonmobile group: 3.27.
[b]Mean response for mobile group: 2.25.
Note: The two-tailed t-test is significant at the .001 level.

demonstrated relatively little interest in working outside the wood-products sector. Nearly half were still without work when we interviewed them seven months after the layoffs. It is true that these men are generally aware of a future decline in wood-products jobs. Will the decline affect them? Do they have any options if it does? Their past work experience suggests that the answers to these questions lie outside their control. Perhaps this is why they express resignation.

Men in the mobile group, on the other hand, appear to have forged a much more active adaptation to unstable employment in the sector. They bounce back and forth between jobs, averaging not much more than a year for each. They quit work frequently—a behavior that is much less apparent among the nonmobile workers—and they rely heavily on jobs outside of wood products to maintain incomes. They have demonstrated to themselves, through their own active adaptation to unstable work, that they can scrape together a living. They are job hustlers, and they are pretty good at it. No, things do not happen regardless of what they think or do about them. They make things happen. They find work in a variety of places despite the reputed scarcity of jobs in

Oregon; they quit if they have a beef; they develop self-reliant, resourceful means of coping with economic hardship; they see themselves getting out of mill work; and they believe that anything is possible if they just put their minds to it. What they want, regardless of the sacrifice that has to be made, is to control their own economic futures. To have control, however, is a goal that nonmobile workers have learned from their experience is next to impossible.

A Division of Labor: Workers Make Wood Products, Capitalists Make Profits

From 1850 to as recently as a decade ago, there seemed to be an unlimited number of trees in Oregon. Oregonians had more trees than they knew what to do with. No more. A shortage of trees, high prices of wood products, closure of small mills, and declining employment have all followed as a gradual consequence of the great land grab that was underway at the turn of the century and of the ensuing concentration of production. The availability of vast amounts of inexpensive timberlands, and the use of these lands for purposes of speculation, enabled a small number of companies to realize windfall profits and assure themselves of a continuing supply of logs for the mills they would later build.

Some of the original land-grabbers, like Weyerhaeuser, are still around. Other large wood-products corporations, like Georgia-Pacific, acquired their timber holdings and mills by buying up small, independent firms in the wave of mergers after World War II. Regardless of the historical route, ownership of timberland has become the critical factor influencing productive longevity and the ability to make profits. The big corporations that own the land now have an even tighter hold. They have increased their timber holdings, diversified production, and moved on to other areas with unexploited timber reserves. It is abundantly evident from observing substantial yearly increases in profits that the "tree famine" has not starved the treasuries of these corporations (Table 2.10).

Small mills without their own timber holdings continue to go under. In Lane County, Oregon, the heart of the softwood country, six small sawmills shut down in 1976 alone because they could not get timber. These shutdowns permanently cancelled the paychecks of 2,000 men and women, and the closures continue.

Meanwhile, George Weyerhaeuser boasted to the New York Society of Security Analysts that his corporation has "freed" itself of its West Coast operations in order to "capture the growth in the export markets" and acquire "major Indonesian operations" (Lembcke, 1976:10). In the past decade Weyerhaeuser's foreign ventures have included the purchase of 700,000 acres of cutting rights in Malaysian Borneo and the Philippines, acquisition of a 250,000-acre timber concession in Indonesia, and acquisition of International Timber Company in Indonesia, which owns cutting rights to 1.5 million acres. Recently, the company also made known its interest in Brazilian timberlands (Lembecke, 1976:14). Thus, when the last tree has been cut from

Weyerhaeuser's holdings in Oregon and Washington, the company will have somewhere else to go. When it gets there, it will not lack company, because Georgia-Pacific, Boise Cascade, Evans Products, International Paper, and others have also been busy buying up timberland in Southeast Asia. Clearly, these corporations will not be caught with a timber shortage.

Table 2.10. Profits in the Wood-Products Industry[a], First Nine Months of 1976.

Company	Reported Profits (Loss) ($ Million)	Increase (Decrease) Over a Year Ago (Percent)
Boise Cascade	69.8	39.0
Champion International	79.3	76.2
Crown Zellerbach	71.1	48.4
Evans Products	22.8	159.1
Georgia-Pacific	161.7	43.4
International Paper	205.9	43.6
Medford Corporation	2.0	(16.7)
Pope and Talbot	3.4	(1.8)
Potlatch	35.3	22.6
Weyerhaeuser	220.2	43.8
Willamette Industries	31.2	19.1

[a]All firms listed in the table have production facilities in Oregon.

The IWW recognized the loggers and mill workers of the Pacific Northwest as fierce, proud men. The Wobblies said they learned their best lessons about courage and persistence from these "timber beasts." Although many mills are not unionized, most wood-products workers need no longer fight for the right to have a union. The resistance by workers is now a response to much more subtle exploitation than that which prompted the Wobbly-called strikes. The lack of historical accountability and commitment to the wood-products work force is now manifested in log exports (which might just as easily be called "job exports"), a rapid rate of mechanization (or wholesale job loss), movement of production to the Southeast and overseas, unilateral and frequent layoffs and closures without warning, uncorrected work hazards, and the corporations' outrageously hypocritical statements that they are against wilderness areas because they are "for jobs." In a multitude of ways the large wood-products firms show that in fact they are for profits, not jobs, and are concerned about productivity, not the welfare of their workers.

The reaction to this cavalier and exploitative treatment takes many forms. The mobile, mostly younger workers treat the job as casually as they are treated—quitting frequently, continually searching for a new job, acting on their dreams of leaving wood products and being their own boss. They react to the cyclical insecurity of wood-products work through activities aimed at achieving self-reliance and individual freedom. It is important to note, however, that these men are not cavalier about work as an activity, but only about the choice of jobs and employers available to them. They commonly complained that work was so undemanding and the product of such poor quality that they could no longer get pride and a sense of satisfaction from their work. More satisfaction from work, as well as greater security, was the motive behind the job turnover.

The nonmobile workers, not all of whom are older, have more seniority and hence more job security with any given company. They have made a different adaptation to the capriciousness of wood-products employment: They wait out layoffs and stick to one company. This does not mean that they are more satisfied with their work or more approving of their employers. A majority of both groups of workers said that companies were not justified in laying off workers to protect profits. Similarly, both groups reported that they did not feel pride in the product they were making. However, the nonmobile workers, in developing a strategy that maximizes both their job security and their earnings, have relinquished a larger measure of control over their lives. They appear to perceive this in their fatalistic admission that things tend to happen regardless of what they do.

In the larger picture all wood-products workers have very little control indeed. No matter how imaginative and self-reliant their private lives are, how persistent their search for more satisfying work, or how dedicated they are to present jobs, the rapid mechanization of wood-products work and the shift of company activities overseas will eventually deny them the means to a livelihood.

Since workers, like their employers, are accustomed to regarding trees primarily as a productive resource and are kept deliberately misinformed about the most important causes of the impending reduction in jobs, they are naturally inclined to support the timber companies in their selfish desire to increase the cut from public lands. They are encouraged by the companies to direct their wrath toward environmentalists, whose interest in preserving natural resources makes them a convenient scapegoat. Such exploitation and ideological manipulation can be justified by the companies only on the self-serving grounds that "that's the way things must be" for them to make profits. That such outcomes are a "necessary part of doing business" in a free-enterprise system is a very unappealing explanation when placed alongside the human costs that are involved.

Notes

1. No one knows for sure where this nickname for loggers originated, but it appears in early poems and stories from the region.

2. A detailed account of timberland acquisition in the Pacific Northwest is to be found in Meany (1935). Our abbreviated discussion is based on Chapter V, "Timber Depredation, and the Concentration of Timber Ownership through General Federal Legislation," and Chapter VI, "Concentration of Timber Ownership through Federal Land Grants."

3. In conventional usage, the contemporary wood-products industry includes those occupations that fall under Standard Industrial Classification (SIC) numbers 24 (Lumber and Wood Products) and 26 (Paper and Allied Products). The following breakdowns give a more specific idea of the occupations involved in each of these two sectors. Industries included in SLC 24 are:

241 Logging camps and logging contractors
242 Sawmills and planing mills
243 Millwork, veneer, plywood, and structural wood members
244 Wood containers
245 Wood building and mobile homes
249 Miscellaneous wood products

Industries included in SLC 26 are:

261 Pulp mills
262 Paper mills, except building paper mills
263 Paperboard mills
264 Converted paper and paperboard products
265 Paperboard containers and boxes
266 Building paper and building-boards mills

4. This survey was carried out under the direction of Joe B. Stevens, Department of Agricultural Economics, Oregon State University. The funds for data collection and analysis were provided by the Oregon Agricultural Experiment Station, while the Oregon Employment Division provided complete records from which the initial, random sample of 2,000 workers was drawn. The ensuing discussion of this survey draws heavily on Stevens's (1976) description and analysis of it in a report to the U.S. Forest Service.

5. This figure was computed from 1972 employment and earnings data, Bureau of Economic Analysis, U.S. Department of Commerce.

6. As will be the convention throughout, the people in this chapter are given pseudonyms.

7. Altogether, forty additional questions were asked. They were phrased in the form of questions or statements to which the respondent was asked to react. A continuous scale was provided, marked with five intervals: (1) strongly disagree; (2) disagree; (3) neither agree nor disagree; (4) agree; and (5) strongly agree. The men were handed the several pages containing these questions, asked to read through them, and then mark their reaction to each on the scale provided below it. We coded the responses from 1 to 5 and calculated a "numeric" equivalent for each answer. Thus, an "X" placed midway between "agree" and "strongly agree" was coded as 4.5. If one makes the assumption that the five intervals are equidistant from one another, then any point on the line can be given a specific numeric value.

3 A Company Town with a Hole in the Ground, and No Company

Mining for Profits

The early mining camps of the Southwest have a militant labor history that is not generally known. The obscurity of this story is understandable, for it is comprised of shameful and shocking events. The "bad guys" are large American corporations, state, local, and federal governments, and the courts. Neither historians nor their readers seem to have much stomach for writing or reading narratives about incidents in which, for example, vigilante committees, state militia, and armed mine guards wrecked the homes and meeting halls of miners, machine-gunned union meetings, and beat and killed individual union members.[1]

In 1917 Bisbee, Arizona, was the scene of a particularly bizarre and brutal conflict between the Phelps-Dodge Corporation and its workers, the story of which has been passed down through several generations of miners. Miners refer to the events described in this story as "the deportation," and, along with other stories about past labor struggles, it forms part of a militant history with which contemporary miners are still in touch. The miners' remembrance of the deportation is important because it is partly responsible for current mistrust and bitterness toward the company. Miners do not believe that the interests of Phelps-Dodge coincide with theirs, nor do they believe what the company tells them about the reasons for its actions.

In 1974 Bisbee was the scene of another conflict. Once again both the Phelps-Dodge Corporation, now a large multinational corporation with holdings in South America, and its workers were involved. The company closed down its copper mines, after nearly a century of operation, and laid off 1,050 workers—most of Bisbee's labor force. Unlike the dramas of earlier years, there was no violence this time, only a pervasive cynicism about the company's motives and intentions. Amid expressed fears by public officials that the town was facing economic disaster, miners voiced sullen doubt that the closures were necessary or permanent, and many stayed around to wait it out.

Class consciousness may be manifested in ways other than direct action, although this form of expression is perhaps where it is more anticipated. Consciousness as a state of awareness is more difficult to observe, of course, than the collective action that might come from such awareness. However, when workers theorize about their employer's intentions—manipulation of tax laws, deception of the public and government agencies, and trickery, all in pursuit of more profits and with harmful consequences for workers—they are describing a structure wherein their economic interests and those of their employer are in conflict. This structural awareness is class consciousness. Why it does not lead further, to action, is a basic question asked in this book. The lessons learned in Bisbee about how a company uses subtle means to keep its workers disorganized and powerless comprise part of the answer.

The miners were wrong about what would happen in Bisbee, and public officials were wrong, too, in their dire predictions about economic disaster. What has actually happened is something neither group anticipated. This chapter is a revealing depiction of how human beings, cast aside because their skills are outmoded or their strength diminished by toil and age, become invisible, as well as obsolete. As an invisible group, the miners have invisible problems that do not appear to need a solution.

Working Down in the "Glory Hole," 1878–1974

Bisbee is and always has been a mining town. Its beginnings date back to 1878, when it was born as a copper camp in a narrow canyon of the Mule Mountains of Arizona, about eight miles from the Mexican border. A glorious future seemed assured when a large body of high-grade ore was discovered under a rising piece of land called Queen Hill. The main mine shaft to the ore was called the Copper Queen, although the miners nicknamed it the glory hole, a term eventually used to refer to the Copper Queen Consolidated Mining Company, which operated the mine as a subsidiary of the Phelps-Dodge Corporation. By 1890 Bisbee was by far the greatest of all the southwestern high-grade ore districts, producing 12 million pounds of ore a month, an amount equivalent to the combined production of all other mines in the United States in 1880. The Copper Queen's rich ore continued to be mined for decades, yielding Phelps-Dodge more than a hundred million dollars in profits. A second and highly successful competitor to Phelps-Dodge was the Calumet-Arizona Company, which in 1890 made a rich strike of its own in a mine called the "Irish Mag." The two companies continued as rivals for new claims in the Bisbee area, thus allowing the town to thrive.

A letter written from Bisbee in 1900 describes the town as

. . .an odd little corner of the world . . . a collection of shanties, adobe huts and a few half-way decent appearing houses, looking as though they had just been dropped down the mountain gorge. All over the [canyon] hundreds of them have stuck fast and the rest of them are piled up in a heap at the bottom. (Mayhall, 1974:22)

Other contemporaries saw in Bisbee a more grandiose present and future, calling it, "the most important town between El Paso and San Francisco." Thirty years after the town's founding, it contained numerous large and elegant brick structures with such names as the Pythian Castle and the Copper Queen Hotel. The town even boasted a large opera house, which brought performing companies from as far away as Europe. Meanwhile, for less cultured miners, a tavern district called Brewery Gulch was open 24 hours a day. Here there was another kind of opera—drinking, carousing, and fighting exacerbated by labor disputes in the mines. The town was indeed a "strange mixture of the frontier and the metropolitan" (Ayer, et al., 1975:11). Thus the mining camp of shanties and huts boomed into a turbulent town that reached a peak population of 18,000 in 1910.

Beginning in 1907 and continuing over the next nine years, there were a series of bitterly fought strikes in mining towns of the West. By 1916 the Wobblies were increasing their organizing efforts in Arizona's four metal-mining regions. After the outbreak of World War I in 1917, the price of copper soared, and with it mining profits. At the same time wages were cut at the Bisbee mine, an action that outraged the miners and eventually precipitated a strike. Demands for wage increases were met by the company's refusal even to discuss the matter. On 27 June 1917 the IWW called a general strike in Bisbee.[2] This action was also supported by the International Union of Mine, Mill, and Smelter Workers and several AFL unions that joined in the general walkout of June and July. The strike committee presented a list of demands to Phelps-Dodge officials, including: "abolition of a regular physical examination, use of two men on all machines, no blasting during working shifts, no bonus and contract work, no sliding scale of wages, institution of a flat minimum wage of $6.00 per shift underground and $5.50 above" (Mayhall, 1974:26). The two companies ignored these demands, claiming that they were "inimical to good government in time of peace and treasonable in time of war" (Mayhall, 1974:36). The companies also stockpiled arms, organized vigilante committees, hired additional guards and gunmen, and publicly declared their intention to remove labor agitators from the area. The local press, which was company-owned, joined in calling the strike a "pro-German plot," accusing the strikers of being "foreigners," and predicting imminent bloodshed.

On 11 July 1917 a meeting of company personnel, law-enforcement officers, and many of Bisbee's civic leaders was held at the Copper Queen Dispensary. The meeting was presided over by the Bisbee sheriff, Harry Wheeler, and the Phelps-Dodge general manager, Grant Dowell. A plan was developed to rid the company town of "agitators and sympathizers," who would be rounded up and shipped by rail to Columbus, New Mexico, where federal troops were stationed. It was hoped the army would then take control. More than 2,000 men were deputized and organized into search parties. The so-called Bisbee Loyalty League began its round-up before dawn on 12 July 1917. More than 1,200 male prisoners (women were warned to stay off the streets) were marched at gunpoint to the baseball park at the edge of town. There a kangaroo court asked prisoners to choose between work, arrest, or deportation. A poem, written by one of the Wobblies present, recalls how the miners were dragged and driven from their homes under threat of death and held for hours in the hot desert sun while they watched water brought to them by their wives and daughters being poured into the sand (Kornbluh, 1964:309)

> . . . Then in haste with kicks and curses
> We were herded into cars
> And it seemed our lungs were bursting
> With the odor of the yards.
>
> Floors were inches deep in refuse
> Left there from the Western herds
> Good enough for miners. Damn them.
> May they soon be food for birds.

Loaded 50 to a car, the dissidents were hauled across the desert to New Mexico. Depending upon which account you read, (i.e., the company's or the miner's), they were either allowed to stay at an army camp in Hermanas, where they were fed and housed for three months, until it shut down; or they were kept without food and water in the desert for 36 hours, then beaten up and taken to a federal stockade to be held without charge for an equivalent period of time. To prevent the clandestine return of deportees to Bisbee, armed guards were posted at the entrances to the town (since the town was located in a canyon, it was easily guarded) and instructed to deny passage to anyone not having legitimate business in town.

An investigation of the deportation was ordered by President Woodrow Wilson, and it was found that the strikes were "neither pro-German, nor seditious, but appeared to be nothing more than [a normal reaction to] the increased cost of living, [and] the speeding up process to which the mine management had been tempted by the abnormally high price of copper (Kornbluh, 1964:294). The government consequently failed to support the actions of the companies. Not only did the governor of Arizona and President Wilson both refuse to send troops to Bisbee during the strike, saying there was no danger of violence, but a mediation commission appointed by the President determined these facts about the deportees:

Of the 1200. . . . 381 were AFL members; 426 were Wobblies and 360 belonged to no labor organization. . . . 662 were either native-born or naturalized citizens, 472 were registered under the Selective Service Act, 205 owned Liberty Bonds, and 520 subscribed to the Red Cross. The foreign-born deportees included 179 Slavs, 141 British, 82 Serbians, and only a handful of Germans [Kornbluh, 1964:294]. [Note: One wonders why the Mexican nationals were not enumerated. They were part of the work force and likely accounted for the balance of the 130 or so foreign-born.]

The events of 1917 were disastrous to the organizing efforts of the Wobblies and other unions in Arizona's copper industry. By 1918, conspiracy trials were underway against the IWW leadership; and in 1919, Attorney General A. Mitchell Palmer launched a series of unprecedented and unconstitutional raids on radical and socialist groups across the country. There was little time and no leadership left for organizing miners or anybody else. It was 1935 before a major strike again erupted in Bisbee.

The conditions of copper mining in Bisbee during the depression were described to us by a respondent whom we shall call "Bill Mayer."[3] Mayer was hired by Phelps-Dodge in the year 1935 when employees worked only three days a week and miners and muckers[4] were paid only $5 and $4.40 respectively for working a ten-hour day underground. Mayer commented as follows: "They ran us around like mules, and when the shift foreman declared, 'I want 100 cars (of ore) out of this son-of-a-bitch by shift's end' we did it or went to the surface and turned in our badge."

Such poor working conditions made the copper workers an obvious target for union organizing, and the AFL and CIO were competing against each other to become the representative bodies. Mayer recalls that the company fought hard against those organizing efforts, causing much bitterness, and was able to break the strike of 1935. Company directors, under the influence of advice from the National Association of Manufacturers (NAM), then undertook a court case to test the constitutionality of the Wagner Act, which prohibited blackballing and lockouts. The case was appealed all the way to the U.S. Supreme Court. Several years and five million dollars later, Phelps-Dodge lost the case, after which its chairman of the board suggested that the company might do better by taking a softer line. His comment was, "We aren't going to make that mistake again." From 1943 on the company increased benefits, tried to organize a "company" union, and adopted a paternalistic stance toward its work force. The company hoped to mute the strength of its organized workers by keeping workers with different crafts and skills in separate unions.[5]

Competition between craft unions continued. In the early 1950s the Mine, Mill, and Smelter Workers, an industrial union of the CIO, appeared to be making considerable progress. Mayer was attracted by the more militant nature of this movement, and he supported the "one big union" concept. He began to organize for MMSW at other mines in Arizona while taking work leaves, which lasted up to six months. This effort proved futile in the early 1960s when the MMSW lost out to two AFL unions—the United Steelworkers, representing mostly underground miners, and the Teamsters, representing mostly aboveground or "pit" workers. This circumstance left many of the copper workers unrepresented. Some workers were even more concerned, however, about just how effectively the giant United Steelworkers Union would look after their interests, since the Bisbee contingent constituted only 2 percent of the national membership: "We're just little people here, and its a damn big union. We don't really get word of what's going on—from the bosses or the union."

It is striking that miners' labor unions arrived on the scene so late, especially in view of the long history of protracted and bitter struggle by miners and skilled organizers. The hard-won unionization also came as only a partial victory. Although underground miners and those working in the pit aboveground shared essentially the same work place and produced the same product, each group was represented by a different union. There were altogether six unions representing various subgroups of the Bisbee copper workers. Obviously, this had the effect of weakening the power of union members vis-à-vis their common employer. Such fragmented union representation is probably one reason why the wages of copper miners lag behind those of other industrial workers, and even more so behind the wages of workers represented by a consolidated union such as the United Automotive Workers.

The wages of copper miners seem especially low considering their working conditions. Working underground is particularly arduous and hazardous. Underground mines are a labyrinth of downward sloping shafts and stopes—small caverns where drilling and blasting occur. Although tall enough for a good-sized man to stand in, the work areas give one an unsettling feeling of dense closeness and of being swallowed up by the darkness. According to one union official, 5 to 8 percent of new workers are "scared out" of the mines by the experience of going underground. The temperature in the shafts is about 45 degrees, and a substantial draft blows through them. The stopes vary greatly in temperature; some are very hot and others very cold. It is damp everywhere. The noise from the work (drilling, blasting, and ore-hauling on tracks) occurs at intervals and is deafening. Perhaps the most pervasive sensation is that of darkness. In the actual work areas the only illumination is provided by lanterns on the miners' hats, while the main shafts are dimly illuminated by strings of lights. Pack mules, formerly used to haul ore and quartered underground in large caverns, went blind if kept underground for six months. Blindness occurred because, in the absence of miners' lanterns, there was no source of light to which the eye might adjust, not even a pinpoint or a crack. No experience is comparable to total darkness 1,500 feet below the surface of the earth.

In a hard-rock mine such as the one in Bisbee, cave-ins and other accidents resulting in death were relatively rare, and Bisbee's safety record was very good compared to that in other mines. However, there was some danger of injury from explosives and heavy equipment. Moreover, chronic back injury was made almost inevitable by constant heavy lifting. Deterioration of the lower back often begins when a worker is in his late 30s or early 40s, which is a relatively young age in his working life. There were still other hazards. Many of the fathers and grandfathers of the men who were laid off from Bisbee's mines died of "miners' con" or consumption, a fatal respiratory disease caused by inhalation of copper-laden dust. The introduction of federal safety standards in mining has now lessened this occupational hazard to a considerable degree, but they have not eliminated it completely.

Despite such hardships, underground miners are proud of their ability to take the pressures of their work. Some of them are third-generation miners. Their fathers and grandfathers before them worked the same mines. They consider themselves, and are considered to be, the elite workers of the industry; the underground work remains a craft.

The fortunes of miners in places like Bisbee are greatly dependent upon the fluctuating price of copper and the quality of ore. Both these factors are capricious, unknowable, and seemingly beyond control. Copper prices, for example, fell during the Depression, rose sharply during World War II, and then fell again. Layoffs at the Phelps-Dodge Bisbee site in 1949 and the closure of a Phelps-Dodge mine in Jerome, Arizona, were directly related to sagging postwar prices.

The fortunes of workers are also likely to be affected by major technological changes. In 1952, for example, Harry Lavender, who was the superintendent of the Phelps-Dodge mines in Bisbee, put into operation a method of surface extraction that created a huge open-pit mine. The use of large machines and heavy blasting meant that lower-grade ore could be exploited because it could be produced and milled in much greater quantities. The introduction of this new technology and the subsequent opening of the pit also meant the hiring of 600 additional employees, mostly in the category of heavy equipment operators, and it probably protected the jobs of underground miners from the frequent company threat of a total and permanent shutdown.

The story of Bisbee miners, however, is not so much that technological developments at various times preserved their jobs, but that they and their families lived amidst constant uncertainty generated by rumors about projected shutdowns and layoffs. Such rumors intensified after 1960, when projections were made that the open pit would soon exhaust its supply of ore.

After years, and even decades, of hearing rumors, miners became conditioned to take each new rumor of shutdown with a "handful of salt." For example, when Phelps-Dodge closed its mine at Jerome in 1949, miners were cynical and refused to believe that the company's action was final. A Phelps-Dodge manager recalls how three old miners reacted when they observed the superintendent padlocking the office door for the last time. They yelled out, "We'll see you back in the morning." The manager then joked, "They're probably still waiting there."

This reaction, although cynical in one sense, is realistic in another, inasmuch as the miners had little alternative but to wait for the company to reopen. They had a very specialized set of skills, not readily transferable to other occupations or industries; and they were not as mobile or hireable as other workers in construction, trucking, or assembly-line work. Thus a realistic assessment of their situation would make them hesitant to move or look for work elsewhere.

Recently Bisbee miners were presented with the same circumstances that existed in Jerome 25 years earlier. In December 1974 Phelps-Dodge closed the pit and laid off 488 workers. Layoffs continued at a slower pace through winter and spring of 1975, and then in June the underground operation was shut down as well. By 13 June only a skeleton crew was left. The layoffs during this period affected more than 1,050 men—virtually all of the Phelps-Dodge payroll in Bisbee.

Closing the "Glory Hole": Why Did It Finally Happen?

Several factors converged to influence the decision by Phelps-Dodge to close the Bisbee mines, and most related to operating costs. The underground mine, for example, was becoming less efficient to work. Shafts and tunnels were getting deeper and longer, meaning that hoist mechanisms and trollies had to cover a longer distance and took more time to haul the ore to the surface. This circumstance also meant that reinforcing shafts and stopes with timber beams and filling in worked-out stopes to avert cave-ins became a more difficult and time-consuming chore. Moreover, passage ways were too narrow and haulage vehicles too small to take out large enough quantities of ore to justify such increasing costs.

The open-pit mine on the surface was also becoming less efficient to operate, for it was dug deeper and the sides were made steeper each year. Although the physical volume of the pit continues to increase as it deepens, it does so at a decreasing rate, because as the ground is scooped out, it gradually produces a bowl with sloping sides rather than a box with vertical sides. Furthermore, extension of the pit on the surface would have swallowed up a major highway, as well as nearby houses and public buildings. Even though the company had the legal right to proceed in this manner, it decided not to risk the consequence of inevitable disruption and public opposition.

In large part, Bisbee's miners were the victims of their company's response to changing technological conditions. Perhaps the most important of the new mining techniques is the "block-caving system," which is used underground to blast large deposits of ore and rock. The debris falls and fractures, allowing miners to remove huge quantities all at once using enormous vehicles and equipment. This system enables one man to mine as much ore in half an hour as could be mined by two men in half a day using the old system. Thus, the new method is more capital intensive and very labor-saving. Since the Bisbee underground mine did not have the correct rock mechanics, the block-caving system could not be implemented. In order to take advantage of the new technology and save on the cost of labor, Phelps-Dodge opened a new underground mine at Safford, Arizona, where explorations had begun in 1968.

Meanwhile, Bisbee's open-pit mine and adjacent ore-milling plant were made relatively obsolete by the development of massive diesel vehicles with rubber tires that move ore quickly from the blasting area to the milling plant. Although the pit mine itself perhaps could have been worked in a way to accommodate the new vehicles, the receiving chutes at the mill were too small to efficiently handle the larger loads. Phelps-Dodge has developed new pits at two other Arizona sites—Ajo and Morenci. The life of the Morenci pit is expected to be 100 years.

Actual refinements have been made in the processing and chemical treatment of ore, which leave the Bisbee mill and smelter at a comparative disadvantage. In fact, one reason why Phelps-Dodge has expanded its South American operations is that none of its Arizona ores is suitable to be chemically treated by a new electro-sulfide process.

Since the productive efficiency of the pit and that of the underground operation were in some respects interdependent, when the pit closed in December 1974, it meant that the closure of the underground mine would soon follow. The milling operation, for example, which was already made somewhat obsolete by technological change, was deprived of a daily average of 23,000 tons of ore when the pit closed. This reduced the daily volume of the mill to 2,000 tons of ore, supplied by the underground mine. Even though the underground ore was of much higher grade, the cost per unit of production for the reduced volume became too high to justify keeping the milling plant in operation.

The exact timing, although not the inevitability, of the Bisbee mine closures was influenced by several circumstances that in a sense served as public excuses for the company's action. The world price of copper had plunged to less than one half the level of the previous few years. Even though current price cannot be considered a significant factor in long-term investment decisions, which are projected over a decade or more,[6] the company was able to point to it as a reason for discontinuing a "high cost" operation. At the same time, a 10-percent investment credit on corporate income tax had been passed by Congress, ostensibly to combat the recession of 1973–74. Phelps-Dodge was able to take advantage of this direct reduction in taxes to pay for the substantial investment in buildings and machines at its new mining sites. Finally, the Environmental Protection Agency, which nowadays is often used as a boogie man by companies threatening to shut down, was also used as such by Phelps-Dodge. The company claimed that new EPA rulings on pollution control forced a 60-percent cut in the capacity of the smelter that processed Bisbee's ore, thus causing unacceptable cost overruns. This appears to be a bogus issue, since it would surely be cheaper to invest in the modification of an existing smelter than to pay for the construction of an entirely new plant at another site.

Company "Monkeyshines": The Miners' Viewpoint

Another major reason for the closure, according to the company, was that the grade of the ore coming from the Bisbee mines was deteriorating. This, however, was not consistent with the experience of the men who worked the mines and knew that high-grade ore was still available. In fact, early cynicism among miners about the permanence of the closure resulted from this perceived contradiction. Since the information provided by the company didn't square with the miners, they adopted alternative explanations and remained convinced that when the company's "monkeyshines" had run their course, the mines would open again.

Ramon Vasquéz, a second-generation miner, told us that his father had worked for more than thirty years for Phelps-Dodge before he died of "miners' con." He himself first went to work for the company in 1946 and was caught in the final layoffs of June 1975. His observations are interesting because they form an alternative explanation of what the company had in mind and account for the wait-and-see attitude taken by the displaced workers. Vasquéz summarized the motives for the closure like this: "Money, Taxes, and Monkeyshines." "Money refers to company greed.

P-D's got people with these little (calculating) machines they've got now. And they figure out where over here you can only make a million and over there you can make thirty million. It's not that they're going in the hole here! It's that they can make more profit somewhere else, and why shouldn't they just kill this town? They can kill this town just like they killed Jerome. I'm telling you, they've got some smart people that work a pencil. And those people over there don't give a damn about anybody over here.

"Taxes" refers to the belief that the company was seeking to obtain some special advantage from the government.

Now if that's the way it is, then shut it up, close it, fire 'em, get rid of everybody! But they don't do that. They just keep doing enough to build their case for whatever it is they want. They've got something up their sleeve. I don't know what they're seeking—some kind of help . . . a cut in taxes, a government loan—but it looks to me like they want it to go bad, and they've been planning on it. They want this place to look bad, so they can get a tax break.

"Monkeyshines" refers to cost-cutting actions preliminary to final shut-down, such as relaxing supervision, allowing mine conditions to deteriorate, and covering up good ore veins when they were found.

In the past two years, as far as I'm concerned, supervision has gone to hell! They've just let loose on everything and I don't understand it, because some of these things they've done, it's not for the good of the company, it's not for the good of the men.

I don't know if you've ever worked underground, but you'd know that if you just let two or three little things go, it really works against everything. Drainage has gone to hell. The tracks are rusted and under water some places. There's one thing they've kept up on and that's radiation and ventilation—doors, big blowers. I think the only reason is because the federal government is constantly coming in to check. But if they don't want some places checked, they just slow it up. If a government man comes in and says "take me to these open-cut places," they say, "Well, we've only got two places going." They slow production up!

I've seen the time, not so long ago, P-D wanted to know as to who, and why, and where. I've seen men now that slack off for four and five hours, and P-D just don't care. They changed the supervision now. One guy is Big Daddy for two weeks, and then he wasn't Big Daddy for another two, and then somebody else is. That just doesn't go. It's just like when you're in the service, and they pull out the captain, the lieutenant, and your sergeant and put in a "ninety-day wonder" and a private who always wanted to be sergeant. See, you lose respect for your boss, 'cause he doesn't know what the hell he is doing. And the boss has no respect for the foreman, and it goes right on up. Everything—all the work—it just goes to hell. It looks to me like they want it to look this bad; they've been planning on it. When they get what they want from the government, they'll come down there and get that supervision straightened up fast.

In November 1974 Vasquéz drilled several 8-to 8 ½-foot test holes at the 1,400 level and found ore at the bottom:

The stope engineer believes that we're sitting on top of an ore body—a big one. But they're not doing nothing. Nothing! And on 1,550 [i.e., at 1,550 feet], I happen to know the crosscut man that would drive in these drifts. They hit one helluva body of ore there last week. They mapped it, and they're not doing a goddamn thing about that either. No, they're having us hit the old gouges, hit the old places, and what have you. I tell you, I personally know that they haven't run out of good ore. That and a few other little things make me believe that there's something—way above what I understand—that they're playing around with.

All of these reasons are also perceived to have something to do with the remoteness of company management. It is known, for example, that the decision to shut down was not made locally; management people in Bisbee were told of the decision to close the pit just before the first scheduled layoffs in December. The Phelps-Dodge Corporation has many mines, including extensive copper holdings in South America; and decisions concerning a particular operation are made against the backdrop of a larger company portfolio. Our respondent was clearly upset when he said: "They can still make a profit here, but they can make a helluva bigger one somewhere else." To him the company seemed awfully cold.

A cynical attitude about company motives was widely shared in Bisbee and was detrimental not only to the adaptations of individual workers but also to the efforts of city officials to develop economic alternatives for the city. As one city official told us:

> City Hall is trying to preserve the crisis atmosphere in the face of mounting cynicism that P-D is merely manufacturing the crisis and will not cut back for long. This attitude is prevalent among all classes of local people, and it is seriously hampering our efforts to mobilize energies to help broaden Bisbee's job base.

The company itself presented an additional problem by not assisting the planning process and not even informing the city of the timing or extent of the layoffs.[7] Miners and other community people maintained their bitterness, cynicism, and expectations of rehiring because of the absence of specific information from the company about why the mine closed and what the company now planned to do. While Bisbee was in a state of unanimated suspension, the company remained unsympathetic. As a Phelps-Dodge field manager explained:

> You see, at some point the mine has to close. And when it closes, it is a final thing, not a close-down-now, come-back-next-week thing. I know some people in this community believe that the closure of the mine is just a manipulative move to secure certain tax benefits; that once we've done that, and eliminated certain undesirable workers, the mines will open up again. But that is not the case: This closure is final. The community does not want to deal with it in those terms, but they're going to have to. We've been telling 'em for ten years that this was going to happen, and I guess we really don't feel a responsibility to do much now.

The Company "Cleans House"

In closing out the Bisbee mines and opening highly mechanized operations at Safford, Ajo, and Morenci Phelps-Dodge can produce a much greater quantity of ore using far fewer workers. We wanted to document and understand the company's selection of preferred workers from the large surplus of qualified labor in Bisbee. Our interest was in part a response to the claim by some miners that the closures were engineered by the company to enable it to "clean house" on its labor force. This theory, and others, can be tested through the analysis of several kinds of data that were collected in Bisbee over a two-and-a-half-year period.

The collection of basic field data began during early spring 1974 and continued through September 1976. These data are rich and varied, ranging from interviews—with scores of local and county officials, public service employees, professional and business people—to notes from ongoing talks with two dozen local families. These field notes comprise a community study describing Bisbee's economic, political, and cultural environment; a corporate portrait based on accounts from inside management; and a series of human stories, revealing the painful adjustment to extended unemployment.

A second set of data, provided by the local Department of Economic Security, was taken from applications for unemployment benefits as filed by miners who were laid off by Phelps-Dodge from December 1974 through July 1975. These files were systematically monitored to provide updates on each miner's status. The final update was conducted during July 1976, at which time some of the miners had been without jobs for 19 months and could no longer collect unemployment benefits. In all, there were 629 useable cases, or about three-fifths of the total number of workers laid off in the mine closures. For each worker there was a basic demographic description, with additional information on occupation, finances, future plans, spouse's status, whether or not employment was eventually obtained, and whether or not the worker left town.

There are two primary questions to which these unemployment data are relevant: (1) What were the criteria by which the company made its decisions about rehiring and transferring workers to the new mines? (2) Has the broader labor market of Bisbee and Cochise County operated with differential effect for some groups of miners over others? Who has fared well and who has not? In the analysis that follows, data from field notes are woven together with a statistical inspection of the 629 cases to examine these questions.

The pivotal personnel decision was whether to transfer, reinstate, or lay off workers. Since Phelps-Dodge had closed down the Bisbee mines, the union was no longer a factor, and the company had control over which workers would be sent to the new pit mine at Morenci and whether they would be *transferred* or *reinstated*. If workers were transferred, they were allowed to keep their seniority; but if they were reinstated, seniority was lost. It appears that most, although not all, of the workers sent initially to Morenci were transferred. This probably occurred because the Morenci mine was already open and in need of skilled pit workers at the time of the December 1974 layoff. The most important statistic, however, is that fewer than one-fifth of the Bisbee open-pit work force was eventually sent to the Morenci mine (Table 3.1).

A final physical examination given to all employees assumed special significance for those whom the company did not wish to transfer directly to Morenci. The physical examination was paid for by the company and conducted by a company doctor. Although voluntary, it was also a necessary prerequisite to reinstatement at any of the mines owned by Phelps-Dodge in the Southwest. Miners felt without a doubt that examination results were used to disqualify unwanted workers from future employment. "Everyone has something wrong," a union official commented. Many workers also discovered that health problems mysteriously appeared for the first time on the day of the examination.

For the most part, workers were powerless either to challenge company

Table 3.1.   Phelps-Dodge Labor Force Changes, 1 December-3 April, 1974-75[a].

Personnel Action	Number of Workers Affected	Percent of Total	
Layoffs	399	64.5	
Reinstatements	15	2.4 } 18.7	
Transfers	101	16.3	
Early Retirement	87	14.0 } 15.5	
Regular Retirement	9	1.5	
Quit	8	1.3	
TOTAL	619	100.0	

[a]This table does not include workers laid off from the underground mine in June of 1975. These figures on company labor force changes are not related to the DES data described elsewhere in this chapter.

policy or to influence the results of the physical examination. Unlike many unions, the Steelworkers' Local in Bisbee had no provision for a counter examination by a union doctor, which could curb the power of the company. Thus, a worker who was not reinstated because of physical ailments had no legal recourse against the judgment of the company doctor. Only a few miners were astute enough to manipulate the situation to their own advantage, as in the following example.

I enjoy good health and, except for a back injury three years ago, I haven't had any problems for some years. When I applied for a job at the Douglas Smelter recently, I had to have my physical, and the doctor asked me about the injury in a sharp tone. I answered by telling him to put my "disability" in writing. [The injury had happened on the job. If the doctor had certified the presence of such a work-related injury, the miner would have had the basis for a further disability claim against Phelps-Dodge.] The doctor backed off fast and gave me a clear bill. I got the job.

There was great suspicion among many miners that Phelps-Dodge was using the physical examination systematically to "get rid of trouble-makers and gripers, certain union people, workers that they don't like, people with seniority, and low producers." This statement challenges three commonly held percepts about work: (1) Decisions to hire or fire are based primarily on criteria of efficiency, rather than on how well employees live up to norms of subservient or obsequious behavior; (2) A relationship of equity usually exists between an employer and hard-working employees, i.e., if you work for a company all your life and feel you've done a good job, you'll be treated fairly; (3) Workers who belong to a big organization have power, i.e., membership in a big union will, at the minimum, provide job security through the acquisition of seniority. When workers find these percepts to be violated, they become angry at having been cheated and "made a fool," and they may become cynical concerning the merit of a lifetime of honest work. As miners' comments suggest, feelings about how they were mistreated will affect their attitude and behavior in future jobs—if indeed they can find any. Many unemployed miners gave voice to these themes.

My father before me, and his before him, we have all worked underground for this company. You could say they also died for it—"miner's con." I am still strong and I do my work well, but they won't even give me the opportunity to transfer.

I worked twenty years as a mechanic for this company and never missed a day, either because of accident or sickness; but people a lot less senior than me were offered a transfer. My brother had to kiss ass to get on at Morenci. I simply cannot swallow my pride and accept the company policy and attitude. A boss I really liked was blackballed from other P-D operations such as Metcalfe. They sure worked around seniority lists! I tend now to lay back and be careful [in job hunting]. I'm determined to stay away from the same predicament.

There is ample evidence that Phelps-Dodge rehired workers, after the layoffs, on the basis of criteria other than seniority or past productivity. One direct, personal account by Felipé Hermanos, a "high-level official" in the United Steelworkers' Local, provides a good example. Hermanos is a third-generation Mexican-American whose father and grandfather were both Bisbee underground miners. He is intelligent, articulate, and has a reputation as a good worker and a strong union man. Although he suffered an injury to his lower back ten years ago at the age of 31, he thought it was completely healed because it had neither bothered him since nor turned up in subsequent examinations. However, upon being examined by the company doctor just after the layoffs, Hermanos was told that Phelps-Dodge could not rehire him to work at one of the new sites because his back would "likely cause future trouble." Sometime later Hermanos was given an alternative explanation by a company foreman, who told him of a personnel meeting in which his transfer was discussed. Hermanos was rejected for transfer specifically because of his union activities. Were other union leaders passed over as well? He wasn't told. Eighteen months after the layoffs, Hermanos was still without work and expressed extreme bitterness toward the company for rejecting him on the "flimsy excuse of possible, future back problems." He wanted to get even with the company and considered starting a lawsuit, but since his prime witness was still employed with Phelps-Dodge, this course of action seemed fruitless. This case, and others like it, are sufficient evidence for many miners that neither hard work, union membership, nor seniority will do you much good if the company wants to get rid of you for some reason.

Retirement was an alternative for some workers who were not rehired by Phelps-Dodge. Only one-sixth of the workers laid off from the Bisbee underground mine took advantage of retirement plans, and only a very few of this number had reached the age of 65 or, alternatively, had reached 60 with 30 years of uninterrupted service to Phelps-Dodge and could qualify for regular retirement (see Table 3.1). Most of those who elected to retire did so under an early retirement plan called the "70/80 option." A worker could qualify for retirement at 55 if he had accumulated at least 15 years of *uninterrupted* service, i.e., $55 + 15 = 70$, or at a younger age if age plus accumulated years of service totaled 80. Although medical benefits were slightly better under the latter formula, other provisions were essentially the same. In either case, an early retiree was entitled to lump-sum severance pay of $5,000. He could also choose to reject severance pay and instead seek other work, although not with Phelps-Dodge. While looking for work, he was eligible for company unemployment benefits, which, like severance pay, came out of a fund that the company and workers had contributed to. Those seeking work could collect $42 for each of the first 26 weeks of unemployment and $75 for each of the remaining 26 weeks. Government unemployment benefits, which averaged $80 a week and and could be collected for a total of 65 weeks, were available to early retirees, as well as to other unemployed workers. Thus it was possible for a worker electing early retirement to receive $7,202 during the first 52 weeks of unemployment and $1,040 during the next 13 weeks.

It could be argued that Phelps-Dodge allowed the Bisbee underground mine to deteriorate in the months before closure as a means of inducing miners to quit voluntarily. If this policy was indeed intended to assist in "cleaning house," it was not successful, for only one to two percent of the miners decided to quit (see Table 3.1). Although many miners were annoyed by increasingly poor and hence more hazardous work conditions, most interpreted the company's negligence as temporary "monkeyshines" rather than as a chronic problem.

In June 1975 Phelps-Dodge closed the Bisbee underground mine, and a group of more than 360 workers were discharged. The percentage of workers rehired by the company appears to be even smaller among this group, although exact figures were not made available to us. This circumstance is especially interesting in light of a statement made by a former officer in the Steelworkers' Local. He said that there were no written provisions governing company transfers in the 1974 contract; but that during the negotiations the company stated that *every* worker laid off during the contract period, "would be given a chance at a job elsewhere." One wonders exactly what kind of protection the union felt this "verbal contract" would afford its members!

Sorting Out Among the Dispossessed

We monitored the ongoing status of unemployed miners by using the records of the Cochise County Department of Economic Security (DES). From this source we constructed a file of 629 complete cases—289 from the initial December layoffs and 340 from the June layoffs. These cases constitute 60 percent of the 1,050 men who were in some way affected by the December through June layoffs. Workers who were immediately transferred to Morenci and those who did not file a claim with the Department of Economic Security could not be included in this sample.

The DES data were analyzed with use of a statistical technique called nonmetric discriminant analysis, which classifies the members of a sample into some specified groups or categories. The categories used in this analysis are "still unemployed," "reinstated by Phelps-Dodge," and "inactive claim." Results of this statistical analysis are stated as conditional probabilities, or decimal numbers, which represent the likelihood of being in one category or another given the presence of a certain prior condition or characteristic. While the methods of nonmetric discriminant analysis are complex, the results are quite straightforward and simple to interpret. We have tried to avoid excessively technical discussions in the presentation and analysis of these results. The technically inclined reader is referred to Reinmuth's (1974) work on nonmetric discriminant analysis.

Examination of DES files several months after the layoffs confirmed worker suspicions that Phelps-Dodge was "cleaning house" on its labor force. Five months after the open-pit miners had been laid off, fewer than one-fourth had been reinstated (rehired without seniority) at the Morenci or Safford mines (Table 3.2). Eight months after the underground miners had been laid off, only 5 percent had been reinstated (Table 3.3). Obviously Phelps-Dodge was using the policy of reinstatement on a limited basis and, regardless of what was verbally promised to the union, never intended to rehire a large majority of its former employees. Miners who had acquired back problems while working for Phelps-Dodge and those whose skills were obsolete in the context of new mining technology were the most readily discarded.

The magnitude of the problem for the miners is indicated by the fact that half of the open-pit miners and 45 percent of the underground miners

Table 3.2. Status of Open-Pit Miners Five Months after Layoffs.

Status	Number	Percentage of Sample
Claim still active		
Worker unemployed	146	50.5
Claim inactive		
Worker reinstated at Morenci or Stafford	65	22.5
Claim inactive		
Worker found other work, or moved and dropped his claim	78	27.0
TOTAL	289	100.0

[a]Forty-one of these unemployed workers are also "retired." Workers who took early retirement could pass up the lump-sum severance pay and file instead for unemployment benefits. In other words, some retired workers were actively seeking employment.
[b]Rehired without seniority.

Table 3.3. Status of Underground Miners Eight Months after Layoffs.

Status	Number	Percentage of Sample
Claim still active		
Worker unemployed	152	44.7
Claim inactive		
Worker reinstated at Morenci or Stafford	17	5.0
Claim inactive		
Worker found other work, or moved and dropped his claim	171	50.3
TOTAL	340	100.0

aRehired without seniority.

remained in Bisbee and were unemployed at the time their records were monitored. A further check on the status of open-pit miners, which was made after 11 months had elapsed, revealed that more than one-third, or 106 of 289, were still unemployed. A similar check on the status of underground miners after 13 months also revealed that more than one-third of this group, or 130 of 340, were still unemployed. At this rate, it is likely that a substantial number of miners remained in Bisbee and were without jobs even after unemployment benefits ran out. These estimates of unemployment are conservative, since it is possible that some workers with inactive claims were unable to find jobs. It is reasonable to assume, however, that these workers moved to places where their particular skills and attributes would make them more employable. Another reasonable assumption is that the unemployed workers who remained in Bisbee had, or at least felt they had, few skills and attributes that would be assets even in a healthy labor market.

The three groups of workers identified in the DES files were compared in order to examine more systematically how Phelps-Dodge made selections in reinstating some former employees at its new mines. Based on comments made by workers about the company's disregard for seniority and loyal service, we expected to find that age and seniority would serve to eliminate many workers from consideration. We also expected to find that certain skills needed at the new mines would otherwise determine which workers would be chosen for reinstatement. In addition to testing our theories about company motives, we were able to examine the salient characteristics of those who had (presumably) found a new job. We expected to find that youth and special skills might improve the likelihood of being hired by someone else.

These employment-office data were further analyzed to determine the specific characteristics of the men in each category, i.e., rehired, unemployed, or inactive claim. We wanted to know, for example, whether such characteristics as union status, age, or ethnicity were associated dispropor-

Table 3.4. A Comparison of Characteristics of Underground and Open-Pit Miners, DES Sample (N=629).
(For selected variables, the standard deviation is in parentheses)

| Variables | Population Means[a] | |
	Open-Pit Miners N=289	Underground Miners N=340
Demographic Characteristics		
Age of worker	42.05 (14.9)	48.95 (10.5)
Last grade in school	10.51 (2.67)	9.96 (2.40)
Anglo	.61	.54
Mexican-American	.39	.46
Married	.84	.91
Wife is working	.18	.18
Divorced	.03	.04
Number of dependents	2.6 (2.03)	2.9 (1.83)
Veteran	.43	.63
Vietnam veteran	.12	.04
Housing Characteristics		
Own house	.46	.80
Own mobile home	.06	--
Rent company house	.28	.08
Rent (not from company)	.16	.11
Live with relatives	.04	--
Monthly cost of housing ($)	54.91 (44.78)	33.60 (45.32)
Occupational Characteristics		
Miner	.36	.59
Mucker, swamper, motorman	.15	.08
Technician (electrician, mechanic, etc.)	.20	.17
Work in shops	.07	.03
Truck driver	.10	.02
General laborer	.07	.02
Security and other	.05	.08
Years of Service with P-D	13.57 (11.15)	21.81 (8.92)
Early retirement	.21	.32
Union Membership		
None	.54	.39
United Steelworkers	.27	.54
Teamsters	.05	.01
Others; boilermakers, machinists, etc.	.12	.02
Future Plans		
Will work in Bisbee only	.31	.38
Will work in Cochise County only	.22	.22
Will work in Arizona only	.25	.27
Will work anywhere	.23	.13
Want mining work and/or	.78	.73
Want any kind of work	.21	.09

[a]All variables except those underlined are coded 0, 1 (0=no; 1=yes). When variables are coded in this way, their means may be interpreted directly as sample proportions. Thus the mean of .39 for Mexican-American underground miners means that 39 percent of the workers in this group were Mexican-American.

tionately with membership in one category or another. Table 3.4 displays mean values for basic characteristics of the overall DES sample for two groups of miners—open-pit and underground. Likewise, the comparisons between the three categories of workers (i.e., reinstated by P-D, unemployed, or inactive claim) were carried out separately for open-pit and underground miners. This was made necessary because the two groups were laid off at different times, as well as by other differences between them (see Table 3.4).

The basic question for this step of the analysis was which types of workers tended to get rehired by Phelps-Dodge, to remain unemployed, or to find other work. Implicit in this question is an examination of the miners' claim that a "weeding out" of the "undesirables" took place. In Ramon Vasquéz's words: "They've got a chance now to clean house without transferring. There isn't gonna be no such thing as a transfer, and the unions that fought so hard for job security—they're not gonna get it." Vasquéz was wrong about the transfers. The company did transfer a small group of preferred workers under procedures that allowed them to keep their seniority. However, about the subversion of seniority in general, he was right. As the following data show, the longer a miner had "given my best days to the damn company" the less likely he was to be rehired, or to be hired by anybody else.

As expected, older workers had the least chance of being reinstated by Phelps-Dodge (Table 3.5). The likelihood of reinstatement for open-pit

---

Table 3.5. The Effect of Age on Employment Status of Miners[a].
(results from a nonmetric discriminant analysis)

Characteristics	Conditional Probabilities					
	Still Unemployed		Reinstated by P-D		Inactive Claim	
Age Levels	Open Pit	Under-ground	Open Pit	Under-ground	Open Pit	Under-ground
16-30	.47	.25	.30	.05	.24	.70
31-40	.32	.19	.40	.16	.28	.66
41-50	.33	.34	.43	.06	.25	.60
51-60	.71	.63	.17	.02	.12	.36
61-65	.71	.64	.07	0	.21	.36

[a]These data represent the status of underground miners five months after layoff and open-pit miners eight months after layoff.

---

miners was .17 for those aged 51 to 60 and .07 for those aged 61 to 65, while the likelihood of reinstatement for underground miners was .02 for those aged 51 to 60 and zero for those aged 61 to 65. Workers with these age characteristics were also more likely to remain unemployed, the likelihood here being .71, .71, .63, and .64 respectively. The types of workers most likely to be reinstated were in the 31- to 50-year bracket. Younger workers between 16 and 30 faired considerably less well, although not as poorly as older workers. This result came as little surprise, since Dick Wilson, the company manager with whom we spoke, had been particularly critical of "today's younger workers," citing their "lack of experience, low work motivation, and poor safety records." He pointed out that the company had uncovered many on-the-job cases of dope-smoking and pill-taking among this group. Despite the prejudice of the company toward this behavior, however, it was still the older workers who suffered the greatest risk of remaining unemployed.

It is clear that Phelps-Dodge disregarded the principle of seniority in discarding its older workers, since the workers with the most service were the least likely to be reinstated and the most likely to remain unemployed (Table 3.6). This pattern was particularly pronounced for those with more than 30 years of service, where the likelihood of reinstatement was .09 for open-pit miners and zero for the underground miners. Among the open-pit miners, those with 16 to 20 years of service were most likely to be reinstated (.41), while among the underground miners, those with 11 to 15 years of service were most likely to be reinstated (.64). These results are consistent with the previous analysis of the effects of age on employment status and indicate that older workers who had given long service to the company were especially justified in feeling "cheated."

What explanation could the company offer for its poor treatment of older, more senior workers? Dick Wilson admitted that until about fifteen years ago, mining companies "had an informal rule that they did not hire men, experienced or not, after age 45." Apparently, the experience of company doctors indicated that miners around 45 to 50 years old begin to show signs of natural physical deterioration, especially in the back. This deterioration was presumably thought to result in lost work time and lower production on the job. Wilson, however, said that he personally felt that men in the 45- to 55-year-old group suffered fewer accidents and carried their own weight,

Table 3.6.   The Effect of Length of Service on Employment Status of
            Miners.
            (results from a nonmetric discriminant analysis)

Characteristics	Conditional Probabilities					
	Still Unemployed		Reinstated by P-D		Inactive Claim	
Length of Service in Years	Open Pit	Under-ground	Open Pit	Under-ground	Open Pit	Under-ground
Fewer than 5	.29	.19	.39	.0	.32	.81
5-10	.27	.21	.31	.32	.43	.47
11-15	.26	.12	.34	.64	.41	.24
16-20	.22	.38	.41	.17	.37	.45
21-25	.43	.32	.32	.38	.26	.30
26-30	.48	.43	.20	.26	.32	.31
More than 30	.81	.72	.09	.0	.11	.28

"because of their experience and desire to work." Why, then, were the older men seldom transferred or reinstated?—a fact acknowledged by Wilson. His explanation was that it was not a matter of deliberate company policy, but rather a consequence of the way the company's pension structure had evolved over time: "A large number of men took early retirement for rational economic reasons."

This statement is not at all convincing, since many of the older miners were extremely bitter at having been passed over by the company in favor of younger, less senior men. They felt strongly that the company should have acted "properly" by following procedures governed by seniority. For those among them who took early retirement, it was often a choice made in the absence of any other alternatives. They said repeatedly that they would prefer to work. Wilson's claim that many workers chose to retire is an obvious case of blaming the victim. Many men "chose" to retire because they were not rehired by Phelps-Dodge, and they needed to support their families. Moreover, retirement pay provided only temporary relief. Why else would so-called retired workers register at the DES to find employment? Furthermore, many senior workers were not old enough to come under the various retirement plans. The company cannot legitimately claim that these men could not be rehired because they chose to retire. It is ample testimony to the company's disregard for its senior workers that nearly 40 percent of this older, unretired group were still unemployed and looking for a job more than a year after the layoffs.

An examination of skill types among open-pit miners shows that having a chauffeur's license, which is necessary to drive a truck, substantially increased a worker's chance of being reinstated at Morenci (Table 3.7). Mechanical and construction skills also seemed to be somewhat in demand by Phelps-Dodge. These results are highly consistent with the new mining technology introduced at Morenci, which is based on the increased use of large machines and therefore needs drivers and mechanics. Construction skills might also have been put to use in building various parts of the new mining operation. Although welding skill presents the exception to the rule as far as reinstatements are concerned, a worker with this skill apparently stood the best chance by far of being hired elsewhere. Those with skills not needed by the company or with no special skills stood a poor chance of being reinstated and were the most likely to remain unemployed. Since 70 percent of the underground miners did not list a special skill, this factor is relatively meaningless in their case and was not subjected to statistical analysis.

Because of the story about the miner who was not rehired because of his active role as a union leader, we decided to examine whether or not union members suffered from systematic discrimination in the reinstatement process. Results were not highly patterned, and in fact they showed the opposite of what was expected (Table 3.8). Union members were likely to fare better in selection for reinstatement. For example, if an open-pit miner was a union member, the likelihood of reinstatement was .44 versus .23 if he was not a union member. It is possible that although Phelps-Dodge viewed some active

Table 3.7. The Effect of Special Skills on Employment Status of
            Open-Pit Miners.
            (results from a nonmetric discriminant analysis)

Characteristics	Conditional Probabilities		
Skill Types	Still Unemployed	Reinstated by P-D	Inactive Claim
Mechanical	.33	.41	.27
Construction	.25	.36	.40
Welding	.23	.0	.77
Chauffeur's license	.14	.58	.28
Other	.48	.22	.30
No special skill given	.41	.23	.36

union leaders as a threat, the general weakness of the union meant that union membership was not by itself a factor in company decisions.

Another check was made concerning racial or ethnic discrimination in the company's reinstatement decisions. There is an old joke about the Phelps-Dodge operation in Bisbee: It is said to be the 3–M Company"—Mexicans underground, Mormons in the pit, and Methodists in the office. It was apparent from our sample of workers, however, that this characterization was not completely accurate. For example, 51 percent of the underground jobs were held by Mexican-Americans, whereas they represent 43 percent of workers overall. This was not a statistically significant difference. Results from the test of discrimination in rehiring cast further doubt on the possibility that the company showed favoritism toward Anglos (Table 3.9). Mexican-Americans were in fact just as likely as Anglos to be reinstated and no more likely to remain unemployed.

No doubt should remain about what the company had in mind. It was able to divest itself of older workers and keep the younger workers, whose specific skills were needed in the new mines. Even many workers who were rehired

Table 3.8. The Effect of Union Membership on Employment Status of
            Miners.
            (results from a nonmetric discriminant analysis)

Characteristics	Conditional Probabilities					
	Still Unemployed		Reinstated by P-D		Inactive Claim	
Union membership	Open Pit	Under-ground	Open Pit	Under-ground	Open Pit	Under-ground
Member	.30	.30	.44	.39	.26	.32
Not a member	.37	.41	.23	.23	.40	.36

Table 3.9. The Effect of Ethnicity on Employment Status of Miners. (results from a non-metric discriminant analysis)

Characteristics	Conditional Probabilities					
	Still Unemployed		Reinstated by P-D		Inactive Claim	
Ethnic identity	Open Pit	Under-ground	Open Pit	Under-ground	Open Pit	Under-ground
Mexican-American	.32	.32	.36	.31	.32	.37
Anglo	.34	.34	.32	.35	.34	.31

lost their previous seniority. The company was then able to avoid being prosecuted under federal law for discrimination in hiring by pointing to the results of a physical examination that showed that the unwanted men were no longer fit for work. No matter what the company doctor said, results here show that widespread and calculated discrimination based on age, seniority, and type of skill did occur.

The Loss of Dreams and Other Things

As unemployment continued for a large number of Bisbee's miners, we attempted to acquire more in-depth information on their personal and financial situations. Through contacts with unemployed miners we identified a set of unemployed men who were statistically representative of those having a high probability of sustained unemployment. This meant that age, indicating relatively younger and older workers, and seniority, indicating workers with the longest service, were the most important characteristics. Eventually, extended interviews were obtained with 12 families. In order to facilitate initial description of these families, background information is summarized in Table 3.10.

At the time of the first interview, the underground miners in this smaller sample had been unemployed for 10 to 13 months and the open-pit miners for 15 to 18 months. Since unemployment benefits had run out for some of the latter group, we were able to acquire information about adjustments to severely reduced income. The miners' stories were eloquent and compelling. It is difficult to convey their impact without simply reproducing them here. In order to allow efficiency of presentation and retain maximum impact, interviews were analyzed for the presence of recurring themes. The themes that surfaced most persistently concerned changes in health, self-concept, and family roles. Two typical responses also emerged from the circumstances of all 12 families, although they were seldom made an explicit part of the interviews. The first of these is a psychological, financial, and sometimes physical adaptation to unemployment that makes looking for and securing a future job less and less likely as time goes on. The second is a strong commitment to stay in Bisbee, going as far in some cases as to mean the rejection of possible jobs elsewhere.

For all 12 men, the matter of physical well-being was a preoccupation. There were many reasons why the men felt, and in some ways even caused, a decline in their health after being laid off. First, there was an abrupt change in their level of activity. Mining is physically demanding, heavy work; out of work, the men quickly began to lose fitness. Most of the men also reported that their drinking increased soon after layoff. Robert Clay, for example, asserted that at first the experience of unemployment "had been a relief, even fun." He had made several trips to Montana to check out the mining possibilities there and had done more fishing and exploring with his sons.

Table 3.10. Summary Data of Twelve Miners Selected for Case Study.

Name of Head[a]	Age	Marital Status	Working Spouse	Dependent Children	Years With P-D	Months Unemployed At Interview
José Navaronne	52	married	no	--	38	16
Alex Singer	30	married	no	3	11	16
Francisco Vallejo	28	married	no	2	8	15
Filipé Hermanos	41	married	yes	3	NR	15
Pepé Martinez	45	married	no	2	6	18
Paul Travis	27	divorced	--	--	5	18
Ramon Vasquéz	46	married	no	--	28	12
Doug Schultz	60	married	NR	--	40	regular retirement
Robert Clay	34	married	yes	2	15	12
Joe Hill	50	widowed	--	--	23	12
Bob Mason	55	married	no	--	30	10
Jay Monroe	41	married	yes	3	21	13

[a]Pseudonyms have been used to protect the identity of respondents.

Gradually, however, he began to drink and gained 25 pounds: "I really began to feel sorry for myself and to drink heavily. You think, 'what the hell. I have time on my hands, don't have to work the next day, can sleep it off, etc.' " Francisco Vallejo's experience sounded similar. He said that he was "really down" for the first three months and drank heavily almost every night during that period. He gained 30 pounds in the process. Even for the men who claimed to have kept their drinking under control, the typical problem was "sitting around home, eating and getting fat."

In addition to substantial weight increases, most of the men reported problems related to tension—headaches, high blood pressure, or fatigue. One commented, "I have been just generally depressed and don't have any energy—to look for a job or do anything." When Robert Clay went to the doctor for a throat infection, he learned that his worry and tension had caused high blood pressure. Declining confidence, lethargy, bitterness, and despair combined to interact with and worsen the real problems of health that accompanied a change of status and activity for these miners.

After a time, poor health took on a different significance; it began to serve to rationalize continued unemployment. Blaming one's circumstances on poor health was easy because Phelps-Dodge used this as an excuse for discarding many workers. Some men received additional reinforcement for this rationalization in applying for other jobs. Of the seven men in this group who were over 40, five were turned down for a new job at least once for "reasons of health." (A sixth man was not looking for work because he was fully retired.) One of the men, José Navaronne, strained his back while working in an underground stope in 1973. Afterward, he was able to handle light duty, such as aboveground work, but on work involving heavy lifting, he continued to have problems until he was finally laid off in January 1975. Navaronne later applied for work at mines in several Arizona towns and, after taking physical examinations, was turned down by all three. "Don't ask us why," the personnel offices told him. Nonetheless, he assumed that poor health was to blame and remained convinced that he was, in fact, incapable of doing any heavy work. Navaronne's doctor confirmed that his back had undergone a great deal of natural deterioration and that he had arthritis. Although these conditions are not sufficient to meet the legal definition of disability, they were apparently enough to disqualify Navaronne from future employment in mining—the only work he knew. "Perhaps I am worthless now," he said, "I am too old, no one will hire me." Our field worker observed cases where men began to stoop, move more slowly, and feel increasingly impaired as time went on, even though medical diagnoses indicated relatively minor back problems. Belief in their own infirmity allowed them to retain some dignity as working men who had inherent worth and many skills but were prevented by disability from finding employment.

Concurrent with the changes in physical health, respondents reported changes in self-concept, which involved a progression of different attitudes toward themselves, the company, and the future in general. Different ways of viewing and coping with free time also emerged. Robert Clay provided a good summary of what seemed to be the typical stages of adjustment. For him the first four or five months were the worst:

At first you can't believe that you are being kicked out by the company which had been your whole life up to that time. You feel you'll be one of the ones that's transferred. Slowly you begin to lose hope that the company will call: "How can they not call; they've got to!" Hope dwindles. Then you begin to feel, "The sons-a-bitches, I wouldn't work for them if you paid me!" I didn't even go by their mine when I was looking for work in Wyoming.

Clay was fortunate; after a year without work he was hired by a potash mine company in New Mexico. He said that he had "broken the psychological lock" that Phelps-Dodge and Bisbee had over him, and he looked forward to making a new start. At 34, his relative youth and willingness to leave Bisbee may have been an advantage.

Like other men, Jay Monroe ran the full gamut of emotions during his year of unemployment. Monroe saw himself as an active, intelligent, and assertive person; and he often was critical of the company "to which I gave 21 years of my life." He was especially bitter that other mechanics with less seniority were transferred and he was not. "They sure worked around seniority lists!" In the next breath he said, "It was just another job. Maybe being off work has been good for me in a way. I'm out of the rut of 21 years, and I've communicated more with people since the layoffs."

For all the men, the first several months saw relief, optimism, and hope turn to concern, perplexion, and fear. Drinking with their buddies and sharing anger against the company was an initial reaction to the worry. Then as they got ahold of themselves, brought the drinking under control, and gave up hope of a call-back from the company, a more calculated reaction set in. They began to canvass the area in earnest for jobs and systematically to cut expenditures at home. Francisco Vallejo's reaction illustrates the vigor with which new starts were pursued. He registered for classes in ambulance driving and emergency medical techniques at the local community college, hoping these new skills would increase his employability. To fill idle time he worked with children as a volunteer at Bisbee's recreation center and was also an assistant coach for a Little League team. "I was real proud of that team," he said. When a position for which he qualified opened up with the local fire department, Vallejo applied. So did 80 other men. The job was reportedly given to a cousin of the mayor. Vallejo again applied for a job when the city advertised for a laborer. The result was the same. These experiences increased Vallejo's bitterness about what it takes to get a job: "It's not experience or qualifications, it's brown-nosing." Still he saw himself as a competent person, "capable of doing a job." At the time of the interview, he was back at the community college taking nine units of law enforcement and hoping to get on with the border patrol. However, the competition for this, or for any other job in Bisbee or nearby towns, was fierce.

As the days without work wore on, many of the men sought odd jobs; parttime bartending, either in Mexico or Arizona, was the most frequent stopgap measure. With typical resourcefulness, Vallejo took care of people's lawns and rebuilt a septic tank. Joe Hill fashioned makeshift income from small projects on his ranch. Alex Singer "turned [his] trumpet into a few bucks" by playing with a band in the night spots just across the border. Pepé Martinez manufactured, sold, and traded individual turquoise jewelry pieces. A local bar provided his "business" phone, and a friend donated a workshop.

On the home front there was much belt tightening. A modest income, say $200 to $300 per month, was typically earned through self-employment or the sale of goods produced at home, while additional food was grown in a garden. Savings were exhausted to keep up bill payments, buy school clothes for the children, or pay medical expenses. Several of the men repaired and painted their houses in return for rent deductions. Some, like Vallejo, cut down on expensive entertainment: "Before, the family liked to go camping and fishing, take drives, visit relatives. Now we drive the car very little and walk around Old Bisbee wherever we go. We stay home at night and the TV is our entertainment."

An ironic twist began to appear in the struggle to make ends meet. If the coping succeeded, a new confidence and sense of acceptance began to emerge: "I can manipulate this situation and survive it!" Job canvassing and course-taking that proved unsuccessful then gave way to other necessary means of hustling to ensure day-to-day survival. As time passed, the men who succeeded in their modest attempts to cope with a jobless situation finally became less employable in regular jobs, for which they now saw themselves as fundamentally unsuited. They reached the point where they could no longer respond, either psychologically or physically, to the promise of new work. These are the men represented in the national statistics that show declining male labor-force participation. We now have some insight as to why. In dealing with prolonged unemployment in a way that permits some shred of dignity, men become increasingly and perhaps irreversibly less employable.

Problems at Home Contribute to Feelings of Worthlessness

The men reported sleeping in late; sitting around home, "doing a helluva lot of thinking, planning, and worrying"; and getting together with their friends for a beer in the afternoon. Petty arguments between husband and wife were an additional problem for some. Perhaps the men's increased drinking occurred in part because, as Robert Clay explained, "My wife got on my nerves much more and we argued a lot, so I couldn't take it and just left for the tavern." Martinez described a more subtle but equally devastating scene: "Several months after I'd been laid off, my wife put the coffee cup down a little harder than usual. She didn't mean it, but the sound rang all through me as a reminder of my no job." Paul Travis's wife was less subtle; she left him six months after he was laid off, taking the two children with her. He conceded that the marriage had problems before, but that economic difficulties, caused by his unemployment, provided the reason for the final breakup. Heavy drinking, before and after his wife's departure, left Travis shaken and run down.

In most of these families traditional definitions of male and female roles prevailed. Of the 11 wives who were present at the time the layoffs occurred, only one was working. (Two wives subsequently found jobs in order to forestall total economic disaster.) This low rate of employment among the miners' wives was echoed in the larger sample, where only 18 percent of the married women were working. The proportion was still lower (13 percent) for the Mexican-American families. Both of these proportions were substantially below the national labor-force participation rate of 48 percent for married women. The men saw themselves as the essential providers and for this reason regretted sending their wives to work in such an emergency. "I don't like it," said Jay Monroe, "She hadn't worked previously, but it seemed a matter of necessity." Although his wife enjoyed her job as a clerk in the local bank, he hoped that she would go back to being a housewife after he found work. That his wife was working damaged his sense of self-worth by calling public attention to the fact that he was of little use to his family as a wage earner. Helping out more around the house, as all of the men reported doing, did not make them feel any more useful; it just filled empty time. Tears welled up in José Navarone's eyes as he talked about his problem: "I've been working all my life and this has been a long year. There is no money coming in, we owe back payments on the house and utilities, and I'm flat broke. . . . [Then, summing it all up] I can't make no promises no more."

Eventually, financial problems combined with emotional and psychological ones. When they were employed, these miners earned annual incomes averaging $10,000 to $12,000. During the first year of unemployment, family incomes averaged $7,000 to $12,000, depending on whether the wife worked. In this group of families, the women who were not working at the time of our interviews were not likely to in the future. Either they felt too old, their health was poor, their English was bad, or their husbands would not allow it. The women who did work earned $5,000 to $7,000 per year. For the other families, incomes after the first jobless year fell to $315 a month, all coming from unemployment benefits. After 15 months unemployment benefits ran out, and several families, like Navaronne's, were living on $200 to $250 a month. At this point four families were eligible for food stamps, but only one was receiving them. The others could not bring themselves to apply. These families desperately resisted giving up what little pride they had left.

It is important to recognize that the Bisbee miners were not acting like the "voluntarily unemployed" people who supposedly contributed to our recent high rates of unemployment. To hear the administration's economists discuss the persistent joblessness of the 1970s, one might well think that being unemployed was sufficiently painless that most nonworking people had lost all interest in finding jobs. Besides being without empirical basis, such a notion impugns the energy and character of working people who, like the ones described in this book, find that their labor is no longer needed.

It is unwarranted to assume that workers, and particularly workers past the age of 40, will automatically move to new places to take advantage of economic opportunities. As Joe Hill stated, "It's not bettering yourself to pick up at my age [50] and go somewhere else, whatever the pay!" His statement suggests that economists ignore factors that are central to families moving or staying. For one thing, people develop loyalties to the places where they live. The Bisbee work force, for example, was very stable over the years. The average length of service with Phelps-Dodge among workers in our larger sample was 21.6 and 13.8 years, respectively, for underground and open-pit miners. Many of these men and women pointed out that their fathers and grandfathers had worked in the Bisbee mines. They wished to preserve their roots and to maintain ties with relatives and friends in established social networks. Moreover, staying in the community had value in the day-to-day struggle for survival. These workers expressed some of their concerns:

It would kill my mother if we left her and kill her, too, if we moved her.

We are taken care of here—we know we will not starve. Meals appear at dinner time; there are "loans" for cigarettes.

We had to sell our car, but people lend us theirs when shopping and interviews come up.

Once I had to go around the neighborhood and collect money for groceries. I felt so ashamed, but everyone had something to give. Now I know I could do it again if I had to.

Mexican-Americans in particular are unwilling to stray from the border. They often have family in Mexico and do not wish to endure the burden of a more distant separation. Since Bisbee is only eight miles from the Mexican border, a great deal of visiting and mutual assistance goes on across this line. Many of these families lead split lives: Their economic and residential lives are in Arizona, while their cultural and psychological lives are in Mexico. Weekends are a time for "going back home."

In addition, living in a depressed area like Bisbee offers certain economic advantages that a new place might not. Housing values, for example, remained low in the absence of demand from homebuyers. Bisbee's rents were incredibly low. The miners in our larger sample were paying rents that averaged $55 a month for underground miners and $34 a month for open-pit miners. In the latter group many of the miners were living in subsidized company housing with monthly rents of $32.50. Obviously if these families were to move, they would be forced to live in much more expensive housing.

Other families simply asserted the preeminence of social goals over strictly economic ones. Such goals can be quite reasonable, as in this case: "Our sixteen-year-old has been outstanding in school—academic and extracurricular activities. We want to make it possible for her to finish school in Bisbee, she's done so well, and then go on to college. We'll make any sacrifice for that." For Jay Monroe's family the problem was somewhat similar. Their teenage son had a serious learning disability that had tracked him into classes for lower-achieving or retarded children. Monroe felt that the Bisbee schools really came to grips with his son's problem and that he might "turn out OK" if he could graduate and enroll in a special work program offered at nearby Fort Huachuca. The Monroes were loathe to disrupt their son's schooling because they wanted him to have a productive future. For many such families the education of their children assumed paramount importance precisely because their own schooling was so minimal, and this gave them all the more reason to make sacrifices for the sake of their children.

Ramon Vasquéz had a more pessimistic view about whether it would be better to move or to stay. He tended to view both choices with a jaundiced eye:

You asked me if I was worried, well I'll tell you. I'm 46 years old—not old enough to retire, not really young enough to go look for a job. I'm sorta undesirable. I have kept my nose clean with this company: I have a helluva good record. I have as good a chance as anybody at going to work, wherever, for this company—as long as this company has a job. Outside of that I will try the right way, but there's not that many jobs all over the country, because this whole damn country is in trouble. So if I can't get it the right way, I'm going to try the other way. If they put me in prison, then they're going to have to have welfare take care of my wife. I'll be well taken care of.

I don't know what the outcome of all this will be. I want to do right: I'll go to work forever. But if they won't let me work, I'll become a thief. It's not that I want to be a bandito, you know. But what's a man gonna do?

Pepé Martinez was also 46, and his tone was one of resignation. Fatigue and despair slowly began to tell on his face as he described his feelings about the future:

You know, the working class only has their little dreams to think of and live for. When they lose their jobs and go on unemployment or whatever, these end, and it's hard. The kind of dreams I'm talking about are boats, campers, iceboxes, a new car, etc.—not the big dreams of the rich. Power is what they want.

The Players Change but the Game Remains the Same:
A Postscript on Bisbee

Until December 1974 the Phelps-Dodge Corporation employed 75 percent of the work force in Bisbee and owned 90 percent of the land on which the town is located. It was estimated by company officials that for every four people on their payroll, an additional worker not directly employed by them provided a product or service to the mines. This estimate leaves fewer than 200 people in Bisbee's work force whose jobs were not directly related to the mines. The next largest source of employment, but a very distant second, was the public sector. Since Bisbee is the county seat, some local jobs were provided by city, county, state, and federal governments. Public utilities also provided some jobs. Other than these, there were no employers with large payrolls. It is thus understandable that there was panic in Bisbee when Phelps-Dodge left. It was grimly joked that as their last act the city fathers would rename the town "Baja Jerome," a reference to the mining town of Jerome, which became a ghost town after Phelps-Dodge left in 1949.

Despite the realism of such fears, Bisbee did not die. One measure of Bisbee's endurance is the stability of city's sales-tax receipts which we monitored before, during, and after the mine closures (Table 3.11).[10] Since sales of goods and services have a very cyclical nature, wherein some months, like December, are invariably higher than others, data on tax receipts must be compared across the same months of different years. The sales-tax receipts for December 1974 and the following two months, for example, were higher than in the previous year. It is not until June 1975, the month of final closures, that there was a substantial drop in sales. Total receipts in that month were 26 percent below the level of the previous year. Sales bounced back up again in July and nearly maintained, or surpassed, the levels of the previous two years until December 1975, one year after the initial layoffs. The receipts in that month were 13 percent behind those of December 1974, and January receipts dropped to 22 percent below the 1975 level. After that, tax receipts lagged for a period of time but then resurged in June 1976. These are not the signs of a dying community.

Undeniable signs of a faltering economy were expected to show in March and April 1976, a point at which state and federal unemployment benefits had expired for the underground miners. Yet the city's sales-tax receipts remained remarkably stable. As we continued to watch Bisbee, this apparent economic resilience was a paradox.

School enrollment data was also examined. The superintendent of schools in Bisbee sent out a questionnaire to parents on 7 February 1975 requesting

Table 3.11. Monthly Sales-Tax Receipts[a] in Bisbee, July 1973 through August 1976.

Month	Receipts, 1973-74	Receipts, 1974-75	Receipts, 1975-76
July	33,443.23	32,739.38	35,726.50
August	25,865.50	28,192.61	27,877.67
September	27,972.22	28,758.91	27,212.23
October	22,249.19	27,378.18	32,032.40
November	22,215.72	20,882.20	26,849.50
December	25,524.65	30,737.74[b]	26,854.95
January	28,552.16	35,457.42	27,644.67
February	33,447.88	34,839.02	30,458.82
March	28,457.26	26,820.91	25,069.00
April	26,427.80	26,176.36	28,609.22
May	27,100.54	27,240.79	28,429.80
June	30,604.02	22,675.16[b]	25,515.24
July 1976			29,337.86
August 1976			26,384.00

[a]Figures are corrected for inflation.
[b]The two major layoffs occurred in these months.

information about enrollment plans for the fall of 1975. Of the parents 80 percent returned the questionnaire, and their responses indicated a projected enrollment drop of 15 percent. In fact, when September 1975 rolled around, overall enrollments were down only 14 percent from the previous year and remained fairly stable until February 1976, when enrollments fell further, to 20 percent below their February 1975 level. This decline in enrollment was enough to hurt school budgets, since 60 percent of the district's operating revenue comes from state subsidies, which are based solely on enrollment; but it does not point to a mass exodus from Bisbee's schools. It seemed that this failed to occur because many miners' families decided to remain in the community for as long as possible.

However, headlines in the *Arizona Daily Star*, one year later, indicated that the exodus had finally come: "Closed Schools Reflect Bisbee's Population Drop" [4 April 1977]. Six of Bisbee's eight public schools had closed by this time, and local school administrators were quoted as saying that the remaining schools would be closed within a year. Apparently it took somewhat longer than we expected for the mine closures to have their impact on other community institutions, such as schools.

In many ways the Bisbee economy seemed quite resilient, as the sales-tax receipts suggested. With so many people unemployed, how could this be so?

Data on utility connects and disconnects provided a clue as to what was happening in Bisbee. The number of total utility hookups existing at any one time, i.e., electrical, gas, and water, remained constant over a three-year period beginning in October 1973. Turnovers, however, were high (Table 3.12). It was apparent that new people were moving into town as others moved out; and this influx of new people kept the community alive.

Table 3.12. Utilities Activity in Bisbee, October through December 1975.

	Total Electrical		Total Gas		Total Water	
	Discon- nects	Recon- nects	Discon- nects	Recon- nects	Discon- nects	Recon- nects
October	169	184	155	152	109	105
November	134	115	119	118	NR	NR
December	134	146	126	137	63	70

Who was moving to Bisbee, and why? In large part they were people who did not require jobs. One group was made up of commuters to nearby army installations at Sierra Vista and Fort Huachuca. Sierra Vista in particular is relatively large, having a population of 20,000, and is not nearly as picturesque as Bisbee. Thus Bisbee serves nicely as a bedroom community for people who work there. Also, Bisbee rents and housing prices were a steal; old homes in good condition could be bought for as little as $5,000 to $10,000. Large numbers of older persons were also attracted to Bisbee's low-cost housing. Bisbee has a dry and sunny climate, which makes it a desirable place to retire.

Bisbee's economy was given a boost by other people drawn there to shop and do "touristy" things. New signs on the highway lured the passerby to see the Copper Queen Mine, which is now operated as a tourist attraction by the city. A tour takes one underground into the deep shafts and stopes that were once the work areas of Bisbee's proud miners. Some timbers still carry the original date of construction—1878. A few stopes are set-up so that the tools and techniques of drilling, blasting, and mucking can be seen and explained. Way down in the belly of the mine there is an old mule "barn" and other remnants of mining from the turn of the century. A cart carries the tourists just as it used to carry miners to and from work. The city has plans to extend the tour into breathtaking underground caverns where brilliant crystalline formations still contain valuable minerals and stones. Several tour guides are former

Phelps-Dodge miners. A small group of former miners were also employed by the city to clear out the shafts that connect the caverns to the Copper Queen Hotel.

The entire setting of Bisbee and the mine tour are surrounded by local color and history. At the tour's end, tourists can sit in refurbished splendor near Brewery Gulch and sip wine coolers at smartly decorated café tables on the patio of the Copper Queen Hotel. Actor John Wayne purchased the old Bisbee jail and was renovating it, with plans to open a museum containing items from his personal collection of Western frontier artifacts, along with historical relics from Bisbee. (One wonders if the Bisbee deportation of Wobblies will be commemorated.) Many crafts shops were opening up to sell turquoise jewelry, antiques, art, and mementos.

As a result of an influx of new residents and visitors, the wave of panic in Bisbee receded, and city officials began to express a cautious optimism. Newfound prosperity, however, was seen by some as a mixed blessing, for Bisbee was apparently being invaded by "hippies." The presence of such people attested to the fact that Bisbee's economy, while holding its own, was undergoing a metamorphosis. A national magazine[11] described this new interest in old Bisbee:

> The word has gotten out to Aspen, to San Francisco, to New York, that hidden away in the mountains of the great nowhere of southern Arizona is the new Jerusalem. A town that looks like San Francisco half a century ago, with abandoned houses on the hillsides free for the taking, or for sale at prices that haven't changed since Sheriff Harry Wheeler's days. Cool nights, warm days, cheap Mexican dope, enough tourists to support leather and craft shops, saloons that still look like saloons.
>
> Strange men from other parts hang out at the St. Elmo Saloon, where Harry Wheeler was known to stop in for a little sip once upon a time. The cow horns he sat beneath are still there, but a funk band spreads out under them nowadays, putting out music that would have made Sheriff Harry flat puke. Up in the city park, where the Wobblies used to whoop and holler, the new Strangers pitch horseshoes, smoke funny cigarettes and set up tents to sell things nobody in his right mind would have any use for.
>
> There's beauty abundant for the Strangers and few hassles. Nobody can really afford to hassle them these days in Bisbee. They bring money with them.

It is now easier for newcomers to get to Bisbee. Federal and state monies were secured to improve the airport, and plans were underway for an industrial park nearby. With the help of federal money, estimated at $49,000 for Bisbee in 1975, the city hired an economic development specialist to recruit light industry to the area.

Even though things were really looking up for Bisbee, none of this had much to do with the future of the miners. As Jay Monroe put it, "There's no future here for us at all." His statement merely recognized that city efforts, to encourage tourism had no relevance for the miners, who themselves were part of the historical scene upon which the city was hoping to capitalize. Monroe also felt that the search for industry would arrive too late for the men laid off by Phelps-Dodge: "Many will have gone already, we'll all be displaced." Many of the miners, like Monroe himself, will remain in Bisbee, despite their bitter appraisal that the town holds no future for them. They will stay because they feel they must; because they think they are too old and worthless; or because they believe that things are not much better anywhere else. If Bisbee appears to be slowly making an economic comeback, it is because the miners, in their adjustment to life without work in Bisbee, have become invisible: to other Bisbee residents, to the state and federal governments, and to the rest of America.

Miners Today Never Had It So Bad

The economic survival—indeed the apparent resurgence—of Bisbee created the illusion that the company had done nothing harmful at all and that workers and communities, if determined enough, can find their own solutions to problems of economic stagnation and decline. The realities of community powerlessness, strikingly exposed in the inability to prevent or influence a company's unilateral decision to close the mines, are repressed or forgotten in the frantic search for a new economic solution. Bisbee's solution, relying heavily on tourism and public-sector dollars, is most fragile. Worse, it is a deceptive solution. The problem caused by closure of the mines was massive unemployment of the town's industrial work force. This problem is altered not in the least by boutiques, new tourist facilities, and the mine tour. Whether or not Bisbee survives by trading in on its quaintness, a large group of miners will remain unemployed.

The plight of Bisbee miners is representative of that faced by many other industrial workers in America. As large corporations continue to mechanize production or move it to foreign countries, an increasing number of workers cannot find jobs and eventually stop looking, relying instead on their own resources. The problem of declining rates of male labor-force participation is obscured by the conventional explanation that is caused by a trend toward early and "voluntary" retirement. Worse, the rate of unemployment is highly publicized, while the problem of people simply dropping out of the labor force is ignored. The human cost of perpetuating such public delusions is huge. We must realize that Phelps-Dodge has contributed to this problem, not by acting illegally or immorally, as defined within our system of corporate capitalism, but rather in the pursuit of its own interests, i.e., its profits. Under the present economic rules, the company cannot be faulted for consequences that were not its primary intention. But to leave it at this is to admit that we lack the nerve and intelligence to imagine a way of producing goods without also discarding people.

In 1917 Bisbee miners were deported and locked out of the mines for daring to challenge the prerogative of the mining companies to carve out an increase in profits at a time when prices were rising. Miners raised hell because they were being gouged instead of being allowed to share in the increased returns from the productivity of their work. When Phelps-Dodge closed its Bisbee mines in 1974–75, miners were treated even worse; they lost their jobs after investing years, decades, and sometimes generations of work. The technological advances that made the company rich were making the workers poor. Despite being worried, these modern miners did not raise hell and did not have to be deported by the company. Instead, they were kept off balance by conflicting signals from the company, and in the end they were quietly left behind.

Unlike many wood-products workers in Oregon, most Bisbee miners correctly identified the company, rather than a diminishing natural resource, as the cause of their loss of employment. Their mistake was in believing too much in their own efficacy as workers. After all, in the past the company had threatened to close the Bisbee mines and had never acted. Although the miners were openly distrustful of the company, they felt they were still valuable as members of its work force and that their record of hard work would not be forgotten. It came as a shock to many to find what little regard the company had for them and how powerless they were to forestall the closure. Moreover, the company effectively defused a potentially volatile situation by transferring a limited number of workers while using medical examinations to pronounce many others unfit for work. Since the company was purported to be selecting on the basis of merit, the seeds of self-doubt were sown among those excluded. Even if the company was known to be pulling "tricks," the process of sorting out among the workers placed the ultimate blame on those who supposedly did not measure up. In the final analysis, the company could not be held at fault because it had warned the workers many times before, and it was now doing what it said it would do all along. Without something new to protest, the workers were clearly outmaneuvered and left to cope with the situation on their own.

It must be clear from this chapter that there are inordinate human costs in the dislocation that accompanies the unconstrained movement of capital. At the present time, a firm may move or alter its production process in a way that dramatically reduces its need for labor without giving any consideration—or even advance notice—to the workers and communities that will be affected by such decisions. Indeed, community input in such decisions is unheard of. On the one hand, we are becoming sufficiently worried about natural resources that we sometimes offer public challenges to harmful corporate actions. On the other hand, we are apparently so cavalier about human beings that we overlook the effect of corporate actions on workers and communities.

Notes

1. An ample flavor of this part of America's history can be drawn from any of the autobiographies or biographies of IWW members. For example, Ralph Chaplin, *Wobbly: The Rough-and-Tumble Story of an American Radical;* Elizabeth Gurley Flynn, *I Speak My Own Piece;* Walker C. Smith, *The Everett Massacre: A History of the Class Struggle in the Lumber Industry;* William D. Haywood, *Bill Haywood's Book;* Joseph Conlin, *Bread and Roses, Too: Essays on the Wobblies.*

2. This account of the events following the call-to-strike of 27 June is based on several sources, including versions by participants on both sides and later historical interpretations by partisans of

both. However, we do not mean to suggest that our rendering is impartial. The interested reader is referred to Mayhall (1974), Chaplin (1948), Kornbluh (1964), and Renshaw (1967).

3. The identity of this man, and that of all other people described in this chapter, is protected through the use of a pseudonym. He has worked for Phelps-Dodge for 40 years and was a particularly gracious and valuable source of information. During this time he also worked as a labor organizer for the Mine, Mill, and Smelter Workers of America—a militant union—and was later a union officer for the Steelworkers. His father died of "miner's con," an occupational disease caused by inhalation of copper-laden dust.

4. A mucker is somewhat like a miner's assistant, although he may be equally skilled. In the work cycle of blasting, mucking out, timbering, and drilling to the next blast, he "mucks out," or clears the work area of the rock and debris (muck) that has been broken loose in the blast and shovels it into cars to be hauled away. The miner does most of the blasting, timbering, and drilling.

5. See the excellent article by Ronald Schatz, "The End of Corporate Liberation: Class Struggle in the Electrical Manufacturing Industry, 1933–1950," *Radical America*, vol. 9, nos. 4–5 (July/August 1975), pp. 187–205. Schatz reinterprets the 1930s era of corporate liberalism, toward AFL unions, as an anti-union tactic. In any case, the posture of "progressivism" still characterized a minority of corporations.

6. Over the medium-long run the company is operating on an optimistic assumption that the economy will perform and expand beyond previous highs. Ups and downs are to be expected, and capital-outlay decisions often take an average of ten years to affect production.

7. In field notes for April 1974 there appears a summary of a conversation with the Director of Bisbee's Community Action Program (CAP), a man who is also a long-time local resident. He was skeptical about rumors of an impending shutdown: "Since 1967, P-D has put out announcements of closings or partial closings. This time the odds are 10 to 1 against any serious cutback in operations, partially because P-D is negotiating on a large body of ore next to the Lavender Pit." Five months later, in the fall, a man in P-D management told our field worker, "It is evident that the company is not close to any major cutback in their Bisbee operation within the next six months." What is clearly evident is that the layoffs, occurring just three months later, in December, took *everyone* in Bisbee by surprise.

8. This table is derived from a paper prepared by William Martin, et al., for the 74th annual meeting of the American Anthropological Association, San Francisco, December 1975. The numbers in this table differ slightly from those in the text because it is based on a preliminary construction of the file, which neither included all useable cases nor excluded all unuseable cases from the file. "Useability" here refers to the completeness of information on each case.

9. See Note 8 above.

10. The city's receipts from the sales tax must be corrected for inflation (i.e., increases in the overall price level) so that what we are measuring are net, or pure, changes in the level of sales.

11. See Robert Houston, "Sheriff Harry Wheeler Rounds Up the Wobblies," *Mother Jones*, vol. 1, no. 9 (December 1976), pp. 43–48. The article contains quite a few pictures of the Bisbee deportation.

4 Pineapple in Paradise "No Can No More"

Melting Pot in the Pacific

Hawaii is commonly regarded as a paradise by visitors, who cannot help but marvel at its abundance of natural beauty. Historically, Hawaii has also been a paradise for capitalist exploitation. The first foreigners to come to the Hawaiian Islands were whalers, sandalwood traders, gun runners, and missionaries. Descendents of these early invaders later became involved in the development of a system of plantation agriculture in which most of the land and wealth were concentrated in the hands of a few omnipotent owners.

One of the most important facts about Hawaii is that 80 percent of the privately owned acreage in the stage belongs to twenty individuals or corporations (Gray, 1973:48). It is equally important to note that fourteen individuals or corporations own or lease 40 percent of all Hawaii land. Such concentrated ownership of land originates historically from the machinations of American capitalists who intervened as early as 1850 to undermine the power of the king by changing Hawaii's traditional system of land tenure. Although certain estates were kept as crown lands, 1.6 million acres were divided among 245 high chiefs, who proceeded to sell, lease, or give it away to foreigners. The remainder of the land was made available for general sale in the form of small lots. In the 1860s increased demand for sugar on the world market led to the development of plantation agriculture, which was controlled by a few powerful American entrepreneurs. By 1890 the production of sugar-cane occupied approximately four-fifths of Hawaii's arable land. The exploitative attitude of the early sugar barons, which seems to have changed little in contemporary times, was expressed at a planters' convention by a missionary descendant, Sanford B. Dole. "I cannot help feeling that the chief end of this meeting is plantation profits; and the prosperity of the country, the demands of society, the future of the Hawaiian race only comes secondarily if at all" (Gray, 1973:51).

By 1930 five companies, commonly known as the "Big Five"—Castle and Cooke, Alexander and Balwin, Theo. H. Davies, C. Brewer, and American Factors—controlled 96 percent of Hawaii's sugar crop and every business associated with sugar, such as banking, insurance, utilities, transportation, merchandising, and shipping. In 1932 these companies gained control of the pineapple industry, which made profitable use of land not suited for growing sugarcane, and this became Hawaii's second most important crop prior to World War II. The Big Five totally dominated Hawaii's economic and political

93

life through their influence in the Republican party, until the labor movement partially broke their power after World War II.

In the latter half of the 19th century and first third of the 20th century, more than 400,000 foreign recruits were shipped to Hawaii to provide cheap plantation labor. Just as there was at that time a melting pot in the Eastern United States, resulting from the importation of industrial laborers from various European countries, so there was a melting pot in Hawaii, resulting from the importation of plantation laborers, mostly from various Asian and Pacific countries. Chinese, Japanese, Koreans, Portuguese, Puerto Ricans, and Filipinos were among those brought into Hawaii during its plantation era.

The last such group to be recruited is different from the rest because its members have had less time to assimilate and are left at the bottom of the socioeconomic ladder. Filipinos, having been exempt from immigration restrictions because of the recent colonial status of the Philippines, were the last immigrant group in Hawaii to be imported in large numbers. Unlike previous groups, Filipinos did not find their status automatically raised by a new group brought in to take their place.

During the 1950s and 1960s Hawaii's Big Five became multinational corporations by investing their profits overseas. The trend continuing into the 1970s has been to develop Hawaii to its fullest extent as a tourist mecca, while agricultural industry is exported to underdeveloped countries, such as the Philippines, where the availability of cheap labor contributes to higher profits. The development of tourism has encouraged land speculation and rising prices, which in turn have resulted in plantation closures and the accompanying loss of jobs. Between 1940 and 1970 there was a 64-percent reduction in the work force attached to pineapple plantations and canneries in Hawaii (Choy, 1973:17). Of nine pineapple companies doing business in Hawaii in 1960, only three existed after 1975. The opportunity no longer exists to work on a plantation in order to save enough money to invest in a home. For recently arrived Filipinos, opportunities are further limited by a language barrier and lack of education, as well as by neglect by those in positions of authority.

The example of the phaseout of a pineapple plantation presented in this chapter is meant to illustrate a specific instance in which the prerogative of capitalists is exercised in the interest of profits at the expense of people whose livelihood is at stake. Although the circumstances of Filipinos will be most thoroughly explored, Hawaiians who live on the island of Molokai will be brought into the discussion because they are directly affected by the plans of developers. Together, Filipinos and Hawaiians constitute just under three-fourths of the island's population, and yet they have very little control over its future.

This chapter examines a part of the colonial period in Hawaii when Filipinos were imported as plantation laborers and discusses how the colonial setting has affected the present-day community of Maunaloa, Molokai. The circumstances under which Maunaloa was closed as a plantation camp, the adjustment experience of community residents, and the response of those in positions of authority is analyzed. This case is particularly revealing because of a political context in which the interests of powerful people are being carried out in the name of giving economic relief to disadvantaged people. Although Filipinos remain culturally distinct and have been socialized by plantation bosses to accept their dependent status, conflict ultimately developed over the issue of political interference versus local autonomy as it related to people's desire to preserve their community.

Colonial Heritage

Since the Philippine Islands were under control of the United States government from 1898 to 1946, the sugar industry, acting through the Hawaiian Sugar Planter's Association (HSPA), was afforded two distinct advantages in recruiting Filipino laborers: (1) Filipinos were classified as United States nationals—neither aliens nor citizens—who could travel freely without passport to any territory of the United States; (2) those officials in the Philippines with whom the HSPA would deal were under the control of the colonial government. Two events in 1907 curtailed the plantation labor supply from other sources and made it desirable to recruit Filipinos. The Japanese Government entered into a gentlemen's agreement with the U.S. Government to limit the migration of Japanese to Hawaii, and the Federal Immigration Law was passed to prohibit assistance to alien labor by corporations or private individuals. Full-scale recruiting of Filipinos began in 1909, and a steady flow of workers was insured by about 1915, when sufficient early recruits had returned home with money, thereby encouraging others to migrate. By 1919 HSPA had brought 23,418 Filipino men and 3,009 women dependents to Hawaii (Lasker, 1931:350).

A shortage of plantation labor developed about 1920 because many Filipinos returned home after World War I, a greater number of Japanese immigrants went into private business, and a series of Japanese-inspired strikes occurred. The HSPA turned to recruiting more Filipino laborers as the only way of dealing with the shortage. The period between 1920 and 1929 was the peak of the immigration movement. A total of 65,373 men and 5,646 women dependents were brought to Hawaii by the HSPA during this time (Lasker, 1931:357).

Before 1925 the HSPA transported sugar workers and pineapple workers at cost, and the pineapple companies paid a prorated share of the transportation cost to the HSPA. Later, Filipinos were so anxious to go to Hawaii that the HSPA ceased to subsidize recruiting, and Filipino workers wishing to travel to Hawaii paid their own way.

In 1927 resentment against the importation of Filipino laborers began to build. On the West Coast it was thought that the availability of Filipino workers was the cause of widespread unemployment among United States citizens. When economic depression hit a few years later, racial disturbances occurred in the wake of a movement calling for the repatriation of Filipinos. In Hawaii Filipinos were resented by Japanese labor-union organizers because of their willingness to be used as strike breakers. As a result of union agitation and reduced demand for plantation labor, the HSPA voluntarily curtailed the importation of Filipinos beginning in 1932. By 1935 the HSPA had ceased its importation activities. In order to insure a continuous supply of labor, plantation owners broke a previously unwritten agreement never to hire a Filipino worker who had quit a planatation job. This action reduced the number of unemployed Filipinos in Hawaii and eased tension with Japanese labor unions, who wished to avoid competition from unorganized Filipino labor.

The Tydings-McDuffie Act of 1934 carried a provision that excluded Filipinos from being brought to the United States mainland. Although Hawaii was exempted from this provision, the HSPA brought no more Filipinos to Hawaii until just before Philippine independence in 1946. From 1909 to 1946 the HSPA brought to Hawaii a total of 109,512 men and 9,398 women dependents (Clifford, 1967:28).

The unbalanced sex ratio among Filipino immigrants originally occurred as a direct consequence of HSPA policy, which was aimed at recruiting single men and later was perpetuated by circumstances that made it difficult for Filipino men to find wives. Life in the plantation camps was unattractive, and many men could not afford to transport a wife from the Philippines and support her in proper style. Often the men were obligated to send money back to their families in the Philippines, and what little was left went to pay for a few immediate pleasures. Although women of other ethnic groups in Hawaii were sometimes considered for marriage, cultural barriers as well as financial problems often prevented the final step. The following remarks, selected from our interviews with plantation laborers, illustrate these concerns:

How can marry, no 'nuff money. Us work 10 hours a day, for 10 cents an hour before, not 'nuff for me, so no more look for wife.

Only get little bit money. Not 'nuff for send to Philippines. I come Hawaii so can help my family, they always ask and ask for money. So how can get one wife? By and by, money no more.

I almost get married to one Samoan you know. But my friends they tell me that marry her, and by and by you eat everytime bananas. You know Samoans, huh, they like bananas and coconuts, like that. I never believe, but my boss, him *haole* [white] and he told me to stay careful if marry people of another kind. I get her plenty gifts already and one time she ask me go buy things for her in Honolulu—dress, food and plenty kine [kind] for her family. I go, but I think she bullshit me you know, 'cuz she different already. My boss, him happy kine when I not get married to the Samoan. More good for me, he said.

Filipino workers typically had no control over living conditions and were subject to the authoritarian role of plantation bosses. Since Filipinos were officially classified as United States nationals, they had no Philippine consulate to protect their interests. In the words of one of the older immigrants:

They told us in the Philippines that we did not have to have any kind of education whatsoever. The only thing they were interested in was whether we were hard workers or not. For example, in the HSPA headquarters in the Philippines, we were made to present our hands for inspection by the representatives of the companies. If we had calloused hands, we were accepted there and then. Those who had "student" looking hands were made to come back when they already knew how to do hard work. Another criteria for acceptance was whether we passed the working test, which was to clean the whole day the entire immigration office so that they will have good evidence of our capacity to do work. (English translation)

After arriving in Hawaii workers found themselves increasingly dependent and alienated by the hardships they were forced to endure: "The planter not only had to feed, clothe, house, and doctor his workers, he also found it expedient to establish rules, for their conduct—when they should rise in the morning and go to bed at night, where they might go and what they might do with their leisure time" (Lind, 1969:19; quoted in Choy, 1973:13). Filipinos worked 10 hours a day in the hot sun under the close supervision of hard-driving foremen for a minimum wage of a dollar a day. Cirrhosis of the liver caused by parasites was a common health problem. Workers went home to crude barracks at night and ate distasteful food; they described their life before labor-union recognition as "one hell."

Discontent was expressed in the form of high absenteeism from work or in quitting the plantation altogether. The standard plantation contract was for three years of work, with the option to receive a free trip back to the Philippines at the end of that period. Plantation workers, however, were not indentured and could leave at any time. And many did: A total of 23,285 men and 3,017 women had returned to the Philippines by 1929 (Lasker, 1931:352). A 1927 arrival narrates what plantation life was like before 1946:

Before in the field, they get sassy to you. They tell you—"you gotta do da kine [that kind], fast worker you." If you no do, they gonna scold you or fire you. But some like that you know, some bosses, they wild bunch, high temper, they whack you sometimes, mostly *haole* [white] bosses. . . .

Our house was the worsest place before, plenty mosquitoes, get *pukas* [holes], they no even fix the pukas. We use a wooden stove and firewood. Get no water too. We get water with buckets. . . .

Before we work almost 10 hours a day, six to six. If you go work 23 days, you get 10 cents bonus. In our boarding house, we like cook, but they no like us cook. We hide cooking in the house, we no like food in the camp kitchen—junk them, but no choice. You no can do nothing if you not smart. When you cook, cook in small stove and hide 'em 'cuz get camp check-up time. . . .

When the war came, all of us prayed. Some still work you know. If you no work, they call martial law. They bring you to army major, they say, "How come you no work?" Then we say " 'cuz get rain." Then they fine you $5.00 for talking. If you talk again, $10.00 until you stop. More better you no talk. With planes coming over your head, you still had to work. Some of us think the Philippines *pau* [finished] already. Some come crazy minds you know.

Plantation camps held little in the way of recreation outlets. Activities that were available were closely controlled by the companies. Acting in typically paternalistic fashion, management would donate materials to help stage festivals, and they unofficially sanctioned illegal gambling activities. Dances were held with the use of professional hostesses. Single men could purchase tickets for a dance, the price depending on the desirability rating of the dancer. As prostitution was widely practiced in Hawaii until 1946, bachelor's quarters at plantation camps were visited by women seeking to sell their affections. Prostitutes sometimes posed as magazine salespersons, setting a price and getting the customer to agree to a subscription. The women would return at a stipulated time to consumate the sale. Prostitutes also worked in a local hotel and in the back seat of automobiles for customers, who were brought to them from the plantation.

The main attraction for Filipino men was betting on cockfights staged regularly during a six-month-long season in a designated arena of the plantation camp. At the time of this study cockfights were still extremely popular. On the day of the event a series of fights were held between carefully matched birds. A sharp steel blade tied to the left leg of the bird served as a weapon in a duel to the death. Bets were collected by the house before each fight and awarded to backers of the winning bird. Gambling tables were run near the arena as an additional attraction. When the fights were held on nonworking days, many men spent most of their time at the arena. Management not only looked the other way to sanction this activity but even provided the arena free of charge.

Oppressive conditions confronting Filipino workers were counteracted by a revitalization movement that spread to Hawaii's plantation camps in 1926. The movement began in California in 1925 among Filipinos who were employed as seasonal farm workers. It was initiated both in California and Hawaii by Hilario Camino Moncado, an early immigrant who left the Philippines in 1914 at the age of 21. Moncado and his organization, officially entitled "The Filipino Federation of America, Incorporated," claimed that the spiritual needs of Filipino workers were not being met and they were not being rewarded for living frugally and doing strenuous labor. Followers believed that Moncado was the reincarnation of a famous Filipino martyr who had come to liberate them from economic exploitation. Core members of the movement wore long hair and were admonished not to drink, gamble, play pool, or attend dance halls.

Although the "Moncadistas" organized themselves as a separate religious group, some followers simultaneously maintained membership in the Catholic Church, as was traditional for Filipinos. An 84-year-old Molokai man reports experiencing a religious conversion at the hands of a Moncado disciple in 1935; the two men were standing in a pineapple field when rain fell and failed to wet the suit of the disciple.

Moncado was extraordinarily tall for a Filipino (six feet) and was a gifted public speaker. Adding to his charisma was his immaculate dress and his marriage to a "glamor girl." Moncado, a symbol of nationalist pride, allowed his followers to participate vicariously in his flamboyant lifestyle.

Another early Filipino immigrant, Pablo Manlapit, organized an all-Filipino union, which failed in its 1920, 1924, and 1936 strike attempts. As a result of his actions, Manlapit was deported on two occasions and finally was kept out of the country.

Where Manlapit failed, Moncado succeeded: He maintained his leadership because he made an accommodation with the power structure. As a wave of unionism led by Japanese organizers swept through Hawaii in the early 1930s, Moncado stood up for unorganized Filipino workers, who were resented by the Japanese for undermining the strength of the union movement. Moncado is quoted as saying: "Naturally, we are not in favor of a strike as a means of settling labor dispute [sic]. We prefer peaceful negotiation and conference [sic] for that purpose" (Moncado, n. d. : 204).

In October 1937 Filipino employees of the Molokai pineapple plantation owned by McNeill and Libby (and later by Dole) went on strike for higher pay. "Moncadistas" were transported by barges from the nearby islands of Lanai, Maui, and Oahu to break the strike. Because of his anti-union stance, Moncado gained recognition among non-Filipinos and was feted by politicians and officials in Honolulu. This development had a detrimental affect on Moncado's followers, who dwindled in numbers from a peak of 2,500 in the late 1920s to 700 in 1941. Unionization across ethnic lines during this period represented a more realistic approach to the problems of Filipino workers and further diminished Moncado's influence. Today, only a few elderly members of the Filipino Federation of America, Inc., survive in Honolulu.

The last wave of Filipino plantation workers to enter Hawaii—unlike Moncado's followers, who were used as strikebreakers—played a key role in solidifying the power of the union movement. The HSPA brought in a total of 6,000 Filipino men in 1946, just prior to the deadline for Philippine independence, because this was their last chance to take advantage of virtually unlimited restrictions on the importation of Filipinos for plantation work. The advent of Philippine independence meant that Filipinos would no longer be considered U.S. nationals by the Immigration Service and that severe quotas would be placed on their entry into Hawaii as immigrant workers.

A shortage of plantation labor had developed during World War II, and it appeared that this would be made more severe by Filipino laborers returning to their newly independent homeland. The HSPA was particularly worried that the cumulative labor shortage would give leverage to the ILWU (International Longshoremen and Warehousemen's Union) in winning a critical 1946 strike. It was no secret that the companies intended this last wave of unrestricted immigrants to break the strike and to shore up their strength against the demands of the union. The union, however, was able to infiltrate the ranks of the new immigrants as they were being shipped to Hawaii. Upon arrival, this group joined forces with other plantation workers to lead the union to victory.

Nine thousand ILWU workers in Hawaii staged a combined strike against pineapple and sugar companies in April 1974. It was the first such effort since 1946. Filipino workers on two Molokai pineapple plantations, one owned by Dole and the other by Del Monte, did not take part in this strike. The union excused these groups from striking because the phaseout of both plantations had been announced by the companies. Since many workers were only minimally employed during the phaseout, a total cessation of work would only have increased their hardship, with no effect on the bargaining.

Despite the inability of the Molokai workers to strike, the union proceeded to negotiate for the job security of these workers and for others who might be similarly affected in the future. Assuming that workers would be willing to move to plantations on other islands, the union sought to guarantee the right to a job. As negotiations proceeded, however, the union was embarrassed to find that Molokai workers were unhappy with the objectives being pursued. The union consequently backed away from its demand for jobs and instead pushed for liberalization of the provisions concerning layoffs and increased separation pay (*Negotiation News*, 29 April 1974). The strike ended, after three short weeks, with standard gains in wages and fringe benefits for the majority of workers. Regular workers in Molokai received a separation allowance amounting in total to nine days pay for each year of service and the right to remain in company housing under the current low rental schedule (about $32 per month for a three-bedroom house) until 31 December 1980. This settlement meant that short-term problems were at least partially solved, but that the long-term fate of the people in the two Molokai communities was still in doubt.

Pineapple Town

The Molokai plantation camps that did not strike in 1974 were established during the peak period of Filipino immigration to Hawaii. Libby, McNeill and Libby, the same company aided in 1937 by Moncado's strikebreakers, began its operation at Maunaloa on the west end of the island in 1923,[1] and Del Monte began its operation at Kualapuu, on the central portion of the island, in 1927.[2] In 1970 Libby, McNeill and Libby sold out to Dole, which is a subsidiary of Castle and Cooke, one of the Big Five corporations.

The largest landholder on the island of Molokai is the Molokai Ranch, which owns 45 percent of all land, or 73,975 acres. Eight other private owners account for 22 percent of the land. The Hawaiian Homes Commission holds a 16-percent share, while state-owned land constitutes another 15 percent of the total (Forman, 1976:276). Only two percent of the land is held in small private lots. King Kamehameha IV was the first to control extensive lands on the west end of Molokai, establishing a sheep ranch there in 1859 (Forman, 1976:22). Kamehameha V used part of the area for a cattle ranch and set aside the remainder of the west end for hunting. In 1884 these lands were deeded to Bernice Pauahi Bishop, who then deeded them to her husband. Twelve years later, more than 70,000 acres were sold for $150,000 to a syndicate, which formed the Molokai Ranch. In 1908 Charles Cooke bought out the other parties in the ranch, and today it is still owned by shareholders who are second-and third-generation members of the Cooke family.

The 1970 census reports that 5,089 people reside on the island of Molokai. Of this population 33 percent are of Filipino ancestry and 39 percent are of

Hawaiian ancestry. The remainder of the population consists of persons having Caucasian, Japanese, or other ancestry. The commercial center of Molokai is Kaunakakai, a seaport with a population of 1,074. The next two largest towns are Maunaloa, with 872 residents, and Kualapuu, with 441 residents. Sixty-seven percent of the Filipinos on the island live in these two towns (Anderson, et al., 1973:17). Thirty-six percent of Molokai adults with full-time jobs in 1970 were employed by Dole or Del Monte in plantation agriculture.

The data on Maunaloa presented in this chapter derive largely from a survey of 144 adult Filipino residents conducted by Sheila Forman during December 1975 and January 1976. A questionnaire was given to all Filipino adults in the community, except those who arrived after the phaseout announcement in October 1972 and those who were absent for a period of six months or more between the phaseout announcement and the start of the interviews.[3] Three resident interviewers estimated that approximately 200 Maunaloans met these requirements. Several eligible respondents may have been missed because they were vacationing in the Philippines during the time of the interviews. Three attempts were made to arrange an interview before a respondent was dropped from the list. There were only three outright refusals. Altogether 73 percent of the eligible adults in the community were interviewed. Thirty-two families known to have lived in Maunaloa in early 1974 have since moved away and are not included in this group. If there is any systematic bias, it is perhaps the exclusion of elderly, unmarried males, who were probably not as easy to find for interviews in their homes.

In our analysis, we have also used field data from intensive interviews conducted with 37 families in Maunaloa. The interviewer maintained contact with most of these families over a period of 18 months in order to observe the impact of the plantation phaseout on their lives.

The demographic characteristics of Maunaloa are influenced both by the large number of single males who immigrated prior to unionization and by changes in immigration patterns during three distinct periods after 1946 (Table 4.1). During the period 1947–65 migration from the Philippines tapered off under the limited quota system. By 1965 the pineapple industry was faltering: A few marginal plantations had already closed, and rural communities had slowed down their activity. Honolulu had grown commercially as the tourist industry began to boom, drawing some Filipinos (particularly locally-born males) from the plantation towns into its orbit.

In 1965 Congress passed a new immigration act that eased quota restrictions and allowed wives, siblings, and children to be brought into the country. The law increased the chain-migration effect dramatically during the period 1965–72, resulting in more women, children, and well-educated persons coming to Maunaloa. During the same seven years only a few additional men came to perform plantation work, for the demand for labor had slackened considerably. Older men, who had remained single for many years either because of immigration restrictions or because of their previous lack of financial resources, began to marry younger women from the Philippines. In some cases a man would vacation for several weeks in the Philippines and select a suitable mate to bring back, while in other cases a sister or a cousin of a woman in the community would be brought from the Philippines to examine the single men and choose among them for a husband. Consequently, a sizeable portion of the marriages among Filipinos in Maunaloa involved extreme differences in age, often as much as 25 or 30 years. Many of these couples had children, so that at the time of our study it was not uncommon for a man over 60 to be raising young children.

A majority of men were old enough to retire by the time pineapple operations ceased. Few of the remaining men had special work skills other than those required to be a common field laborer. Most of the immigrant men were native speakers of Ilokano (a Filipino dialect) and were functionally illiterate in English. A sizeable number of women (about half) had entered the labor force. Family income reported by Filipino men in Maunaloa, including ten men who never married, was below $5,000 in more than three-fifths of the cases. Only five percent reported income of $10,000 per year or more. Maunaloa residents exhibited the lowest income on Molokai.

Table 4.1. Year of Immigration to Hawaii by Sex.

	Locally Born (Percent)	Before 1946 (Percent)	1946-1965[a] (Percent)	After 1965 (Percent)
Male	7 (26)	38 (100)	24 (89)	6 (11)
Female	20 (74)	0 (0)	3 (11)	46 (89)
TOTAL	(100)	(100)	(100)	(100)

[a]All but two came in the year 1946.
Note: Numbers in parentheses are percentages.

In 1972 President Ferdinand Marcos placed the Philippines under martial law and severely restricted emigration. Passports, tax clearances, permits to bring money abroad, and other documentation necessary to emigrate was strictly scrutinized, while at the same time the United States Embassy began to process only those persons in its first two preference categories: unmarried children of U.S. citizens and unmarried children and spouses of permanent residents. The action taken by the Philippine government and the U.S. Embassy was widely believed by Filipino immigrants in Hawaii to be a response to rekindled resentment by U.S. citizens against Filipino immigrants coming to Hawaii and either competing for scarce jobs or going on welfare roles. The effect of the 1972 change in policy was to slow down immigration in Maunaloa to a trickle. It is not altogether a strange coincidence that Filipino immigration to Hawaii was slowed down the same year Dole began to phase out its operations in Maunaloa.

Paradise Lost

The phaseout of the Dole and Del Monte plantations over a three-year period was first announced in the fall of 1972. Del Monte changed its plans, and in March 1974 announced an extension of its operation through the end of 1977. Again, in March 1975, Del Monte announced a further extension, to the end of 1978. Del Monte's indecision tended to give false hopes to Dole workers, who half-heartedly expected that Dole would also announce an extension. Dole, however, followed through with the initial announcement and ceased its planting operations. Since three harvests can be gathered from each planting, the summer harvest of 1975 was the last for the Dole plantation. Aside from working on summer harvests, Maunaloa residents were employed for three years on a part-time basis, usually about four days per month, which was little enough to qualify them continuously for unemployment compensation, averaging $95 per month. Despite a petition circulated in the community asking Dole to stay and vague speculation about future harvest by county officials, Dole closed on schedule. Termination notices were received by 175 workers on 14 August 1975, and actual termination occurred on 12 September 1975.

In the simplest economic terms, the pineapple industry was no longer profitable. Dole readily admits that it made a mistake in purchasing the Libby, McNeill and Libby operation.[4] The cost of the purchase was $9 million, and another $1.3 million was invested in permanent improvements to the camp. Dole also assumed a lease agreement, involving more than 7,000 acres, with the Molokai Ranch for a period extending to 1980. Another 3,000 acres were leased from the Hawaiian Homes Commission. When it became clear that Dole would not reclaim its investment within three to five years, the phaseout became inevitable. The reasons given by Dole for profit failure were yields 10 percent below those on other islands, high irrigation costs, extra costs for transporting pineapple by truck the 20 miles from Maunaloa to the Kaunakakai wharf, and lower recovery of final product at the Honolulu cannery.

Perhaps the most important reasons for Dole's decision to leave Molokai were those not explicitly stated by the company. Both Dole and Del Monte are launching pineapple operations in the Philippines, where workers are compensated at rates equivalent to those paid in Hawaii in 1930. Under the Marcos regime in the Philippines, labor-union activities are illegal, and special trade agreements with the United States protect the interests of multinational corporations, who find it profitable to hire cheap domestic labor. Foreign investment credits allowed on tax bills and the lack of any tariffs or quotas on the importation of foreign pineapple add further incentive for Dole and Del Monte to expand pineapple operations in the Philippines while phasing them out in Hawaii. Moreover, it is no more expensive to ship pineapple from the Philippines than from Hawaii, since Hawaii-based companies must use American carriers, which cost two and a half times as much as foreign flagships.

The advantage to using cheap labor in the pineapple industry is greater than in the sugar industry. Mechanization has proceeded swiftly in the sugar industry, eliminating the human labor required to cut the cane, bulk it, and carry it to railroad cars. With the introduction of diesel cane-hauling units and other new technology, labor requirements have been cut by two-thirds since 1950. Labor-saving technology, along with the historical existence of trade embargoes, may contribute to the easier survival of the Hawaiian sugar industry despite recent closures at Kahuku on the island of Oahu and at Kilauea and Kohala on the island of Hawaii. In contrast, little mechanization has occurred in the pineapple industry. Since labor is still a critical input to production, it is of great advantage for this industry to operate in a protected foreign environment where cheap, unorganized labor is assured. Despite these differences, however, both pineapple and sugar companies are expanding abroad while cutting back at home.

There are several possible reasons why Del Monte delayed its departure from Molokai. The Del Monte lease covers only 6,000 acres, a little more than half the acreage leased by Dole; in comparison to Maunaloa, Kualapuu is about half the distance to the Kaunakakai wharf, and Kualapuu is closer to the island's source of nonsaline water. Del Monte also may have been waiting until it completed ongoing experiments to determine the feasibility of an alternative crop.

While phasing out its Maunaloa camp, Dole continued to operate a similar pineapple plantation in Lanai. According to the company, Lanai is a better pineapple-growing island than Molokai. Another reason for staying in Lanai is that Dole owns, rather than leases, the land and was willing to run the operation at a break-even level until a more profitable use for the land could be found. Dole will probably continue to raise pineapple on Lanai until the phaseout on Molokai has faded from the public memory. Speculations were heard that Dole eventually expects its land to be rezoned for tourist development.

One additional factor precipitating Dole's hasty departure from Molokai was the eagerness of the Molokai Ranch Company to develop tourist facilities on a portion of its land holdings on the west end of Molokai. In 1967 the Molokai Ranch obtained a ruling from the State Land Use Commission and the Maui County Council allowing its land to be rezoned for hotel development. This rezoning was granted despite a report by the State Land Use Commission staff noting a lack of sufficient research into several problems, including the availability of water. Development plans were delayed for eight years by court battles in which environmentalists claimed that the state-owned island water system, which was built in 1969 with $4.5 million in federal funds, could not be diverted (against state law) to nonagricultural use. Hawaiians also opposed development because they deeply resented tourist encroachment on one of the two remaining islands without a major development complex. After winning an extended battle in the courts, the Ranch finally gained access to the state water system in November 1976.

By allowing Dole to ease out of its 1930 lease agreement (for a cost of $3 million), the Ranch was able to acquire Dole's private water system. After Dole's lease agreement was terminated on 1 January 1976, construction began on a road and additional water lines to service a hotel and golf course as part of the Kaluakoi Hotel Development Project on the west end of Molokai.

Kaluakoi now rents space in the state irrigation system for the transmission of more than 2 million gallons per day. It replaces the water it uses with an equivalent amount from the Del Monte well, which has never been pumped to a capacity greater than 1.5 million gallons per day and presents the real possibility of bringing up brackish water (*Hawaii Observer*, 8 December 1976:20). For obvious reasons, Kaluakoi developers would rather use water from the state system than subject resort patrons to Del Monte's water. Thus, farmers who irrigate their crops must use the substituted Del Monte water.

The partner of the Molokai Ranch in the resort development is the Louisiana Land and Exploration Company of New Orleans, a wealthy company that holds 600,000 acres in several southern states and engages in oil and natural gas exploration in the continental United States, Canada, and the North Sea. Why this company should be diverting funds from energy development into unneeded tourist facilities has not been publicly answered. The Molokai Ranch, as mentioned earlier, is owned by the descendants of the Cooke family, who also own Castle and Cooke, of which Dole is a subsidiary.

The termination of Dole's lease agreement with the Molokai Ranch also meant that the Maunaloa plantation camp reverted to the control of the Ranch as of January 1976. The union-negotiated agreement allowing Filipino residents of the community to remain at reduced rates in company housing was thereafter enforced by the Ranch rather than by Dole.

"The Union Won't Let You Down"

After winning the 1946 strike, the ILWU became a dominant force in Maunaloa. Its new role of strength was symbolized by the fact that it replaced the company in contributing material support to ceremonial gatherings and community festivals. As the pineapple industry prospered, the union continued to gain settlements favorable to its members. Wages went up and working conditions were vastly improved. Especially among the pre-1946 immigrants, unionization was considered the demarcation point between unhappy, oppressive conditions and a more free and secure environment.

Bad times before, but now get union so no more da kine [that kind] humbug foremen. They treat us more better 'cuz if not, the union will get 'em.

Is good this one, the union, 'cuz you can fight back. Before we only get little bit pay, and those guys get bad temper too. Now we go strike if we no like 'em do something to us. We get high pay, too, and get increases everytime, but before no more.

Before Dole terminated its operation, Filipino workers in Maunaloa were represented in the Molokai union local by a Filipino immigrant who acted as a patron and was an articulate spokesman for the community. The union representative was looked upon not only as a leader for union members but also as a community authority figure. Sympathetic to the needs of the members of the community and highly sensitive to their demands, he played the patron role to its fullest extent. He was called in to help sort out family problems, intervene in community disagreements, find prospective brides, arrange trips to the Philippines, emcee and coordinate social functions, help sign forms, and push his fellow workers to improve themselves. He spoke for the community at public meetings and represented Maunaloa in various island-wide programs.

Since many older men in the community were illiterate and poor speakers of standard English, they did not attend public meetings conducted in English. They felt they would *lose face* if they dealt with people of higher status outside the community. It was regarded as particularly shameful to ask officials or a boss for a favor and get turned down. The union representative was therefore valuable as an intermediary to convey requests to such important persons. As he was personable and approachable, he earned the respect and loyalty of the workers.

The union so successfully exploited the personal attachment to the union representative as a controlling device that it was said that going against the union, the institution, was in effect going against the man. Most members of the Maunaloa community felt, and perhaps still feel, a personal obligation to express their appreciation for the services of the union representative. It was common for people to send him gifts of vegetables from their gardens, and at election time they were expected to demonstrate further loyalty by voting for union candidates representing the Democratic party.

In recent years the fortunes of the union in the State of Hawaii have changed. It can no longer deal as successfully with the managers of pineapple and sugar companies because the companies are going out of business or moving their operations abroad. On Molokai the weakness of the union is illustrated by a recent, unsuccessful attempt to organize hotel workers. Employees of a small luxury hotel, previously the only tourist accommodation on the island, went on strike for eight months in 1974, only to run out of steam in the end. It was apparently assumed that the ILWU would lose to the more solidly entrenched AFL-CIO Hotel Workers Union in any attempt to control hotel workers on the island. Since the interests of the ILWU were not served by continuing the attempt to represent the interests of the striking workers, the ILWU withdrew its support, and the strike was broken with no unionization and no gains for the workers.

Weakness of the union, which was evident in the failure to organize hotel workers and to forestall plantation closures elsewhere in Hawaii, has contributed to decreasing loyalty among Filipinos in Maunaloa. In recent elections Maunaloa voters have not supported union candidates as strongly as they have in the past. In the 1974 state elections, for example, the union presented a list of endorsed candidates and proceeded to give its members explicit voting instructions. Although there was little open discussion or protest among Maunaloa residents, when asked whether they were indeed going to vote for union candidates, a number of workers said, "Only some, not all." In fact, several workers campaigned for an opposition candidate of Filipino ancestry in the county mayoral primary. One of the more independent workers put it this way:

There is no question that the union has really helped us a lot, but it cannot dictate its every wish to us, and we cannot follow its every command blindly. They can run our affairs where our work is concerned, but when it seems to run counter to what we want, they can only go so far. Of course, we do not protest openly, nor do we make our opposition open, we just go ahead and do what we feel we should do. Anyway, when election time comes, how would they know who I voted for? It's a secret ballot anyway. As long as we don't hurt anybody's feelings, we do what we feel like doing. We are just careful we do not cause anybody to lose face, or us [to] lose face.

A few members of the community, particularly the younger, well-educated immigrant women, became more vocal about their problems and were less willing to allow union officials to speak for them. They felt that union officials did not adequately express the fact that most people wanted to remain in Maunaloa and preserve the community. In some instances they resented that union officials publicly opposed the wishes of the community. For example, the union representative and the head of the union's Maui County chapter halted the circulation of two petitions among residents of the community during the phaseout: One petition asked Dole to stay for two more years, and the other expressed people's desire for the opportunity to own their own homes.

Other controversy over the role of the union representative centered around his opposition to the traditional Filipino Flowers of May Festival, which he considered to be "inappropriate for an American community," and his insistence that he alone should represent Maunaloa residents in securing jobs and public services. His criticism of young wives for "talking too much" also caused resentment.

After the Ranch assumed control of the plantation camp, the union representative, whose power in the union had diminished, was hired by the Ranch as a "communicator." In exchange for the use of his power of persuasion, the Ranch provided him with a rent-free house. As president of the local PTA, the union representative was able to use the meetings as a forum for expressing the views of the Ranch to the Maunaloa community. His message to the people was simple and consistent with his past advice—avoid controversy and cooperate with the Ranch in order to gain the favor of the powers that be. For example, he opposed a petition by 22 chicken owners requesting a community-wide referendum on the issue of whether chickens could continue to be kept in backyards. A housing committee headed by the union representative also proved futile in mediating possible evictions and in gaining a voice for the community in screening future housing applicants. Later, a new chairman was elected to the housing committee, perhaps indicating that the ineffectiveness of the old chairman was generally recognized.

"The Company Will Look After You"

Shortly before terminating its lease with the Ranch, Dole began to tighten its policy with regard to managing the plantation camp. In September 1974, for example, the company placed severe restrictions on access to its beach park at the west end of the island near Maunaloa. Gates to the beach were closed to persons who were not members of Dole workers' families. Even workers and their families were forced to fill out forms and request a gate key before being allowed access to the beach. These restrictions were requested by the Molokai Ranch ostensibly to help prevent cattle rustling and deer poaching. The Ranch apparently suspected Hawaiians and Filipinos of causing losses to its inventory of livestock.

Recreational outlets in Maunaloa decreased further in the fall of 1974 when the pool hall and the movie theater closed. The pool hall was a gathering place enjoyed by teenagers, while the movie theater was especially popular with older men because they were able to view films made in the Philippines.

In October 1974 the company opened vacant housing to outsiders—as it happened, mostly to Hawaiians and low-income whites ("hippies"). It was particularly disturbing to Maunaloans when five "hippies" moved into the community. Shortly afterward the local store was robbed three times. The "hippie" families were then blamed for the robberies and for being a bad influence on the children in the community. The arrival of the outsiders was a concern not only to families with children but also to men who were interested in working for the new resort. Newcomers posed a threat to these men because they were perceived, perhaps rightly so, as competitors for scarce jobs.

What little power could be exercised by Filipinos to maintain their community seemed lost when the Molokai Ranch gained control of the plantation property in January 1976. Before the phaseout was announced, Dole had agreed to rewire all plantation housing, since exposed wires and faulty connections presented a substantial health and fire hazard. By the time the Ranch took over, only 20 houses had been completed. The Ranch immediately stopped all rewiring and sent bills to residents whose plumbing had been repaired.

Although the Ranch was officially obligated to keep Dole's agreement to allow residents to remain in plantation housing until 1980, the actions of the Ranch gave cause for some doubt. A new list of rules designed to set the stage for eviction was established: (1) garden plots were to be kept neat by trimming untidy banana trees; (2) all chickens were to be removed from town and raised only in designated areas; (3) drinking in public was not allowed; (4) parents were to be held responsible for the behavior of their children; (5) and all infractions would be dealt with by eviction. In order to enforce these rules, the Ranch hired a camp manager of Japanese ancestry who had previously worked as a labor supervisor for Dole and was reported by Filipino respondents to be a strict disciplinarian. Seven residents were threatened with eviction between January and May 1976. For the most part the reasons stated by the Ranch related to keeping chickens in the yard. One man was threatened with eviction because his son was caught in town speeding in an automobile. The Ranch also threatened to take over garden plots where banana trees were "untidy."

At first the Ranch claimed that its rules were inspired by county health regulations and by complaints from outsiders moving into the community. Inquiries made by a community resident at the Department of Health and with outsiders in the community failed to find evidence for the claims of the Ranch. Maunaloa residents did not miss the irony of the Ranch position, for many recognized that the faulty wiring in their homes was a far greater health hazard than keeping chickens in the backyard.

According to Forman, the 22 residents of Maunaloa who were threatened with eviction for chicken violations eventually arranged for the assistance of a federally funded, legal-aid lawyer. They protested that they were not given a chance to express their opinions at previous meetings of the housing committee because the former union representative monopolized meeting time. The lawyer suggested that a community-wide referendum be held to determine how many residents supported or opposed chicken-raising. The Ranch manager was quoted in an interview with a news reporter as agreeing to abide by a majority vote (*The Maui Sun*, 18–24 February 1976:5). The referendum was never held. The meeting of the housing committee at which the issue of the referendum was discussed did not include the lawyer or any potential evictees who had asked the lawyer to represent them. The lawyer was not invited to the meeting despite the fact that she had informed the committee chairman in writing of her interest in the case.

One of the intended evictees was known to have openly challenged the authority of plantation supervisors in the past. The Ranch, apparently aware of his reputation, sought his eviction even after he had moved a chicken coop that did not comply with county health regulations. A test court case began to develop at one point around the Ranch's attempt to obtain eviction under its own house rule. The defendant, who was assisted by the legal-aid lawyer, eventually dropped the case on the advice of another lawyer, after the original lawyer became ill and could not continue. The case itself came to have less meaning later when chicken owners moved their coops outside of town and the Ranch refrained from carrying out the intended evictions.

Early in 1976 the Ranch began hiring construction workers from outside the community to work on its resort complex. It was rumored to have spent $10,000 to improve tennis and basketball courts in Maunaloa, which would serve as a recreational facility for the new workers. Although a few Filipino men participate on a community basketball team, no one was known to play tennis. The nature of the improvements suggested to older residents of the community that the Ranch was looking forward to replacing them with other tenants.

In April 1976 fear gripped the community in the wake of two brutal murders. The victims were a Filipino man in his early fifties and his wife in her early thirties, the father and mother of three small children. Following the night of the murder, bystanders gathered in the street to organize a neighborhood patrol to avenge the murders. Members of the patrol were quick to blame a group of Mexican nationals who had been brought in only a few days earlier to work on an experimental potato farm and who were living in temporary quarters near the community. Although the patrol was persuaded by the union representative to desist from making a violent attack, fear in the community did not subside. Doors usually left unlocked were bolted carefully, and people stayed off the streets after 6 o'clock in the evening. All cockfights and other public celebrations and gatherings in April and May were cancelled.

Several families requested that they be allowed to move to vacant houses in safer locations. The Ranch, however, insisted that those who moved would have to pay outsider rates—three or four times as much as the normal rates for former Dole employees. The Ranch also used the murders as an excuse to encourage the police to harass persons whom they regarded as troublemakers. Young rowdies, suspected poachers, and old men who commonly engaged in social drinking near the clubhouse (recreational center) were questioned and falsely accused. Installation of street lights was the only concession made by the Ranch to increase the safety of community residents.

In contrast to Filipino laborers who were laid off and then subjected to additional hardships, Dole's supervisory personnel were well treated; they received company transfers, acquired jobs with the Ranch, and were hired by the University of Hawaii Extension Service. Interviews with several supervisors during the phaseout revealed that they possessed substantial savings and property assets, as opposed to the Filipino workers, who had virtually none. It was evident that the supervisors would experience no economic difficulty.

Resources for a Community

Despite economic difficulties experienced by many families during the phaseout, the feeling persisted that Maunaloa was a good place to live. People retained a sense of community spirit and self-reliance, which enabled them to endure hard times.

This community is a good place to bring up the children. They know everybody and everybody is concerned with everybody.

I come crazy mine when I go to the big city. Here you can go fishing, crabbing, hunting, man the good life!

An abundance of fictive kinship ties among Filipinos in Maunaloa, as is typical of many plantation communities throughout the world,[5] contributed to the sense of a secure social environment. They appeared to serve as a substitute for extensive networks of natural kinship ties that exist in the Philippines,[6] for a majority of both men and women had 30 or more fictive kinsmen. The existence of such formal ties implies an obligation to give and help another person in a way that mere friendship does not. Social networks in

Maunaloa were woven around fictive kinship and continually supported by mutual exchanges involving such items as garden vegetables, freshly caught fish, and babysitting services. The exchange of babysitting services in particular was important to women who did not trust their older husbands with this responsibility.

Breakdown in a fictive kinship tie may occur if one person demands too much or another fails to meet his or her obligation. For the most part, however, a deep feeling of obligation for past favors perpetuates the relationship. In the Philippines fictive kinship ties are often extended beyond the village in relationships of economic or political patronage. In Maunaloa fictive kinship ties existed primarily within the community and functioned to maintain a high degree of solidarity among its members. During the phaseout most families continued to rely heavily on relationships established within the community.

The economic importance of cooperation and sharing within the community was underscored by the way food resources were consumed. Most families cultivated vegetable gardens and ate fresh vegetables yearround. Any surplus of fresh garden foods was shared for efficient use. In order to obtain fresh meat, groups of families often pooled their resources to buy a pig, transport it to Maunaloa, butcher it, and divide it among the families.

Cockfights continued to be held in Maunaloa and in two nearby communities on a rotating basis, and attending these cockfights was a favorite pasttime of many men with idle time on their hands. Some women also attended in order to socialize, but they usually did not get involved in betting activities. Betting patterns tended to reinforce the solidarity of community and friendship groups, as several bettors often cooperated to put money on the same bird. Many men also raised fighting chickens in their backyards. A syndicate of local men organized the cockfighting events in Maunaloa under unofficial sanction of the plantation owners. The syndicate took five percent of the winnings from each fight in return for guaranteeing that no one was cheated. Proceeds were used to pay any fines that might be imposed by the police (cockfights are illegal and sometimes raided) and to sponsor an annual party with free liquor and snacks for regular participants of the sport.

It was characteristic of the women of Maunaloa to attend church and engage in church-related activities. One of the major activities sponsored by women in the Catholic Club was the Flowers of May Festival, in which unmarried daughters of the community were contestants for the honor of being chosen Miss Flowers of May. This festival was the most important social event of the year for Filipinos in Maunaloa because it was organized internally as opposed to other events in which organizations outside the community played a part. Preparations lasted for two months and consisted of such committee and individual activities as setting up a program, sewing costumes, practicing songs, raising funds for the queen candidates, and selling tickets.

In 1974 the phaseout had the effect of demoralizing the preparations for the festival. At the annual planning meeting only two queen candidates surfaced, and no money from the community had been donated. Members of the

Catholic Club expressed disappointment that some women in the community were more concerned with working for a wage in the fields than with working for the festival. In 1975, however, the community rallied to the support of the festival. Four queen candidates emerged, and it became a lavish affair symbolizing the community's identity. Despite the continuing objections of the local union representative, the festival was well attended by an estimated 300 people. Sheila Forman, who was residing with her family in the community at the time, observed, "Of the celebrations we attended . . . it drew by far the largest crowd (Forman, 1976: 109). It is also significant that the union representative was given only a peripheral role in the celebration. The success of the Flowers of May Festival suggests that the community was pulling together on its own initiative before the final closure of the plantation.

Young Wives and Old Husbands

One of the most difficult problems caused by the phaseout involved strains in the relationships among married couples and their children: The role of the wife was made stronger, the role of the husband was weakened, and the problem of how to discipline children became more critical. By virtue of being younger, more energetic, and better educated than their husbands, the women of Maunaloa assumed a dominant role in the household. A typical wife attended PTA meetings, met with her children's teachers, signed papers for her children, took them to the doctor, disciplined them, paid the bills, filled out forms for social security and unemployment, and established contact with public agencies. One wife discussed her role:

He is not interested at all in the school affairs of the children. He feels ashamed, maybe because he is old already. When our daughter was a candidate for queen last May, I worked hard to make her win, and it was one time he helped out. But I am always the one to attend meetings, sign papers, attend baseball games for our son. But I have gotten used to it already.

The status of the husband derived from his being primary breadwinner for the family—a role that did not, however, include authority to discipline the children. Many fathers of Maunaloa children were elderly, and they treated the children as leniently as would a grandfather. This was a source of concern for a number of wives, one of whom commented: "My husband is very gentle and quiet. I do the disciplining in this household. My kids are troublemakers at times, so occasionally I whack them with a slipper or belt. My husband doesn't say anything if the kids misbehave. He's too softhearted."

The phaseout of the pineapple industry in Maunaloa undermined the husband's role as primary breadwinner and, from his viewpoint, robbed him of the right to receive respect from his wife and children. Some wives went to work in the onion fields or corn fields to help support their families during the economic crisis. We found that those wives entering the labor force were younger and better educated than those who remained as housewives, and their earnings contributed to a significantly higher family income. Even so, many husbands resisted their wives' decision to work. One such husband refused to talk to his wife for a week after she started working. Another expressed his discontent, saying, "I'd rather have my wife stay home than be out working. Anyway, there is no urgency in her working. I'll be retiring soon, and we can still support ourselves with my salary. Her first responsibility should be her family." Many wives felt equally strongly that they should work. One such wife threatened to leave her husband if he opposed her. Working wives often suffered from the disapproval of their husbands: "He cites that I have a bad heart and that I get short of breath easily. One time I insisted on working in the fields and fell ill. I never heard the end of it from him since then."

As husbands began to spend more time at home during the phaseout, wives became more worried. They claimed that their husbands were always in the way and interfered with disciplining the children. They also expressed apprehension about working and leaving the children in the care of their lenient fathers. As one wife said, "I can just imagine when I shall be out of the house and my husband is left to care for the kids. I don't think I'll have control over them anymore."

Some wives recognized the loss of breadwinner status as a problem for their husbands and constantly reminded the children that their fathers deserved respect because they had sacrificed and worked hard for many years: "I never fail to impress upon my sons that their father worked really hard to feed them, clothe them, send them to school, and the only way to repay him for his hard work is that they do well in school and get out of trouble."

For other women, coping with an older husband who had lost his job and his self-respect was an agonizing duty.

I don't like my children to have greater respect for me than they have for their father. That is not healthy. But I can't do anything because my husband is so timid and spineless. I have to push him everytime, and the children see me doing it.

Our oldest son is very close to his father. He is always with him wherever he goes, and that's fine with me because I have my baby to take care of. But the thing that I object to is that he takes the boy with him gambling, and sometimes he gets drunk when he is with his friends. I don't like that at all, but he gets angry when I tell him that.

"Please Leave Politely"

During the phaseout county officials and union leaders publicly declared that most Maunaloa residents would prefer moving to the Philippines and that they would be better off doing so. At the same time, a 1974 survey of Manualoa, purporting to show people's real wishes, was "lost" by county officials and conveniently unavailable for public scrutiny.[7] Forman's survey of Maunaloa residents in December 1975 and January 1976 revealed, contrary to official pronouncements, that a large majority of Maunaloans wished to stay in the community. Only 15 of 75 family heads still residing in Maunaloa expressed a likelihood of moving, while only eight had actually made any moving preparations.

This reluctance of many Filipino families to move away from Maunaloa was in good measure because their fictive kinsmen, friends, and neighbors represented *social capital,* which they were unwilling to exchange for an uncertain future. There were also basic economic reasons why people stayed in Maunaloa. Housing was much cheaper—at $32 per month for a three-bedroom house—than could be found anywhere else, retired men received social security checks and those still young enough to work received temporary unemployment compensation. While predicting, and perhaps hoping, that people would eventually leave, union leaders and county officials held out the alluring prospects of decent housing after 1980, hotel jobs, and possible employment in a succession of proposed development projects. It is clear that these promises and proposals, as well as the optimism caused by Del Monte's extension through 1978, induced people to take a wait-and-see attitude rather than to risk moving into a new and untested situation. Many older residents also expressed a fatalistic outlook based on past experience as a reason for staying in the community.

No can do nothing. These guys in the company strong guys. Us, only small potato; small potato no can fight big potato.

God will not leave us alone. Something will come up somehow. We should all pray and ask God's mercy.

We will be able to get out of this economic difficulty; I've gone through the Depression and the Second World War, and the big sugar strike, and I am still here.

Despite the strong desire of most families to remain in Maunaloa, several families moved to other islands in Hawaii. By the fall of 1974 eight families had moved to Honolulu and another eight families had moved to Maui. Those moving to Honolulu were able to do so because they had saved for the future and, unlike most plantation families, possessed modest financial resources. Men who were married at an early age were given their wives' encouragement to plan and save for their children's future. Since these families had planned for many years to live in Honolulu, they were prepared to move when the phaseout was announced.

When I first came to Hawaii in 1946, I already had a wife and family, so I was forced to save every penny I earned. I then sent for them. Thinking that my children would soon be going to college in Honolulu, I might as well invest in a house and lot there, and instead of paying dormitory or boarding house's fees, I'd pay for the loan to the house. I really anticipated moving to Honolulu so when the announcement of the phaseout came, it was a smooth transition for me.

Other factors contributing to the decision to move to Honolulu, in the four cases on which information is available, included lack of involvement in gambling activities; deviant religious affiliation (e.g., Jehovah's Witness rather than Catholic); having friends of different ethnic (non-Filipino) background; and being peripheral to the social networks in Maunaloa. Other more typical families, in which the head of the household married

late, did not have the financial resources to move to Honolulu. Before getting
married, a single men spent their earnings on immediate pleasures. Now
faced with the reality of a diminishing income and rising prices, it was very
difficult, if not impossible, for these men to move their families.

The male heads of families moving to Maui averaged 32 years of age, which
was much younger than the average for the community, and had worked only a
few years for the plantation before leaving (Anderson and Pestaño, 1974). All
had ties to union leaders, which could have led to jobs, and they were able to
stay with relatives, who provided temporary support upon their arrival in
Maui. In one case, 19 people were living in a three-bedroom house. Seven of
the eight families who moved to Maui were part of the same social circle while
living in Maunaloa, and they obviously influenced each other to move.

One woman who moved to Maui was an organizer of the petition drive
requesting that Dole extend its operations for two years. When she became
frustrated with the union's opposition to the petition, she and her husband
moved, even though her husband did not have a job in hand. At least seven of
the eight men were later able to find jobs: four as laborers for sugar companies;
one as a dishwasher; another as a golf-course caretaker; and the last as a
construction worker.

Agreements reached in the 1974 strike settlement increased the attractiveness of returning to the Philippines. Special benefits were provided by the
company for former Dole employees who agreed to undergo repatriation and
not return to the United States. The offer was a lump-sum pension payment
with free fare to the Philippines and separation pay based on eleven days pay
per year of work as opposed to nine days pay per year of work agreed upon for
nonreturnees (Negotiation News, 29 April 1974). At least three families
violated the expectations of the company by moving to the Philippines,
collecting the lump sum, and then moving back to Hawaii. One family even
persuaded the company to pay for shipping furniture and appliances, which
were then sold at a profit in the Philippines before the family returned to
Hawaii.

Sixteen of the Maunaloa families who moved were known to live in the
Philippines. Six of these families were interviewed in October 1976. The
whereabouts of the other ten families and the circumstances in which they
were living remained unknown. Moving to the Philippines was facilitated by
the Molokai union representative (now the ranch communicator), continuing
to act in his patron role. The returnees reported that the union representative
talked with them and encouraged them to move. They still received letters
from him and his wife, keeping them informed about happenings in
Maunaloa. All family heads among the six known returnees were already
retired when they left Molokai and received social security pensions averaging
$350 per month. Although none was employed, all invested in small
businesses and rental properties in the Philippines, such as farm machinery,
farmlands, fishponds, stores, market stalls, and apartments. Five families who
received a lump sum from Dole built their own houses, worth between

$14,000 and $20,000. Like the families moving to Honolulu, they seem to have saved for the future, as the husbands were not avid gamblers and infrequently attended cockfights in Maunaloa.

The six families expressed contentment with life in the Philippines. The main difficulty was sadness over the circumstances of relatives who were found not to be well off financially. Investments by the returnees, made with the lump-sum payments and past earnings, were designed in part to tie up resources and prevent excessive demands by relatives. A strong element of Filipino culture involves financial obligations to one's extended family: Those who have more resources are expected to help those who are less well off. If the returning families had not put their money into concrete and nondivisible assets, there would have been a good deal of pressure to distribute it among relatives. Hard feelings would have resulted if they had declined.

The families were ambivalent about martial law under the Marcos regime and expressed reservations about high prices. An apple or an orange costs $1.25, or 10 pesos, which is the minimum wage for a day's work in the Philippines. The returnees, however, were able to indulge their children once in a while with "Hawaiian food."

When asked whether they would encourage other families to move to the Philippines, they said that pensioners should be the only ones: "The young ones can still find jobs in Hawaii, but the pensioners should consider coming home because it is hard to be old in Hawaii, especially for the single men." Indeed, among those still in Maunaloa, elderly men were most interested in moving to the Philippines, where they might be able to recapture status as primary breadwinner for the family.

Husbands and wives in Maunaloa often disagreed over whether moving to the Philippines would be a good idea. In one instance, a husband who favored the move argued that he had relatives in the Philippines; the family would have a house to live in after 1980; his pension would go further in the Philippines; and his wife could stay home and would not have to work. His wife wanted to stay in Maunaloa, arguing that she was not eager to cope with a wife and children whom her husband had left in the Philippines; his pension would not go far enough even in the Philippines; they could make it financially if her husband would allow her to work; her children would get a better education and have more opportunities in the United States; and she could remain active in the Catholic Club and community affairs in Maunaloa.

Women with the most children were least interested in moving to the Philippines and most resistant to leave the community. Although many immigrant wives were disillusioned when they first arrived in Hawaii and discovered that life would not be as easy as expected, most bore children and, like the wives in the Philippines, had strong ambitions to see their children achieve upward mobility in the United States. Many of these women were relatively well educated, had taken out citizenship papers, and had ambitions of their own to work and support their families.

An additional deterrent to returning to the Philippines was the fear that interaction with relatives and friends might not be as harmonious as it was in the past. Women in particular might be stereotyped as "gold diggers," who married old men for their money. Obligations to share financial resources with poor relatives was also a source of concern. Some felt that they would create resentment by refusing to honor the demands of relatives. One respondent expressed the dilemma:

Over here you can plant vegetables, raise chickens, have good neighbors, turn to friends for help, share foods, while at the same time drive a car, see a movie, watch color TV, fill up the freezer, eat good food, bathe in hot water. In the Philippines, you only have either, usually the richness of friendship, but none of the material comforts.

For many families, and especially those in which the husband had not yet reached retirement age, the availability of government support in the United States and lack of it in the Philippines was an important consideration. Although most families were proud of having a strong work ethic, welfare in the form of food stamps was acceptable to some as a last resort. Maunaloans have seen others subsisting on food stamps and felt that Filipinos deserved at least as much consideration because they had worked hard for many years in the pineapple fields.

This is where Hawaii is very much ahead of the Philippines. Here, the government will not let you down. When you are poor, there is the welfare program to turn to.

Why should we have compunctions about going on Welfare? The hippies do it, the Hawaiians do it, so we do it too.

Despite these feelings, very few families were food-stamp recipients. Wives of families receiving food stamps were all of local origin. Having been raised in Hawaii, they may have been less resistant to prevailing trends toward welfare dependence outside the Filipino community. Since fathers were present in almost all cases, few, if any, families qualified for aid to dependent children.

Development Schemes on Molokai

A few months after Dole and Del Monte announced their intended departure from Molokai, anxiety about future employment among Molokai residents grew to a crisis of major proportions. Since the island's official unemployment rate was already 20 percent, and nearly half of the island's adult residents were receiving some kind of welfare assistance, the phaseout of the pineapple industry had to be regarded as a severe problem by public officials.

In June 1974 a state law was passed that enabled Maui County (in which Molokai is located) to organize an economic task force to explore various means of easing the crisis. The county mayor, who had risen to power with the backing of the union and the Democratic party, was given control over appointments to the Molokai Task Force and its activities. Members of the Task Force were appointed from among county officials and the ranks of existing leaders on Molokai. In order to cope with various aspects of Molokai's economic ills, the Task Force was divided into subcomittees on agriculture, commerce and industry, manpower and training, tourist industry, and housing. Initial funding of $200,000 had already been given to the county for feasibility studies prior to formation of the Task Force. In July 1974 an additional $5 million was allocated by the state legislature to be spent through June 1979 on Molokai economic development projects (*Ka Molokai*, 16 May 1974). Spending priorities were to be determined by the mayor and his Task Force.

A Task Force newsletter dated September 1975 listed 74 members, of whom only eleven (or 15 percent) were from Maunaloa, only four (or 5 percent) were Filipinos from Maunaloa, and only one was a first-generation Filipino from Maunaloa (Forman, 1976:128). All of the above classes of people were vastly underrepresented on the Task Force. That Maunaloa was one of the two communities cited in the state legislation and that first-generation Filipinos were experiencing some of the worst hardship made the problem of underrepresentation even more critical. The people who had the most to gain (or lose) were not given a voice in planning for the future.

It is not surprising that various projects considered by the Task Force raised and then dashed the hopes of Maunaloa residents. One proposal was to raise experimental monkeys and provide jobs caring for the monkeys and raising their food. A problem with disease control apparently scuttled this scheme. Another proposal was to establish a garment factory under the management of Malia Enterprises, a manufacturer of women's dresses. Malia decided against the project, probably because of transportation and marketing difficulties. However, before reversing its plans, the company held a sewing test to screen future employees, and it announced afterward that an insufficient number of Maunaloan women had passed. Most of the women who took the test considered themselves to be experienced seamstresses and were upset to have their competence questioned and to have the failure of the project blamed on them. A project discussed by the University of Hawaii to employ Filipinos on several small guava farms met with little enthusiasm from potential operators, primarily because of high capitalization costs and a wait of several years before profits could be returned.

The only project actually started was a potato farm operated by a man from California. One hundred acres for the farm were leased from the state under an agricultural parks program subsidized by the Task Force. The farm operator hired 30 to 40 potato pickers from Maunaloa, paying them a wage of $2.50 per bag. A move to unionize began almost immediately, whereupon the operator announced plans to close. In order to bring in the last of the harvest, he imported 20 Mexican nationals from California. The operator was later held in disfavor by county officials because he failed to register as an employer with the State Department of Labor. The presence of the Mexican workers and the subsequent closure of the potato farm were particularly disturbing omens to Maunaloa residents who had hoped to find agricultural employment. As of May 1976 there were no leases in the agricultural parks program.

"We're Trying to Help You":
Other Crops,
Retraining, and Tourism

Two types of constraints limit agricultural development on Molokai: natural constraints, which consist of a shortage of water, salinity in the water supply, and the presence of high winds from which root systems need protection (Anderson, et al., 1973:47–52); and more important, institutional constraints, which relate to patterns of land ownership, the interests of large landowners, and the economics of transportation and marketing.

The Molokai Ranch, which holds 74,000 acres, amounting to most of the agricultural lands on the island, maintained a herd of 3,000 head of cattle at the time of this study; but following the phaseout, the Ranch did little to investigate alternative agricultural uses for land previously planted in pineapple. Instead, it became involved through a subsidiary, the Cooke Land Company, in property sales and real-estate speculation. It sold about $1.3 million worth of its holdings near Kaunakakai as part of a longer-term plan to sell land worth a total of $2 million. In addition, the Cooke Land Company was involved in developing a 20-acre parcel of ranch land near Kaunakakai into eighty house lots.

The Ranch's lack of interest in agricultural development is perhaps best explained by the scarcity of water on Molokai, a circumstance that would be prohibitive to Kaluakoi hotel and resort development if water were used extensively for agriculture rather than diverted to the island's dry west end where the resort is located. Hawaiian homesteaders felt that Kaluakoi developers would use their influence to rob them of irrigation water, and some spoke out against the development. Hawaiians in opposition to the Kaluakoi project were then branded as "irresponsible troublemakers" by the Ranch. The following comment by the local Ranch manager reveals his patronizing attitude.

I can't understand how anybody on Molokai could oppose Kaluakoi. I think the Hawaiians should do what they can do best. They make very good heavy equipment operators, cowboys, entertainers, and they work well in the tourist business. I would think they would welcome tourist development in Molokai. (*Hawaii Business*, May 1975:61)

Negative reaction to agricultural alternatives by Maunaloa residents was undoubtedly a partial function of the pronouncements of the union and the Task Force that such projects would not pay. The lack of frequent barge service to Molokai was one of the barriers most often cited by the Task Force as inhibiting the development of diversified agriculture. A transport barge visited Molokai only once a week, since a low volume of business prohibited more frequent shipping service. The Task Force indicated that Young Brothers, Ltd., the firm operating the barge service, "has not been cooperative" in providing transportation for agricultural products to Honolulu markets. The president of Young Brothers, Ltd., however, stated in a press release that they could increase scheduling and operation of service if more agricultural products could be shipped. He added that a government subsidy would be necessary for daily service if the volume of goods remained low. The Task Force, for reasons unknown, did not propose that a portion of the $5.2 million available in state funds be used for such a subsidy.

The Task Force had only about 700 acres to lease to farmers in its agricultural parks program. This program spawned only two agricultural ventures that offered employment opportunities to Filipinos. One project involved raising onions on 110 acres of state land, while the second involved growing a drought-resistant strain of seed corn on scattered small plots. It was in these operations that many of the young wives in Maunaloa found employment. The jobs were not strenuous and paid only $2.50 per hour, the legal minimum wage according to state law. Women were hired on a daily basis both from Maunaloa and from Kualapuu. Resentment among job seekers was expressed at times regarding which community was more in need of jobs and which should be given preference in the hiring.

The Hawaiian Homes Commission holds 10,000 acres in central Molokai, most of which has been used by Dole and Del Monte for pineapple cultivation. This land was originally allocated in approximately 35-acre parcels for the use of Hawaiian homesteaders by the Hawaiian Homes Commission Act of 1920. Homesteaders farmed the land themselves until 1926, when they over-pumped their wells and drew saltwater onto their fields. As a result only a few of the 200 Hawaiian homesteaders in residence on the land engaged in farming before the phaseout. Although leases of homestead land may be technically illegal, land was made available to the pineapple companies under planning agreements that were never challenged in court.

After agreements for pineapple cultivation was phased out, many home-steaders appeared ready to return to farming and to make use of the new state water system. Difficulties for Hawaiian homesteaders were many, however. Few of them possessed the necessary machinery and sufficient knowledge of farming to work with soil made highly acidic and depleted of nutrients through many years of single cropping and chemical abuse. Meanwhile, the appointed director of the Hawaiian Homes Commission issued a warning: "Use your lands or lose them" (*Hawaii Observer*, 8 December 1976:21). When home-steaders complained that they needed equipment, training, and time to rehabilitate the land, the director replied, "We are not going to take them by the hand and show them how and when to plant. They had five years' warning before Dole left." Although experiments with growing alfalfa to restore nutrients to the soil proved successful, the cost of machinery could make the growing of alfalfa on small acreages uneconomical.

All available evidence points to the conclusion that without investment capital from a large corporation, future agricultural ventures on Molokai will be small scale and piecemeal. The Molokai Ranch, the largest land holder on the island, shows little or no interest in furthering agricultural development. The state holds only a few hundred acres to lease to farmers, and Hawaiian homesteaders are without sufficient capital or markets to develop anything beyond a one-tractor operation. Even small-scale ventures are of questionable viability since barge service for transporting the product is infrequent and expensive for shipments of small quantities. Some of these specific problems could have been alleviated with funds allocated by the Task Force. Such was not to be.

The promise of retraining, often treated as a panacea for unemployed groups, was used in what can only be called a particularly manipulative way on Molokai. To begin with, temporary employment and training opportunities were almost as scarce for Filipinos as permanent jobs. Initially, Del Monte hired on a seasonal basis, 70 of the 175 workers laid off by Dole. This source of employment typically generated only a few weeks of work during the harvest season, and it offered no long-term prospects.

Only five persons from Maunaloa were given six-month jobs in federally funded programs, such as CETA. A worker in the government office indicated that Filipinos were often barred from such programs because it was against unofficial policy to hire noncitizens. Many Filipinos were noncitizens only because they were illiterate, and the McCarren-Walter Act of 1954 made literacy a requirement for citizenship.

Many Maunaloa residents were interested in receiving training as evidenced by the fact that 20 men, aged 45-59, enrolled in a six-week carpentry class sponsored by the Task Force. Unfortunately, only three men graduated from the course because the curriculum was too difficult. Most Maunaloa men were unable to read or understand the workbook, which presented mathematics and geometry, even though they received individual tutoring outside of class. The objective of the course was to teach the men to read blueprints so that they could become apprentices and get construction jobs. The usefulness of the course in this respect was questionable since a higher paying job could be gotten as a common laborer rather than as an apprentice. Despite the fact that 20 men from Maunaloa received at least some training, only three or four got jobs on road work when construction of the Kaluakoi resort began. Since the company brought in many outsiders to work, members of the Maunaloa community began to take a dim view of alternatives in construction work.

In order to ameliorate the economic crisis on Molokai, the Cannon Business School was given $60,000 by the National Institute of Education (HEW) to train local people in need of jobs. The withdrawal of the pineapple industry was cited as justification for the project. The courses offered were bookkeeping, accounting, and hotel management—all subjects presupposing at least a high school education. A list of enrollees showed none from Maunaloa or Kualapuu. People in Maunaloa who were asked about the program said they had never heard of it.

When the Molokai Task Force was formed in June 1974, the island's unemployment rate was approximately 20 percent. Almost two years later, in March 1976, the official unemployment rate on the island had jumped to 34.5 percent, and only 95 of the original 175 employees laid off from Dole had either retired, relocated, or found new jobs (Forman, 1976:223). It is obvious that the Task Force failed in this period to find alternative means of providing training and jobs for workers affected by the departure of the pineapple industry.

Another failure was the lack of recognition that many young women married to retirees needed to work to support young children. In fact, the need for training opportunities was most often expressed by younger, better-educated women with preschool children. It is clear that training programs did not serve the needs of the community and, in particular, this important group of women.

The lack of market alternatives for development enabled island leaders to safely advocate tourism as the only feasible source of jobs in the future. The issue of resort development then became the issue of jobs, and some Filipinos were led to believe that Hawaiians and environmentalists opposed to hotel development were also opposed to Filipinos.

[The mayor and his supporters] have little patience for those who argue against them, and the major dismisses the likes of Walter Ritte [a major island opponent of the hotel] as an irresponsible minority who are unconcerned by their own joblessness, as well as that of those around them. It is a comfortable explanation, well supported by tradition and leads many to condemn out of hand, or to marvel at those who disagree. (*Hawaii Business*, May 1975:61)

The head of the county chapter of the ILWU was among those who supported hotel jobs as an alternative for the residents of Maunaloa. He blamed environmentalists for holding up construction of the hotel and depriving Filipinos of jobs. When asked why the union was not doing more to find jobs, he pointed to the fact that the union offered plantation jobs on the islands of Hawaii, Lanai, and Maui. Demonstrating his insensitivity to people's desire to preserve their community, he blamed the workers for not wanting to improve themselves. What the union leader did not say is that the jobs proposed by the union did not offer enough financial compensation to justify leaving the security of close relatives and friends. Workers from Maunaloa, most of whom were older and had established several decades of seniority, would have been forced to start again at the bottom of the seniority list. Wages at such a low level would not have justified the expenses of moving and giving up severance pay from Dole. Furthermore, there was no guarantee that plantations on the other islands would continue to operate indefinitely into the future.

At the same time some Hawaiians became angered because many Filipinos supported hotel development. Although Hawaiians had substantial reasons for opposing tourist development, Filipinos were not generally aware of these reasons because of what they have been told by union leaders and county officials. The county mayor stated that only one hotel development would be allowed in the west end of Molokai and that it would be for the sole purpose of providing work for local people in need of jobs. Plans as announced called for the construction of a golf course and a 300-room hotel, costing a total of $14 million. Of the 300 rooms, half would be rented and the other half would be sold as condominiums to help finance the cost of the development. The mayor's office projected that 500 jobs would materialize.

Another picture emerges when the full extent of the plans and financial backing of Kaluakoi are taken into account. On the basis of the developers' projection of *2,750 hotel rooms and 5,210 villas, cottages, townhouses, and houses to be built by 1979*, the County Planning Commission and County Council granted developers enough urban zoning to construct 6,000 to 8,000 rooms without seeking further approval! Kaluakoi's proposed development involved 6,762 acres adjacent to 44,000 additional acres held under option to the development company for further project expansion (Anderson et al., 1973:53). It was predicted that nearly 13 million gallons of water per day would be needed in order to fully implement Kaluakoi's development plans (*Hawaii Observer*, 8 December 1976:20). This compares to a limit of seven million gallons per day available from the state water system. The Louisiana Land and Exploration Company, which receives approximately one hundred times the $2.5 million revenue of the Ranch, was a partner in Kaluakoi, thus insuring that investment capital for extensive development was available. This company guaranteed $8.6 million in loans for Kaluakoi, while at the same time developers were "soft-peddling" the potential for expansion, hoping to keep opposition to a minimum.

Strong protest was registered by the Hawaiians, who formed an organization called Hui Alaloa in April 1975 to protest lack of access to public land. One year later a successful march was held through property that had been closed off by the Ranch despite the existence of a state-owned easement to beaches on the west end of the island (*Honolulu Advertiser*, 19 April 1976). Also in April 1975 the state Land Use Commission held a public hearing on a petition by 67 Hawaiian homesteaders to down-zone Kaluakoi land and prevent construction of the hotel. The petition cited social and economic costs, the importation of masses of outsiders, land speculation, and the probability of higher property taxes and housing costs. In addition, the petition claimed that jobs would not be available for unemployed pineapple workers.

The housing construction that has taken place with tourism growth is not for the needs of local families but rather to satisfy wealthy outsiders. In addition, past experience shows that the best jobs in the tourist industry go to outsiders instead of local folk. The need for jobs on Molokai is frequently used to justify the Kaluakoi Project. Yet the people who are being laid off the pine[apple] fields will not be the prime competitors for resort and construction jobs. (Land Use Commission files, Hearing on Sam Peters and sixty-six other petitioners, Molokai, 22 April 1975)

The Task Force and island leaders, including the local union representative, opposed this petition, citing the need for jobs as a primary reason. The response of such leaders at the hearing is characterized in the following report:

The proponents of development were in no mood for indulgence. Drill field fashion, they stepped confidently to the rostrum to talk about their communities' needs, the desirability of more jobs, and their wish to provide young people, including presumably those present, with the economic chance to live out their lives on their native islands. Those who spoke for the development represented the recognized power structure—labor leaders, businessmen, political figures. (*Hawaii Business*, May 1975:66)

One precedent that bears upon the controversy occurred at Kahuku, on the island of Oahu.[8] After closure of a sugar plantation, only 55 local Filipinos were hired by the Kuilima Hotel, a resort development that had taken the place of the plantation. Many Filipino applicants were said to have been turned down because of their poor ability in English. The number of Filipino workers hired went up to 135 following a strike, but the pay in such jobs was little more than $6,000 per year, much less than needed to achieve a modest living standard in Hawaii even with two family members working.

It is evident, despite Task Force pronouncements to the contrary, that the prospect of hotel work did not have wide appeal or credibility among Filipinos in Maunaloa. Fewer than one-fourth of the adults in the community expressed any interest in such work. Interest in hotel work was exhibited almost exclusively by locally born women (Table 4.2) and men who were either locally born or came as immigrants in 1946 (Table 4.3). Here the influence of the ILWU is apparent insofar as locally born Filipinos and 1946 immigrants tended to be under greater union influence. Members of the 1946 group were organized aboard ship before arriving in Hawaii and, like the locally born, had no work experience in the absence of a union. Their expressed interest in hotel jobs can therefore be interpreted as a reflection of well-advertised union support given to the Task Force in its pursuit of hotel development.

A number of respondents indicated that they regarded hotel work as unsatisfactory because the pay was too low. As might be predicted, three-fourths of this group were women (Table 4.4). Only one of the 16 women opposed to hotel work was locally born, and more than three-fourths had preschool children.

In addition, more than three-fourths had entered the labor force. These results suggest that a number of women who needed to work to support young children regarded hotel jobs as inadequate for this purpose.

The failure of various development schemes and training programs to serve

---

Table 4.2. Birthplace by Expression of Interest in Hotel Work (women only).

	Locally Born (Percent)	Immigrant (Percent)	Total (Percent)
Interest in hotel work	13 (35)	3 (6)	16 (23)
No interest expressed	7 (65)	46 (94)	53 (77)
TOTAL	(100)	(100)	(100)

Notes: Corrected Chi Square = 24.44 with 1 Degree of Freedom pl .0001. Numbers in parentheses are percentages.

Table 4.3. Year of Immigration to Hawaii by Expression of Interest in Hotel Work (men only).

	Locally Born (Percent)	Before 1946 (Percent)	1946-1965[a] (Percent)	After 1965 (Percent)	Total (Percent)
Interest in hotel work	6 (86)	2 (5)	9 (37)	1 (17)	18 (24)
No interest expressed	1 (14)	36 (95)	15 (63)	5 (83)	15 (76)
TOTAL	(100)	(100)	(100)	(100)	(100)

[a]All but two came in the year 1946.
Notes: Corrected Chi Square = 24.51 with 3 Degrees of Freedom pl .0001.
Numbers in parentheses are percentages.

the needs of Filipinos was the result of planning that did not include consultation with the residents of Maunaloa. The people who plan the future of Molokai are politicians, corporate executives, businessmen, real-estate salesmen, and major landholders, who are more interested in obtaining personal profit from hotel development than in promoting the welfare of the people of the island. They assumed that their positions of power carried the right to "speak for the people." Little opposition was manifest despite this presumptuous behavior, because illiterate and undereducated people feared "loss of face" and the possibility of worse circumstances if they should present a challenge. Moreover, these fears had some foundation in reality, for Hawaiian dissidents in the past reported being blacklisted for jobs by the political establishment in Maui County.

Despite a general lack of public protest, the Molokai Youth Congress was organized in the spring of 1975 by a few concerned parents and teachers. Local political leaders representing federal programs, the county government, the union, and private business were invited to appear and answer students' questions concerning the phaseout of the pineapple industry. The perform-

Table 4.4. Expression of Dissatisfaction with Hotel Work by Sex.

	Male (Percent)	Female (Percent)	Total (Percent)
Dissatisfied with hotel work	6 (8)	18 (26)	24 (17)
No dissatisfaction expressed	69 (92)	51 (74)	120 (83)
TOTAL	(100)	(100)	(100)

Note: Corrected Chi Square = 7.21 with 1 Degree of Freedom pl .001.

ance of the leaders was typified by the mayor's comment that Molokai did not have an unemployment problem. Several students asked embarrassing questions about hotel development and the whereabouts of funds appropriated by the state legislature for economic relief. That this new political awareness among students threatened some of the leaders was indicated by one of them cautioning that it was best "not to rock the boat."

A Community Without Homes

Uncertainty continuously surrounded the housing situation in Maunaloa after the phaseout of the plantation was announced in October 1972. Anxiety heightened early in 1974, when the county government proposed consolidating the primary school in Maunaloa with the one in Kualapuu and busing Maunaloa students several miles to the other town. Consolidation was called off only after 85 Maunaloa residents expressed unanimous opposition to the plan at a public hearing. The threat to the existence of the community was vague, however, until the Molokai Ranch began to release specific information about its plans. At a meeting of the Maunaloa Community Action Council on 9 May 1974, the Ranch employee who was later to be named manager of the plantation camp gave the first indication that the community was going to be uprooted. The information contained in the following report was also confirmed by the same Ranch employee in a January 1976 interview with Sheila Forman.

A Molokai Ranch employee surprised the 65 people at the meeting by announcing that they would not be able to buy their homes such as the Del Monte employees are counting on because Maunaloa would probably be relocated. This was due to plans being made by Kaluakoi Corporation. "There is big money here," said [the employee] in reference to the decisions being made concerning the future of west Molokai. (*Pukoo Examiner*, vol. 1, no. 5, undated, but probably June 1974)

The feeling that Maunaloa might not exist after 1980 persisted from that time forward. A quote from a five-year-old child illustrates that such expectations are indeed pervasive: "By and by all the trucks are gonna come and bust up our houses already" (Forman, 1976:217).

At a public meeting in October 1974, the union tried to ease people's minds by proposing to convert Maunaloa into a subdivision, including the standard features of suburbia, such as supermarkets and shopping centers. The feasibility of this plan was suspect because a low-income project already in the works for several years had been "delayed" for the reason of probable cost overruns. Construction bids came in too high to meet the standard limit of $35,000 per unit to qualify for a government subsidy. The union proposal was simply unrealistic because few Filipino families could afford such a price even if hotel jobs were to become available. The leader of the Maui chapter of the union, who conducted the meeting, did not invite discussion on the issue of cost. Instead, he tried to persuade his audience to rely upon the union and not to worry about housing difficulties.

The labor union has proven itself to all of you. We have delivered the goods in the past.

We haven't let you down before. I don't see any reason why we should now. Don't panic! We are on top of this thing. The union will not stand still. We gonna take care. These guys (Filipino workers) have been loyal to us and we will not leave them alone.

So be patient with us and we are going to plan housing for you. We will explore things in detail and all of this will be for you. We will convert Maunaloa into a subdivision so you will have decent housing, not the kinds of shacks you live in now.

Housing for retired men, many of whom have young children, was a critical need. Although a grant of $400,000 to purchase a site for an elderly housing project had already been received from the federal government, no immediate action was taken on construction of the project. The project was postponed at least in part because the Task Force wanted the site to be located near the commercial center of Kaunakakai, whereas Maunaloa residents wanted the project in Maunaloa so that friends and relatives could remain together. The Task Force also persisted in refusing to consider the housing needs of elderly men with children, who needed larger units than ordinarily would be provided. Because of a federal regulation, applications requiring larger units appear to have been ignored and left unprocessed by county officials. The failure to recognize such special problems was consistent with a previous ruling preventing elderly fathers from bringing their children on a free bus that transported senior citizens between Maunaloa and Kaunakakai.

The Task Force promised to finance the construction of 90 houses in a low-income housing project. Shortly after the project was announced, applications were received from 150 families residing in five different Molokai communities. It was not likely that needy Maunaloa residents would fare well in the competition, for several were told by county officials that separation pay, which could not amount to much more than $10,000, would count as an asset, thus making them ineligible to receive mortgage assistance from the Farmers Home Administration. The loss of regular income from the closing of the plantation would also make it impossible for many to obtain conventional mortgages.

For a while there was talk about the possibility of employee housing being constructed for future hotel workers. Later, it became clear from statements by a representative of Kaluakoi that no such housing would be built.

Appearing before the Maui Planning Commission last month, Endre Mott-Smith of Kaluakoi said the company is not planning to provide employee housing at the proposed resort site. He explained that the problem on Molokai is not housing, but rather the lack of jobs due to the phasing out of pineapple production by Dole and Del Monte. (*The Honolulu Advertiser*, 30 January 1975)

Contradictory signals, however, were sent to the community by the Ranch, which began renting houses in Maunaloa to outsiders employed by Kaluakoi. The Ranch sent a letter to tenants, dated 1 January 1976 and received by tenants on 15 January, which stated that the "critical housing shortage on Molokai" compelled them to take a hard line on requiring prompt rental payments (Forman 1976:227–28).

The community formally made clear its desires on the housing issue in April 1976 when a housing committee consisting of representatives of local residents voted almost unanimously to pursue the option of buying existing homes and lots. At an earlier housing committee meeting, a planner from the state government gave assurances that amendments to building codes and zoning ordinances necessary for such a course of action were possible. In January 1976 the Ranch manager changed his position slightly and indicated that homes might be sold to the people living in them. In other public statements, however, the Ranch spokesmen consistently refused to express willingness to sell existing homes and lots to renters, often citing building codes and zoning ordinances as prohibitive factors.

Lack of appropriate action by the Task Force and lack of concern by the Ranch meant that the problem of housing for Maunaloa residents went unresolved. Difficulties with many proposed alternatives and conflicting information from island leaders perhaps served to rally people around the cause of protecting their existing homes. Nevertheless, the wealth and power of the developers still gave *them* the prerogative to determine what would happen to the homes in Maunaloa.

Maintaining the Appearance of Accountability

The departure of the pineapple industry from Molokai was the cause of great public concern soon after the phaseout of Dole and Del Monte operations was first announced in 1972. State money was appropriated, an economic task force was formed, and much talk was expended on possible remedial actions. Yet after Dole closed its Maunaloa camp at the end of 1975, the unemployment rate on the island rose from an already high 20 percent to an incredibly high 34 percent only a few months later. Necessary relief was not given to Filipino residents of Maunaloa, and prospects were that the community would be dissolved after the housing agreement expired on 31 December 1980.

Filipinos responded to the problem in rational and predictable fashion. A few who were lucky enough to possess the necessary resources moved from the community, either to other islands or to the Philippines. Most, however, had little chance to obtain a good job elsewhere and remained in the community. It is understandable that past reliance on the company and the union conditioned the response of some who did not wish to move. It would be a mistake nonetheless to assume that such conditioning was the only factor involved. Unemployment compensation, severance pay, and pensions provided a cushion that enabled families to survive. Many young wives in the community were also committed to working, if possible, and building a future for their children centered around the economic and social resources of the community. With nowhere else to go, the decision to stand firm and protect the community was entirely reasonable.

The hardships endured by Filipino residents of Maunaloa and their uncertain future were direct consequences of corporate decisions based solely on the profit motive. Dole closed its pineapple operations on Molokai because more profit could be obtained by shifting its capital overseas, where colonial conditions still exist and labor is available at very little cost. Dole was also influenced by its corporate connections with the Molokai Ranch Company, which brought in additional capital from the Louisiana Land and Exploration Company in order to begin the development of a hotel and resort complex.

These companies acted against the public good not only by disregarding the needs of former plantation workers and their families but also by proposing to divert large tracts of land and scarce water from basic use in growing food to serve a less essential purpose in providing more tourist facilities. The main island of Oahu is already suffering from overcrowding because of tourism and from the construction of too many high-rise buildings. It was of no concern to the companies that Molokai was one of only two major islands in the Hawaiian chain that had not yet been developed and exploited, and that it should have been protected from the all-too-well-known and ugly consequences of tourist blight.

In addition, it was not in the public interest for the Louisiana Land and Exploration Company—a corporation that has prospered from exploiting its ownership of energy resources—to be funneling profits into tourist development while the nation was experiencing a critical need for additional sources of energy. Having thus contributed to and profited from one problem (the energy shortage), the company used its prerogative to create another—the imposition of hardships on the people of Molokai.

The issues mentioned here are perhaps familiar by now because they have been given attention in the media. Many people recognize the need for increased corporate responsibility in preserving land and water for agricultural use and avoiding overcrowding, which causes pollution. Many, however, do not recognize that lack of accountability to the communities in which they are located allows corporations to exercise very little responsibility precisely in the areas where increased responsibility is needed the most. The companies operating on Molokai, as a case in point, did not act responsibly toward Filipinos and Hawaiians, who together constitute 72 percent of the island's population. Company policy is either to remove these people from the scene or to cajole them into taking low-paying hotel jobs, while better jobs, at least according to past precedent, are likely to go to outsiders. If they could be held accountable, the companies would not be able to carry out such purely self-serving development plans. It is thus essential to their strategy to appear to be accountable by defining the interests of the local population as being similar to their own. In this case, they claimed that hotel development was the only means of providing jobs for people who desperately needed to earn a living.

The function of maintaining the appearance of accountability was assumed largely by political leaders, the list headed by the mayor of Maui County. "He . . . lauded tourism for helping break the old "plantation syndrome" . . . and he called for a new "peaceful revolution" where tourism would help the community solve its social problems (*Honolulu Advertiser*, 24 April 1976). It is no mystery why the mayor's Task Force did not find a feasible alternative to

Molokai's unemployment problem except hotel development. The Task Force, although not accountable to Filipinos in Maunaloa through its membership, maintained the *appearance* of serving community needs through public statements designed to validate its mission and discredit opposition.

The role of local union officials was not only to assist the Task Force in maintaining the appearance of accountability but also to use persuasive power and personal influence to defuse the opposition. In the past, union leaders were the exclusive agents of the Maunaloa community acting in a larger political context. As the power of the union waned, these leaders lost the right to represent their natural constituency, i.e., former union members. In order to preserve their status, they identified developers and politicians as an alternative constituency and opposed initiatives by members of the community to act on their own behalf. The developers and politicians sanctioned the leadership of the union officials in such matters as long as they were able to mute protest or block collective action that might prove embarrassing to officials or harmful to corporate interests.

Although initiatives originating among members of the community were officially discouraged and usually thwarted, collective responses aimed at gaining some degree of community autonomy or control continued to arise spontaneously. Two aborted petition drives, opposition to consolidation of the Maunaloa primary school, closing ranks around the traditional Flowers of May Festival, challenging the Ranch and its rule to prohibit keeping chickens in the backyard, and voting almost unanimously to pursue the possibility of purchasing present residences are all examples of such spontaneous, collective responses.

Feelings expressed within the community, however, were given little or no public attention. After all, official solutions were being proposed with enough fanfare to obscure the happenings in a small and isolated community. There were also some members of the community who maintained faith in the union and were persuaded to wait patiently for hotel jobs to materialize. It is clear that unemployed pineapple workers and their families were being manipulated, either to gain their support or stall their opposition, while their unemployment was used as an excuse for developers to pursue profits at the expense of a delicate environment and of the many people who depended upon it for a livelihood.

Epilogue: Mission Accomplished?

After June 1976 we lost contact with events in Maunaloa. Therefore, a short return visit was made in June 1977 in order to update our information before this book was completed.

The first phase of the Kaluakoi resort development opened in March 1977. The hotel hired 150 employees, a number that falls far short of the mayor's prediction of 500 jobs, even with a multiplier effect of 1.2 in the remainder of the economy. Of the 70 former Dole employees and their wives still living in

Maunaloa and available for work at that time, only 25 were hired by Kaluakoi, and after three months only 15 were still on the payroll. Complaints were heard from Maunaloa residents about harsh supervisors, arbitrary firings, and rules that prevented workers, especially housekeepers, from socializing with hotel guests or even among themselves. One woman was fired, for example, because she wanted to stay home for one day with a sick child. Of the remaining 15 employees, 13 were working in menial jobs as housekeepers and groundskeepers, while only two worked at better-paying jobs in the dining room. Moreover, only two in 10 housekeepers had full-time jobs; the other eight were on call and averaged only two days of work per week. At one point, the hotel sought to lay off workers over 50 years of age, a move that would have left even the groundskeepers without jobs. Fortunately, the ILWU, which retained jurisdiction on the hotel grounds (while the AFL-CIO Hotel Workers Union acquired jurisdiction inside the hotel) was able to forestall this move.

Of six persons who received federal training specifically for hotel jobs, only two were working for the hotel. One widow who went to Maui for training with the assurance that she would be offered a job was not hired by the hotel. Afterward this woman made two unsuccessful trips to Maui to try to find work to support her daughter and her aging mother. Respondents reported that she had lost hope and was suffering from severe trauma over her predicament. Meanwhile, good jobs in the hotel, such as personnel manager, social director, and dining-room hostess, were reported to have been given to persons from other islands who were related to political supporters of the mayor.

In May 1977 the official unemployment rate on Molokai had reached the staggering figure of 40 percent. Nonetheless, a primary leader of the now inactive Task Force had already departed from Molokai to pursue other business. A former Maunaloa resident heard him explain his departure with the incredible statement that the Task Force had "completed its work" with the opening of the hotel.

The Molokai Ranch continued to deny Maunaloa Filipinos the right to purchase their homes. The local housing committee consequently abandoned its efforts to preserve the community. One respondent commented that "nobody wants to live here much anymore." The truth of this statement was reflected in the fact that a number of families had moved to other islands and that others were soon to move. (None was reported to have left for the Philippines, probably because that option was rejected earlier.) One family, for example, invested its life savings of $18,000, part from severance pay and part from the wife's earnings, in a one-half-acre lot on Maui shared with another family. When asked where the family would live, the wife commented that they would "put up a hut." Respondents estimated that only one-third of the families still in Maunaloa are Filipinos.

The low-income housing project, now offering three-bedroom units for about $40,000, was finally underway; but there was little chance that former Dole employees without sufficient income to obtain mortgages could be accommodated. Moreover, 300 families had put in applications for the available 90 units. In gestures of transparent motive the Ranch promised to donate 200 acres of land for the purpose of building housing for future hotel employees, and the mayor promised to provide money for construction loans. Such self-serving plans were not meant to benefit Filipinos, who have largely been excluded from hotel jobs. One respondent cynically asked, "Why didn't the Ranch donate the [plantation] camp?"

Indications of community disintegration were apparent among those remaining in Maunaloa. There were no more holiday celebrations after the Flowers of May Festival in May 1975, and there were no more baptisms or weddings in the community clubhouse. The only party, a 1976 Christmas gathering sponsored by the Ranch, was not attended by Filipinos. Cockfights had been removed from local control and taken over by three men from Kaunakakai who began keeping fees collected from participants for personal use and no longer paid police fines. It was reported that regular bets had risen from $100 to $200 or $300 and that it was common for "outsiders from Hilo and Kuai" to attend the fights (outsiders had been mostly kept away in the past). As a result, some participants from Maunaloa were said to have been "squeezed out."

The University of Hawaii was sponsoring an experimental alfalfa project near Maunaloa, which had produced a green and flourishing crop. However, the mayor's permission was required for the continued use of the state water system for the project. Respondents reported that the mayor was reluctant to give his approval and had questioned the project's value. He was quoted as saying, "What good is it to Maui County?" Despite the mayor's preference for resort development at the expense of agricultural development, the feasibility of several crops, in addition to alfalfa, was being demonstrated in four university-sponsored projects on homesteader farms. Crops that would not spoil in shipping to Honolulu—watermelon, cantaloupe, onions, potatoes, corn, pepper, tomatoes, and soybeans—were being grown successfully. Three seed-corn companies were also conducting successful operations, thus providing a few jobs for Maunaloa residents. It is clear that Molokai, despite certain natural limitations, has the potential for increased agricultural development and that the key question concerning its future will be answered in the competition over scarce water.

It was at least somewhat encouraging to find that a rush of tourists to Molokai did not immediately occur in the numbers hoped for by hotel owners. The Sheraton-Molokai was sorely in need of business and was offering special cut-rate packages to attract visitors. A brief look at the hotel site itself revealed that the same high winds often mentioned as a deterrent to agriculture might be an even greater deterrent to tourism. Winds were consistently strong enough to be annoying both to sun bathers and to golfers. In addition, the "private and secluded beach" near the hotel is unsuitable for swimmers because it has a rocky bottom and a dangerously steep drop-off just beyond water's edge. Finally, Molokai does not yet offer any of the night life or shopping that commonly attract tourists. In Honolulu one is likely to hear that Molokai is "the island where there is nothing to do." The proponents of tourism, however, are determined to change this image and have launched a promotional campaign to turn Molokai's lack of commercial development to their advantage by advertising it as the "Getaway Isle," where one can enjoy a "yawning lifestyle" while the island "gradually joins the twentieth century" (*Mainliner*, May 1977:63).

If the Molokai Task Force was intended to create jobs and housing for unemployed people on Molokai, it did not accomplish its mission. If, however, it was intended to preside over the destruction of a community, which represented the last resource of its members, and to establish a foothold for selfish corporate interests in the pursuit of profit, it succeeded in large measure. It is abundantly evident that the attitude of social irresponsibility expressed in the last century by sugar baron Sanford B. Dole is fully characteristic of the beliefs and actions of his corporate contemporaries operating in Molokai today.

Notes

1. An earlier account of social life in Maunaloa is contained in Norbeck (1959).

2. A comparative description of Maunaloa and Kualapuu is contained in Peterson (1970).

3. For further information on this survey data, see Forman (1976), particularly p. 50–54. Analysis of data presented in this chapter has been generated independently from raw data files and is not necessarily intended to duplicate Forman's approach and presentation of results.

4. "The Closing Down of Pineapple Operations on Molokai," a report by the Pineapple Companies of Hawaii Negotiating Committee, 28 January 1974.

5. The forms of social structure that typically exist in plantation communities are discussed by Mintz (1943, 1954).

6. A general overview of family and kinship patterns in the Philippines is provided by Eggan (n. d., probably about 1961).

7. Results of the survey for the county as a whole are contained in a report by Baxa (1973:20). No separate reporting of the data obtained from Maunaloa is included in this document.

8. The problems experienced by Filipinos in the wake of the recent closure of the plantation at Kahuku is discussed by Garside (1972).

5 Adapt or Die: Resist and Perish

> The class of citizens who provide at once their own food and raiment may be viewed as the most truly independent. . . . It follows, that the greater the proportion of this class to the whole society, the more free, the more independent, and the more happy must be the society itself.
>
> —James Madison, 1787

> Adapt or die; resist and perish. . . . Agriculture is now big business. Too many people are trying to stay in agriculture that would do better some place else.
>
> —Earl Butz, 1955[1]

Exactly What Is the "Farm Problem?"

In the early days of our country James Madison, Thomas Jefferson, and many other Americans believed that farming was to be valued primarily as a way of life. Today, farming is primarily valued by consumers for what can be provided to them at an inexpensive price and by corporations for what can be produced at a profit.

This change in our attitude toward farming is a result of the loss of farm self-sufficiency and an increasing reliance over many decades upon an expanding industrial sector for supplying the means of production and a wide variety of consumer goods (Perelman, 1977:69–72). Although many sentimentalists still like to think of traditional farming as a desirable way of life, in actual practice the lifestyle of many farmers has drastically changed. Even agricultural economists point out that "some farms have changed so much that we hestitate to call them farms anymore" (Nikolitch, 1969:545). The words of former Secretary of Agriculture Earl Butz, presented above, rudely awaken us to the fact that in recent decades many small farm operators have not been able to adapt to modern circumstances and have left farming. The number of farm operators has not only greatly declined, but average farm size has continued to increase, while corporations and wealthy individuals have gained control over an increasing number of farm-related enterprises.

Standard explanations by agricultural economists for the failure of small farms suggest that "economies of scale" dictate lack of efficiency for the small scale-farmer. Since the small farm operator holds less land and receives less income, so the argument goes, he cannot afford expensive machines and chemicals that could raise his productivity to a competitive level.

Economic studies show that as the labor cost rises, it is economical to use more and larger equipment. Larger equipment can handle bigger acreages, so it becomes

134

economical to increase the business size. Machinery developments such as mechanical harvesters can often handle acreages beyond the size of many existing farms. Therefore, the farmer must increase the size of his business to use his equipment efficiently and to operate at the lowest cost per unit. (Burlingame, Parsons, and Reed, 1972:3)

Some agricultural economists, in step with their famous colleage Earl Butz, are fond of telling us that the elimination of small and so-called inefficient producers is a necessary evil if an increasing quantity of food is to be made available to consumers at a sufficiently low price. Taking the opposite side on this issue, Harold Breimeyer points out that the cost of this efficiency may be a price that is too high to pay: It is robbing Americans of a competitive marketing system.

The efficiency in size, which can reduce the number of firms, conflicts with the need to retain many firms in order to keep the market competitive. Perhaps the advantages of a self-regulating competitive marketing system can be had only by foregoing some of the physical economies possible from large size. To maintain a sufficient number of firms at some cost of efficiency may be a part of the cost of freedom. (Breimeyer, 1965:28)

Despite Breimeyer's seemingly good intentions in proposing that production be sacrificed for more important goals, he has not raised the fundamental question of political power relationships. Economic and political power in the United States is distributed in such a way that the advocates of production will prevail over the advocates of "freedom." The normative argument for a competitive market will be regarded as weaker than the coercive argument for production, and large farms and corporations will continue to control the marketplace at the expense of the small producer. By validating the proposition that big is better, agricultural economists, no matter how they stand on this argument, have merely provided a convenient rationalization for those who are wealthy and powerful and wish to accumulate even more wealth and power.

The apparent contradiction between efficiency and a competitive market is spurious because institutional variation is not taken into account. Big is better only in the context of modern capitalist institutions, which have been structured to serve the interests of agribusiness. It is also true that those who benefit from institutionalized rules of the game, the wealthy and powerful, are those who make the rules of the game. The small farm operator does not make the rules and does not benefit by the rules. In fact, he is put at a severe competitive disadvantage by rules that he does not make.

The purpose of this chapter is to examine the experience of small farm operators to show that, contrary to the beliefs of many agricultural economists, *the economic efficiency[2] of the small farm is not so much affected by natural disadvantages because of smallness as by institutionalized penalties of scale.* In other words, the profits of the small farm operator are insufficient because he is inflicted with institutionalized rules penalizing his smallness. If, however, this handicap is taken into account, the strategies employed by small farm operators to minimize costs and maximize production are indeed efficient. Even without considering such institutionalized penalties, it has been argued that small farms are more efficient in terms of economizing on farm inputs and actually show a greater net income per acre (Perelman, 1977:97–98). A survey of a number of studies of economies of scale, involving different types of farms in different parts of the country, also shows that the cost per unit of production for one or two person operations on small acreages is no higher than for larger farms (Madden, 1973). The main difference between larger and smaller farms was found instead to be in the size of the profit margin. Thus it can be argued that, since his profits are not high, the small-scale farmer must be productively efficient because his survival depends on it.

Another purpose of this chapter is to examine the loss of independence suffered by the small farm operator. Former Secretary of Agriculture Orville Freeman several years ago predicted the following change in the status of the small farm operator: "A food industry . . . closely integrated from production to retail outlet . . . could reduce the farmer to the status of a hired employee, and in many cases an employee without any of the benefits found in most employer-employee relationships."[3] In many respects this prediction seems to have come true. With the disappearance of a competitive marketing system, small farm operators have begun to resemble hired employees because much of their freedom to make essential decisions has been curtailed. Like many blue-collar workers, they must take what comes their way, and in the process many become frustrated by their impotence. Those who maintain even a small degree of independence must struggle to do so.

Colusa County, a rich farming area in the Sacramento Valley of northern California, provides the setting for this study of small farm operators. Many Americans are already familiar with the problem of loss of farm land to urban sprawl. As city dwellers move to the suburbs, farm land surrounding the metropolitan center increases in value, while property taxes also increase to provide needed public services. Farmers who own the land often find that they cannot pay the taxes and prefer to sell the land at an inflated rate for future homesites. Colusa County lends itself for study because it is little affected by this problem. The county's largest town, also named Colusa, has a population of only 3,842 (U.S. Bureau of Census, 1970), and the nearest metropolitan center, Sacramento, is too far away to be within commuting distance. The existence of problems for the small farm operator, such as inflated land values and pressure to sell out, therefore cannot be blamed on creeping urbanization. Instead, basic changes in the nature of farming and farm organization are at fault.

The difficulties experienced by small farm operators, like those experienced by workers, are caused by a social system in which profit is used to manage the choices and in which economic incentive is provided neither for productive efficiency nor for other worthy social and environmental goals.

Modern Jeffersonian idealists are concerned with the preservation of such small farms as still exist—although precariously and in limited numbers—in

Colusa County. Overwhelming institutional odds against the economic success of the small farm operator and the frustrations of farm life lead one to wonder how there are any of his kind left to preserve at all. Earl Butz took it for granted two decades ago that the small farm operator would not survive the institutional climate of agribusiness. This chapter is the story of small farm operators in Colusa County who struggle to challenge the oddsmakers.

Agricultural History: The Political Economy of Land and Water in California

The origins of concentrated landownership in California revert to the days when the state was a Mexican possession. Between 1828 and 1848 the Mexican government granted title of private use, mostly for cattle grazing, to a number of large plots of land in California. Many of these plots were as large as 11 square leagues (about 47,700 acres) in size. Some of the recipients were Americans, most of whom became naturalized Mexican citizens in order to qualify for the grants. After the war with Mexico in 1848, California was ceded to the United States with the understanding that the rights of Mexican landowners would be respected. The United States government had complete control over the remainder of the land under the provision of the Constitution that gives it "Power to dispose of and make all needful Rules and Regulations respecting the territory or other property of the United States." One year after California became a state in 1850, a claims commission was established to act upon the validity of Mexican land grants. Out of 813 cases considered, 553 grants involving 8,850,000 acres (an average of 20,954 acres per grant) were eventually confirmed (McGowan, vol. 1, 1961:37).

Corporate control over land, initiated by the Pacific Railroad Act of 1 July 1862, granted the Union Pacific Railroad and the Central Pacific Railroad alternate odd-numbered sections of land for 10 miles on each side of the road. In 1864 the distance was increased to 20 miles. Similar grants were made in 1866 to four other railroad companies. All but one grant, which was later forfeited, were taken over by the Southern Pacific Company upon its incorporation in 1884. Altogether, about 11,588,000 acres were included in the grants made directly to or for the benefit of railroad corporations (McGowan, p. 44). Cash sales, chiefly through public auction, were responsible for disposing of 8,631,000 acres. The Homestead Act of 1862 and subsequent homestead acts allocated another 11,433,000 acres in small holdings, usually 640 acres or fewer. These acreages total 20 percent of the land in the state, just slightly less than the acreages granted to railroad corporations. As a result of these policies, more than half (51 percent) of the land in the state was given either to the holders of Mexican land grants, to railroad corporations, or to those wealthy enough to purchase it.

The town of Colusa was established in July 1850 as a steamboat terminal on the Sacramento River. As many as fifty stagecoaches per day were loaded with freight to continue the journey north from Colusa. It was not long before the river passage above Colusa was cleared, allowing steamboats to carry freight 60 miles farther to Red Bluff, which by 1853 had replaced Colusa as the northern-most steamboat terminal.

Colusa County, including what is now Glenn County, was established by the California legislature in 1850. The town of Colusa, already designated as the county seat by the legislature in 1851, was confirmed as such by an election in 1853, which gave Colusa 310 votes to Monroeville's 52 votes. Later, increased population in northern Colusa led to the division of the county and the creation of Glenn County by special election in 1891.

Treaties were signed with the Indians in 1851 at the town of Colusa and at the major ranches bordering the Sacramento River. The first reservation in the Sacramento Valley was opened on "less desirable land" in 1854 and was intended to minimize Indian "interference" with white settlers (McGowan, p. 137).

The cattle industry continued to flourish in the Sacramento Valley for a brief period after the end of Mexican rule. Colusa County had 47,000 head of cattle in 1859 (McGowan, p. 158) and held the lead in cattle production among all counties in the valley between 1859 and 1870. A series of natural disasters contributed to the decline of the cattle industry after 1865. Plagues of grasshoppers, years of drought, a flood, and a snowstorm resulted in heavy losses to herds. Sheep became numerous in the valley only after the Gold Rush. The advent of the Civil War provided great incentive for sheep production, for the supply of cotton in the east was low and the demand for cotton to make army uniforms was high. This situation created abnormally high prices for wool and justified increased exports of wool from California. Although natural disasters affected sheep as well as cattle, sheep proved hardier, particularly in withstanding drought. Colusa had 100,000 sheep in 1866 (McGowan, p. 159) and held the lead in sheep production among valley counties from 1866 to 1872.

Cultivated land was restricted to an area one or two miles on either side of rivers and creeks until 1867, when it was discovered that the adobe soils of the inland basins could be farmed successfully. In the same year officials of the California Northern Railroad filed a map for an intended railroad line through the valley, therein establishing a claim for half the land within 20 miles on each side of the track. It was reported that the railroad advertised it would give persons already on the land first option to purchase and would not charge for improvements already made. When it came time to sell, however, the railroad set the price higher than that for any land previously sold in Colusa County (McGowan, p. 235).

Railroad towns that sprang up on the plains of Colusa County became the shipping points of large volumes of wheat. None of these towns, however, contained more than 200 people. The town of Colusa itself was bypassed by the railroad and found its early growth irreversibly thwarted. The town financed its own connecting line, which began operating in 1886 and closed in 1915 because of financial failure.

Several factors in addition to the availability of convenient shipping on the railroad contributed to the wheat boom. It was found that wheat could be farmed without irrigation if moisture was preserved in the soil by letting the land lie fallow for one year between crops. The development of the gang plow enabled one man and eight horses to plow more land than fifty men could do with earlier techniques. These two developments occurred in the late 1860s, shortly after a wheat shortage developed in Europe and the international price rose, making it much more profitable to ship wheat abroad than to sell it in California. The final stimulus to wheat farming was the invention of barbed wire in 1868 and the repeal of the "No Fence" law in 1872, which stated that cattlemen were not required to fence in their lands.

Colusa County reached first place among valley counties in wheat production by 1873 with 200,000 acres planted (McGowan, p. 244). Colusa County continued to lead the valley, raising its wheat acreage in 1882 to 400,000, the equivalent of 6,400,000 bushels. At this time Colusa County produced 2 percent of the wheat crop of the entire United States. Only two states in the union produced more wheat than Colusa County. Wheat farming was dominant until about 1893, when profits were reduced by foreign competition and the market collapsed as a result of a worldwide depression.

In the shift to wheat farming it was found that acreages originally well adapted to cattle raising were too large to be efficient with the use of existing technology. On small owner-operated farms, horse-drawn reapers cut the grain stalks close to the ground, leaving them to be bound and shocked by hand while waiting for the arrival of the thresher. Big wheat ranchers, with ten to twenty thousand acres of grain, which had to be harvested in a relatively short period of time before the kernel fell to the ground, found this procedure inefficient.

In response to the needs of the wheat ranchers a machine called a "header" was invented to speed up the harvesting process. The header was a frame on wheels pushed by four to eight horses into a standing field of grain. It cut the stalks a few inches below the kernel and dropped them onto a revolving belt into a wagon pulled along side, and then dumped the grain into a central pile to wait for the thresher. The header could cut a swath 16 to 28 feet wide, depending on the width of the cutting blade (McGowan, p. 249). One header could reap 30 to 35 acres of grain per day.

Most farmers with fewer than 5,000 acres had their threshing done by an occasional neighbor who owned a machine. One such horse-operated machine is reported to have averaged 1,500 bushels per day for 31 consecutive days moving between 28 different farms. From this activity, now commonly called "custom work," the owner of a thresher could earn $100 per day and up to $6,000 per year. A steam thresher that could handle more than 3,000 bushels per day was developed to serve the needs of the big ranchers. The largest such machine was reported to be so enormous that it required 50 mules to move it from one location to another, 70 men to operate it, and 6 headers with 18 header wagons to supply the stalks fast enough.

A steam-traction engine for plowing and a steam combine were later inventions. Even after much experimentation the steam-traction engine remained impractical until wheat began to decline as the dominant crop. The steam combine appeared about the same time (1899), but it was regarded as much too expensive and cumbersome to be used economically by the average farmer.

The large size of the ranches in the Sacramento Valley in the 1870s is illustrated by the fact that 132 persons in Colusa County owned an average of 3,651 acres apiece (McGowan, p. 256). Moreover, the average size of the largest ranches increased between 1873 and 1890. The public began to object to large holdings when it became clear that settlers found it difficult to acquire land. In 1877 a wagon train of 1,644 persons from the drought-stricken San Joaquin Valley came looking for a place to settle. Critics pointed out that these persons were forced to continue north to Oregon because all the land was taken.

The largest estate in the Sacramento Valley was owned by a Missouri medical school graduate, Dr. Hugh Glenn. Glenn acquired a total of 55,000 acres in northern Colusa through a series of purchases between 1867 and 1874. One story is that Glenn won $10,000 in a poker game and used it to pay for his first purchase. Glenn's operation was so large that he used 100 eight-mule teams working in concert to plow his fields (McGowan, p. 259). A full day was required for the team to complete the trip around one 20,000-acre wheat field. The ranch work force included 715 men, 50 of whom were at work constantly repairing machinery housed in two large buildings. At the time of his death (he was murdered) in 1883, Glenn owed a million dollars in debts, and his heirs were forced to sell much of the property to meet the claims.

The issue of land monopoly, as represented by Glenn's vast holdings, came to a head in 1879, when Glenn ran for election as governor of California. Glenn was characterized by his detractors as greedy, unpatriotic, an unfair employer (because he hired Chinese workers), and an enemy of the homesteader. The opposition candidate pointed to the contrast between lands divided into small prosperous farms and Glenn's territory in northern Colusa, where there were no signs of prosperity, no villages, no schools, no children, no homes, and just one big ranch. A local newspaper, the *Marysville Appeal* claimed that Glenn should be paying four times the amount of his present property-tax contribution, and that if Glenn's ranch were subdivided, it would provide homes for 375 families, or 1,770 people.

> Dr. Glenn is an individual, and as such has no business to own fifty thousand acres. He is occupying lands that belong to a hundred persons. If Glenn were justified merely because he paid a fair price for his land, then one could rightfully own the entire state if he could pay for it. (*Marysville Appeal*, 1879)[4]

Glenn and the monopolistic practices he symbolized were soundly rebuked in the September 1879 gubernatorial election. Glenn, however, was greatly responsible for leading the way in experimenting with farming as big business and successfully competing against smaller operators.

The cultivation of fruit trees was made commercially possible by the development of factory canning techniques that could preserve large quantities of fruit long enough to be sent to distant markets. It was common for canneries to hire school children during the summer to work during the peak canning period. The first successful fruit cannery was established at Sacramento in 1882. A canning cooperative was established at Yuba City, not far from Colusa, in 1883. Colusa had its own cannery for five years, between 1889 and 1894.

Decline in wheat prices about this time caused a number of wheat farmers to subdivide and put in fruit trees. A noticeable expansion of fruit acreage occurred in Colusa County in 1885. I. F. Molton was the biggest fruit-grower in the county at that time, with 200 acres in orchards and vineyards and plans for 1,000 acres in pears and prunes the following year. Colusa County had 1,741 acres in fruit trees in 1889 and 19,500 acres by 1920 (McGowan, p. 11).

The introduction of irrigation to valley wheat lands was an additional stimulus to the expansion of orchard crops. The Wright Irrigation Act, authorizing the creation of taxable irrigation districts, was signed into law in March 1887. The Orland Irrigation District established in September 1887 to serve Colusa and Tehama counties was the first in the state to be organized under the Wright Act. Although only two districts were successfully organized under this act, it stimulated interest among cooperating farmers and private developers who financed their own projects. Private developers were able to sell irrigated land at a 300-percent mark-up over unirrigated land. The amount of irrigated land in the Sacramento Valley increased from 100,000 acres in 1880 to 206,000 acres in 1902, and to 300,000 acres in 1909 (McGowan, p. 399). Beginning in 1885 the break-up of large wheat farms and the introduction of orchard crops began to reduce average farm size, and this trend continued until 1925.

Rice farming, although dependent on irrigation, was introduced only after a period of experimentation with various crops as a replacement for wheat. A valley farmer named William Grant began testing the possibilities of rice cultivation about 1905. In response to a letter of inquiry, the United States Department of Agriculture sent him 250 varieties of rice seed, which he planted in separate plots for the purpose of obtaining comparisons. By 1908 Grant had found a variety good enough to win a medal at the Seattle Trade Fair in 1909.

Rice growing began in Colusa County (its boundaries now excluding newly formed Glenn County) with 75 acres of rice in 1911, increased to 12,000 acres by 1915 and increased again to 53,000 acres by 1920 (McGowan, vol. 2, 1961:202). This rapid expansion of rice farming was at least partly caused by high prices accompanying the heavy demand created by World War I.

In addition to aiding the growth of orchard and rice crops, the advent of irrigation prompted the cultivation of alfalfa and mixed-vegetable crops. Five crops of alfalfa per year could be harvested enabling a dairy operation using alfalfa as feed to be successful on a small acreage. Irrigation also allowed one to make a good living on a family-sized farm, where a variety of crops were grown. In 1920 Colusa County had 193,000 acres in grain crops, 17,000 acres in alfalfa, and 12,000 in field crops (McGowan, p. 236).

Aircraft technology was first used for agricultural purposes in 1919, when farmers in the Colusa area signed contracts with a pilot to herd ducks away from their rice fields. In 1929, when late rains delayed rice planting, two flyers experimented with seeding from the air and found that planting could be accomplished ten times as fast. This event triggered the use of airplanes to spread chemicals, at a time when the use of chemicals had already begun on a limited basis.

Widespread use of the automobile and the advent of the 40-hour work week in the 1930s enabled many hunters from the populous San Francisco Bay Area to travel to the Sacramento Valley to hunt fowl. Between 1935 and 1948 in Colusa County the hunters' booty in ducks increased from 45,000 to 233,000, in geese from 8,000 to 132,000, and in pheasants from 3,000 to 71,000 (McGowan, p. 371). The popularity of hunting, and particularly hunting to supply restaurants in the city, led to the creation of several wildlife preserves and the introduction of stiff penalties for commercial hunting.

By 1930 the need for water conservation in the Sacramento Valley had become critical. The use of well water for irrigating small plots of land had increased to the point where the underground water table was dropping. Another problem concerned the low level of the Sacramento River during the summer irrigation season. In dry years such as 1930–31, 70 percent of the channels at the river delta became filled with saltwater because of a reversal in the flow of the river at high tide (McGowan, p. 293). On occasion, sewage from Sacramento was reported to have been carried as far as six miles upriver. It was hoped that a series of dams and canals connected to the Sacramento River and its tributaries would conserve sufficient water not only to irrigate the Sacramento Valley but also to supplement water flowing to the San Joaquin Valley, which had twice as much irrigable land and only half as much water available from the San Joaquin River. The sale of electric power generated by the project was expected to cover half of the financing. Without this feature the cost of water to farmers would have been prohibitive.

California voters approved a bond issue in 1933 for construction of the Central Valley Project, but the bonds could not be sold during the Depression years of 1934–35. Congress was finally persuaded to fund the project as a relief measure, and construction of the Shasta Dam was begun in 1938. The Shasta Dam was completed in 1944, and integrated use of the project began in 1951.

During construction of the project, strong opposition developed among big landowners because federal regulations contained in the Reclamation Act of 1902 would limit the number of acres supplied with water to 160 in the case of individual ownership, or to 320 in the case of family ownership. There were strong demands that control of the project should be returned to the state so that federal policies would not prevail. Big landowners need not have worried because the law has not been enforced. Despite the intent of the federal government to subsidize family-farm operations, it is estimated that at least 900,000 acres of California farm land are receiving publically developed water in violation of regulations written into the law (McGowan, p. 294).

Farm Labor and Mechanization

The first farm laborers in the Sacramento Valley were displaced Indians. John Bidwell, the owner of a large farm, not only hired Indians but also nurtured a settlement of Indians on his property and was sometimes accused of running a "slave camp." Bidwell's stated purpose in forming the settlement, as the story goes, was to teach Indians "to know the living God" while giving them a "chance to make a living." Later, he built a church on land set aside for the Indians and deeded the land to the Indians when he died.

Transient labor was introduced later because of the seasonal demands of enormous wheat crops. Many workers were immigrants from Europe or the Midwest. Irish, German, and English customarily operated the machinery, while Chinese, Mexicans, and Italians were hired as cooks or field hands. Chinese immigrants provided much of the farm labor in the Sacramento Valley between 1870 and 1900. They earned a reputation as diligent workers and were resented by unemployed whites, who felt that the Chinese were being hired at their expense. Numerous acts of mob violence, arson, and murder were perpetrated on the Chinese in the 1870s and 1880s. Employers of Chinese also became targets of public anger. John Bidwell, who was regarded as the first to import Chinese contract labor, found his soap factory burned to the ground in 1877. When Chinese workers demanded equal pay in 1882, a movement was begun in Colusa to replace Chinese domestic workers by hiring young women from the cities of Europe and the United States. After 1884 the federal Chinese Exclusion Act made immigration from China illegal. It was not long before most Chinese had either left the state or moved to cities such as Sacramento and San Francisco. The number of Chinese in California declined from about 130,000 in 1882, to 72,472 in 1890, and to 33,271 in 1919 (McGowan, p. 138).

After 1890 Japanese immigrants began to arrive to replace the Chinese as agricultural laborers. When the United States annexed Hawaii in 1898, contracts with foreign laborers were cancelled, and thousands of Japanese were free to migrate to California. Ten thousand young Japanese men, both from Hawaii and Japan, arrived in the year 1900 alone. Sentiment against Japanese grew strong about 1910, when the total number of Japanese immigrants reached 40,000 (London and Anderson, 1970:8). Japanese immigrants began to work in California as farm laborers, and many soon began leasing land on a share basis with the owner. By 1909 Japanese settlers leased or owned one-fourth of all irrigated land in the Sacramento Valley (McGowan, p. 308). As a result, a series of laws was passed, between 1913 and 1923, to prohibit aliens from owning land. During World War II Japanese farmers were finally eliminated from the Sacramento Valley as landholders when their property was expropriated with little or no compensation, and they were herded into "internment camps." Given the choice of remaining idle in the camps or doing farm labor, many chose to do farm labor.

East Indians immigrated to the Sacramento Valley about the same time as the Japanese, although in small numbers. (They were called "Hindus" to distinguish them from American Indians.) By 1919 they owned 1,293 acres in the Sacramento Valley and had leased another 44,605 acres, including 10,000 acres in Colusa County (McGowan, p. 141). The federal Immigration Law of 1924 prevented further immigration of East Indians, Japanese, and Europeans, who had also arrived in substantial numbers. By 1940 Colusa County's foreign-born segment had been reduced to about 10 percent of the total population.

The importation of Filipino laborers who qualified as U.S. nationals was made desirable after the Immigration Law of 1924 excluded other Asians from migrating to the United States. The California farm-labor force included about 30,000 Filipinos by 1930 (London and Anderson, 1970:11).

Mexican laborers began moving to California in substantial numbers about 1910. The outbreak of revolution in Mexico and a shortage of agricultural labor that developed during World War I gave many immigrants incentive to move across the border into California. By 1930 there were 9,695 Mexicans residing in the Sacramento Valley (McGowan, p. 308). The use of Mexicans as agricultural laborers was interrupted by the Depression. Between 1935 and 1939 as many as 140,000 destitute persons driven from the "Dust Bowl" and other hard-hit areas of the United States arrived in California to look for work (London and Anderson, 1970:12). Many Mexicans returned to their homeland during this period, for Mexico by this time had become politically stable. California agriculture received special dispensation from the federal government to use Mexican contract laborers, or *braceros,* during World War II. A predictable labor shortage and the urgency of war were apparently sufficient reasons for the government to spend more than $21 million in the year 1945 alone to subsidize recruitment, transportation, food, housing, medical care, and general administration for about 50,000 workers (London and Anderson, 1970:14). The bracero program continued until 1964 and provided a substantial supply of workers each year; 25,000 in 1953, 51,300 in 1957, and 32,000 in 1962 (*California's Farm Labor Problems, Part I.* California State Assembly, Mexican National Labor in California Agriculture, 1963:78).

The end of the bracero program did not halt the immigration of Mexican laborers. Under the McCarron-Walter Act of 1952 Mexicans are allowed to cross the border if they have a letter guaranteeing employment. The latest wave of legal immigrants have come as "green carders," i.e., those who carry a green card to indicate that an employer has guaranteed permanent entry for the purpose of working. Illegal immigrants, or so-called "wetbacks," have crossed the border from Mexico in large numbers since the early 1950s. In 1954 approximately 84,000 wetbacks were apprehended in California and deported (*California's Farm Labor Problems, Part I,* 1963:72). This number dropped to 11,000 in 1960, but it has risen steeply since then. In 1976 alone 266,000 deportable aliens were apprehended at the Chula Vista border in California (*Portland Oregonian,* 11 September 1977). Although many early Mexican immigrants have moved to the city, a significant number of recent immigrants are still involved in agricultural labor. Mexicans have not been absorbed as independent farmers, as were earlier immigrant groups (Table 5.1).

Labor-union organizing among Mexican and Mexican-American agricultural laborers began in the late 1950s. The first series of strikes was called in 1960, and a long struggle between workers and the big growers has followed and has not yet been settled. It is perhaps not coincidental that experimentation with mechanical harvesting of tree and vegetable crops was accelerated after 1957, at the same time farm labor began to organize. Almonds and walnuts were the first tree crops to be mechanically harvested because nuts would not be damaged by falling to the ground and being picked up by a mechanical device. A machine called a "knocker," or a "shaker," was developed to shake the nuts loose from the tree, and by 1960 most nut growers had adopted the use of this machine. Mechanization and planting new trees closer together, along with irrigation made possible by the Shasta Dam, are probably responsible for a reported increase in yield of almonds per acre from 400 pounds (in shell) in 1940 to 1,240 pounds in 1973 (Reed and Horel, 1975:2).

Table 5.1. Spanish Background vs. Occupation for Persons Employed in California Agriculture.

	Persons of Spanish Language or Spanish Surname (Percent)	Others (Percent)	Total
Farmers, owners and tenants	3,984 (3)	32,271 (24)	36,255
Farm laborers, wage workers	52,680 (40)	43,997 (33)	96,677
TOTAL	56,664 (43)	72,268 (57)	132,932

Source: U. S. Bureau of the Census, 1970.
Note: Numbers in parentheses are percentages.

A prune harvester developed a year or two later works on the same principle, but it drops the fruit delicately onto a canvas, where it rolls down inclined sides into a catcher. The savings brought to the large grower on cost of labor are readily apparent. In one case, for example, a mechanized prune harvest was reported to be one-third the cost of an unmechanized harvest the year before (McGowan, p. 357). Other mechanical harvesters have been developed for peaches, apricots, tomatoes, and numerous other crops to allow similar savings on the cost of labor. In recent years heavy investments in machinery specific to one crop and the increased availability of fertilizers have meant significant changes in farming methods. Whereas in the 1940s rice crops were rotated to renourish the soil and increase the yield, in the 1970s rice is cultivated year after year on the same land. In this way the machinery is put to most efficient use, while the soil is subjected to heavy applications of fertilizer.

Population and Farming Trends

Colusa County has always been rural and continues to be rural despite extremely rapid population growth in other parts of California. In this century the population of California has doubled approximately every 20 years, while Colusa County's population shows an increase of only 62 percent over a period of 70 years and a slight decrease between 1960 and 1970 (Table 5.2).[5] The rural character of the county is reflected in the fact that well over half (1,913) of the county's 3,569 employed persons are working in agriculture or agricultural services (*Colusa County Profile, Economic Resources Survey*, prepared by Colusa County Chamber of Commerce, March 1977).[6] Manufacturing employs very few people, most of whom work on a seasonal basis in food-processing plants. Unlike retail businesses in many areas of California, those in Colusa County primarily serve the local population and are not oriented toward tourists.

Table 5.2.   Colusa County and California Population Statistics.

	Colusa County	California
1900	7,364	1,485,053
1910	7,732	2,377,549
1920	9,290	3,426,861
1930	10,258	5,677,251
1940	9,788	6,907,387
1950	11,651	10,586,223
1960	12,075	15,717,204
1970	11,896	19,779,156

Source: California Statistical Abstract, Sacramento, California, 1970.

Because more than half the farm laborers who work for a wage in California are of Spanish language or surname, it is likely that such persons constitute a significant portion of Colusa County's agricultural labor force. Seventeen percent of the county's total population is reported to be of Spanish language or surname (*California County Fact Book*, 1973). In Colusa County 90 percent of those of Spanish language or surname are of Mexican descent (Moles, 1976:16).

The total value of Colusa County's agricultural commodities remained steady between 1966 and 1972; it then increased dramatically over the next two years, reaching a peak in 1974 (Table 5.3). The years in which this increase

Table 5.3.   Ten-Year Chart of Colusa County's Agricultural Commodities.

Year	Total Dollar Value of All Commodities
1975	$134,164,000
1974	153,894,000[a]
1973	128,675,600
1972	66,551,400
1971	55,225,000
1970	55,071,100
1969	60,388,800[b]
1968	59,668,810
1967	48,211,700
1966	51,214,400

[a]The preliminary 1974 Census of Agriculture reports this figure as $104,407,000.
[b]The 1969 Census of Agriculture reports this figure as $47,820,015.

Source: Annual Report Crop Statistics of Colusa County, 1971 and 1975, compiled by Colusa County Department of Agriculture.

Table 5.4.   Colusa County's Leading Agricultural Commodities, 1974.

Crop	Dollar Market Value	Harvested Acreage
Rice	$78,450,000	119,000
Safflower	11,830,000	26,000
Tomatoes	11,315,000	9,220
Sugar beets	10,165,000	9,540
Wheat	6,435,000	33,000
Almonds	5,985,000	13,600
Prunes	4,320,000	6,050
Vine crops (seed)	3,885,000	6,300
Cattle and calves	3,266,000	15,000 head
Grain sorghums	2,277,000	11,000
Barley	2,242,000	19,000
Beans, dry	2,025,000	5,000
Field corn, grain	1,688,000	4,500
Walnuts	1,554,000	3,500
Sheep and lambs	1,080,000	30,000 head
Alfalfa hay	1,072,000	3,300

Source: Annual Report Crop Statistics of Colusa County, 1975, compiled by Colusa County Department of Agriculture.

Table 5.5. Trends in Number and Size of Farms in Colusa County.

	Number	Average Size (acres)	Total Land in Farms	Value of Land and Buildings (per farm)	Production Expenses (per farm)
1974	578	766	442,512	$480,782	$109,963
1969	632	766.3	484,331	305,483	55,020
1964	601	885.4	532,151	276,545	NA
1959	768	639.5	491,128	135,087	NA
1954	746	802	597,968	116,000	NA
1950	813	656	532,778	60,277	NA
1945	894	566	505,940	29,730	NA
1940	730	599	437,030	28,323	NA
1935	870	572	497,375	29,150	NA
1930	894	539	481,604	37,805	NA
1925	1,139	394	448,976	36,586	NA
1910	667	783	522,376	25,893	NA
1900	582	945	550,002	20,142	NA

Source: 1969 and 1964 Census of Agriculture; Preliminary 1974 Census of Agriculture.

occurred correspond to a period of inflation in the national economy and also to a period of expanding rice production in the county. In 1971 rice was harvested on 81,600 acres—compared to 53,000 acres in 1920—with a total crop value of $21 million. By 1974 harvested acres of rice increased to 119,000 with a total crop value of $78 million, almost four times the 1971 value (Table 5.4). Among other leading crops, such as safflower, tomatoes, sugar beets, wheat, almonds, prunes, etc., none has more than 15 percent of the value of the rice harvest.

Colusa County differs from the state insofar as its farms are, and always have been, on the average significantly larger. But a trend toward fewer and larger farms between 1925 and 1964 is clear both for Colusa County and for California (Tables 5.5 and 5.6). Between 1964 and 1974 it appears that the trend toward larger farms ceased as a continued decrease in number of farms was offset by a decrease in the amount of land in farms. It would be tempting to conclude from these figures that the epitaph of Earl Butz was premature and that the small farm is making a comeback despite creeping usurpation of agricultural land. This conclusion is especially tempting when it is noted that in Colusa County the number of farms with 50 acres or less increased over this ten-year period, while the number of farms with 2,000 acres or more decreased (Table 5.7).

Evidence to partially invalidate this conclusion is that an increase in the number of small farm operators has not been accompanied by a return to the lifestyle of the family farm. In fact, the trend away from family-operated farms seems to have continued. For instance, in both Colusa County and California

Table 5.6.   Trends in Number and Size of Farms in California.

	Number	Average Size (acres)	Total Land in Farms	Value of Land and Buildings (per farm)	Production Expenses (per farm)
1974	73,549	455	33,499,588	$304,615	$83,200
1969	77,875	458.7	35,722,348	217,730	45,600
1964	80,852	457.8	37,010,925	214,650	NA
1959	99,274	371.6	36,887,948	131,212	NA
1954	123,075	307.1	37,794,780	69,620	NA
1950	137,168	266.9	36,613,291	41,192	NA
1945	138,917	252.3	35,054,379	25,084	NA
1940	132,658	230.1	30,524,324	16,331	NA
1935	150,360	202.4	30,437,995	15,466	NA
1930	135,676	224.4	30,442,581	25,203	NA
1925	136,409	202	27,516,955	23,111	NA
1910	88,197	316	27,931,444	16,447	NA
1900	72,542	397	28,828,951	9,758	NA

Source: 1969 and 1964 Census of Agriculture; Preliminary 1974 Census of Agriculture.

as a whole the number of operators in residence on their farms has declined in recent years, while the number of operators not in residence on their farms has increased (Table 5.8).

During approximately the same period, the number of farm owners and

Table 5.7.   Farms and Land in Farms in Colusa County, 1969 and 1974.

	1969		1974	
	Number	Acres in farms	Number	Acres in farms
All Farms	632	484,331	578	NA
Farms with --				
1-9 acres	37	142	40	NA
10-49 acres	104	2,806	107	NA
50-179 acres	133	13,945	121	NA
180-499 acres	159	50,070	122	NA
500-999 acres	73	52,900	78	NA
1,000-1,999 acres	62	83,028	62	NA
2,000 acres and more	64	281,440	48	NA

Source: Preliminary 1974 Census of Agriculture and 1969 Census of Agriculture.

unpaid family members employed in farming has decreased substantially (Table 5.9). In Colusa County the number of hired workers, including both domestic and foreign contract workers, has remained roughly the same. If the number of illegal aliens employed in agriculture could be counted and added to the total number of hired workers, the results would probably show an increase in both Colusa County and in California. In any case, there appears to be a trend away from reliance on family labor to more complete reliance on hired labor.[7]

The latest statistics for the year 1974 indicate that farming in Colusa County and California must be regarded in partial measure as a secondary activity of persons who have primary occupations other than farming, for 20 percent of the farm operators in Colusa County and 48 percent of the farm operators in the state fall into this category (*Preliminary 1974 Census of Agricluture*)[8] It is understandable that the number of nonfarmers in farming is greater for the state as a whole, where the average farm size is smaller than in the county. Smaller farms are more likely to go up for sale and to be offered at a reasonable price. An increase in the number of very small farms thus would seem to reflect increased participation by those who engage in farming as a sideline. A trend in which outsiders bid up the price of farms is indirectly evident from a two-thirds increase in the average value of land and buildings per farm between 1969 and 1974 for the county and state. This has occurred along with a decrease in the amount of land in farms, indicating that some investors are purchasing farmland at rapidly increasing prices even while some farmers take land out of farming because they cannot make a living. The corresponding

Table 5.8.   Farm Operators by Place of Residence, Colusa County and California.

	1974	1969	1964	1959
Colusa County				
Residence on farm operated	NA	328	395	NA
Residence not on farm operated	NA	244	NA[a]	NA
Total farm operators	NA	632	601	768
California				
Residence on farm operated	NA	51,044	65,409	80,518
Residence not on farm operated	NA	18,420	13,210	12,946
Total farm operators	NA	77,875	80,852	99,274

[a]This figure would necessarily be lower than the 1969 figure since the number of operators residing on their farms decreased and the total number of farm operators increased. For farms with sales of $2,500 or more the number of absentee farm operators increased from 121 in 1964 to 217 in 1969.

Source: 1969 and 1964 Census of Agriculture.

Table 5.9. Agricultural Employment by Type of Worker, Colusa County
and California.
(annual averages based on mid-month estimates)

	Farmers and Unpaid Family	Hired Domestic, Regular and Seasonal	Contract Foreign
Colusa County			
1955	840	1,080	190
1963	810	980	120
1970	600	1,110	0
California			
1955	115,400	211,200	40,200
1963	93,900	196,500	28,000
1970	78,900	210,400	0

Source: State of California Department of Employment
Report 881M #4, December 1965 and January 1971.

decrease in the number of very large farms in the county can be explained by
an across-the-board decrease in the number of farms of all but the smallest
size. Steeply rising production costs, which doubled between 1969 and 1974
for farmers in Colusa County and nearly doubled for farmers in the state,

Table 5.10. Production Expenses[a] for Colusa County Farmers, 1969.

Major Items	Number of Farms	Total Cost All Farms	Cost per Farm
Fertilizers	506	$3,000,045	$ 5,928
Other chemicals	394	1,605,051	4,073
Gasoline	619	1,606,011	2,594
Hired labor	458	6,637,179	14,491
Contract labor, custom work and machine hire	419	2,753,449	6,571
All Items	632	$34,773,008	$55,020[b]

[a]Not counting unpaid family labor or costs of machinery.
[b]239 farms, or 38 percent of all farms, listed as under
$10,000.

Source: 1969 Census of Agriculture.

provide further evidence that the family farm is increasingly being replaced by a more industrialized form of organization (Tables 5.5 and 5.6). As this trend progresses, a distinct difference can be observed between farms that have followed the trend and farms that have not.

The average cost of farm production in Colusa County in 1969 was $55,020 (Table 5.10). The most expensive items were fertilizer, other chemicals, gasoline, hired labor, and the category of contract labor, custom work, and machine hire. Despite the high average cost, however, the total production cost of 239 farms, or 38 percent of all farms, was under $10,000. This circumstance indicates that the distribution of farms across production cost was a bimodal in character, i.e., most farms either had high costs or low costs, with few farms in between having close to average costs.

Ownership of machinery and equipment was similar to production cost in separating most farms into two distinct groups. Although the average value of machinery was $37,000, slightly less than half the farms reported an average of $68,000 while the remainder reported an average of $7,000 (Table 5.11). Another way to view it is that slightly less than half the farms had 90 percent of the machinery and equipment based on its market value while the remainder had 10 percent of the machinery and equipment based on its market value.

Table 5.11. Machinery and Equipment on Place in Colusa County[a], 1969.

	Farms Reporting	Dollars
Estimated market value of all machinery and equipment, total	604	$22,358,239
By value groups:		
$1 to $999	26	17,635
$1,000 to $4,999	94	267,155
$5,000 to $9,999	93	647,250
$10,000 to $19,999	96	1,325,918
$20,000 and over	295	20,100,281[b]
Average value of machinery and equipment for all farms		$37,000
Average value of machinery and equipment for 295 farms reporting a value of $20,000 or more		68,000
Average value of machinery and equipment for 309 farms reporting a value of less than $20,000		7,000

[a]Actual cost of machinery to the farmer would be greater than its estimated market value or depreciated value for tax purposes.
[b]295 farms have 90 percent of the machinery and equipment based on its market value.
309 farms have 10 percent of the machinery and equipment based on its market value.

Source: 1969 Census of Agriculture. 1964 data not available.

It appears from this analysis that there are two distinct strategies of farming—one to maximize income and the other to minimize costs. The family farmer who has little outside income on which to gain advantages from tax write-offs is forced to minimize costs.

The Problems of Small-Scale Family Farms

In order to learn more about the difficulties of the small-scale family farmer, a sample of 39 respondents was drawn from Colusa County. Since there was no precise means of defining a small farm, the procedure employed was to locate respondents by word of mouth on a hit-and-miss basis.[9] Most of this information was provided by the county farm adviser, government agencies, and various farmers who had knowledge of each other's circumstances. Even after initial contact with a respondent was established, it was difficult to assess the farmer's precise status because of the number of potential variables involved. It was puzzling to decide whether land, fixed capital, payroll, crop value, income, debt status, etc., was the most important criterion; and information on all such factors was not obtainable without conducting extensive interviews.

Despite its frustrating nature, this approach yielded a number of small-scale family farmers receiving relatively low incomes. When measured against Census of Agriculture statistics on a number of important criteria, respondents in this sample were almost uniformly below the norms of the average farmer in the county. Of 34 active farms in the sample, 94 percent operated with less than the average of 766 acres and had land and buildings valued at less than the average of $480,782; 91 percent had equipment valued at less than the average of $58,877; all reported production costs less than the average of $109,963; and 91 percent reported crops valued at less than the average of $180,630. For these 34 farmers the average number of acres farmed in 1973 was 284; the average value of land and buildings was $188,000; the average value of equipment was $30,000; the average production cost was $17,000; and the average value of the crop was $78,000. With only a few exceptions these respondents fell into the category of small operators whose strategy, as previously identified, must be to minimize costs rather than to maximize income. These comparisons are based on 1974 data for the county and 1973 data for the sample respondents. Although dollar figures for 1974 are somewhat inflated over those for 1973, the number of respondents below average would not likely change even if estimates were provided for the same year. That is, inflation alone cannot begin to account for the differences.

The sample of 39 respondents includes five who ceased active farming before 1973. Farm income figures for these five and eight others could not be calculated owing to poor record keeping, inconsistent reporting, etc. Of the remainder, approximately one-fourth had net farm incomes below $7,000; one-fourth were between $11,000 and $20,000; one-fourth were between $21,000 and $50,000, and one-fourth were over $50,000.[10] Only three had incomes high enough to disqualify themselves as small scale farmers. All three of these were rice farmers with 1973 incomes of $136,000, $207,000, and $309,000.

Income from custom work was an important supplement to farm income for one-fifth of the active farmers, who earned between $7,500 and $50,000 in 1973 by this means alone.[11] Income from other sources, such as nonfarm work, returns on capital investments, gifts, welfare, and social security, was also important for supplementing farm incomes. One respondent received as much as $120,000 in outside income from such sources in 1973. One-third of all respondents received between $10,000 and $50,000, while another third received income of less than $10,000. On the average, custom work and other sources added $12,000 to total yearly income[12] One-fourth of the respondents indicated that their main occupation was other than farming. Occupations listed by this group include a number not directly related to farming, such as airline pilot, flight engineer, chemist, auto-parts dealer, construction contractor, and fertilizer-chemical retailer. Farm-related occupations among this group were indicated as beekeeping, custom work, and, in two cases, acting as a manager for a larger farm. None of the respondents had more than three full-time paid employees. Of the active farmers, 65 percent had no full-time paid employees. Approximately half of this group still had debts relating to the purchase of farmland, owing an average of $69,000 per farmer. Among the total group of 39 respondents, 29 percent sold at least part of their land sometime between 1964 and 1973. Of those who sold land, only one appeared to have sold out completely. One respondent received welfare payments, and 10 percent received social-security payments.

Orchard crops were the primary concern of two-thirds of the respondents, and rice crops were the primary concern of one-fourth of the respondents. Two reasons other than simple bias could account for the inordinate representation of orchard farmers. One is that orchards are less profitable financially than rice, and the other is that orchards do not require planting every year and lend themselves more easily to part-time commitment among older persons and those pursuing other occupations. In the present sample all but one of ten farmers with a part-time commitment cultivated orchards as a primary crop, and none of the part-time farmers was a rice farmer. Moreover, the three most prosperous farmers all cultivated rice as a primary crop.

Immediately the question arises as to why rice farming should be such a profitable activity. One answer is that from 1957 through 1973 the government regulated the amount of rice that could be grown by allocating a limited number of growing rights, or "rice units," among farmers. The government could, of course, arbitrarily raise or lower the total number of rice units, but failing government action, a farmer could acquire rice units only by purchasing or leasing land from another farmer. One effect of such limits placed on rice cultivation was a staggering increase in the market value of rice. In a period of three years, from 1971 to 1974, the rice acreage cultivated in Colusa County rose by 46 percent, whereas the value of the rice crop rose by 265 percent. Neither inflation nor technological innovations could account for such an increase. The only possible explanation is that increased demand on the world market and an insufficient increase in production pushed the price up.

Another question concerns why small farm operators, and poor orchard farmers in particular, did not switch to rice cultivation. One obvious answer is that orchards are fixed resources and give the farmer little choice but to raise the same crop year after year. If an orchard farmer were to change to rice farming, it would involve abandoning a long-term investment in trees and acquiring new technology at prohibitive expense. Other small-scale farmers, although not committed to orchards, would face similar difficulties in acquiring new technology appropriate for rice and in meeting excessive production costs. Moreover, extreme fluctuations in the value of the rice crop can occur from one year to the next, making it risky to change crops. In 1975, for example, the effect of lifting restrictions the previous year was already being felt, for rice acreage increased by 9 percent and the value of the rice crop decreased by 14 percent.

Of the respondents 38 percent indicated a recent immigrant background, with 15 percent reporting that either Spanish or Italian was spoken in the home. Three-fifths came from farm families. Two-thirds were between the ages of 48 and 57, while one-fifth were between 62 and 71 and the remainder between 32 and 44. Three-fourths had at least completed a high school education, and more than one-fourth had some college experience. All but two respondents were married, with wives on the average having a slightly higher level of education than husbands. Only 15 percent had children under 12 years of age. More than half, however, had children between 13 and 18 years of age. Well over half also had children older than 18. And 36 percent were living in two-person households.

The family background of several respondents indicates that parents and grandparents were involved in agriculture either before or during the early part of this century, when diversified farming was being introduced into Colusa County. The grandfather of one respondent obtained a grant of 160 acres to begin farming in 1855. Another respondent reported that his father came to start farming in Colusa County in 1884. He was still living in the house that his father built in 1909. Another respondent of Spanish ancestry reported that his grandfather fought with Maximillian in Mexico before coming to California and obtaining land through a Mexican grant. His wife's father, also a farmer, lost his land during the Depression and was forced to work as a farm laborer. The parents of still another farmer came from Spain to Hawaii in 1907 on a five-year contract to work for the sugar industry. The company gave them a few acres for their own use, and they were able to save enough from this source of income to migrate to the mainland and enter farming.

The route into farming for those who entered before 1965 but did not inherit a farm came generally through working as laborers or managers for other farmers. Experience often was gained over a period of several years working for an uncle, a cousin, or a neighbor. In at least one case farm work was begun in childhood under conditions of severe hardship. The respondent's father died, forcing him to help his mother pick fruit for a combined wage of $3 per day. In another case the means to becoming an independent farm operator was provided by an employer who gave the respondent land to farm as a substitute for pay.

Perhaps the most interesting group in this sample were those who entered farming after 1965. They tended to have little previous experience in farming, or at least less than those who began earlier. Farming was attractive to them as a way of life and as a means to support themselves through their retirement years. The common ingredient that made it possible for them to farm was the possession of investment capital, either in the form of outside income or proceeds from selling previously owned assets.

Several examples follow of small-time investors who wanted to become gentlemen farmers. A man who owned a drugstore in San Francisco for many years sold his business and purchased a small almond orchard. His reason for abruptly changing occupations was "to get away from the rat race." An airline pilot bought an orchard ten years before retirement, using his salary to finance new walnut plantings. A white-collar employee of an oil company bought a few acres of almonds on which to make improvements and to hold for his impending retirement so that he could "live in the country." A factory foreman resigned from his job in a coastal town after living there for many years because he and his wife "got tired of the fog and the people." They had a septic-tank business on the side that was later sold but initially sustained investments in farming. Finally, one who left Colusa County as a young man and operated an auto-parts business for 27 years went back into farming because "he was tired of dealing with the public." Despite suffering losses in farm income for four years in a row, he was able to continue farming by using up a nest egg obtained from selling the auto-parts business.

It is most likely that the entry into farming of persons from other occupations is responsible for the increase in the number of small farm operators in Colusa County between 1964 and 1974. This phenomenon has been verified by several respondents, one of whom observes: "Small farming is coming back in a new form now with city people moving out to small acreages and commuting to regular city jobs. This is good for these people since the country is a better place to raise a family."

The critical role of outside income to the financial success of farming is illustrated by the case of an aero-jet worker who bought a small farm "to spend tax dollars on." The farm operation was set up as a "break-even proposition" to be subsidized by his aero-jet salary. One month after he bought the property, he was laid off, and it became necessary to farm for a living. He tried to farm for eighteen months before selling out. During that period he sustained a $9,000 operating loss. In order to improve the operation financially it was necessary to pay for new plantings to replace an old orchard. Since it would have been several years before new trees were in production, it was impossible for him to borrow enough money to continue. After the sale he had netted only about $10,000 for his efforts over eighteen months, but he was relieved to be off the hook. He commented, "if the place hadn't sold when it did, it would have really caused me some trouble."

The lack of viability of small farms with no outside income is a factor preventing young people from entering farming. One respondent claimed that small farms will be sold rather than inherited unless they are large enough for a family to farm for a living. Most respondents felt that it would be impossible for a young person starting out to farm for a living unless he or she had a very substantial inheritance. Inheritance taxes are another obvious factor in making it difficult for young people to farm for a living. One consequence of such barriers is that young people move away from the county to find employment.

Farming as Big Business: The Strategy of Operating for Losses

The farming interest of nonfarmers can be at least partly explained by the desire to obtain a tax shelter. A distinct financial advantage can be gained by a wealthy individual who invests in farming. First, all capital expenditures can be deducted against income from other sources. For example, an investor is lodged in the 60-percent tax bracket, primarily because of a substantial nonfarm income, with capital expenditures for farm production of $50,000. This "farmer"-investor would receive a government subsidy of $30,000, or 60 percent of his total production expenses. In comparison, a real farmer with no outside income, the same capital expenditures, and the same revenue from crop sales would receive no subsidy. In this case the *net expenses* of the farmer would amount to $50,000, or two and one-half times as much as the $20,000 in net expenses for the investor. If the investor sells his crop at a loss, say for $30,000, he is still ahead by $10,000, an amount that he is free to put in his pocket. If one who farms for a living sells his crop at the same price, he has *lost* $20,000 and is in difficulty not only because he depends exclusively on farm income for his livelihood but also because he did not cover his costs and cannot reinvest in next year's crop without borrowing. We begin to see how operating at a "loss" makes sense as a strategy for the wealthy farmer-investor.

Second, an accelerated depreciation schedule can be used by an investor to rapidly depreciate machinery, equipment, cattle purchased to build up a herd, etc. Depreciation, like capital expenditures, can be deducted from income and likewise gives the investor in a high tax bracket a greater write-off than a farmer in a low tax bracket.

That tax write-offs enable wealthy investors to make profits by farming at a loss is supported by 1965 data from the Internal Revenue Service, which shows that wealthy individuals engaged in farming are more likely than those with lower incomes to report farm losses! Among individuals engaged in farming, farm losses were reported by 87 percent of those with $1 million or more income, 84 percent of those with $500,000 to $1 million, 73 percent of those with $100,000 to $500,000 income, 60 percent of those with $50,000 to $100,000, 44 percent of those with $20,000 to $50,000, and only 36 percent of those with $15,000 to $20,000 (Fujimoto and Zone, 1976:3).

Government price-support policies give further advantage to large farms. A study by Phillip LeVeen of the University of California at Berkeley reveals that if price supports had been withdrawn in 1971, the typical large farm would be earning about 3.75 times as much as the typical small farm, whereas with price supports it was earning 9 times as much (quoted in Perelman, 1977:84). Considering all forms of government payments to farmers, including price supports and the soil-bank program, it is evident that a greatly disproportionate share goes to large farm operators. In fact, the disparities in such payments are so pronounced as to suggest that "the rise of the large commercial farmer in the United States is in large part the result of his political power rather than his market efficiency" (Ford, 1973: 50–53).

It is not surprising that large farm operators appear to be unaffected by the competition from "big-city investors." Large farm operators themselves are investors in a sense because they have a consistently higher volume of sales and receive more from tax write-offs and government payments. The farmer who is likely to encounter trouble is the small operator whose income falls low enough to put him at a competitive disadvantage. Even the middle-sized farm operator, with a fairly high capital investment and considerable production expenses, would in all probability be quite vulnerable to a low-income year because of market fluctuations and thus would go permanently into the red.

Information obtained about small farm operators who were in the process of selling out revealed that "big city investors" were purchasing a great deal of land in Colusa County. A common pattern was for the farmer to sell out and become a farm manager, either on a larger farm or on what used to be his own farm. As one small farm owner put it, "There used to be thousands of farmers around here; now we all work for the big guys." By selling to a wealthy investor a financially unsuccessful farm can actually be transformed into a successful one even though the farm operation must bear the additional expense of a manager's salary.

Wealthy investors are not interested in farming and do not live on the farm itself. They are easy-chair farmers, interested only in advantages realized in calculating their tax bills or in land speculation. Respondents, a few of whom sold to wealthy investors, reported that a group of doctors and lawyers, under the name of "Arbuckle Almond Orchards," bought several orchards in Colusa County and was interested in acquiring several more. The group was said to own other land in the San Jose area in addition to its Colusa County property. Its orchards in Colusa County were managed by the Dusche Nut Company of Oreland. One of the farmers who sold out wanted to manage the operation, but Dusche was reported to have brought in their own relatively inexperienced manager because they felt the farmer would exercise too much independence. The president of a Hawaiian bank was mentioned as another investor.

Lack of attention to management is one symptom of the interest of wealthy investors in profits and not in production and efficient land use. Another symptom is that land is sometimes bought on speculation and sold soon after it is acquired in order to realize capital gains. Dusche, for example, was reported to have sold some of its newly acquired land because the price went up. The flames of land speculation are fanned as investors continue to buy more farms, convert them into subsidized operations, and add to their capital value by acquiring more machinery, equipment, and buildings. Frequent buying and selling at inflated prices is further encouraged by depreciation schedules, which can be started anew, based on purchase price, rather than on already depreciated values. The incentive to use capital gains as a tax dodge is particularly great, for a 25 percent ceiling on the capital-gains tax does not apply to regular income earned from farming. The attraction for the wealthy investor is well explained by noted agricultural economist Philip M. Raup.

To him [the wealthy investor], the primary advantage of an agricultural investment lies in the high ratio of durable assets to total assets. Assets that can be treated as capital, and taxed under capital-gains tax provisions, are an invitation to the man of wealth to acquire them and seek ways to convert the largest possible amount of income into an appreciation of his asset values. (Raup, 1971, 1972:4416)

The impact of wealthy investors on small operators who farm for a living goes beyond the obvious creation of subsidized competition. It also raises the value of the land and the farm operation well above its worth as an asset to be used in farming for a living. The price goes up to match its value as a write-off in a tax shelter and the increased value of subsidized capital investment. This means that a small farm operator can often sell out and be in a better financial position than if he had continued to farm. It also means that the assessed value of land for property-tax purposes will increase and add to the tax burden of the small farm operator, thereby increasing pressure to sell out.

One respondent whose family had been farming in Colusa County for five generations decided to sell his property because he "kept getting deeper in debt" and felt that he "shouldn't be working so hard." When he received a good offer, he reluctantly took it rather than face the eventual prospect of a quick sale to pay insurmountable debts. After he sold out, he commented, "I don't have to worry so much anymore."

During interviews respondents constantly complained about the pressure of increasing taxes and the bidding up of land values by big-city investors. One respondent even made the following tongue-in-cheek suggestion to cope with the problem: "We should have neighbors sell land back and forth to each other cheaply to cut the assessment rates." Unlike wealthy investors, small farm operators who farm for a living are not businessmen. Their primary activity is to perform farm work, and hence most of them have little time for record keeping. Records kept by respondents were often poorly organized, and detailed budgets were mostly unheard of. In several cases, records were virtually unusable. One respondent had records scattered all over the house in different files, and he kept jumping up to find what he needed to answer questions. The accounting system of another consisted of old bills kept in shoe boxes in the basement.

Another reason for poor record keeping is that small farmers cannot afford to hire outside accounting help and rely instead on spouses or other family members. In one case, the 77-year-old mother of the farmer was responsible for the bookkeeping. During the course of the interview with this farmer and his wife, numerous errors were found in the records. In another case, household and farm accounts were combined by a wife acting as bookkeeper. Eventually the farmer discovered that his wife had spent fertilizer money for household expenses. In the few cases where an accountant is hired for tax purposes, the highest reported fee was $1,000. In general, respondents were aware that they needed better means of keeping records. One suggested that the university should provide an accounting service instead of advice about growing crops. Another was hoping that the purpose of the present study might be to provide information to him about the size of his income!

The advantages of having a sophisticated tax-accounting system were apparent in one case, where the son of the respondent became a lawyer and later assumed power of attorney over farm finances. He set up a nonprofit corporation to shelter farm income and pay his father "benefits," not taxable income, for farming leased land. The corporation also built a shop next to the farmhouse, which belonged to the corporation and was not taxed as personal property. The actions of the lawyer could be viewed cynically, but it is virtually certain that no other means would have sufficed to save the family farm. In this case, complicated financial and legal maneuvering succeeded where methods of farming had supposedly failed.

The Problems of Tenancy

Arrangements whereby landowners lease land to farm operators were common. In 1974 more than half of the farmers in Colusa County were either tenants or part owners–part tenants (Preliminary 1974 Census of Agriculture). Half of the active farmers interviewed for this study leased an average of 249 acres. In some cases, leased land constituted a majority of the land farmed. Of all respondents, including those who had quit farming, 46 percent, leased an average of 122 acres to other farmers.

For the landlord, leasing arrangements are a means of acquiring income from the land and allowing it to appreciate in value without putting effort into farming. For the tenant, leasing is a means of acquiring land to farm without paying an expensive purchase price or property tax on the land. In the past, tenancy enabled immigrant farm laborers to acquire more easily the use of land and to raise their status to farm operators. Later, it allowed farmers to acquire additional land, which increased their sales to the point where they were more "efficient," i.e., they could take better advantage of tax write-offs. Recently, leasing has become a convenient way to preserve large estates when heirs elect not to divide the property and farm it themselves. One large estate of more than 5,000 acres in Colusa County, for example, was managed collectively by the heirs and leased out to other large farms.

Leasing may occur for the first time when a farmer reaches retirement age and does not want to sell out because he has a sentimental attachment to the land. Leasing may be equally attractive to a farmer faced with the prospect of changing to a mechanized operation and investing large sums of money. If the capital requirements are too high, the best perceived option may be to lease out the land. As one respondent put it, "I made more money leasing out the land than I would have made farming."

Another reason for leasing may be to take advantage of the benefits of a partnership. One farmer, who had leased the same 600 acres since 1948 without a written contract, traded machinery and labor with his landlord, who also farmed some of his own land. In this case, the landlord benefited by reducing his costs for machinery and labor, thereby increasing his overall success.

The greatest risk in leasing land is borne by the small-scale farmer, who may not know from one year to the next whether or not he will have land to farm. One respondent reported that he leases a different piece of property every year. Another, who farmed 650 acres in 1973, was reduced to farming only 250 acres in 1974 because his landlord sold 340 acres the day before his sale options expired for that year. There is little the tenant can do about the sale of leased land, even though it is common for him to have first option to buy. In this case, the tenant was quoted a price based on the offer of the intended buyer. Since the tenant could not afford the price, he had no way of preventing the sale. It was particularly discouraging for this farmer to lose his leased land because, he said, "I put a lot of work into improving some orchards."

Another small-scale farmer eventually was forced to sell his own land because adjacent plots he had leased were sold by his landlord. Not only did he lose the benefits of having a larger and more profitable farm, but his new neighbor began hauling machinery across his land between the two adjacent plots. The farmer finally sold out because hauling machinery "wrecked the land."

Large farm operators by contrast suffer little risk in leasing land. One large-scale farmer was known to lease 2,000 acres from six different landlords, including land in two heirship estates. If he were to lose one of the leases, say for 340 acres, he would not be forced out of business, as would the small-farm operator. Furthermore, the large-farm operator was highly mechanized and subsidized by outside sources of income and could offer his landlords the best possible returns for the use of their land. Under such circumstances there is much less chance that one of the landlords would sell out. The lack of risk in this situation is perhaps best illustrated in one case where a large farming corporation offered to buy, not the land, but the farm operation. The offer was refused.

In order to further investigate land tenure patterns in Colusa County a survey of all landowners, based on tax records, was conducted by mail. One hundred thirty-eight landowners, or approximately 30 percent of this group, reported owning more than 510 acres, an amount far below the average farm size of 766 acres reported in the U.S. Census of Agriculture. Three reasons for this result are apparent. First, response bias would tend to exclude large landowners who might be apprehensive about revealing the extent of their holdings. Second, smaller parcels are often not used as farmland and would not be figured into average farm size. Third, it is common for owners to lease their land to farm operators who accumulate the land owned by others into larger units for farming purposes. Only 34 percent of the landowners reported farming any of their own land in 1973; while 33 percent reported leasing at least some of their land to others.

According to survey responses, altogether 61 separate parcels (a few with the same owner) were not farmed in 1973. Among the reasons given for not farming the land were economic difficulties, 26 percent; incapacity due to old age, retirement, or widowhood, 26 percent; use of the land commercially for recreational acitivities, such as duck hunting, 28 percent; and absentee ownership, 7 percent. No reasons were given for not farming an additional 13 percent of these plots. Smaller sized parcels were less likely to be farmed. Land used recreationally, for example, tended to exist in smaller plots.

The more important determinant in land being farmed by the owner in 1973 was whether or not he was among the 29 percent who owed money on the land. More than half of this group farmed their land in the previous year. In sharp contrast, only one quarter of the group that owned their land debt-free had farmed it in 1973. Indebted owners were also more likely than debt-free owners to be among the 15 percent who leased additional land. Eighty percent of these tenants leased more than 200 acres, and one leased a total of 3,000 acres. Virtually all indicated that economic concerns, such as improving income and efficiency, prompted them to lease more land. Obviously this group had a greater need for additional income to maintain a viable farm operation. In sum, the indebted owners are much more likely both to farm their own land and to lease additional land for farming.

Whether or not an owner decides to lease his land to someone else to farm depends on several factors. One of the most important of these is the number of acres at the disposal of the owner. We found that the greater the acreage, the more likely it was for the owner to lease it out. One-third of the farmers were leasing some portion of their holdings; but among those who owned more than 240 acres (30 percent of the sample), the proportion engaged in leasing was close to 60 percent. Small parcels are not usually leased out, probably for the same economic reasons that they are not farmed by the owner, i.e., it would be neither convenient nor profitable to farm several small, isolated plots of land. The exception to this rule would be river-bottom land well suited for intensive cultivation of row crops.

Another determinant of leasing land was whether or not the land was inherited or purchased. Owners who inherited at least some of their land, approximately 28 percent of the total, were twice as likely to lease it out as owners who purchased all of their land.[13] One reason for this circumstance, as previously noted, is that leasing is a means to prevent the division of property among heirs. It is consistent with this finding that land acquired before 1941 was likely to be leased, while land acquired after 1968 was unlikely to be leased.

Leasing arrangements are commonly made with persons who are well known to the owner. Half of the leasing arrangements in our sample were made with neighbors, friends, or relatives. Of the leases 44 percent were given to unknown individuals and 6 percent to corporations. Unknown tenants were selected either on the basis of general reputation in farming, or on a recommendation from a trusted source.

In one-third of the leasing arrangements, payment for the landlord was specified as one-third of the crop. Rent was paid in cash for another 22 percent of the leased parcels. The remainder of the parcels were rented for one-fourth or one-fifth of the crop or a combination of percentages for different crops. Fifty-eight percent of the leasing agreements called for the landlord to assist in paying production costs for items such as fertilizer, chemicals, spraying, and water. It was most common for the landlord to pay one-third of the cost of the items specified in the agreement. In a few cases, the landlord paid the full cost of one particular item, such as irrigation.

Leasing arrangements were most often renegotiated on a yearly basis. Only half of the tenants held their leases for 5 years or more, and only 9 percent held their leases for 15 years or more. Leasing arrangements were informal and fluid in that contracts were not put in writing. One farmer suggested in an interview that a formal contract would "not be worth the paper it is written on." Lease agreements usually do not involve permanent commitments, since only 9 percent of the tenants resided on their leased land.

Future plans expressed by survey respondents would lead to a 20 percent decrease in the number of parcels being farmed by owners and a 14 percent increase in parcels leased for others to farm.[14] This would mean a net decrease of 6 percent in the number of parcels specifically intended for farm use. Of the parcels 7 percent were to be sold or deeded to heirs. No plans were expressed for 18 percent of the parcels.

Supplies, Machines, and Workers: Examples of Institutionalized Penalties of (Small) Scale

The cost of supplies is rising faster than the small farmer can absorb it. Overall production costs nearly doubled between 1969 and 1974 for farmers in Colusa County and California. In just one year (1973–74), examples of cost increases reported by individual respondents were $42 per ton to $112 per ton for fertilizer and 26¢ per gallon to 44¢ per gallon for fuel. Tax write-offs on production costs make it possible for corporate manufacturers and suppliers to sell fertilizers, chemicals, and machines at expensive prices that would otherwise certainly be regarded as too costly and wasteful of energy and natural resources, even for large farms. The small-scale farmer is not only forced to compete against such artificial shortcuts to higher production but also must bear the penalty of volume discounts given by retailers to large-scale operators. One respondent reported that large farm operators were paying only $85 per ton for fertilizer, while he was paying $110 per ton. Another reported that his fuel dealer gave a 2 percent reduction in price for buying more than 4,000 gallons of gasoline, diesel fuel, or oil in a year.

Discounts to attract high-volume customers have been shown in other studies to be as much as 10 percent for fertilizers, 14 percent for insecticides, and 25 percent for crop dusting.

It is not unknown for farm-supply retailers also to be engaged in farming. One retailer of farm machinery in Colusa County, for example, owned farm acreages and retail outlets in several counties. Imagine the advantage to an operator who sells machinery to himself at factory rates and uses profits from his business to obtain tax write-offs on much of the remainder of the cost.

The main tactic used by small farm operators to insure steady supplies, but not necessarily at a reduced price, is to establish a regular relationship with a dealer. There are obvious advantages to such a relationship, both after a poor harvest when a small farm operator may want to postpone payments and during a shortage when supplies cannot be obtained elsewhere. During the oil shortage of 1972, for example, farmers were unable to obtain fuel unless they had a direct relationship with a distributor or knew someone who did. In contrast, a common tactic of the large farm operator is to maintain accounts with several suppliers, so if one goes out of business he can still get supplies. For the small farm operator who does not deal in large volumes, this tactic is, of course, impossible. Price reductions are usually obtained by small farm operators only if they have friends or relatives who work for suppliers. One respondent, for example, received a discount because his cousin was the local distributor for an oil company. The wife of another respondent worked for an auto-parts store and received a discount on spare parts for farm machinery.

High prices and lack of special treatment by suppliers forces a number of small-scale farmers into severe cost-cutting practices. Payments for fuel, of course, can be largely avoided by remaining unmechanized. Several respondents also reported that they did not use fertilizers or sprays on their orchard crops. One of these respondents, who had done little or nothing to improve his orchard, indicated that his yield was only 10 percent below the county average. Even if he could raise his yield to 10 percent above the county average, it would certainly not pay him to mechanize and use fertilizers and sprays.

It appears that small farm operators, through very hard work and personal care of their orchard crops, are able to compensate for not using fertilizers and sprays. They also show more ecological awareness than large farm operators or big-city investors who do not live on the land. One respondent compensated for lack of spraying by setting traps for squirrels and making sure that all nuts were knocked from the trees so that worms in the old nuts would not infest the next year's crop. Another farmer, sensitive to environmental pollution, stopped spraying his trees when he noticed in a recent year that the Orioles did not return. A third farmer did not spray because he did not want to "kill the good bugs along with the bad bugs."

The use of fertilizer by small farm operators with diversified rice and vegetable crops is likely to be less intensive than the use of fertilizer by large farm operators with similar crops. Many respondents were constantly experimenting with intercropping patterns to minimize the use of fertilizer without setting aside fallow land. The common practice on large farms is to rely totally on intensive use of fertilizer.

Perhaps the most dramatic example of the penalties of scale is in regard to farm machinery. The cost of mechanization is prohibitive for many small farm operators. Not only is the purchase price too high but also added costs are attached to leveling orchard land to accommodate the machines, hiring trained men to operate the machines, paying for the fuel to run the machines, and taking machines into the shop for repairs. The cost of repairs and spare parts was said by one respondent to be "staggering." Another pointed out that it was difficult to avoid making repairs because, "The machines you buy are junk even though you pay outrageous prices for them."

The immediate advantage in using machinery to harvest orchard crops may also be offset by increased costs in the long run. One almond farmer, for example, reported that using a limb shaker lowered the productive capacity of his trees and decreased the life span of his orchard. A final cost is the trauma of going to the bank for a loan and having the bank usurp the right to manage the farm.

Farmers who do not mechanize or are only partially mechanized are usually able to get along by relying on family labor, hiring custom machine operators, or borrowing machines when necessary from willing neighbors. Although a few individuals hesitate to lend machinery and incur the possibility of extra repair bills, most neighbors appear willing to lend machines without charge and without specific obligation on the part of the borrower. As one respondent stated: "Loaned equipment can be misused. But I don't want to rent equipment because it's too much hassle and unsociable. I would rather just loan it for a few days."

The decision to mechanize can be precipitated by a number of factors. In one case, a respondent's regular custom-machine operator died, whereupon he was forced to buy his own equipment. In a second case, a respondent's children had grown up and moved away from home, thereby forcing him to find a substitute for family labor. Another common reason for mechanizing is to overcome the uncertainty of the availability and performance of hired labor in an increasingly industrialized labor market.

Two factors appear to contribute to allowing the small farm operator to mechanize without fatal cost overruns. The first is that many small farm operators are capable of doing their own repairs. An analysis of open-ended interviews showed that at least 15 respondents had mechanical or welding experience, either on the job while in military service or in trade school, and did much of their own repair work. A few even built their own rigs for spraying or applying fertilizer. As one respondent put it, "The small farmer has to be something of a mechanic." The second factor is that informal partnerships are easily formed with other farmers for the purpose of sharing machinery and reducing the amount that each farmer has to purchase. Although one respondent claimed that there were not enough "little guys" left to go into partnership, several other respondents had current partners.

No matter what shortcuts are taken, mechanization is a risk to a small farm operator. At least two failures reported by respondents were due to mechanization. One respondent said he sold out because he was "forever repairing things." Another went into custom work full time as a result of mechanizing and suffering heavy cost overruns.

While the small farm operator most often finds it too expensive to mechanize and can barely afford partial mechanization at best, the large-scale farm operator has little difficulty in purchasing all the machinery he wants. Resentment against the special tax treatment given to large farmers was expressed by one respondent like this: "The big guys buy new machinery every year for a tax write-off even though they don't need it. Year-old machinery sits on their property rotting away."

The third area in which institutionalized penalties of scale are apparent is that of labor. Frequent complaints were heard from respondents about the availability and quality of workers. These complaints probably would not have been heard during previous decades, when docile foreign immigrants were in abundant supply to work as farm laborers. After 1965, when legal immigration from Mexico was halted, the supply of such eager workers was confined to a lesser number of illegal immigrants and to a few families who had been loyal workers for periods between 10 and 40 years. Special ties with Mexican families, however, are now less significant because a federal law preventing children under 12 from working has reduced both the supply of workers in the family and the income of the family. The shortage of workers is often felt most acutely at harvest time, as noted by one respondent: "I used to get four to five carloads of laborers looking for work around harvest time. Now they're getting hard to find."

The character of the labor force has also changed since the days of legal Mexican immigration. Most importantly, *farm laborers have become part of an industrial system, while farmers have become business executives.* Although farm laborers in Colusa County are not unionized, they are less willing to perform part-time work for low wages—$2.00 to $2.75 per hour—as paid by small farm operators. It is said that the only laborers available are the temporary kind who work in the summer for six months and go on welfare in the winter, because it is reasoned that good workers get full-time jobs. In the eyes of the farmer, present-day laborers do not work as hard and tend to be more irresponsible than their counterparts in the past. One respondent claimed that his biggest problem was "getting good-quality labor that doesn't always go off and get drunk and never come back." A second respondent told of an incident in the preceding year when his laborers got drunk and were thrown in jail. Since he was left without help, he hired his nine grandchildren to gather the harvest. A third respondent had a similar experience in hiring workers who stayed overnight, had breakfast the next morning, and then disappeared.

Many small farm operators must rely on high school students or the children of local families at harvest time. In addition, daily Mexican and "Hindu" labor pools in the county are on call; in rare instances foreign students are available on agricultural exchange programs; and sometimes transient youth ("hippies") appear unannounced and stay to work through the harvest.

Hiring laborers to operate machinery presents additional problems, for high school students under the age of 16 are not allowed by law to operate heavy machinery, and farmers find it difficult to train and teach safety standards to Mexican workers because of the language difference.

A number of respondents were quite outspoken in expressing a preference for hiring illegal aliens because, like their immigrant predecessors, they are docile workers. In the words of one respondent, "Mexican nationals know the value of hard work and are glad to get it." Another respondent stereotyped them as a vital source of labor because they are "happy being fruit tramps" and "do not want full-time work." If it weren't for regular inspection tours made by the county sheriff, respondents claimed that a great number of illegal aliens would be working on small farms at harvest time. As it stands, it is said to be risky to hire illegal aliens because they could be rounded up at a moment's notice by the sheriff, thus leaving the farmer without help at a critical time.

The subsidized farmer-investor, in contrast, seems to have less difficulty acquiring responsible laborers because he can afford to offer full-time work and to pay more. In one case, where 250 acres of orchard land was sold to a big-city investor, the new owner could afford to replace the farmer and one laborer (who together ran the whole operation) with a manager and five laborers.

A final contributing factor to the labor problems of the small farm operator is that as farms have grown larger the number of farmers available for the exchange of labor has decreased greatly and correspondingly increased the need for hired labor. In this respect, the cooperative aspects of farming and the harvest feasts in which neighbors and workers participated are a phenomena of the past. Although the small farm operator still resists, he is forced to cope with the reality of a largely industrialized farm-labor force.

Despite the fact that small farm operators are critical of farm laborers and are generally against unionization of farm labor, the two groups are both adversely affected by the growth and mechanization of large farms. Laborers have been displaced in large numbers by machines and have been forced to deal with the monopoly power of large farms in negotiating contracts. If small farms were more numerous, financially above water, and in a more competitive position, operators could not only offer more satisfactory wages to laborers but also increase the quality of labor available to themselves. Even as things stand, some small farm operators are known to pay higher wages.

Survival Through Economic Imagination

Cost-cutting activities and working toward self-sufficiency are a necessary means of survival. Two-fifths of the active farmers among our respondents exchanged equipment rather than purchase it or pay for custom work. Three-fifths of the active farmers obtained at least some farm labor from another member of the family. Wives helped in 38 percent of the cases, sons in 45 percent of the cases, and daughters in 18 percent of the cases. Two-thirds of the families produced goods directly for household consumption. The major activities involved in producing goods for the home were canning, freezing, and gardening; raising livestock for meat; sewing clothes; and repairing houses, appliances, and automobiles. Half of the families engaged in at least three of these activities.

The role played by the farmer's wife in maintaining a viable farm operation was often a critical one. Analysis of open-ended interviews revealed that the activities of these women were indeed important. [15] Seven of the women kept books for the farm operation; eight performed physical labor on the farm; five operated heavy equipment, such as shakers, hullers, and pick-up machines; and one woman participated in planting and caring for all new walnut tree plantings.

Women usually did most of their work at harvest time or at other times when the need for short-term labor arose. Only one woman helped in daily chores, and this was a special case because it involved caring for livestock. Several women indicated that they would take over management of the farm when their husbands did custom work and were away from the farm for a period of time.

Some wives found employment off the farm to supplement the family income. In the sample of 37 farm wives, 35 percent worked off the farm (including six full-time and seven part-time) for an average of $355 per month. Jobs held by these women included a variety of occupations, such as bookkeeper, store clerk, bank teller, nurse, schoolteacher, music teacher, insurance agent, secretary, cook, and domestic servant. Four other women expressed interest in working, and one of these was particularly disappointed because Colusa County had so few job opportunities.

The main occupation of the farm wife is at least in part related to the occupational status of the farm operator. We found that the wife of an operator whose main occupation was *not* farming was three times as likely to work off the farm as the wife of a "pure farmer." This pattern is clearly related to the crucial role played by many wives in helping the family farm survive. Her unpaid labor on the farm is more important than the potential income from off-farm employment.

Several other women contributed to family income without leaving the household to work. One woman earned $20 per month by sewing clothes, while another did artwork on T-shirts. A third woman wrote articles for a local newspaper, earning about $60 per month. Two women who did not work also accounted for outside income, one receiving a retirement pension as a former teacher for $275 per month. The women with sources of outside income account for almost half of the women in the sample.

Marketing Cooperatives and Corporate Control

Corporate control in agriculture seriously erodes the viability of the small farm. The extent of this control, however, is often well concealed and should be exposed to full public view. Both illegal corporate ownership of land originating from the early history of California and the present-day complicity of marketing cooperatives are contributing factors to massive corporate power.

In 1969 only 5.0 percent of the farms in Colusa County and 3.6 percent of the farms in the state were owned by corporations of any kind, including family-owned corporations *(1969 Census of Agriculture)*. In 1974 these percentages increased to 5.6 percent and 5.3 percent, respectively *(Preliminary 1974 Census of Agriculture)*. Although the number of corporate farms is not alarming, the amount of land they control is staggering. A survey conducted in 1969 by the Agricultural Extension Service of the University of California, in cooperation with the Economic Research Service of the U.S. Department of Agriculture, revealed that 45 corporate farms, representing less than one-tenth of one percent of the commercial farms in the state controlled 3.7 million acres, which is nearly *half the farmland* in the state (Fellmeth, 1973:12–13). A Ralph Nader task force also found in their own survey that the top 20 landowners in rural California counties controlled between 25 and 50 percent of the private land (Fellmeth, p. 21).[16] Moreover, the owners of large portions of private land sit on interlocking boards of directors of powerful corporations. Safeway's board of directors, for example, includes men who own approximately one million acres of California's richest agricultural land (Fellmeth, p. 19). A special report prepared for the State of California indicates that 5 percent of California's farms, with annual sales of $500,000 or more, control 61 percent of all sales of agricultural commodities, and that 10 percent of the farms, with 1,000 acres or more, control 57 percent of the state's irrigated land *(The Family Farm in California*, 1977:7–8).

U.S. Census of Agriculture statistics for 1969 indicate that corporations *farm* only 38,235 acres, or 7.8 percent, of the farmland in Colusa County and 5,128,655 acres, or 14.4 percent, of the farmland in the state. The lack of consistency between these figures on farming and those reported above on ownership and control is difficult to explain. It is likely that corporations lease a large share of their land to other farmers, which would explain why corporate ownership is not accurately reflected in the census data. The Southern Pacific Company, for example, is known to lease 3,000- to 5,000-acre parcels to ranchers in northern California (Fellmeth, 1973:12, and Perelman, 1976:71). At the same time, they are opening up large tracts for development and selling land to speculators, which would explain the loss of farmland even to large farms in recent years. This circumstance is consistent with our earlier observation that the owners of large farms are not interested in producing crops, but rather in using their holdings for tax or speculative advantages in the pursuit of profit.

Moreover, evidence exists to suggest that USDA figures in the Census of Agriculture are wrong. A count made by Richard Rodenfield in Wisconsin found that the census missed 252 farm corporations in that state while underestimating the amount of land owned by corporations by 37 percent and the number of acres rented by 269 percent (Hightower, 1975:190).

Even disregarding landownership and operation of farms, it is evident that corporations control markets and have usurped great power from the independent farmer. Tenneco, a corporate giant that entered agricultural production as late as 1967, has already sold much of its lands in order to concentrate on obtaining greater profits from the control of marketing and distribution (Perelman, 1977:87–88). Senator Gaylord Nelson has characterized the situation as follows: "There is evidence that much of this country's corporation farming is a nearly invisible type operation aimed at control of farm commodities at the producer level and bypassing of traditional markets rather than direct operations of farms or ranches" (Fujimoto and Zone, 1976:4).

In the past, marketing was not of excessive concern to the small farm operators. Buyers appeared on the scene to look over the crop before it was harvested, and they paid cash on the spot. Today, farmers must first harvest their crops, haul them to the buyer, and wait for the price to be determined without receiving immediate payment. However, in the contemporary situation—monopolistic control of markets for agricultural commodities—it is common for wholesale buyers, transportation companies, processors, and retailers to be vertically integrated, so that all steps in the distribution of food to the consumer are under control of one organization. The link to the farmer often is established through a contract that obligates the farmer in advance to sell his crop to a particular outlet. Under such an arrangement, the farmer loses his prerogative to sell on the open market and becomes a mere vassal of the conglomerate. An investor with income high enough to benefit from tax write-offs can farm at a loss and accept a contract without looking for the best price. One who farms for a living often cannot afford a contract.

Another option for the farmer is to join a marketing cooperative, which will sometimes engage in preliminary processing activities and has the authority to hold the crops of its members until the best price can be obtained. Prices obtained throughout the year are averaged so that the per-unit payments to each member are the same. Payments are made in two to five installments. The last installment is sometimes not paid until after production expenses are due for the following year. Votes are commonly allocated among members according to the volume of business they give to the cooperative. Since the policy of the cooperative is influenced by the voting strength of large farm operators, prices received for crops are often lower than small farm operators can afford.

Even large farm operators may have little direct control over cooperative policy, because the organization is run by a group of professional managers. Managers are not hired and fired, and their salaries are not at the mercy of the same market fluctuations that affect farmers. The cooperative is therefore run independently to serve its own interests and those of its managers. Hence, marketing cooperatives, which in principle are supposed to work for the benefit of all farmers, in practice serve the interests of vertically integrated corporations by allowing them to obtain the farmer's product at a lower price.

Cooperatives often control large portions of the statewide market, and managers often wield an inordinant amount of power over cooperative policy across the state through overlapping membership on the governing boards of local cooperatives. In some cases, cooperatives have even formed partnerships with corporations (Kravitz, 1974:63).

Many small farm operators refuse to join marketing cooperatives or have dropped membership in order to avoid being manipulated by professional managers over whom they have no control. Only 36 percent of the respondents in this study were found to be members of a marketing cooperative.[17] A grievance frequently expressed by respondents was that cooperatives paid for only part of the crop when it was sold. Payment schedules extending throughout the year in three to five installments made it difficult for respondents to cover production costs for the following year without either borrowing from a bank or from the cooperative itself. The cooperative, although holding the farmer's money without paying him interest, is willing to lend money back to the farmer only if the farmer pays interest to the cooperative. A respondent who quit the cooperative put it this way: "I got fed up with having to pay interest to get my money back sooner than the payment schedule allowed. I didn't like paying double interest."

A further focus of complaint by respondents concerned the degree of control exercised by cooperatives and processors over the prices received by the small farm operator. Even if the farmer avoids the cooperative and signs a contract directly with a processor, he is still likely to get his money a "little bit at a time," and the price he receives is not likely to be any better than the price he could get from the cooperative. The cooperative can set its own price because in large measure it exercises monopoly control of the market. Respondents estimate, for example, that the California Almond Exchange controls 70 to 75 percent of the growers in the state. Other buyers were reported to have minimal influence, in that they wait to announce their price until the Almond Exchange has set its price!

The control exercised by the cooperative also extends to its own membership. Membership meetings were said by respondents to be held for advertising products, such as new pesticides, and were not meant for serious discussion. The circumstances of the small farm operator and his particular grievances appear not to be taken into account even when serious discussion does occur. The Almond Exchange, for example, was reported to hold most of its meetings in Sacramento, a convenient site for an absentee owner, but not for a small farm operator who lives on his land. One respondent commented that a small farm operator once stood up in a meeting to express his opinion, and before he had a chance to speak, he was told to "shut up and sit down." Lack of responsibility is further illustrated by two cooperatives that reportedly owe $7,000 and $10,000 each to two respondents who were former members. One of these former members indicated that he might be forced to go to court to get his money.

A final complaint leveled against cooperatives was that the farmer does not receive any benefits in the long run from the financial success of the cooperative. Sunsweet, a cooperative for marketing prunes, was accused by one respondent of being "unfair" because farmers could not sell their shares at increased value. This respondent bought in at $28 per share and was not allowed to resell his shares at the current value of $80 per share. Rather, he was required to sell his shares back to the cooperative at the original price, while "the association kept the difference." Another respondent registered a similar complaint about the Almond Exchange: "The Almond Exchange is run like the mafia. If you join the cooperative your orchard belongs to them for five years. They say after five years they start giving you your money [entrance fee] back. But there is no interest on your money."

Given the power and managerial practices of cooperatives and the lack of control exercised by cooperative membership, it is no wonder that many small farm operators remain independent and sign contracts only after their crops are harvested. The price extracted by the cooperative in exchange for guaranteeing a market outlet is too high. One respondent summed it up by stating, "I couldn't continue to operate unless I was independent."

Small farm operators who remain independent must either take pains to find and cultivate rare marketing outlets through personal contacts or take time to travel around the region keeping up with the "coffee crowd," which provides the latest market information. One respondent reported that such tactics were necessary because prices on the open market often change greatly in the period of just a few days.

Superficially, it would appear that consumers might benefit from a well-integrated marketing system by obtaining lower prices for food. Despite tax advantages given to wealthy farmers, however, vertical integration and control of the market mean that corporations acting as processors and middlemen are in a position to take a large profit, leaving prices even higher for the consumer. The profits of major food chains, for example, increased dramatically during 1974 at the same time the price of food was undergoing rapid increase (Zwerdling, 1976:43). Perhaps this circumstance explains why 75 percent of the rise in food prices in recent years is because of nonfarm costs (Green, 1976:57). The consumer loses on still another account because his or her taxes assist indirectly in subsidizing the lower prices paid by corporations at the wholesale level. Overall, it is difficult to find the competitive markets that economists tell us still characterize the production and sale of agricultural products.

Finally, many small farm operators say that financing is their biggest problem. Three respondents reported that they were able to secure financing only because they had a friend at the bank, and one was unable to get a loan after a friend left his position at the bank. Another obtained initial financing for his farm operation by bringing in a large-scale farmer as a co-signer. Sources of financing used by other respondents included the Production Credit Association, the Bank of America, Crocker Citizens Bank, and the Farmers Home Administration, which is federally funded and serves as a source of last resort only after financing has been denied by at least two other credit institutions. The PCA is owned by shareholders, most of whom are wealthy farmers, and it is run by a professional staff. The head of the PCA local board of directors at the time of this study operated one of the largest farms in the county and was known to employ more than 100 hired workers in the peak season. Preferred credit risks are, of course, large farm operators. The credit system works to the lesser advantage of small farm operators because interest payments on production loans are tax deductible.

Perhaps the most bitter complaint of respondents against farm credit institutions was that they serve the interest of the large farm operator, at the expense of the small farm operator. One respondent reported that he was turned down for a loan at the PCA in 1969 because it was a bad year and large farm operators were given all the loans to bail them out of financial trouble. This respondent was advised to give up his own farm and find a job as a farm manager for a larger farm where the PCA had its money invested. He indicated that the PCA was worried about several large farm operators whose alcholism led to mismanagement. A second respondent, whose farm operation was in the red, needed capital to run a more successful operation, but he was turned down by the bank and advised to sell to someone who did have the capital. A third respondent was told that he could not get a loan at the bank unless his deed of trust for the purchase of land was paid off. This individual reasoned that if he had the money to pay off his debt, he could use it to cover production costs and therefore would not need a loan. He concluded by saying, "its Catch 22. If you don't need the money you can borrow, but if you need it you aren't eligible." A large farm operator who was a board member of the PCA confirmed that credit was not given to those who needed it the most; otherwise, he contended the PCA would not have a perfect success rate over a period of several years in avoiding defaults because of farm failures. He pointed out that the Bank of America was even more conservative in its loan policy than the PCA.

Another criticism of credit institutions concerns high interest rates, which the small farm operator cannot afford because the write-off on income taxes does not give him the same advantage as the large farm operator. Interest rates that were usually set between 6 and 7 percent in 1965 went up to 12 and 15 percent in 1974.

Production loans to unprofitable farm operations are sometimes extended on the basis of appreciating land values alone rather than on the basis of profits. This procedure allows some poor farmers to sacrifice their financial position from year to year in order to maintain their commitment for farming. Eventually, yearly losses take their toll and force poor farmers to sell out to cover their debts. Meanwhile, creditors are careful not to allow debts to rise above the value of the farmer's property.

Concern about the security of loans has caused credit administrators to dictate management practices to the small farm operator. The terms to which the small-scale farmer might have to agree were reported to include specifications for the use of fertilizers and pesticides; a requirement that some recreational property or farmland must be sold to pay past debts; the adoption of a fixed budget for the farm operation; and a limit placed on the amount of money used for household consumption. The farmer might also have his operation checked periodically to insure that he follows directions. Such procedures, of course, rob the farmer of his independence and make him little more than a farm foreman for the bank.

Although the FHA gives loans to farmers who cannot get financing from other sources, the agency was found unsatisfactory by respondents, because its household allowance was considered too low (for one farmer the difference was between $250 from FHA and $500 from Bank of America) and its staff was said to be incompetent.

FHA is a joke. They'll tell you one thing one day and another the next day. They don't know much about farming.

Farmers who have been forced out of farming would be the best people to work at FHA. Most FHA people don't know a cow from an elephant.

Difficulties in obtaining loans and the control over management by the credit institution make it either necessary or desirable for the small farm operator to get along without taking loans. Only 35 percent of the active farmers in this study took production loans in 1973. Many of these respondents expressed a desire to avoid interference from credit institutions.

Social Stratification Down on the Farm

Small-scale farmers in Colusa County lament the fact that there are fewer landowners and farmers than in the past. Young people in particular have fled the area because of the lack of opportunity to enter farming. At the same time, newcomers have replaced some of the older families who have moved away. Old social networks that facilitated cooperation among neighbors have broken down and have been replaced by a system of stratification dividing the operators of large and small farms. Large farm operators were said to run the affairs of the community through participation in various organizations in which small farm operators were not welcome or to which they could not afford to belong. As one respondent commented: "When farmers get rich, then they aren't neighborly anymore. People don't visit, say hello in town, help each other with canning or let you pick a little fruit like they used to. There is no community spirit around these days. To socialize with people you have to belong to the right churches or clubs."

Regardless of whether they were old-timers or newcomers, respondents felt left out and usually did not join organizations or attend club meetings. The exception to this rule was that some belonged to fundamentalist or unconventional churches. But standard denomination churches that wealthy farmers attended were regarded with suspicion as just another institution through which the large farm operator could place a financial burden on the small farm operator. One respondent, for example, was asked to contribute money for a new church building, although he was only a nominal church member. He refused because, he said, "When I build a building on my farm no one is going to help me, so why should I help a church."

From their position of relative isolation and powerlessness, small farm operators look with skepticism on the "success" of large farm operators, who were criticized by respondents for idling away time in a pool hall every morning, drinking too much, and for not working hard enough. The success of the large farm operator was not attributed to his efforts; rather it was viewed as having happened because of his privileged status and *despite* his lack of effort. In contrast, the respondents regarded austerity and hard work as the key to their own well-being. One respondent told of a farm couple who went bankrupt because they kept two houses, hired domestic help, and generally "tried to live too fancy." Another respondent expressed a typically strong work ethic and a determination not to give up when he said, "Someday it will come down to survival of the fittest. People like me who know about hard work will be the few that survive."

A Futile Struggle

In the 19th century California farms were large and were run by enterprising capitalists. Incredibly grotesque machines were developed to assist those farmers, particularly in the production of wheat on vast plots of land. Their success, however, was relatively fragile and short lived. The inputs of production in those days were justified only by direct returns from crop sales. When the world market faltered and social opposition arose to the use of cheap foreign labor, large farms went under and subdivided because they could no longer exploit others for profit. Farms gradually grew smaller as irrigation made it possible to farm a variety of different crops on small plots of land.

After World War II an abundance of cheap (and often illegal) Mexican labor and, later, development of sophisticated but perhaps still grotesque machines, again made larger farms economically viable. The present system of agricultural production, although ecologically fragile and socially undesirable, is different from the system 100 years ago in the sense that it is shored up by artificial supports. This system will continue regardless of its real efficiency because corporations and wealthy investors can farm at a loss and still make profits. Losses are more than made up by taking increased profits from food processing and marketing, or even from business enterprises unrelated to food production.

Farms can no longer be viewed as separate economic units that depend on the work ethic and farming knowledge of the farmer for their success or failure. There is, instead, a vast series of external relationships to other firms and institutions that primarily determines the farmer's fate. Such relationships may include leasing land for a share of the crop, joint use of machinery and equipment, securing financing from a bank or other credit institution, membership in a marketing cooperative, prior contract agreements with buyers, acquiring inputs to production from suppliers, having outside income from another job, having other financial assets, running another business or several businesses, and having access to tax lawyers or other financial experts. Knowing how to farm and working hard at farming are simply less important than knowing how or possessing the resources to properly manage these critical external relationships. Under these circumstances it is inevitable that the successful farmer has become the businessman that Earl Butz predicted he would be two decades ago.

The income-tax system and the marketing system in particular have served to increase economic distance between the small farm operator and the large farm operator. As a result, small farm operators have become socially isolated and resentful of the success and power of large farm operators. The problems of the small farm in fact are related to institutional privileges accorded the large farm. In a way, small farm operators are analogous to workers embroiled in a class struggle against wealthy farmer-investors and the managers of credit institutions and markets. Those against whom the small farm operator struggles control the income that flows, or does not flow, to him for efforts that are never adequately rewarded. They have also usurped many of the decision-making functions of farm and household management that originally belonged to the farmer and his family. In some instances, small farm operators, although nominally independent, have been reduced to the status of hired hands. In other instances, they have sacrificed their financial position in an attempt to preserve a way of life in farming. They barely survive by severe cost cutting, by selling portions of their land, and by avoiding entanglements with banks and cooperatives. Such farmers live by the work ethic, and most fail to understand fully the nature of their struggle and to what extent the odds are stacked against them. After all, they are not big businessmen and have no way of knowing about the intricacies of corporate control and the tax system that oppress them. The realists among them sell out, but they seem to have only somewhat more understanding that they are inevitable losers.

Ironically, indirect programs designed to help the small farm operator will likely only help wealthy investors in farming—at the expense of the small farm operator. The regressive nature of tax write-offs ensures that whatever new inputs of production are developed to make farming more efficient will cost less to the wealthy farmer than to the poor farmer. Direct government subsidies would be more helpful to small farm operators, but such programs are not needed by wealthy farmers and therefore gain little support among politicians who depend on the farm lobby (corporations and wealthy investors) for campaign support. In fact, whatever direct subsidies exist are likely to be phased out because they are highly visible to the taxpayer and can be handily attacked in the name of fiscal responsibility.

The Rural Environmental Assistance Program, in effect since 1936 to promote water and soil conservation practices, provides a good example. Two hundred farmers in Colusa County were affected when this program was eliminated by Earl Butz in 1972 (*Colusa Sun*, 21 January 1973). The installation of equipment to prevent animal wastes from running into drainage ditches could no longer be subsidized by this program. Farmers were then forced to cover the costs themselves to meet the specifications of a state law. The rationale for the cutback was that the subsidy was no longer needed and that the federal budget deficit had to be cut.

Eliminating incentives for ecologically or socially desirable kinds of farm improvements and letting the so-called free enterprise system operate freely serves primarily to allow profit seekers to act irresponsibly toward the public. The consequences are far-reaching. Small increments in productivity and purported savings to the consumer are used to justify large expenditures on machinery, the purchase of which is subsidized by taxpayers, even though these expenditures would not bring commensurate returns without tax subsidies. If the use of scarce fuel or potentially dangerous chemicals leads to increased profits in the short run, it occurs without thought to the long-term shortage of a needed resource or damage done to the soil. Since it is more profitable to concentrate on one crop and compensate for intercropping and proper soil management with intensive use of fertilizers, strip mining of phosphates (such as is conducted by a number of major corporations in central Florida) proceeds out of control and causes permanent damage to land and water supplies. The dilemma posed for us by the corporations is to continue to destroy the environment or lose our inexpensive food supply. This, of course, is a false dilemma because it is predicated on the existence of the present system of capital-intensive agriculture.

We must revise the notion, often expressed by agricultural scientists and businessmen, that the present system of food production supplies the public with relatively inexpensive food when compared to the rest of the world. The trend in which farming has become a business instead of a way of life has lead to taxpayers heavily subsidizing production costs. In addition, experimentation with machine development and the use of chemicals and fertilizers is directly subsidized by large amounts of tax money that support agricultural experiment stations in land-grant universities in every state in the country. The seemingly futile struggle of the small farm operator, thought perhaps by some to be unimportant, is prophetic in a larger political context because it tells us something about outselves. Our way of life, our environment, and our material well-being are beyond our control. Most important decisions on these matters are made in corporate boardrooms and concentrated in the hands of a few people whose overriding concern is to make profits regardless of the consequences.

Notes

1. "California Living Magazine," *San Francisco Sunday Examiner and Chronicle*, 20 March 1977.

2. Efficiency is commonly measured by agricultural economists only in economic terms, i.e., costs and returns. Efficiency should also be measured in terms of energy expended per unit of energy produced. On this basis, it has been found that U.S. agriculture is extremely inefficient. For example, it takes six calories of energy in fuel to produce one calorie of food energy, whereas traditional wet-rice agriculture in China uses one unit of energy in fuel and in human labor to produce a harvest of 50 calories (Perelman, 1977:12).

3. Statement of Hon. Orville L. Freeman, Secretary of Agriculture, U.S. Department of Agriculture, *The Family Farm*. Hearings before the Subcommittee on Family Farms of the Committee on Agriculture, House of Representatives, Eighty-eighth Congress, First Session, 3–5 June, and 10–11 July 1963, pp. 139, 142. Quoted in Breimeyer (1965:302).

4. Quoted in McGowan (vol. 1, 1961:339).

5. The Colusa County Chamber of Commerce, perhaps anxious to convey the impression of growth and prosperity, reported an increase in population between 1960 and 1970 from 12,075 to 12,431 (Colusa County Profile, Economic Resources Survey, prepared by Colusa County Chamber of Commerce, March, 1977). The latter figure appears to be based on projections beyond 1970.

6. This estimate of employed persons covers the period July 1973–July 1974.

7. Similar observations about the decrease in family workers are made by Sosnick (1973: 4.3–1).

8. No data on primary occupation are available in census taken before 1974.

9. Difficulties in sampling are described as follows by those who participated in fieldwork:

We encountered a methodological difficulty in isolating criteria that differentiated small from large family farms. From reviewing the literature on economies of scale in agriculture and discussing the problem with specialists dealing with factors of production, we initially decided to look at the number of acres farmed, gross income and/or number of full-time employees. However, we encountered problems in attaining the needed information prior to interviewing the farm families. The tax records of the county government only record the farmers who own land and not those who lease. Gross income could have been used to identify small family farms. However, we did not have access to this information until after several visits to each of the families and even then the accuracy of the farmers' financial records was sometimes open to question. Our inability to identify small farms made drawing a representative sample impossible. At last resort we located the families to be interviewed by talking to the farm advisor [county agent], representatives of governmental agencies and other farmers. Thus, it is not known if the sample we drew was representative of the small family farm population. (Moles, Blomberg, Love, and Thompson, 1975:5)

10. Farm income was calculated as the difference between production costs and income from the sale of crops and livestock. Production costs include payments for purchased and leased land, property taxes, equipment, labor, irrigation, custom work, fertilizer, pesticides, fuel, electricity, and interest on loans.

11. Several other respondents report doing custom work, but they earned less than $2,000 in 1973.

12. Income from custom work and income earned by spouses is not included in this calculation of outside income.

13. Of 38 owners with inherited land, 29 have purchased no part of their land.

14. For most of Colusa County there are no restrictions such as zoning for exclusive agricultural use. Only 22 percent of the owners indicated any restrictions placed on the use of their land.

15. Content analysis of open-ended interviews with these farm wives was done by Judith Thompson, Department of Anthropology, University of California, Davis. The information presented here is contained in her unpublished paper, "The Contribution of Women to Small Farm Operations." Information obtained from open-ended interviews does not lend itself to rigorous analysis, since some topics may not have been systematically covered in the interviews.

16. The Nader task force found information about land ownership difficult to obtain because many county controllers' offices and corporate land owners remained secretive about this information. It is also difficult, if not impossible, to trace the nexus of subsidiaries through which a corporation disguises its holdings.

17. Information on the particular cooperatives dealing with Colusa County farmers was obtained only from farmers. No attempt was made to interview cooperative managers; it was politically perilous and may have threatened the continuation of this study.

APPENDIX: A *Spring Flooding*

A special problem concerning the operation of the Shasta Dam confronts several small farm operators whose land is on the east side of the Sacramento River bypass weir. Excess water is stored in the Shasta reservoir during the winter months to ensure that enough water will be available in the summer for irrigation and recreational use. Late season rains often cause an overflow, which is released from the dam in the spring months and results in the flooding to farmland. Both rice farmers and orchard farmers among our respondents reported that crops are severely damaged by such spring flooding. One rice farmer who was forced into a late planting by wet grounds reported a 20-percent drop in crop yield. Orchard farmers reported up to a 50-percent drop in crop yield and the total loss of many young trees. They contended that they would be better off without the dam because winter floods, which occur when the sap is not flowing, are harmless. Spring flooding, however, was said to cause "drowning" and "root rot." Two respondents reported that their homes as well as their trees were threatened by the flood waters. In one case, the respondent was forced to take his dogs across the flooded area in a boat in order to take them for a walk, and in another case the respondent was forced to open his first-floor doors and move all his furniture upstairs. In some cases, the extra hardship caused by the flooding has resulted in farmers selling out. One farmer, for example, tried using a better grade of fertilizer and whitewashed the trunks of his trees to reflect more sun. His effort was to no avail. He said that he was "tired of pumping money into the place without any return," and he sold out.

All farmers affected by the flooding complained bitterly, but they were unable to do anything about it. A drive to get the state legislature to deal with the problem apparently failed, and a lawsuit by one farmer against the state to compensate for flood damage was lost. Given the need in northern California to store water for urban and recreational use against the possibility of drought, it is unlikely that the grievances of flooded-out farmers will be addressed by those in positions of authority.

6 Closing the Frontier: "I Miss Not Being My Own Boss"

A Smalltown Drama

It is unquestionably a part of the American character to want to be materially self-sufficient and spiritually independent. Pioneers who came to the West during the 19th century exemplified in actual practice what has now become a cultural ideal that few persons can attain. As pointed out by Braverman (1974), the heyday of the farmer or craftsman who possessed a wide range of related skills and set up his own business to sell his own product or services is long past. With the rapid development of assembly-line techniques of production came extreme specialization of tasks for American workers. Goods produced en masse became cheaper than those produced by craftsmen. Inevitably, small and less efficient producers, made obsolete by modern factories, have disappeared from the scene, gradually effecting a profound change in the quality of American life. Most workers are now employed by large organizations. They have little control over their individual destinies and have little hope of ever accumulating the capital or gaining an opportunity to establish an independent business. Even managers of branch offices and chain stores are constrained by executives in higher positions of authority to follow company policy. Hobbies that involve "doing your own thing" are popular, perhaps as compensatory devices; but they are at best diversions rather than adequate substitutes for meaningful work experience.

However, anachronistic pockets of small-time entrepreneurs do exist as a stubborn exception to these historical developments. Business opportunity still can be bought for very little cost in semi-ghost towns of the rural West, which for all sound economic reasons should have disappeared long ago. Ironically, it is the very lack of vitality and doubtful future prosperity of such towns that may produce enticing opportunities for the common man seeking to be his own boss. A steady decrease in customers in a town, for example, reduces business income and in turn lowers the market value of the town's businesses. In order to stay in business an owner may be forced to cut back on repairs and improvements, a strategy that contributes to the appearance of a deteriorating community and lowers the value of surrounding businesses. The existence of many unused and delapidated buildings also reduces the cost of renting or buying business space to an affordable level for almost anyone. All too often, however, those who purchase and attempt to maintain a small-town business are doomed to failure. This fate is dictated by the trend toward large, industrialized farms in the surrounding countryside, as discussed in the

180

previous chapter, and inevitable population decline, the effects of which also have been examined by Goldschmidt (1947) in the context of another setting.

The illusion that opportunity still exists allows the last segment of the drama of the American frontier to be played out in small, dying towns. The frontier ethic, emphasizing hard work and individual initiative, persists in these towns despite prevailing circumstances that contradict the utility of the ethic and prevent would-be entrepreneurs from controlling their own destiny. Those who participate in the drama are sometimes descendents of the pioneer era seeking to preserve their heritage, sometimes hobbyist-craftspeople seeking to combine a set of skills with a livelihood as was possible in the past, and sometimes idealists searching for a secure community and a less complicated way of life. More instructively, the participants are sometimes escapees from the world of blue-collar work—the miners, mill workers, loggers, and field laborers described in earlier chapters, who yearn to elude the tyranny of bosses and the meaninglessness of their work by becoming their own boss. It is especially in this sense that the story of the small-time entrepreneur represents the closing of the last frontier. Against the expressed dreams of the common worker—to have autonomy, dignity, and freedom—stands the reality of places like Lincoln County, Washington, and the unavoidable demise of the craftsperson/entrepreneur as a viable entity in American economic life.

Like the workers and small farm operators discussed in previous chapters, shopkeepers in the small towns of Lincoln County in eastern Washington are faced with impending obsolescence. Many also come from basically the same social class as small farm operators and blue-collar workers. In fact, a number of them have farm backgrounds and have done or are now doing blue-collar work. It is not uncommon for them to have incomes at or below the poverty level and to suffer both materially and psychologically from this hardship. The unexpressed realization that they cannot avoid failure undermines their sense of control and erodes self-esteem. The strength with which they hold to the frontier ethic means that defeat is neither easy to accept nor possible to understand. This chapter is about their problems of survival in an age of advanced capitalism that has gradually passed them by.

"Wild Goose Bill": A Frontier Legend

The first entrepreneur and settler in Lincoln County was Samuel Wilbur Condin, otherwise known as "Wild Goose Bill." Condin claimed to have come to the area in 1859, traveling from his native New Jersey by way of Illinois and California. Before early settlers began coming to eastern Washington, Condin owned and operated a cayuse pack train and was engaged in transporting supplies between Walla Walla and other supply depots serving miners, prospectors, and surveyors who were charting a route for the Northern Pacific Railroad.

About 1875 Condin staked off a claim on a site where the town of Wilbur now stands. He built a cabin, disposed of his pack train, and invested all of his available money in horses and cattle. This ranch was marked on early maps used by explorers as "Wild Goose Bill's Place."

Condin was married at different times to two Indian women. According to observers at the time, he had several children, one of whom was crippled and became the object of his special attention and love. Condin also had a reputation as an intrepid Indian fighter, especially when he found Indians interfering in his domestic affairs. After inducing his second Indian wife to leave, Condin took a white mistress, who proved to be his undoing. This woman lived with him only a short time before she tired of it and left to bestow her favors on another rancher. Condin's jealousy motivated him to try to get her back, and he died of bullet wounds during the attempt in January 1895.

Condin received his nickname when he was a young man from an episode that occurred on a hunting expedition. The story is that he spotted a flock of geese on a pond and shot them all assuming that they were wild. Shortly afterward he discovered that the flock was tame and belonged to a woman who lived nearby. Thereafter, Condin was known as the man who mistook a flock of tame birds for a flock of wild ones—"Wild Goose Bill."

Today, "Wild Goose Bill" is celebrated as a symbol of Lincoln County's frontier heritage and the ethic of rugged individualism thought to characterize the past. For example, the present town of Wilbur, which bears Condin's middle name, recently abandoned a failing harvest festival and began holding an annual frontier celebration called "Wild Goose Bill Days." A small restaurant in the town has also been renamed the "Wild Goose Bill Cafe."

A Boom Town in Eastern Washington

The first business establishment to open in Lincoln County was a saloon built in June 1880 to accommodate workers who were grading the railroad that would eventually run through the town of Sprague. In observance of a rule established by the Northern Pacific Company, the saloon was built one mile north of the present town of Sprague, at a place called "Whiskey Rock." During the same month the railroad company also built a commissary store on the future site of the town itself. In May 1881 railroad tracks were laid into town, thus turning Sprague into a boom town. Already there were eight businesses of various kinds other than the railroad that had opened in the space of one year.

A number of settlers in the area were raising sheep, and the railroad was used heavily for shipping livestock. To accommodate the demand the railroad company erected a depot and then selected Sprague as the location for railway shops for its Idaho division. Approximately 350 men were employed to build the shops, roundhouses and other buildings to house company enterprises. Company officials residing in the town also built elegant houses, which contributed to the look of emerging prosperity.

The behavior of the railroad officials in building their homes was the only questionable aspect of Sprague's early development. Many officials were placed on trial and charged with appropriating company materials and using company labor to build their homes. It was claimed that from ten to fifteen houses had been built this way; yet no one was convicted.

In 1882 the railroad shops were opened, Sprague was granted a post office, the first newspaper was established, and a volunteer fire department was organized. The town of Sprague was incorporated by the Territory of Washington in November 1883. Befitting its origin as a railroad town, Sprague was named after General John W. Sprague, who was, from 1879 to 1883, the official in charge of the Northern Pacific Company's interests on the West Coast. At the time of incorporation the town contained about 500 people.

Lincoln County was created from a division of Spokane County approximately at the same time Sprague was incorporated, in November 1883. Although Davenport was designated as the temporary county seat, an election was held a year later to determine its permanent location. Three towns, Davenport, Harrington, and Sprague, contested with each other in the general election of 1884. Sprague won handily over its nearest rival, Davenport, by a margin of more than 400 votes. Immediately following the election, charges of voting fraud became widespread, for there were 1,023 votes cast from Sprague, which had a population of no more than 600 or 700 at that time. Several arrests were made, but no convictions resulted; and the election results were allowed to stand. The citizens of Davenport, however, were convinced that the election had been fraudulent and refused to turn over county records to Sprague. For three weeks the town of Davenport was an armed garrison while its people waited for a court injunction to prevent the seizure of county records. Eventually the defenders returned to their homes and offered no resistance when 60 to 100 armed men from Sprague arrived to claim the records.

Sprague continued to grow during the next several years, reaching a full measure of prosperity in 1890. The population at that time was 1,689, and the town had graded streets, brick business blocks, a large public school, a courthouse, a Catholic school, a railroad headquarters building, many railroad shops, a brewery, an electric light plant, a system of water works, a dairy, a brick city hall and opera house, and a Masonic temple. A boom in real-estate speculation was set off by rumors about the building of a new railroad, about $250,000 worth of planned improvements to the Northern Pacific Company shops, and about the construction of a smelter, which would employ as many as 2,000 men. Great optimism about the future of the town was expressed in the 3 April 1890 edition of the *Sprague Herald*.

Sprague is the scene of a very busy season. Building operations are developing rapidly and as soon as each structure is finished it is at once occupied. Calls are continually being made for workmen. Not enough laborers can be had to carry on the work necessary to the rapid growth of the city. Sprague in the infancy of its growth resembles Spokane during its miraculous advancement of a couple of years ago. This week two real estate offices have been established and the transfers number over one hundred. With all its advantages Sprague is destined to become one of the foremost cities in Washington. At any rate the confidence of those who have been purchasing real estate must be very great or they would not invest so heavily. (*History of Lincoln County*, 1904:80)

As it turned out the rumors about the new business activity proved to be false and the real-estate boom was short-lived. Sprague's prosperity, however, continued for another four years. The *Sprague Herald* of 25 April 1894 reported that a sound business climate existed in the community.

Bradstreet's Commercial Agency gives Sprague the best rating of any city in the state. In effect, it says, it is the soundest and safest city in which to do business in the State of Washington. There has never been a business failure of any significance in the city. (*History of Lincoln County*, 1904:181)

Boom Turns to Bust

The fortunes of Sprague began to wane in July 1894, when the American Railroad Union, under the leadership of Eugene V. Debs, called a strike against the Northern Pacific Company. As the strike was imminent in June 1894, a group of citizens led by Lincoln County farmers met in Sprague to express support for the strikers. This group adopted a resolution condemning the railroad company for mistreatment of workers and offered support to the strikers:

Resolved, That we as a body assembled hereby pledge ourselves to do all in our power to alleviate any condition of suffering or want, and that we are willing to contribute everything within our power that may be needed, for the purpose of the strikers or their families. (*History of Lincoln County*, 1904:102).

The issue of support for the strike came to a head after violent resistance was offered against a train operated by strikebreakers. Striking demonstrators threw rocks at the engineer and "scab" crew causing the train to crash into two idle box cars. Meanwhile, other protestors set fire to two trestles, one of which burned to the ground. As a result of the disturbance martial law was declared, and two companies of U.S. Army soldiers were brought in to repair the trestles and occupy the town.

Shopkeepers in Sprague became uneasy because the violence created an inhospitable business climate both for themselves and for the railroad company. They were also concerned that the resolution adopted by the farmers did not represent their views. On 16 July a meeting of businessmen and other citizens of the town was held to express opposition to the strike and the violence that was a part of it. The businessmen included a statement as a part of the resolution adopted on this occasion:

Resolved, That for the purpose of indicating the attitude of the businessmen in this matter, and in order to preserve law and order and aid the authorities in protecting the employees and property of the Northern Pacific, should such aid be necessary, we organize ourselves into a law and order league, the members thereof to be sworn in as deputy sheriffs. (*History of Lincoln County*, 1904:103)

Shortly after the strike ended, the fears of the Sprague shopkeepers came true, for the Northern Pacific Company announced its intention to move its division headquarters and eventually its shops to the larger city of Spokane. The *Lincoln County Times* on 27 July 1894 carried an article blaming the strike for the company's decision to move.

The division headquarters of the Northern Pacific have been moved from Sprague to Spokane, and Superintendent Gilbert is quoted as saying that the shops would in all probability be moved also. This would prove a severe blow to Sprague and a loss to the entire county. The taxes derived from the location of the shops in the county is by no means inconsiderable and their removal would be unfortunate. This action of the railroad company has been hastened, if not entirely precipitated by the apparent sympathy for, and the support given to the strikers, in most they have done, by the citizens and businessmen of Sprague. If the public meetings recently held there denouncing unlawful acts and pledging support to the laws had taken place at the beginning of the trouble as they should, it is not probable that the headquarters or anything else would have been moved. (*History of Lincoln County*, 1904:182)

To what extent the strike motivated the actions of the company is an open question even to this day. Nonetheless, it is clear that the company was unwilling to rehire those who were considered "agitators" in the strike. It is also obvious that the company could exercise greater control over its workers in a city where a larger labor force was present. The loss suffered by the town in business and the loss to the county in tax revenues was unquestionably great, because the Northern Pacific Company possessed twelve times the taxable property of the next largest business in the county.

A second catastrophic event occurred in Sprague a year later and only a few months after "Wild Goose Bill" had died in a gun battle. On 3 August 1895 a huge fire broke out and nearly destroyed the whole business section of the town. At one time more than 200 buildings were burning, and only six business houses were left standing. The losses suffered by the Northern Pacific Company to its headquarters, trains, shops, equipment, and supplies was estimated at more than $700,000. The fire undoubtedly hastened the departure of all railroad operations to Spokane and ruined many businessmen who had no insurance. During the next several years the population of Sprague declined precipitously, reaching a total of 695 in the year 1900.

A final blow to the town of Sprague was struck by the citizens of Davenport, who still wanted to reclaim the county seat for their town. They had tried unsuccessfully to do this in a special election held in 1890. In the general election of 1896, they tried again and obtained an overwhelming victory over the recently devastated and depopulated Sprague. On 11 July 1897 the Sprague courthouse and jail and lots on which those buildings stood were put up for public auction. Facilities that had cost Lincoln County $10,000 twelve years earlier were sold for a mere $300. Hence Sprague was deprived of the chance to fulfill its destiny "to become one of the foremost cities in Washington." If Sprague had not been so affected, the economic picture of Lincoln County today would undoubtedly be quite different.

Some Demographic Effects of Wheat Farming

The earliest settlers in Lincoln County engaged mostly in raising cattle, horses, and sheep. Livestock could be raised with little labor and driven long distances to market on foot. As one early settler reported: "Some of the stockmen here (Lincoln County) drove herds of cattle of 2,500 or 3,000 all the way to Cheyenne, Wyoming (a distance of 1,500 miles), where they were put on cars and shipped to Chicago, Omaha and Kansas City" (Yoder, 1942:184).

The range was not fenced and cattle were allowed to graze anywhere. Round-ups, which took a month or longer, were necessary to separate and brand the cattle. All this changed, however, with the advent of the railroads, which gave wheat farmers transportation access to eastern markets. Many settlers soon flooded the area, giving rise to the growth of a number of small towns serving as railroad depots and supply points. An increase of wheat farming in the area also meant the end of open grazing land for the cattlemen. One early settler made this observation: "All the government and railroad land was soon homesteaded and bought up by the settlers. When they began to farm and put up fences, the cattlemen had to get rid of their herds" (Yoder, 1942:183).[1] By 1900 the wheat yield in Lincoln County was 6,750,000 bushels, almost half as much as the yield in the whole state of Oregon and already more than half the yield of 12,533,711 bushels reported for Lincoln County in 1969 (1969 Census of Agriculture).

Shopkeepers in the county were instrumental in assisting new settlers to get started in farming. Although the price of goods was relatively high, shopkeepers made up for this by carrying credit accounts for up to two years until farming began to pay off. Credit was given on a personal basis without knowledge of past credit reliability. It became common practice for farmers to settle accounts once a year after crops had been harvested and sold.

Between 1900 and 1910 the county prospered greatly and increased in population from 11,969 to 17,539. The town of Sprague was also given new life by the wheat farmers, and it increased in population from 695 to 1,110. Since 1910, however, the population of Lincoln County as a whole has steadily declined, reaching a low of 9,572 in 1970. The population of Sprague fell to 550 during the same period (Table 6.1).

Population decline over the years is largely related to changes in farming practices. When wheat farming was first begun in Lincoln County, the average size of farms was relatively small. Later the development of sophisticated machinery increased the profitability of farming larger plots of land and decreased the profitability of farming smaller plots. As smaller farms consolidated into larger ones the average farm size in Lincoln County went from 303 acres in 1890 to 565 acres in 1910, 906 acres in 1930, 1,335 acres in 1959, and 1,606 acres in 1969 (1969 Census of Agriculture). Increased efficiency led to a decrease both in the number of farm operators and in the number of laborers required to work on farms. Consequently, the population *outside* of the county's incorporated towns fell from a peak of 11,694 in 1910 to 5,092 in 1950

Table 6.1. Population Changes in Lincoln County, Washington, 1890–1970.

Community	Year of Incorporation	1890	1900	1910	1920	1930	1940	1950	1960	1970
Almira	1904			368	450	339	466	395	414	376
Creston	1903			308	317	216	281	268	317	325
Davenport	1890		1,000	1,229	1,112	987	1,337	1,417	1,494	1,363
Harrington	1902			661	882	519	545	620	575	489
Odessa	1902			885	1,050	830	816	1,127	1,231	1,074
Reardon	1903			527	420	422	422	410	474	389
Sprague	1883	1,689	695	1,110	822	639	641	598	597	550
Wilbur	1890		595	757	870	737	1,011	1,043	1,138	1,074
Lincoln County	1883		11,969	17,539	15,141	11,876	11,361	10,970	10,919	9,572

Source: 1970 Census Data Book, pp. 440–449.

and to 3,932 in 1970 (*1970 Census Data Book*:297). A Lincoln County shopkeeper who observed this change over the years described the situation: "Every couple of years a farmer will retire—or die—and his neighbor will buy his land up. Forty-fifty years ago, there were farm families on every section. Now one person will farm three to four sections." With the exception of temporary increases in 1940 and 1960, the population of incorporated towns has followed a similar downward trend. The overall cause and effect relationship between mechanization in wheat farming and the loss of population in the incorporated towns of Lincoln County seems clear.

The population decline has had predictable demographic effects. Changes in the age structure of Lincoln County's population have occurred because many young adults have moved away to find jobs elsewhere. In the entire county in 1974 only 215 persons were working in manufacturing jobs, which exist in such few numbers that they afford little in the way of potential employment opportunities (*Davenport, Washington: A Standard Community Industrial Survey*, 1975). The departure of young people has left a residual population of older people: Despite a net population decrease between 1960 and 1970, the number of persons 55 years of age and over increased during this period from 2,357 to 2,649 (*1970 Census Data Book*:294). Altogether, persons in this age group represent 28 percent of the population of Lincoln County and only 18 percent of the population of the state as a whole.

Economic stagnation in Lincoln County resulting from population decline is reflected in an extremely depressed real-estate market. The number of year-round housing units in Lincoln County increased only 2.5 percent between 1960 and 1970, while the number of such units in the state as a whole increased by 23.9 percent (*County and City Data Book*, 1972). In Lincoln County 77 percent of all housing structures were built prior to 1950 and only 11 percent after 1960; whereas in the state as a whole only 51 percent of the structures were built prior to 1950 and 29 percent after 1960. Consistent with the existence of many older buildings is the fact that the market value of housing is well below the norm. In 1970, 49 percent of the housing units in Lincoln County were valued at less than $10,000 and only 15 percent were valued at $20,000 or more; whereas in the state as a whole only 14 percent were valued at less than $10,000 and 42 percent were valued at $20,000 or more (*1970 Census Data Book*:298). The vacancy rate in Lincoln County in 1970 was relatively high—10.5 percent compared to 8.2 percent statewide.

In turn, retail business in Lincoln County has been critically affected by demographic trends. Reports by local residents indicate that failures and/or closures are commonplace, as business districts deteriorate and lose their capacity to attract customers. For example, in Wilbur three gasoline stations closed in one year alone and two grocery stores closed within four years. Only 28 small businesses remain in Sprague, and between 1972 and 1974 it is reported that at least five businesses in this town have been forced to close. One motel owner illustrated the bad business climate by saying that only eight tourists had stayed at his motel during the first three months of 1974! Blacksmiths, handymen, and others who could do plumbing, electrical work, auto work, appliance repair, and carpentry work have all but disappeared throughout the county.

Lincoln County not only has economically depressed towns but also qualifies as a "medically underserved" area according to a recent newspaper account (*The Wilbur Register*, 21 August 1974). Overall, Washington has a ratio of one physician to every 556 residents. Lincoln County is one of 10 eastern Washington counties in which the average ratio is one primary-care physician to every 2,059 residents. Moreover, the average age of these primary-care physicians is 51.5 years, indicating that there is also a shortage of recently trained, young doctors and foretelling an even worse problem in the future. In Lincoln County itself, there are only six doctors, four of whom practice in Davenport and staff the county's only hospital. One of the doctors not residing in Davenport is over 70 years of age and is semiretired. He continues to see patients only because the town has been unsuccessful over the last several years in finding a new doctor. Residents of the smaller towns are sometimes said to be treated for minor ailments by "semiretired nurses" or "firemen with first-aid cards." Most Lincoln County residents not living in Davenport are required to seek medical treatment for serious illness either in Davenport or in a town in another county. Even services provided by the Davenport hospital are in jeopardy because it is difficult to raise tax money to meet standards required by the state.

Police protection is another difficult problem in a county plagued with various types of criminal activity. Newspaper accounts reveal the persistence of cattle rustling, alcohol and other drug-related offenses, burglaries of homes that have been locked up and abandoned, auto theft, vandalism of public and private property, and burglaries of local businesses. Only 13 full-time peace officers were employed in Lincoln County in 1973, including four state troopers, six deputy sheriffs and three local police officers. That an insufficient number of peace officers patrol the county is illustrated by reports of worsening incidence of vandalism to county road signs. County road crews estimated in 1973 that 60 percent of all road signs in the county were damaged by vandals. One road sign, for example, had 125 holes shot in it. The county engineer reported that in the first six month of 1973, $1,730 had been spent on replacement signs. He is quoted as saying, "This vandalism is just like taxpayers lighting a flame to dollars" (*Davenport Times*, 29 November 1973).

The town of Davenport began to discuss the hiring of a second policeman after it was reported that its one existing officer had filed reports on 203 cases and booked 25 people for criminal offenses during the first six months of 1973 (*Davenport Times*, 19 July 1973). The county sheriff reported the following list of activities in a nine-day period during the summer of 1975.

Aug. 5   picked up two juvenile runaways
Aug. 6   arrested a man for growing marijuana
         received a report on a house burglary in which clothing was taken
         arrested a man for possession of marijuana
         investigated the theft of a 10-speed bicycle
Aug. 7   arrested two juveniles for possession of alcohol and marijuana

Aug. 8   recovered a stolen beer truck from which 155 cases of beer had been taken
            received a report on someone with an air rifle shooting holes in three
               windows of a residence.
Aug. 9   received a report on 80 stolen hogs valued at $8,000 to $9,000
Aug. 12   received a report on an assault at a tavern
Aug. 13   burglar alarm at a grange store sounded and a window was broken
Aug. 14   burglar alarm at a drugstore sounded and two juveniles were later arrested
              for burglary
              found broken window in drugstore, a safe opened and drugs missing. (*The Wilbur Register*, 21 August 1975)

It is not uncommon for several businesses in a town to be burglarized in the same night or for the same business to be robbed more than once in a period of several months. The most popular items for theft from stores include liquor, cigarettes, and drugs, in addition to cash. Many of the offenders who are apprehended turn out to be young adults or juveniles.

Shopkeepers in Small Towns: An Endangered Species

In order to understand the problems of retail businesses in small towns, we conducted interviews with a number of local shopkeepers. They were selected from among the owners of 301 businesses found to be actively engaged in retail trade in Lincoln County during 1973.[2] Many businesses were eliminated from consideration because they were not truly "local" businesses. Branch banks and chain stores, such as Safeway, for example, were eliminated because their parent companies are not constrained by total dependence on the local market. The sample was further limited to include businesses owned by the same person for at least five years, for it was regarded as most important to understand the problems faced by well-established businesses and long-term resident-owners. An additional criterion was invoked to eliminate all businesses not based in a conventional business building. This procedure eliminated agricultural spraying companies and other such operations that are not tied to one location by fixed capital. The owners of 98 businesses that met these criteria were contacted for interviews. Information was eventually obtained from 43 owners operating 44 businesses in the county (Table 6.2). Although not a random sample, the interviewees are nevertheless representative of typical shopkeepers with businesses that are locally dependent and face severe adjustment pressures. A response rate of less than 50 percent, somewhat lower than expected, can be explained in great measure by general distrust of outsiders in small and isolated towns (some towns, such as Odessa, being less hospitable than others). Two project interviewers working in Odessa were threatened with arrest and asked to leave town by a local policeman. At this point only three interviews had been completed. The reluctance of Odessa shopkeepers to be interviewed may be related to a 1962 survey made by the local Chamber of Commerce. A survey report issued to each business pointed out deficiences and recommended improvements. A former member of the Chamber of Commerce recalled the reaction to the report: "Everyone hid in a corner to read it, complained about it, and threw it away."

One year after we conducted the initial survey, the same 43 shopkeepers were again contacted for interviews. All but four agreed to answer additional questions. This follow-up survey was designed to monitor changes in circumstances and attitudes over time.

Supplemental interviews were conducted with six shopkeepers who had in recent years sold or abandoned their businesses and left the county. This sample was obtained by way of words of mouth and fortuitous circumstances and was not intended to be random. The six cases so identified are important because respondents typically expressed themselves more freely than others who remain in the county. They lend a distant perspective not otherwise obtainable. An attempt was also made to meet briefly with several shopkeepers who had moved to Lincoln County within the last five years and to monitor the entry of new businesses. Such interviews, however, were not exhaustive or systematic. All of the above-mentioned samples are used as sources of information in the following discussion. All tables and numerical tabulations are based on the original sample of 43 shopkeepers unless otherwise specified.

The sample of 43 respondents included owners of 14 retail stores, such as those selling building supplies, garden supplies, groceries, drugs, hardware,

---

Table 6.2. Number of Firms in Each Community, Fall 1973.

Community	Number of firms	Number Meeting Criteria	Number Responding
Almira	12	6	6
Creston	9	7	0
Davenport	71	22	11
Edwall	7	5	2
Harrington	24	6	1
Odessa	56	17	3
Reardon	29	4	3
Sprague	28	6	6
Wilbur	62	22	12
Other Places	3	3	0
TOTAL	301	98	44

[a]Unincorporated.
[b]Interviewers were prevented from contacting all owners meeting the criteria.
[c]Two businesses with same owner.

Source of first two columns: Barkley, 1974; p.10

furniture, jewelry, and antiques; 18 service establishments, such as hotels, restaurants, taverns, funeral parlors, newspaper publishers, electricians, and blacksmiths; nine automotive dealers, such as gasoline stations, service garages, and auto-parts stores; and two general establishments that involve both retail and service aspects. Of these businesses, 34 were owned as proprietorships, two as partnerships, and only seven as corporations.

The ages of the respondents ranged from 28 to 82, although there were many more older than young persons within this group. Two-thirds were 50 years of age or older, while only one-seventh were under 40 years of age. All but a few had completed a high school education, and almost half had at least one year of college.[3] Women accounted for eight of the 43 respondents.

A definite pattern of upward mobility appears when educational attainment and occupational traits are compared across generations. Two-thirds of the fathers of the respondents reached only the eighth grade or less. More than half the fathers worked at blue-collar occupations or trades; one-third were farmers or ranchers; and only one-sixth were in white-collar or professional occupations.

For the most part the shopkeepers in this survey did not start in business with large amounts of capital or extensive experience. Three-fourths had work experience of various kinds in other occupations. One-third worked for another employer immediately before starting in business. Only one-fifth were previously self-employed, while only one-seventh started in business as debt-free owners. One-fourth began their involvement with the business as wage earners or salaried employees unrelated to the family of the previous owner. One-fourth also had relatives previously involved in the business.

Respondents were about evenly divided between those from Lincoln County and those from other places in Washington, with slightly less than half in each group. One-fourth had fathers who grew up in Lincoln County. In one instance, a business was inherited through three generations after the respondent's grandfather bought the business from a "Swede" in 1919. In another, the father of the present owner started the business in 1906. Although the premises of this business appeared quite shabby, the owner still occupied the original building.

The involvement of a majority of owners with their businesses began before 1960. In one case, the owner held the same business for 51 years. Because of sampling restrictions, there were no respondents who started in business after 1970.[4]

Most owners ran their businesses on a very small scale; three-fifths had two or fewer paid employees and less than one-tenth had more than seven paid employees. A substantial part of the labor involved in running these businesses came from the owners and their spouses. Almost half of the owners reported working 60 hours per week or more, while all but a few worked at least 40 hours per week. In fact, the burden of running a business was so demanding on time and personal health that many owners were given to complain: "I'm getting old and have had the business for ten years. I'm getting tired of it. Being an owner and operator plus the cook is a lot of hard work.

Your net income is so much money, but after you remodel and make repairs plus other expenses and wages for help, you don't make too much money."

Two-fifths of the spouses of respondents performed services for the business as uncompensated workers, and one-fourth had jobs outside the business, whereas only one-fifth worked exclusively as homemakers. The feeling among many shopkeepers was that the spouse's work represented an essential contribution to family income. The main constraint on the spouse working was the presence of young children in the household. However, more than half the families no longer had children living at home.

The small scale of most businesses was further reflected in low net income figures. One-third of these businesses showed a net income of $8,500 or less; two-thirds had net income of $14,000 or less; and only one-seventh had net income of more than $20,000. These figures can be decreased further because on the average only about half of this income was reported to be returned to the household and treated as "family income."[5]

Half the respondents reported either no increase or a decrease in profits between 1972 and 1973. Even more than half may have been suffering from lack of a profit increase, since interviewers sometimes found the reporting of these trends to be systematically distorted. Respondents commonly expressed optimism about profits despite other visible indications of downward trends. The most realistic note of optimism was perhaps sounded by the owner of a funeral parlor, who took consolation from the presence of an elderly population in the town. He expressed the belief that "the last business to collapse in a small dying town is the funeral business."

In many cases, it appeared that household income was adequate only because the spouse brought in supplemental income. One-fourth of the spouses worked for another employer, while one-eighth operated businesses of their own. In addition, two-fifths of the respondents themselves worked for other employers to supplement their incomes. Respondents and spouses who worked for others reported an average addition to family income of $9,000 per year.

Even with a significant amount of nonbusiness income, it is difficult to understand how some of these families survive unless the absence of significant household expenses is considered. Two-thirds, for example, owned their homes debt-free and did not have to make mortgage or rental payments. Even those who had mortgages or lived in rental units were not burdened with excessive payments. On the average, payments were $133 per month for those with mortgages, and one rental was reported at $110 per month. Most families also had few, if any, expenses connected with raising children. Fewer than one-fourth had more than one child under 19 living at home.

Living on a small income, even though expenses are low, does not provide extensive latitude for investment. If large amounts of capital are allocated for business improvements, the risk of total failure increases greatly. Accordingly, most respondents employed a strategy of maintaining steady but low levels of investment. Half maintained inventories valued at $10,000 or less, whereas only one-fourth maintained inventories valued at more than $20,000.

One shopkeeper who was caught with a $100,000 inventory and only $20,000 in yearly sales was forced out of business. Another carried so little inventory that a neighbor who was hoping for more business in the area was heard to complain about the store's lack of variety and attractiveness:

He has so much space available and yet the store is almost empty. He carries as few lines as possible, and when he goes to reorder something, he reorders the smallest quantity possible. He is the only businessman I know who would order one bottle of aspirin.

Although the absurdity of the situation is obvious, there are nevertheless good reasons why it is impossible for many shopkeepers to carry a large inventory. One respondent explained his troubles:

One year I wanted a lot of selection for people so I could compete with larger businesses in larger towns. So I bought a whole truckload of appliances. If I couldn't get rid of them in one year, I would have had to run a sale at the end of the year to get rid of that year's model. And that's exactly what happened. It wasn't worth it financially. In a small town you have to be very selective about your merchandise. You must know what sells and how much of it to buy that will get bought up in one year.

Expenses related to fixtures were also kept low, allowing shopkeepers to get by with a low profit margin. Although many buildings were old and in need of repair, investments were made only if absolutely necessary. For example, a tavern owner put up a new front and a new sign costing approximately $2,000. When asked why, he replied: "I had to. The empty building next door starting falling in, and bricks fell into my building breaking part of the side wall in and collapsing the front. I had to spend the money because I had no insurance."

A crisis sometimes occurs when major repairs are required to meet safety and health regulations. In such a case the owner must either make a large investment or be forced to shut down. The following example, describing a restaurant and hotel business, was reported in a local newspaper.

[The owner] said she and her employees originally operated the upstairs half of the building as a hotel when she first undertook the business. She said that, given the lack of housing in town, and the reasonable three dollars a night room, the hotel was a service to the community as well as a sound business venture.

However, the state inspector, after looking over the premises, recommended to [the owner] that she close down the operation or the state would.

Since that time, the upstairs has deteriorated substantially for lack of upkeep [the owner] said. Particularly the plaster ceilings are in need of repair, she said.

If major repairs can be avoided, however, expenses incurred by occupying business space are generally quite low. Two-fifths of the respondents owned their building debt-free, and the rest paid very little on rent and mortgages. Half the rentals, for example, were below $200 per month. A landlord who might like to raise the rent in order to improve his building had little recourse in renegotiating the contract because the renter could easily move to another vacant building. On the average, rents had not been negotiated for more than six years. In three cases, the rent had remained the same for fourteen, fifteen, and sixteen years. One landlord began renting out his building after he went out of business and found that he could sell neither the building nor the business. He explained the renters' advantage:

> Those other businesses are now in the building renting. There is still space for one more business. The occupants now pay a very, very low rent, but I can't do anything about it. They refuse to pay more and at the time [the rental agreement was made] I was caught in a bind and needed the money. I have to pay taxes and up-keep of the building. Had to put a new roof on the building two years ago for $2,000. I sure wish I could sell that building.

Most respondents maintained a low level of financial commitment with regard to personal as well as to business property. This phenomenon is reflected in the fact that the total level of combined business and personal indebtedness was $14,000 or less for three-fourths of the respondents. It was regarded as essential not to borrow or extend oneself too far because savings were not sufficient in case of emergency. All but one-eighth of the respondents had $5,000 or less in savings.

Keeping Your Friends by Going Broke

Small businesses in Lincoln County survive on the good will of customers. Owners must often work overtime and go to extra trouble to cultivate relationships with customers. One kind of special treatment given to a customer is indicated in the following example:

> I bend over backwards to help my customers and give services which a large business would normally refuse. One time I ordered a special, large refrigerator for a customer. After the contract had been signed and the merchandise delivered, the customer changed her mind about the purchase in preference to something else. I took back the refrigerator, sold her what she then desired, and later was able to sell the large, specially ordered refrigerator during one of my business sales. I came out ahead on the deal, the customer was happy, and thus, good business relationships were established.

Most shopkeepers extended credit to customers as a standard and expected practice. Only one-sixth of the respondents failed to extend any credit in 1973, while three-fifths extended credit in amounts from $12,000 to $144,000. Some of this credit, as was customary even in pioneer days, was extended to farmers who pay their total bills once a year after crops are harvested and sold. Credit was also given to friends as a means of doing favors. Credit based on friendship was given by 44 percent of the respondents.

Although friends may be loyal customers, familiarity may place extra demands on the merchant and make him vulnerable to default. A 60-year-old handyman who ran a business in Lincoln County for twenty years before moving to Spokane provides a good example of how the desire to keep friends may cripple a business.

> Money was always slow coming in. That's a big problem in small towns—credit. People expect to have credit automatically. The farmers will say they'll pay you back after harvest, but they don't say what harvest.

In a small town you don't get rough with any of your customers because the others in town will get mad and go elsewhere. They have even called someone in Spokane when they were mad at me. In Spokane it is different. You don't know your customers and can ask how do you plan to pay for it, and if they don't you can take them to court. You could never do that in a small town.

When I got to Spokane, I had $23,000 worth in bills from the folks back in town. Many bills were years old. I got so disgusted that I burned them all. I probably got back a total of $5,000.

Other businesses in town have credit problems, but they wait it out. I couldn't wait; just got sick of the whole thing.

Maintaining good relations with customers is less important if the merchant has a local monopoly. The owner of a grocery store who enjoyed such a position admitted setting prices without regard for public sentiment. Townspeople complained about the prices and felt they were not getting a fair deal, but lack of good will did not stop them from coming to the store. The owner stated that profits did not exceed $5,000 and that prices had to be set high in order to keep the business open.

In another town four gasoline stations closed between 1969 and 1973, leaving the market to be shared by two remaining stations. Since the two owners did not want to engage in ruinous competition, they soon got together and decided to cut off credit to all customers except those on commercial accounts. As a result, the total volume of credit carried by one of the owners was reduced from $5,000 to $1,600 a month. In this case, the owners determined that business was more important than friendship.

Obligations to the Community

The vitality of the business community in the three largest towns in Lincoln County has been severely affected by chain supermarkets, which have located outside central shopping districts and drawn customers away. In both larger and smaller towns business closures have reduced the variety of goods available and detracted from the desirability of shopping in the central district.

Some respondents considered it a duty to keep their businesses open so that others in the central district would not lose customers. The effort to keep a business open may involve considerable personal sacrifice by an owner: "I was sick for five months in the winter of 1973 and had to hire help. That's where the winter profit went. I would have been better off to close the cafe up for the winter, but I couldn't since my cafe is the only one in town." In another case, an owner claimed to have bought a second business simply to save it from bankruptcy and thereby help the community. Although one of his neighbors perceived this gesture as a normative attempt to gain influence, the owner's motive was no doubt sincere.

Although pressure against closures exerted within the business community was considerable, the location of chain stores could not be influenced and not all closures could be prevented. Lack of control over these circumstances was often combatted by existing businesses taking over the product lines of businesses that had closed or moved. During the period 1968 to 1973, for example, thirteen respondents added product lines, and only one dropped product lines. Adding product lines, which in other circumstances might indicate increasing prosperity, signals in this context that the main product lines may not be selling well and are not in themselves sufficient to attract customers. Typical cases include a hardware merchant who began stocking grain bins, a newspaper publisher who began selling office supplies, and a furniture dealer who began carrying kitchen appliances.

Some pessimistic owners refused to add new product lines because they had given up: "I would not add more product lines because I lack faith in the community." Other owners preferred not to diversify but did so anyway because they saw it as necessary for survival. The following example is from a young druggist:

I realized that I couldn't make it by selling drugs alone, especially in a small town. This is particularly true now, since grocery stores handle so many drugs themselves, like aspirin, etc. People go to the grocery store more often than the drugstore and are inclined to pick up such drugs while they are grocery shopping. When the variety store next to my business when up for sale, I borrowed money from the Small Business Administration to buy it. Then I tore down the wall separating the drugstore from the variety store and expanded. I added more gift lines like toys, hobbies, crafts, cards, cameras, summer hats, and glass items.

My main interest is still working with drugs strictly as a pharmacist. I don't want to bother with front-line products, but it is expected of me and it is a financial necessity.

Additional product lines are intended to compliment and not compete with lines already offered by existing stores. For example, the drugstore mentioned above did not add baby clothes because another drugstore in the same town carried this item. Competition between the two druggists was minimized because both sought to maintain a good public image and avoid the appearance of engaging in cutthroat business practices.

The addition of work skills, like the addition of new product lines, is often necessary for merchants who offer repair services. Since the demand for repairs was low, full-time specialists were few. Dealers found that they had to compensate by providing a broad range of services themselves in order to keep customers satisfied. One merchant, for example, was known to do plumbing, electrical work, auto work, TV repair, and carpentry work.

A small-town norm emphasizing community involvement was observed, at least to some extent, by volunteer fire departments that carried on a historical tradition of cooperative firefighting. An ambulance service to the county hospital that depended on volunteer drivers was also regarded as important to maintain because there was only one hospital to serve the county's elderly population. Approximately one-fourth of the respondents served as volunteer firefighters and drivers or as organizers of annual frontier festivals, such as "Wild Goose Bill Days." However, Chambers of Commerce were found virtually nonexistent in the smaller towns of the county. In fact, more than half of the repondents were not members of a Chamber of Commerce. The last organization resembling a Chamber of Commerce in these towns folded in 1974 because of "lack of interest" and the poor health of the president. It is reported that only six persons usually showed up at the meetings and that four of these were clergymen.[6] The Chambers of Commerce in the three largest towns were still active in sponsoring festivals in order to attract visitors and at least temporarily to boost business sales. Not all respondents, however, were enthusiastic about joining the Chamber of Commerce. One reported that a little friendly coercion was necessary to get him to join: "I didn't want to become too involved, but joined the Chamber because of pressure from members. One of the members told me, 'Join us and we will do business with you; don't join and we won't.' Now I want to see if it [joining] will help my business any."

Newspaper accounts and recollections of county residents reveal that participation in community-service activities was much more evident in the past. Townspeople, for example, would cooperate to paint storefronts to add to the attractiveness of the community. Today, one is more likely to hear a shopkeeper complain about lack of cooperation, such as a neighbor who fails to shovel the snow off of his sidewalk or neglects to keep his store neat and attractive.

Newcomers to the business community are often enthusiastic about living in a small town and are eager, at least at first, to get involved. Such persons are perhaps in many ways responsible for whatever vitality remains in Lincoln County communities. Some have come to Lincoln County in recent years with the purpose of fulfilling a dream to become gainfully self-employed, as opposed to working for an employer, and to find a wholesome environment for their children.

When the newcomers first arrive, they expect the people to be friendly and the problems of life to be fewer and less severe. The following excerpts from a recent edition of a county newspaper describe the expectations of a hopeful immigrant who left a company job in California.

A tall California native who says owning a hardware store was one of his longtime dreams is the new proprietor [of a hardware store in town]. . . . The family was familiar with this town long before the move. They had spent vacations here for several years. [He] said he never could get along with the big city. He said he likes the small town atmosphere. "And the friendliness," he added. "That's a big plus." "Life seems to run at half-speed here in comparison with California," said the new merchant, who grinned and said he didn't miss the freeways at all. "I don't know the demands [on the business]," he said. "I'll have to keep my eyes and ears open . . . and I hope people will tell me what they want."

Initial enthusiasm for small-town life inevitably wears off as newcomers realize that they are not readily accepted in the community. It is especially difficult if one must compete against another shopkeeper who offers the same product or service and has been in town for a longer period of time. Customers sometimes maintain their loyalty to established businesses even after several years have passed and despite the newcomer's service to the community. Two newcomers expressed their feelings this way:

I am still a stranger after five and a half years. Many people in the town feel that you have to live here at least twenty years before you actually become one of them—a citizen. For example, my wife wrote a letter to the newspaper. It was printed and did express the feelings of the vast majority of residents. However, several local residents came into the store and told me that my wife had no right to voice their opinion like that because we weren't "citizens" yet. I own a business in town, belong to the Chamber of Commerce and the Lions Club, and yet I wasn't considered one of them.

The townspeople are narrow-minded, petty, jealous people—which is typical of small towns. The town will never grow or be a thriving community because of this. Many people grow up in small towns and after high school don't leave but stay right in town. They never learn to see how others live. Their pettiness and jealousy is also a drawback. The townspeople didn't like who a young female proprietor was dating so they took it out on her business, and she gets very little business.

The number of older people living in the towns was perceived by some newcomers as a further barrier, not only to their participation but also to community progress. An ex-shopkeeper whose tenure as a tavern operator in one of Lincoln County's smaller communities lasted less than two years, found that older people strongly resisted his attempt to get the town "on its feet" by initiating a number of civic-improvement projects. He succeeded temporarily in getting Christmas decorations put up and in reviving an annual frontier festival that had previously been discontinued because of "lack of interest and help." He was, however, unable to promote any lasting changes, and he complained bitterly about his failure.

I tried many times in talking the town into tearing down old, empty, delapidated buildings, but the older residents don't want to. These older buildings are momentos to them and tearing them down would be upsetting to them. One older citizen told me, "Anyway if we tore those old buildings down, the wind would blow through the town."

Another ex-shopkeeper, who was born and raised in a Lincoln County town, claimed that established merchants were basically selfish and did not have the interest of the community at heart. He pointed to several instances where they could have acted constructively but did not.

In 1952–53 the Chamber of Commerce appointed a committee to try to get more businesses into town. The committee made several trips to Olympia, where there is a list of businesses that need a location and a list of towns that need businesses. But the whole thing faded away. The Chamber ran out of money, and no one wanted to take the time to help.

In 1960–62 an alcohol company wanted to build an alcohol plant near town. They had the site all picked out, and electrical power, railroad facilities, etc. When it came time to buy the land, the owner wanted an enormous price for it, which was outrageous for the rocky, scabby land that it was—no good for farming. And the town refused to go in together and buy it from him either. Everyone was out for themselves and no one could see that the plant would help stabilize the community.

In 1969 a potato plant was proposed to be built near town. But when the town heard about this, the farmers and businessmen had a fit over it. They didn't want any of those "dirty spics" around. They especially feared the thought of having migrant workers' children in their school.

One of the most fondly held ideals of Lincoln County shopkeepers—and of other Americans who take a nostalgic view of the past—is that small towns are good places to raise children. It is a basic tenet of conservative American ideology to believe that children are better off in a small town, where presumably they will not be exposed to the evils of the world around them. Both newcomers and oldtimers among Lincoln County shopkeepers shared such views.

In reality, however, these ideals seem as difficult to implement in Lincoln County as in larger cities. The juvenile-court officer for Lincoln County reported to a group of concerned citizens that as many as 30 percent of the students in one high school had been involved in criminal activity. During 1974 alcohol possession was said to be the leading type of juvenile-court action handled by the county, followed by possession of marijuana, second-degree burglary, assault, auto theft, runaway, no driver's license, vandalism, petty theft, driving while intoxicated, reckless driving, and ungovernable lewdness (*The Wilbur Register*, 9 January 1975). Concerned citizen's meetings were held in all three larger towns to deal with the problems of alcohol abuse and juvenile delinquency. The problem with alcohol abuse was particularly severe, as explained by the county juvenile-officer in the following newspaper account.

From re-referrals he is now getting, he explained, some 5th and 6th graders of the community are apparently experimenting with alcohol; they begin attending parties in junior high years and are drinking regularly in high school.

"Parents aren't really that concerned," he said he has learned when one or both are asked to report with their juvenile.

There are kids in Lincoln County schools who are alcoholics, [he] stated in relating that he has seen them "walk into school at 9 a.m., drunk." (*The Odessa Record*, 10 April 1975)

Despite the expression of general approval of small town and rural schools as an ideal type, the people in this study did express disapproval about a wide range of actual circumstance, which include the lack of anything for young people to do, a cheerleader who came drunk to a basketball game, discrimination against a student, who was not treated as well as the children of "wealthy farmers," lack of funds, second-and third-rate teachers who acted as "pals" and did not discipline students, sloppy dress, and declining test scores. It is evident that widespread disillusionment and bitterness in the business community was also felt by the young people of the county and that they were no more immune to the influence of the outside world and no less alienated by small-town life than their parents. The alienation of young people in turn could serve only to increase the dissonance of elders, whose ideals are being contradicted.

It is doubtful that the future will bring many prosperous businesses to Lincoln County to give life to its communities. The existence of "plenty of empty buildings in town to be purchased for a business" is not a sufficient inducement to attract large amounts of capital, and even if new businesses could be attracted, mixed feelings exist about the desirability of encouraging an economic boom, which would bring an unwanted increase in population.

Although several businesses were recently established by newcomers, none was economically significant. The types of recent entries included shops selling rocks, guns, saddles, arts and crafts, a special kind of Hawaiian barbeque sauce, flowers, and a fortune-teller. All of these businesses were hobbies intended to make use of special skills or interests of the owner and were not likely to be financially profitable. Many of these hobbyists were content to break even while relying upon other sources of income, such as military retirement pay or the wage of a working spouse for primary support. In some cases, local people regarded the hobbyists as "weird." Even some newcomers who had taken over legitimate businesses were regarded this way. The owner of a gasoline station, for example, bought the business in order to support himself and still have free time to pursue his main interest, which he described as "studying hypnotism, metaphysics, and parapsychology." Owners with such off-beat interests do not become a force in the community, and as soon as their interests wane, their businesses quickly disappear.

Big Farmers and Small Shopkeepers

Relations between shopkeepers and farmers in Lincoln County improved little over the eight decades following the time when farmers supported striking railroad workers and shopkeepers supported the railroad in order to keep the railroad shops in the town of Sprague. Since farmers have now become large landholders and employers, they are no longer champions of distressed workers; but the few farmers who remain in the county are thought by shopkeepers to care very little about the fate of local communities. Frequent complaints were heard from respondents, who claimed that farmers did not patronize local stores and did not support community development projects.

The farmers do not deal with the locals. They ship their wheat to grain elevators, then in turn to the world market. In a sense, the farmer is independent. He doesn't have to make the wheat flour and haul it into town to sell on the street. If he did, this town would be altogether different and certainly larger. The farmer would have to be friendly and sociable with locals, since he would have to depend on them for a livelihood. No wonder why all the businesses fail in town, with so many farmers so against the townspeople; they don't want anything to do with us.

A watershed project would serve as a flood control for the town and also be a recreational site. There would be a lake for fishing, swimming, boating, and a picnic area. The problem is, though, that people in the district don't want additional taxes, especially the farmers who own most of the land. The local businessmen would like to see the project go through since flooding losses amount to $100,000 in a bad year in the downtown area, and $100,000 would pay for the project with matching [federal] funds. The problem arises from the farmers who are against it. They can't see how they can benefit from it, other than the recreational aspect of it, and they're the ones who will end up paying for most of it in land taxes. So the farmers are setting up a petition against the dam project.

The wealth here is in the hands of twenty percent of the townspeople, who are farmers that live in town. This has a negative impact. The town needs a sewer system badly but cannot get any federal funds for it because the average income in the town is too high for assistance. But they fail to realize that ninety percent of that wealth is in the hands of twenty percent of the people and that the twenty percent are very reluctant to spend money on the town.

Another sore spot with respondents was competition from farmer's cooperative supply stores, which were organized by local granges in the early part of the century. Grange retailing has prospered even up to the present, as evidenced by the following account from a local newspaper early in 1975.

A ninety percent sales growth with a forty-seven percent expenditure increase and a 263.5 percent increase in profits over a two-year period were reported to the Grange Supply Company membership at the annual meeting of patrons on Wednesday afternoon.

The manager indicated that sales had increased from $1,504,194 in 1972, to $1,972,060 in 1973, to $2,867,408 in 1974 for the 90.6 percent increase.

The profit picture took a big jump, starting with $81,710 in 1972, going to $97,449 in 1973 and to $296,997 in 1974.

Cash returns to patrons totaled $85,602, the manager stated.

The effect of the expansion of grange cooperatives was not lost on local shopkeepers. One respondent was able to point to several specific examples of business failures resulting directly from the addition of competing product lines by the grange.

Large businesses that answer to corporate offices and not to the informal pressure of local residents were resented by respondents for the same reason farmers were resented. That is, like most farmers, they did not regard themselves as members of the community and were thought to show no responsibility toward the community. Chain supermarkets, as previously mentioned, have located apart from other downtown stores and have drawn away customers. Branch banks present a similar problem. A local electrician, for example, complained bitterly about a branch-bank manager who obtained electrical wiring service from a Spokane company and not from him. Upon hearing the complaint the bank manager remained unperturbed. The fact that some businessmen and farmers were not bound to follow the norms of the community was particularly demoralizing to those who regarded the observation of such norms as a necessary sacrifice.

I am people-oriented. I am always willing to help those who need it, regardless of their ability to pay. If an individual in this area needs my service, I am more than willing to help him out, regardless of the payment period, and in fact knowing that repayment may never come. I get angry with bigger businesses [farms and corporations] that owe me money. They can afford to pay it, but they chisel me out of every cent they can.

A lot of dishonesty goes on when a company or corporation gets a tax number and is able to purchase goods wholesale. With a tax number, you can buy not only items wholesale that pertain to your business, but anything wholesale, like groceries. I have a tax number but would never consider buying wholesale food with it. It isn't fair.

I used a few tax loopholes in order to pay less taxes last year. I paid more taxes than Nixon the year before, so I decided to do everything possible to lower my taxes. Large-income recipients aren't paying taxes, so why me.

Some shopkeepers had even more reason to feel intimidated because they were directly under the control of large distributors, such as oil and gas companies. In 1975, for example, a service-station owner was told to liquidate his assets because his distributor, an oil company, wished to sell the land and building he was leasing. Another example concerns an independent retailer who was under constant threat of having supplies cut off by his wholesaler. By confining this client to 30-day contracts, the wholesaler was in a position to terminate the relationship at any time and begin retailing on its own. The retailer was particularly worried that the wholesaler would take over his business if it became too lucrative. Meanwhile, the retailer was assuming the risk involved in operating a small rural business.

Trapped in Smalltown, U.S.A.

The activity involved in buying and selling businesses, at least in the case of businesses that have some market value, is substantial in Lincoln County. For example, one restaurant and hotel business changed ownership in 1934, 1948, 1953, 1965, 1967, 1972, and 1975, a total of eight times after it opened in 1926. Other businesses for which information is available had a similar history of being bought and sold several times, particularly in the period since 1946. There were also instances of family businesses that remained off the market during most of their existence, but in recent years they were sold several times following the retirement of the original owner. One café, for example, changed hands six times in six years following the retirement of the original owner. Rumors passed among shopkeepers suggested that the first buyer mismanaged the business; that the second buyer was unsuccessful in trying to be his own cook because he drank on the job; and that the third and fourth buyers drank too much and went bankrupt. The original owner then repossessed the business and leased the premises to the present owner.

Change of ownership keeps new capital flowing into a business at periodic intervals and often leads to needed improvements and repairs being made. At the time of this study, however, not much new capital was being provided by new owners. In one recent case, a business was repossessed within a year after being sold because the new owner failed to put $5,000 into repairs, as written into the contract. The futility of making large investments is illustrated by an owner who put $33,000 into repairs and improvements that did not produce an expected boost in sales. A grandiose plan to put even more money into the business then had to be abandoned. The owner was forced to sell out at a loss and finally was humiliated by the criticism of other shopkeepers, who charged that he had run a "slovenly" operation. Thus it is understandable that newspaper accounts and interviews rarely revealed more than a few thousand dollars being invested either by new or old owners. Most owners are likely to fail in the long run either with or without making investments, because businesses will continue to lose market value as customers disappear.

There were many instances in which owners wished to sell out but found, to their chagrin, that the value of their businesses and buildings had dropped to nothing. As one respondent put it: "Anyone would be a fool to buy this business because it would take fifty years to make it pay." Older shopkeepers in particular may be trapped into hanging on until retirement and squeezing what they can out of a hopeless situation. More than half of the respondents said they were faced with a situation that made it impossible to move to another location. Only one-fourth of the respondents had considered moving. Both the financial impossibility of moving and advanced age significantly influenced the lack of consideration given to moving. One trapped and disheartened shopkeepers described the situation this way.

I would like to leave, but I must think about income. What would I do if I didn't have this store? But at least I'll be able to retire soon. A young person can leave and learn something else, but not at my age. I am the owner of the building and I can't just leave it. I would have to find a buyer for it; it's not like someone who just rents the building.

Things will get worse, The town is slowly dying. Most of the present owners are older people, and when they retire, probably no one will buy their businesses.

If, as in a few instances, a newcomer is unwise enough to invest in a business that has no value, a financial failure can occur almost immediately. A young couple who bought a tavern in one of the smaller towns had such an experience. The tavern was a marginal operation from the start, and it required the full-time attention of both the previous owner and his wife to make it pay. The tavern was sold after the owner's wife had a heart attack, and the owner found that he could not afford to hire additional help. The buyers made the mistake of investing $15,000 for remodeling, and within eight months the tavern was closed and abandoned. Such an incident verifies the truth of a statement made by an older shopkeeper in the same town: "This is certainly no place for a young person to have a business."

Getting Out After the Getting Is Good

In the year between the original survey of 43 shopkeepers and the follow-up survey in April 1975, four respondents sold their businesses, and two others began to try to sell out. In three cases, the common complaint was that too much time was being spent in running the business, and in two other cases the owner was ready to retire. In the remaining case, the mother of the owner, who served as a cook, had suffered a heart attack, forcing the business to close. None of these businesses seemed to be financially solvent even when run by new owners. Three of the former owners gave up without having any specific occupational alternatives in mind. At the time of the follow-up survey, these three persons were unemployed, and two others had no idea where they would go or what they would do to earn a living.

Interviews with six shopkeepers who had left the county before 1974 revealed motivations similar to those expressed above. Financial losses, health failure, and extensive demands on time and labor were mentioned as reasons for quitting in at least three of the six cases. In the following example all three reasons were involved. The respondent in this case had operated a combination furniture, carpet, linoleum, and large appliance store, a business that had belonged to his family for more than forty years. At various times new product lines had been added to compensate for a steadily decreasing volume of business. In the end his physical and psychological burdens became too great for him to continue.

As the small farms disappeared, my market slowly diminished. I had to travel further and further away to get business. I developed a large trading area and it took a lot of time and energy. I had to run twenty to thirty miles to do the same amount of business as I did before running ten to fifteen miles. I worked six days a wekk, 8 AM to 6 PM on the average. Of course, there were many times when I worked until 10 PM on Sundays. It came to the point where it wasn't worth it.

There was also a problem of getting help. There was no one I could get that knew how to lay carpet or service appliances. Another problem was wages. I wouldn't be able to pay a helper much anyway—not as much as he could get working in a city. And I couldn't charge the regular "urban" services charges. People wouldn't pay it. Several times I tried, but the customers refused and ended up calling in someone from Spokane anyway.

Then I had a serious back problem. I already had an operation and just couldn't handle lifting furniture and appliances by myself anymore. I couldn't get help and I needed a second back operation, so I folded up the entire business and left. Business was going downhill more and more every year anyway.

Only one of the six shopkeepers who left Lincoln County was still self-employed, and he had been able to survive only by carrying an entirely different type of product that required little capital to be tied up in inventory. The remainder had no choice but to give up their businesses and look for other means of support. One was forced to retire at the age of 57 because of a chronic illness, and then he was in and out of hospitals while relying on his wife's income. Three others took blue-collar jobs—as a security guard, gas-station attendant, and electrician. Another ex-shopkeeper worked as a floor manager and clerk in three stores and as a salesman for a large company after leaving Lincoln County.

Spouses of all but one of these six shopkeepers took jobs. All five women were working in traditional female occupations, which included coffee-shop manager, sales clerk, nurse, receptionist, and bookkeeper. Two of the five started working only after moving away from Lincoln County. The spouse of one ex-shopkeeper was unable to work because of illness.

Although escape in many ways brought relief, the experience of leaving behind relatives, friends, and a lifetime commitment to a community was painful for some families. One woman who was 52 and had lived all her life in the same community found the adjustment particularly difficult. Her husband gave the following account:

It was really her idea to move. She was tired of having no money and of not being able to pay the bills, so we moved. But we had to leave our 'dream house.' This is the house we planned and built together. Selling it really upset my wife. For the first few months in Spokane she went through a violent depression.

Although financial losses involved in business failure were a hardship for ex-shopkeepers, an even more important hardship was the psychological adjustment made necessary by the loss of freedom that goes with being one's own boss. Although working for another employer may be easier and less burdensome, the feeling was that the personal rewards are not as great.

I don't work as hard now. I have a regular set of hours I put in, plus only a five-day work week instead of six. Working for others is more secure. I get a fixed income, insurance, retirement benefits, etc. But I would prefer my own business to working for others. With my own business I had a certain amount of freedom. I miss not being my own boss.

The feelings expressed here are similar to the rationale given by shopkeepers who stayed in Lincoln County despite all the problems. It is ironic that the shopkeepers who hang on, trying to preserve their freedom, gradually lose it as they become increasingly powerless and vulnerable to external forces. They suffer not only from population decline, burglary, neglect by local farmers, competition from retail cooperatives, and absence of concern by the corporate offices of chain stores, but also from lack of understanding and increasing pressure from government. As the situation slips further out of control, more and more complaints are heard about the government, a visible and convenient target toward which festering resentments may be expressed. High taxes for such purposes as social security and unemployment compensation, numerous health and safety regulations, and extensive accounting requirements were the most frequently heard targets of complaint. Lincoln County shopkeepers expressed the feeling that the government was not interested in their problems, but only in the problems of larger businesses and corporations.

There are more and more government requirements and regulations every day, like price controls, the Occupational Safety and Health Act, the U.S. Department of Labor, and the Washington State Health and Safety Board.

The federal government will never get off small businessmen's backs, so it doesn't do much good to talk about it. But the federal government could give more exemptions to the small-small businesses to eliminate a lot of bookkeeping tasks that are now required. I am required by various government agencies to fill out papers every month. A lot of this work actually requires a great deal of time on the part of the owner, and, really, one almost needs to hire a bookkeeper to take care of it for him. But what small-small businessman can afford to hire one and to take care of the requirements and regulations imposed on them by the government?

Also, there really is no federal program or agency to help the small-small businessman. The Small Business Administration doesn't mean businesses that employ four to five people. It is directed toward those small businesses that employ fifty people (or more), so actually small businesses in a rural town don't really exist in the eyes of the government.

Specific resentments were accompanied by general pessimism and bitterness. At the time of the follow-up interviews, conducted in the spring of 1975 such feelings were even stronger than in the previous year. The World Exposition in Spokane had ended by this time, and some respondents who had expressed optimism about a boom in tourism were now despondent. A lumber mill located between Davenport and Wilbur was also shut down for several months in 1975, laying off 85 to 100 employees, and on the national scene the economy was undergoing a recession while the military was executing a final (humiliating) withdrawal from South Vietnam. These circumstances were perceived as final proof of the ineptitude of government. The failure of the government was found difficult to reconcile with strong belief in the "free enterprise" system and an unwavering commitment to patriotism. Frustrations were compounded by unsettling feelings of doubt, as revealed in the statement: "The country is in a mess. I am disgusted with the Vietnam situation. We should have dropped the atomic bomb on them long ago . . . but we have the best country in the whole world and I wouldn't trade it for anything."

Frustration with the government was directly experienced in the planning and construction of new highways designed to bypass the towns of Lincoln County. During the 1960s highway bypasses were responsible for the failure of a number of cafés, restaurants, hotels, and gas stations. In 1969, for example, an interstate highway was constructed near Sprague and began diverting traffic that previously went through the town. A few shopkeepers are reported to have banded together to petition the state government for permission to put up a sign on the bypass containing a list of Sprague businesses. A blueprint of the billboard design was sent to the state capitol with the letter of petition. The government responded that a state law prohibited billboards on the interstate highway, but that the sign could be put up on another highway as long as it was not visible from the interstate freeway. The billboard petition may have been one of the last, if not the last, serious efforts by shopkeepers to reverse the declining fortunes of one of these towns. This circumstance is perhaps symbolic of the modern age, with its large farms, powerful corporations, and insensitive government, which has passed these people by.

Capitalists Made Obsolete by Capitalism

Lincoln County was born in the days of the frontier, when opportunity was abundant, laissez-faire capitalism flourished, and the government stayed out of people's business. The conditions of the frontier no longer exist in Lincoln County except in memory and in unfulfilled ideals. Today, opportunity has been severely curtailed, most small businesses are perpetually on the verge of failure, and the government is found increasingly burdensome with its many legal restrictions and tax requirements.

The shopkeepers of Lincoln County are above all else believers in the capitalist way of doing things because they themselves are archetype capitalists—small-time entrepreneurs whose success or failure depends upon how hard they work and how well they exercise judgments over their investments. The difficulty is that even though they work hard and do not squander their money, they are doomed to ultimate failure. Their efforts will only help them to succeed temporarily in coping with inevitable decline. Before some realize what has happened it will be too late; their assets will have no value and they will be trapped into a marginal existence. Others unable to tolerate financial, physical, and psychological stress will be forced to give up and leave after investing much time, effort, and money in a hopeless cause.

There are many reasons why Lincoln County has lost a viable business community. In the most general sense all these reasons have something to do with the modern capitalist world rendering small towns and shopkeepers obsolete. Lincoln County towns are now of little importance either as railroad terminals, highway stops, or as supply centers for farmers. Resentments are expressed by shopkeepers against farmers, corporations, government, and even each other, but there is little or nothing that they can do except to gripe. Their only way of exercising control is to show hostility to the outside world and thereby avoid further annoyance or embarrassment from having strangers meddle in their affairs. Thus it follows that a company interested in locating in the area or researchers attempting to understand the situation would be regarded with suspicion.

A respondent in Sprague, upon being asked to participate in the present study, informed the interviewer that a team of community-development experts from the University of Washington came several years earlier to conduct a study and make recommendations. The team is reported to have concluded that a number of improvements were in order: (1) Business buildings in current use should be painted; (2) old condemned buildings should be torn down; (3) a cocktail lounge would be advantageous; and (4) a doctor and a dentist were needed.

These recommendations must have had a hollow ring to local residents who do not have the capital to invest in any of these projects and would certainly suffer losses even if they had the capital and made the investments. As might be expected, the recommendations were followed only insofar as a few storefronts were painted. Such obvious lack of understanding shown by experts from a famous university can only serve to increase alienation from the outside world. Thus it is not surprising that many potential respondents refused to participate in the present study and that many of those who did participate expressed the view that the study would be of little if any use.

With the views of our respondents in mind we cannot make any self-serving claims about the "usefulness" or "relevance" of this study. It has not produced any answers to liberal-minded questions such as "What should shopkeepers do to improve their profits?" Our intention is not to advocate individual solutions to complex social problems. Instead, we have tried to describe the complexity of these problems by showing what the closing of the American frontier means for a forgotten group of people. It should be well understood that the present economic system gives scant preference to small-scale capitalists as opposed to small farm operators and workers in distributing its burdens. Changes in economic and social structure over the years have in effect made it nearly impossible for the common person to be a successful capitalist. Many who believe and try, like those in Lincoln County, will ultimately fail in reaching the goal of economic self-sufficiency. A newcomer who makes a serious effort often does so only because he or she has miscalculated or overlooked inevitable losses. Opportunity exists primarily for those content to be regarded as misfits and hobbyists who can do as they please with nothing to gain or lose.

Perhaps the most severe consequence of obsolescence to the shopkeeper is the loss of freedom to control his own work life. Since the ideal of freedom in this sense can only be realized by being a successful capitalist, the failure of small business diminishes freedom. It is clearly ironic that a capitalist society should allow those who practice and believe most strongly in the system to lose their freedom. The persistence of the frontier ethic, however, means that this irony is misunderstood and that the loss of freedom is experienced as a personal failure and a constant source of misery for many who wish to but cannot be successful entrepreneurs.

Identification with the ideology of capitalism and the experience of personal failure combine to produce an extremely conservative or right-wing political posture. Resentment is focused against the government for showing favoritism to big business and big labor at the expense of the small-time entrepreneur. Hence the most obvious solution to the problem, as cast in these terms, is to reduce government involvement in the economy so that the ordinary person can again become economically competitive. Over the last several decades the obsolescence of large numbers of people in the marginal capitalist class, perhaps even including many workers who dream of becoming entrepreneurs, has no doubt contributed to the current strength of the right wing in American politics.

On the local scene the adaptation to experiencing business problems as personal failure occurs in two stages. The first stage is represented by a few relatively prosperous shopkeepers in Lincoln County's three largest towns. There persons remain active in community affairs and maintain a façade of respectability that belies the economic stagnation of their businesses. The second stage is represented by the marginal and destitute shopkeepers trapped in Lincoln County's smallest towns. These persons have no escape from failure and have withdrawn in bitterness from community life altogether. In fact, their communities have no life and no active existence. The reactions characteristic of either of these two groups are likely to occur among members of the marginal capitalist class. Whether they go through the motions as a means of changing reality or whether they withdraw completely, the result is self-defeating. Such individualistic solutions result in a futile affirmation of the very system that oppresses these people and presents a formidable barrier to meaningful change.

Notes

1. Ultimately the changes in land-tenure patterns and agricultural practices mentioned here affected the raising of sheep and horses more than cattle. The number of cattle and calves in Lincoln County in 1970 was 39,766, compared to 21,642 in 1890. The number of sheep and lambs was 3,191 in 1970, compared to 12,724 in 1890; and the number of horses and ponies was 838 in 1970, compared to 15,863 in 1890 (*1969 Census of Agricluture*).

2. The surveying of businesses in Lincoln County and the subsequent sampling was carried out by Paul Barkley. The *1972 Census of Retail Trade* counts only 133 businesses in the county, as opposed to 301 counted by Barkley. It appears that many of the small, unlicensed establishments are overlooked in this census.

3. Lincoln County towns are reasonably close to several colleges and universities in Spokane and also to Washington State University in Pullman.

4. The original intention in conducting the sampling was to exclude businesses started after 1968. Three businesses started in 1970 were inadvertently included because the owners had lived in town since 1968.

5. It is very difficult to arrive at a meaningful figure for net income, since, in family businesses of this type, business and household finances are not calculated separately. The amount of income that goes to the household is not precisely known and could be reported by the respondents only as a rough estimate.

6. The clergymen were perhaps looking for shopkeepers to join their churches, for only one-fifth of the shopkeepers sampled currently are church members.

7 Building Toward Economic Democracy

Survival of the Fittest

As our study of the five sites described in this book proceeded, three questions become central. First, how were individuals, families, and communities adapting to persistent unemployment and deterioration of their economic position? Second, why did people affirm the necessity and propriety of capitalist development, which made them the victims and destroyed their communities? Third, what were the factors that limited political mobilization and radical change?

One important characteristic of the adaptation in each of the five sites was a tendency for most people to stay in the same community, reduce their standard of living significantly, and use the resources of family and friends in the community as a means of survival. In some cases, moving out of the community was regarded as too risky, while in other cases it was not economically possible. Up to a certain point our respondents displayed a great deal of resourcefulness and resiliency in the face of economic hardship. It appears, however, that prolonged adaptation to unemployment or economic stagnation of a business enterprise eventually erodes self-confidence and the capacity to fight back. Older persons, who have already put in many years of hard work and are less flexible in being able to adapt to the current requirements of an increasingly restrictive labor market, are the most vulnerable to being broken in spirit. They are often forgotten because they do not appear on the unemployment roles and are regarded as "voluntary" labor-force dropouts. As they are left isolated in rural enclaves or as other industries such as tourism are brought in to stimulate economic activity, obsolete workers, farmers, and shopkeepers become invisible victims of what is regarded as "inevitable economic progress."

A second important characteristic of the adaptation of the people we studied was their assertion of individual independence while organizational support collapsed around them. In the three sites involving company closures the existing union had been weakened to the point of ineffectiveness in protecting the interests of discarded workers. Likewise in the case of small farm operators and shopkeepers, existing mechanisms of formal cooperation were not effective. Farm cooperatives originally designed to assist all farmers now serve only the interests of large farms and corporations. Shopkeepers acting through a depopulated Chamber of Commerce also have little political clout compared to the chain stores and large-scale farmers in their communities. Workers, farmers, and shopkeepers alike were cynical about participating in organizations that for them had lost their *raison d'être*. Many felt specifically betrayed

211

and generally distrustful of organized attempts to represent their economic and political interests. Protest that might otherwise be expressed in a political arena was often translated into affirmations of individual independence and expressions of antigovernment, antisocial sentiment. To drop out of the labor market is thus to affirm that one can take a job or leave it, and to cut costs to operate a small farm or a small business is to affirm that one's livelihood need not be dependent upon those who are economically and politically powerful.

A third important characteristic of the adaptation to economic hardship was that resistance, when it occurred, was manifested in efforts to preserve the community. The tendency toward community preservation was particularly evident in Maunaloa and the towns in Lincoln County. Former pineapple workers and their families were acutely more interested in keeping their homes and maintaining personal ties within the community than in taking make-shift jobs that would require them to disperse to other islands. They resisted the loss of their primary school and on two occasions started petitions, one requesting the company to stay and the other requesting that they be allowed to purchase their homes. Although the interference of political brokers effectively stopped the petition drives, collective action and protest aimed at confrontation arose spontaneously around the issue of preserving the community.

In Lincoln County resistance to economic stagnation occurred in the context of trying to initiate and obtain funds for public-works projects that would enhance the attractiveness and improve the business climate of the towns. Efforts along these lines were also made to keep existing businesses from folding up, to revive frontier festivals, and to attract new industries to these towns. Although the opposition of large farm operators, lack of government interest, and widespread apathy prevented such efforts from succeeding, the fact remains that the issue of community preservation was the focus of some amount of protest and collective action.

The tendency for many of our respondents to lend support to corporate actions taken against their interest can be explained partly by what we have called "frontier ideology." They believe in hard work and that hard work will be rewarded despite company closures and economic stagnation in rural communities. In other words, in the context of a "free enterprise" system the work ethic itself is attributed with survival value. As one small farm operator said: "Someday it will come down to survival of the fittest. People like me who know about hard work will be the few that survive." We found that great emphasis was placed on economic independence by workers as well as by small-scale entrepreneurs. Oregon wood-products workers and the Bisbee miners both expressed dreams, and sometimes even concrete plans, related to establishing business enterprises of their own. Even Filipino pineapple workers, although not as fiercely individualistic as other respondents in our study, believed strongly in the work ethic; and a few who had the chance ultimately invested in small business ventures in the Philippines. As explained earlier, the primary goal sought by small farm operators and shopkeepers even in the face of great adversity was to maintain control of their own work lives. Since the dreams and goals of our respondents were directed toward successfully exercising capitalist prerogatives through their own initiative and hard work, it was not regarded to be within the realm of possibility to challenge others, especially those who were extremely powerful, who would exercise the same prerogatives. In other words, it was unthinkable to erode the ideological foundation upon which one's own hopes and dreams were built.

Another essential observation about the reactions of workers is that they were manipulated by false information and forecasts about opportunities they had little way of knowing would not materialize. In the case of Oregon's wood-products workers, there was the promise of holding onto their jobs if only more trees were cut, and in the case of Maunaloa's pineapple workers there was the promise of new housing and hotel jobs. In both cases, campaigns were conducted to popularize false promises and to mislead the public about environmental problems. Although environmental abuses have raised public consciousness about corporate behavior and have taught the lessons of vigilance, workers in extractive industries who rely upon an exploitive relationship to the environment for their livelihood are especially vulnerable to being persuaded that exploitation must be allowed. Miners in Bisbee were misled, despite a relatively high degree of historically nurtured class awareness, because they thought the company was "crying wolf," as it had done many times before. When the company finally closed, they were given no advance warning, and they were too stunned to mobilize against what was actually happening.

One final reason for the prevalence of "false consciousness" among workers was that in the past they had trusted the union to look after their interests. As long as the union was able to guarantee them a small share in the company's prosperity, the actions of the company were not held in question. What the workers in Oregon, Bisbee, and Maunaloa did not count on is that their unions were rendered powerless by plant closures, thereby making it possible for the companies to cheat workers out of their jobs.

By answering the first two questions raised in our study, we have already answered the third question. The factors limiting political mobilization and change were inherent in the adaptations and ideology that typify our respondents, for they turned inward toward their communities and close acquaintances and stayed away from organizational entanglements. They also maintained strong belief in the work ethic and the basic principles of a free-enterprise economy. Although they became increasingly proletarianized, they were left with no rationale for mobilizing politically to seek radical change. The only issues that precipitated collective action were those centered around community preservation. The futility of such efforts and the discouragement generated by coping individually with long-term unemployment and financial hardship comprised the final limiting factor. When self-doubt and cynicism became stronger than the work ethic, workers became psychologically incapacitated and unable to help themselves. Thus the final indignity suffered by those who had been made obsolete was that they were robbed of the work ethic, which was the key to their psychological well-being in its being regarded as essential to their economic survival.

On one hand, it is an indictment of the American economic system that many productive people have been made obsolete and robbed of their self-respect; on the other hand, it is a tribute to many workers and small-scale entrepreneurs that they are able to survive by their wits and still fight to maintain their communities despite enormous odds against their success.

Economists As False Prophets

Americans are rarely asked to consider serious or realistic suggestions for how our institutions—and hence our daily life—could be significantly and constructively altered for the better. Much of what is presented in movies, television, newspapers, magazines, and books either implicitly accepts the system the way it is or takes off on a wild flight of fantasy that allows escape without stimulating new thought. In both instances, there is a decided lack of courage and critical vision. To make matters worse, professionals and experts who are respected as being knowledgeable also spend a good deal of time validating the status quo. In fact, economists, among whose ranks are found the worst offenders, have long served as advisers to business and government and as rationalizers of social inequities and environmental abuse. Their excuses and explanations are phrased in both pretentiously complex and patronizingly simple terms for the consumption of the general public. Such behavior reached grotesque proportions during the Nixon years, when the Council of Economic Advisers became political pawns and simply lied about the present and future state of the economy to suit the needs, ambitions, and neuroses of the Administration.

Although other social scientists are not without fault for attempting to rationalize inequalities in the existing social order, they do not enjoy the high professional standing of economists—a standing that results from their pretending to make a mathematically objective interpretation of capitalist economic growth. Economists are widely employed by private industry and are often appointed to important policy-making bodies and governmental positions, including the President's Cabinet. Since the subject matter of other social sciences is not regarded as particularly relevant to policy, sociologists, psychologists, anthropologists, and the like are relatively powerless. In fact, they often busy themselves trying to prove how helpful they can be and end up not doing much of anything.

In the last few years the increasingly important role of economists in providing theoretical support for an American-based, worldwide system of economic exploitation has been recognized by the award of a Nobel Prize in economics and the bestowal of "scientific" status upon its practitioners. It is precisely because the ideology of economists has been certified as "objective" and "value neutral" that it is so dangerous. Economists have at their disposal a plethora of pseudoscientific axioms and euphemisms that are commonly used to dull and confuse the analytic capacities and moral sensibilities of the ordinary citizen, who is often regarded as a mental dullard and forced to accept extremely narrow limits on what he or she is allowed to believe and hope for in the future. We are told, for example, that unemployment is a necessary evil if we are to avoid inflation; that older men who are dropping out of the labor force in ever-increasing numbers are "voluntarily unemployed"; that a need for nutritious food, housing, or social services does not exist because no "demand" is registered for it, when people are often simply too poor to pay; that the unfettered accumulation and movement of private capital is necessary to keep the economy running; and that the rules of the game result in an equitable distribution of economic opportunity for those who work hard and thus are deserving. Evidence presented in previous chapters indicates, to the contrary, that inflation is caused by perverted tax incentives, land speculation, and monopolistic control of markets; that many "older" men face discrimination in the labor market and are becoming involuntarily unemployed; that ignoring needs for housing and social services by economic sleight of hand does not make people's hardships disappear; that the unfettered accumulation and movement of capital just gives us even bigger capitalists, as well as environmental abuse and the exploitation of laborers and small producers here and abroad; and that the rules of the game exacerbate a trend toward greater economic and social inequality. The point here is that we Americans are turning to the wrong people to seek advice on how to solve so-called "economic" problems.

Economists have no yardstick to measure what is socially desirable and what is not. Their concern is confined to making judgments about whether there is a sufficiently healthy economic climate so that corporate investment—the motor force of capitalism—will be forthcoming; that is, economists want to make sure that investments will bring profits, regardless of other consequences. An extreme example of the utter depravity some economists exhibit is a recent declaration that public institutions, such as universities, should not divest their stockholdings in corporations that do business in South Africa. One reason given was that most of these corporations actually "resent apartheid" because it *forces* them to build separate toilets and pay discriminatory wages. Besides, "large and vocal South African business groups are already fighting apartheid . . . political change is inevitable."

Here is another example. A well-known expert on economic development recently attended a conference on Chile's "external financial policy." Topics included the issue of direct investment in Chile by foreign corporations. This economic expert observed that "the government of Chile is largely non-ideological and appears to operate without fanfare for the achievement of social stability and economic order." The majority of Chileans, he says, "are grateful to the Junta for having delivered Chile from the claws of the Allende era." His conversations with government and diplomatic officials satisfied him that "only one political prisoner remains in Chile . . . [although this] does not mean that the government is becoming soft on leftists or even on individuals who . . . insist on political expression." He concludes by expressing the hope that the Carter Administration will reciprocate Chile's desire for cordial relations, for "Chile is an open society and . . . susceptible to American influence."

Such positions directly support two of the most repressive governments in the world. They also support an arrangement whereby American companies take advantage of the availability of cheap labor and an abundance of natural resources to make profits, while native people are kept ignorant by deliberate policy and excluded from sharing in wealth that is rightfully theirs. Whether it is sweathshops in Korea and Mexico, plantations in the Philippines and Thailand, or laborers and small producers in the United States, exploitation is rationalized by economists as a necessary part of a sound investment climate. Americans as well as foreigners are exploited by monopoly capitalism and the moral blinders of the economist give no preference in this regard. This is why economists should not be taken at face value when they promote the idea that what is good for big business is also good for the rest of us. Economists are not the experts they appear to be; they are ideologues in objective clothing, the false prophets and depraved high priests of corporate religion.

The economic problems we face in America are inherent in an undemocratic system of monopoly capitalism that has subverted many essential aspects of political democracy. Watergate, illegal influence peddling in Congress, serious violations of human rights committed by the CIA and FBI, numerous violations of campaign financing laws by large corporations, as well as their outright bribery of foreign officials, are just a few examples. Not only are candidates easily chosen and elected officials easily influenced and corrupted by a large and powerful capitalists, but many political appointees to government agencies are selected from among the wealthy capitalist class and have little accountability to the electorate. The most glaring example at the national level is the Cabinet of President Carter, which includes several key appointees from the Trilateral Commission—a private policy-planning group maintained within the Rockefeller empire. These trilateral appointees include the Secretary of State, National Security Adviser, Secretary of the Treasury, Secretary of Defense, Ambassador to the United Nations, and the Vice-President. At both the national and state level it is common knowledge that having served on one or more corporate boards is requisite to being selected as an appointee to political office (consider President Carter's difficulty in finding "qualified" women with corporate experience to appoint to his Administration). Regulatory agencies meant to serve the public interest are commonly staffed with appointees from the industries they must regulate. Some examples have been discussed in Chapter 1.

Consistent with this pattern is the fact that people who suffer economic problems—such as laborers and small producers—are absent from the ranks of either elected or appointed officials. This phenomenon is directly related to what has been shown in this study, namely, that ordinary working people have been exploited economically and that they lack political power to prevent further exploitation. Conventional capitalist solutions to problems of economic decline and unemployment, such as bringing in a new industry, dissolving communities, extracting nonrenewable resources in ever greater quantities, and passing out unemployment checks, merely serve to shift the burden from one work force to another, from one community to another, from one generation to another, or from the private to the public sector. What we have been offered in addition to our problems are hucksters' shell games, impotent commissions "to study the problem," irrelevant policies, and impoverished programs. What we need are *political solutions* that will alter the undemocratic structure of the economic system itself.

A Unifying Goal

The present study has identified four general problem areas that must be addressed in any program of political and economic change. These problems are briefly summarized here so they may be kept in mind as the discussion turns toward suggesting immediate strategies for change. One problem concerns *capital flight,* wherein a company closes or moves elsewhere because its operation is found to be "uneconomical" or less profitable than it might be in another place. Capital flight typically results in the slow death of dependent communities; the abandonment of American workers in favor of cheap foreign labor; discrimination against older workers in layoffs and rehiring; and chronic unemployment in the economy as a whole.

A second problem concerns *capital concentration* in the hands of large firms and conglomerates at the expense of small producers. The tax system gives special advantages to large companies and has fostered the uncontrolled development of an inefficient and socially undesirable technology that replaces workers and makes them economically obsolete. Meanwhile, few restrictions are placed on monopoly capitalists who use their profits to invest in land speculation, excessive extraction of nonrenewable resources, chemical poisoning and other abuse of the land, and conversion of good farmland to nonessential, nonagricultural uses. In fact, there are a multitude of incentives for all these antisocial and destructive behaviors. The overcrowding and pollution of urban areas and the lack of opportunity for young and old alike in rural areas are a direct result of capital moving from the hands of many to only a few. There are many other examples.

A third problem concerns the lack of *political power* among workers, their inability to exercise control over their work lives, and the vulnerability of their communities to economic shocks. Not only the workers' right to maintain their livelihood but also the conditions under which they work are largely out of their hands and are controlled by professional managers. Laborers who have suffered physical ailments and have grown old while in a relationship of dependency to unions and employers are quickly discarded when employers default. (In some cases, cited in this book, "old" means over 40.) Workers in general are unable to challenge capital flight in the absence of class conscious union leadership and collective organizing strategies. A lack of political power exists not only among laborers but also among petty shopkeepers and small-scale farmers who have been stripped of their decision-making prerogatives. Small producers without capital are likely to find themselves eventually trapped in bankruptcy or forced to sell out against their will. This can happen regardless of their good business sense, hard work, and community spirit. These qualities are causally irrelevant to the experience of being made obsolete by the increasing capitalization of other economic units.

A fourth problem concerns *lack of knowledge* on the part of workers and small producers about the systemic inequities that rob them of the ability to control their lives. Many are misled to think that they can form an unholy alliance of sorts with their oppressors, while others hope to win out in the end because they possess moral superiority and are doggedly determined not to be beaten by the system. In either case, almost all share some resentment against big business and government and are capable of identifying particular circumstances of their own that are oppressive. At the same time it is true that they do not understand the structural incentives that subsidize monopoly capitalists and determine how the political and economic system operates. Economists who cloud the issues for us, as previously explained, are a large part of the problem. They contribute substantially to the ideological manipulation through which monopoly capitalists maintain control. Lack of understanding also results from a basic scarcity of accurate and reliable public information about the size of corporate profits, how they are acquired, and how they are used. The government is generally not charged with the responsibility of collecting such information, and what is presented by large corporations in media advertising is extremely shallow, manipulative, and often deceptive. Lack of clear understanding derives as well from the historical dulling of political consciousness, which, as described in previous chapters, was nourished by the abundance of the frontier and has receded as we have been cajoled into substituting consumerism for the more enduring satisfaction of performing meaningful work.

A final factor that inhibits understanding of the system in which we live appears to be a widely held, fundamental belief in the rightness of "free enterprise." Although the term "free enterprise" is hackneyed and has been used by monopoly capitalists *incorrectly* to describe themselves, it perhaps evokes better than any other concept the ideals that Americans have for their country. The term suggests that people are able to control their own economic activities and to shape their own destinies. This Jeffersonian ideal of free enterprise persists strongly in people's minds as a basic attribute of the American system, no matter how bureaucratic and undemocratic the workings of the system have become in practice. In other words, frontier ideology, with its emphasis on free enterprise, has survived while the frontier itself has not. This perhaps explains why many Americans, as with some of those interviewed for this study, complain bitterly about large corporations and corruption in government and yet react with extreme defensiveness and patriotic fervor against well-meaning criticism of the system.

Despite its antiquity, it would be a mistake for us to dismiss the general belief in free enterprise as anachronistic and totally inappropriate as a foundation for bringing about change. There are two reasons why it must be recognized as important. First, it is deeply felt and perhaps impossible for some persons to disavow and, second, it reflects a realistic dissatisfaction with the way the system has evolved, partially to compensate for its own defects. Moreover, it is the *compensatory features* of the system (such as welfare programs) that are made most visible to people and seem to threaten their ideals, especially the work ethic, the most. Thus there is widespread resentment against waste, inefficiency, and corruption in the provision of government service; for example, lethal hazards in sawmills go uninspected, uncorrected; a task force with $5 million cannot find a working solution to the continued unemployment of 135 Filipino laborers. There is exasperation over the regulation of business and private life by government agencies; for example, payment into retirement and unemployment funds brings some small shopkeepers to the point of bankruptcy. Citizens feel the impotence of their state governments and local communities and dislike the arbitrary and heavy-handed actions of the federal government and big business; for example, the fate of a community can rest in the hands of the National Forest Service, the Civil Aeronautics Board, the Department of Transportation, or institutions of banking and credit. It is perfectly consistent for people to value the ideal of free enterprise, and hence "the American way of life," and also to complain bitterly about the many compensatory interventions and regulations that have been devised to curb the worst excesses of monopoly capitalism but which often make life problematic for ordinary working people.

What then are the implications of recognizing that the ideal of free enterprise is salient to and deeply held by most Americans? It means, first, that in constructing an alternate system we should not include features that would ask people to give up important ideals or endorse what they fear or feel is alien to them. Second, we can put the most positive construction upon the tenets of this ideal: In their expressions of disillusionment with the political process and bitterness about a lack of correspondence between their ideals of free enterprise and the actual system in which compensatory regulation is required, Americans are saying that they are ready for a life that is more democratic. It is not difficult to agree with the premise that enterprise should be free for everyone and not just for a class of big capitalists. Finally, *broad-based participation by all people in a truly democratic political and economic system* can serve as a unifying goal. In order to stress this point we have chosen to call such a system "economic democracy."[1]

The discussion of economic democracy that follows is meant to stimulate thought and suggest strategies that have immediate potential for progressive change, given ideological and political conditions as they now exist in America. These suggestions represent a synthesis between democratic (public) ownership and control of the means of production, on the one hand, and free enterprise ideology and anti-monopoly-capitalist sentiment, on the other. We feel they have the potential to unite workers in communities that are in crisis, give people a greater sense of collective purpose, and perhaps erode the destructively individualistic tendencies of frontier ideology that presently pervade American life. We believe that people need to learn through direct experience that public ownership and popular political control are necessary, desirable, and achievable goals. The suggested strategies are designed to promote such direct experience.

Economic Democracy: An Alternative

We believe that it is possible to work toward economic democracy through existing but not normally used means. The transition to economic democracy will require critical structural changes in three areas of the economy— ownership and control of the means of production, tax rules, and the handling of money.

The United States is the only advanced industrial nation that does not have some provision for nationalization of essential industries where mismanagement and ownership by private corporations could adversely affect the public good. In Europe national or state ownership of such basic industries as steel, coal, and transportation is common. In the Canadian province of British Columbia, the National Democratic Party (NDP) pursued a policy of acquiring the province's extractive industries during its recent term in power. One example was the outright purchase of eight separate plywood and sawmill operations from British and American multinational corporations that were planning to close their plants or sell them to other multinationals. These purchases by the NDP were initiated primarily in response to petitioning to take over the plant by members of the International Woodworkers of America. Public ownership helped provide a chance for workers to move toward genuine democracy at the plant level (Lembcke, 1977:29).

In order to get from where we are now, that is, locked into an exploitative system of monopoly capitalism, to where we want to be, that is, full and equal participants in a system of economic democracy, nationalization of basic industries might appear to be a basic first step. However, we are afraid it is neither sufficient nor advantageous at the present time. It is not sufficient because history teaches the lesson that, in the absence of a strong working class party, nationalization does not automatically bring workers more control over the circumstances of the work place. Moreover, it is not advantageous, under the present conditions, for it would serve no useful purpose to transfer ownership from corporate captains to state and federal bureaucrats or political leaders who already act as partners in perpetuating the abuses of monopoly capitalism in the United States. Let us be clear on this issue. We are not rejecting nationalization as a step which is forever unacceptable, but rather as one which is not practical in the absence of popular political control. The existence of a progressive and strong working class party is needed to make state bureaucrats accountable and elect responsible candidates to public office.

In the present, strategies other than nationalization hold more promise for altering the existing patterns of capital concentration and control: namely, worker self-management, worker ownership, and community ownership. All are being tried in various parts of the country. While the issues of ownership and of worker self-management (or control) are distinct, the following discussion combines them in one possible model, that of worker ownership and control. Another possibility, and one which we tend to favor, is that of worker self-management and community ownership. In this model, workers control the processes of production while the means of production are held in trust by the community at large. Both advantages and disadvantages of these forms of organization are included in the following discussion.

Who should own the means of production? "When we speak of workers' control," writes theorist André Gorz, "we speak of the capability of the workers to take control of production and to organize the work process as *they* see best." (in Zwerdling 1978:6) This, of course, is precisely the opposite of present-day capitalist enterprise, where workers are separate from owners and management and regarded merely as another factor of production. Worker control can change the motives for, nature of and output from production. For example, with workers in control, companies will rarely find that it is desireable to move or close down. Under this mode of management, it is up to workers to cut wages, instead of laying off workers, or to do whatever is necessary to survive a temporary economic slump. Workers in control of their own companies will be less willing to harm their own livelihood by shifting capital away from a useful enterprise that provides them employment to a "more profitable enterprise" that does not. Worker-owners as stable residents of a community will have a basic interest in protecting their community from pollution and environmental abuse, unlike absentee corporate owners who do not work and live in the community and, as this book has shown, are quite unaccountable to community needs and preferences. Just because owners are residents of a community, of course, does not guarantee environmental perfection, but the trade-offs should be better reasoned since they are in the hands of people who are affected by goals related both to production (as worker-owners) and environmental protection (as community residents).

Extending democracy to the work place can give workers a sense of efficacy that has not existed in the past. For example, decisions that directly affect workers' lives—such as fixing the percentage of revenues allocated for wages, profits, and benefits and establishing the conditions of work, safety standards, hours, task requirements, and personnel action—are firmly placed under worker control through company-wide elections. If this seems utopian, it is only because the present nature of work in America does not require or utilize the creativity, resourcefulness, and variety of human labor that people possess. The mindlessness of contemporary work does not mean that workers are mindless, irresponsible, or dull. Many examples exist that demonstrate that American workers can capably fulfill the functions of management and of their own work.

One such worker-owned firm, Olympia Plywood, was founded in 1921. Others followed, and sixteen that still operate today range in size from 80 to 450 worker-owners, have gross revenues of between $3 and $20 million, and comprise one-eighth of the American plywood industry. The worker-owned mills have demonstrated their superiority to conventionally owned mills in several ways. First, they are much more productive.

Though they are not professionally trained to run a modern business, worker-owners in [sixteen] plywood firms in the Pacific Northwest have consistently outperformed the industry, their . . . output exceeding industry productivity levels by 25 to 60 percent. (Bernstein, 1977:55)

Second, workers' collectives often have taken over bankrupt or money-losing private firms and converted them into successful enterprises. Third, these collectives generally have run at a higher percentage of capacity than conventional mills. Fourth, during periods of recession when industry wide layoffs have occurred, the worker-owned firms typically have cut wages equally for all members and kept everyone working. Alternatively, workers have loaned part of their wages to the company to keep it open. Fifth, wages in some of the worker-owned plywood companies are equal for all workers and average 25 percent more than in conventionally owned companies. In addition, each worker-owner receives as much as several thousand dollars from year-end division of profits and the full value of his share when he leaves the company. Such shares typically bring $20,000 to $40,000.

A similar success story comes from the Vermont Asbestos Group (VAG) in Lowell, Vermont. In 1975, 175 employees and 125 local residents bought out GAF, a New York-based conglomerate that planned to close a faltering asbestos mill and rob the community of its major source of employment. The mill is now a financial success; working conditions have improved substantially; wage-and-benefit increases have averaged 15 percent a year; and VAG stock has jumped from $50 a share to a current level of $2,000 (*Dollars and Sense*, 1978:6–7).

There are other examples, from all parts of the country, representing a wide range of production situations. While their number suggests they are little more than the exception to the rule (of increasing scale and concentration in ownership), they are still concrete testimony to the ability of workers to fulfill successfully the functions of ownership, management, and labor.

More must be said about the management of worker-owned firms. We propose the following structures. Company boards of directors consist of workers elected on a rotating basis. The single most important principle in all elections is one-person-one-vote. Representation in larger firms is based on departments or work units, so that all types of workers and divisions within the company can be included. Perhaps the expertise to oversee finances will still be provided by managers under the control of the elected directors. Being a manager, however, will confer no special authority, remuneration, or privilege. Managers purchase shares and participate in decision-making as equals to their fellow owner-workers. Basic equality is reinforced by equal pay. Wages are kept within a narrow range; for example, the highest paid worker receives no more than double the pay of the lowest paid. The primary bases for differences in pay are seniority and diligence, as determined by a consensus of co-workers, rather than expertise. Although it is regarded as desirable to give a small bonus for special skills, the primary basis for accepting a position of responsibility is the nature of the job itself and not external rewards, which encourage people to take jobs for reason of self-advancement rather than their interest in performing a service and enhancing the public good.

In the structure of work under economic democracy, it is essential to prevent the formation of undemocratic hierarchies and privilege. This can be done in several concrete ways. First, managers are required to spend at least one month per year doing productive labor alongside other workers, an experience through which they gain intimate knowledge of workers and their problems. A further precautionary measure is to rotate board membership—a structure that allows office-holders a term long enough to acquire needed perspective and yet short enough to prevent self-serving alliances between managers and board members. Approval of the functions performed by managers is always open to a general vote of the workers, so that the power to decide which are matters of general concern is not usurped by managers. A manager is prevented from using his or her special knowledge as a weapon to intimidate subordinates because one essential part of this job is to educate board members and fellow worker-owners about policies and problems of the company. Regularly scheduled seminars and newsletters are used as educational vehicles.

Initial action in personnel cases is to be handled by committees elected from among workers in the same division or work place. In this way, hiring and firing decisions are made by the persons most directly dependent on each other in their work. Committees take applications, screen candidates, and select one candidate for final approval to the board of directors. This procedure is not only fair but also serves to institutionalize an often effective, informal system of selection through interpersonal networks, such as that described many times in this book. However, personnel action is not likely to be the constant headache that it is under the alienating and undemocratic work conditions of monopoly capitalism. For example, worker absenteeism and turnover should be minimal.

As a further benefit, worker control produces more efficient decisions about controversial issues. For example, we expect workers in such companies to abolish forced retirement and allow co-workers to change to less demanding jobs as they grow older. Since the number of people of retirement age has increased relative to the number of younger people in the work force, this kind of flexibility is greatly needed. In other cases, workers may choose to support forced retirement because the safety of all workers depends on the health and skill of older workers. Whatever is decided, however, it is based on criteria relevant to workers' concrete concerns and not on arbitrary rules set by government or professional managers.

Setting production quotas is another touchy issue that is decided differently by worker-owners than by professional managers and union representatives at the bargaining table. Unlike union members, worker-owners are not at odds with the company over its interest in production. As the American situation so amply shows, workers in undemocratic companies do not work up to capacity because they wish to avoid impossible burdens that may be imposed upon them by professional managers. In democratically organized settings the incentives and control of work are markedly different. Since we assume that human beings like to find expression and meaning in work, we fully expect that they will work to capacity in a democratic work place.

As suggested earlier, worker ownership can be made to work and to work well, as has been demonstrated in a number of isolated cases in which firms run uneconomically by professional managers were bought out and salvaged by workers. These cases also amply demonstrate that establishing truly democratic work organization will not be an easy task. Both managers and workers experience considerable frustration in the attempt to behave democratically, as indicated by a recent experiment in running a democratic insurance company in Washington, D.C. (*Working Papers for a New Society*, vol. 5, no. 1:68–81). Workers not accustomed to making decisions shy away because of feelings of incompetence, lack of interest, or resentment over time spent arguing in meetings. Managers not used to listening to what workers have to say are sometimes not able to treat workers as equals or deal with their indecisiveness. Managers also resent having no authority to act without first educating workers and seeking their approval.

A more basic problem is that worker ownership *alone* does not necessarily alter the individualistic ideology of workers or make them more accountable to the economic needs and security of their communities. For example, two prosperous worker-owned plywood firms in the Northwest were recently sold to ITT and the Times-Mirror Corporation, two giant conglomerates. These sales render the local communities vulnerable once again to the common corporate practices of layoffs, closures, and capital flight. Ironically, it is the most economically successful worker-owned firms that are most likely to be sold in this way. Such firms are vulnerable because "success has raised the price of their shares to high levels, making it difficult for new individuals to buy in [and] their economically favorable track record attracts giant companies looking for lucrative acquisitions." (Bernstein, 1977:57). Thus, although worker ownership increases control over the conditions and remuneration of work, it is still private ownership. The crucial matters of community economic stability and the public good are not completely assured because the means of production are not held in perpetual community or public trust.

What of the rights of the community in which production occurs, or those of the people who depend upon or desire the product? Should workers own the plywood or steel mills in which they work, thus controlling the quantity and quality of these essential products, as well as their prices and the price of their own labor? Or is the production of such commodities as wood, steel, and coal so critical to us all that ownership should reside with the people as a whole? There are no obvious answers to these questions, particularly within the context of a political and economic system that sanctifies private-property rights and free enterprise. Further, several different arrangements for equitable ownership could coexist with the development of economic democracy, depending upon the nature of the product or service being produced, the need for capital, and an assessment of the public interest. Now let us consider the alternative of community ownership, an option that may be preferable in some cases to worker ownership.

"Community ownership" refers to circumstances in which economic organizations are controlled or owned by the residents of the area in which they are located. Organizations that can be owned or controlled locally might include such types as business firms, industrial-development parks, housing-development corporations, banks, credit unions, and cooperative ventures. They might also include social and environmental organizations that increase the economic value and energy of the community. Schaaf (1977), for example, has suggested that communities purchase farmland to lease at reasonable rates to persons seriously interested in starting small farm enterprises and that community investments could be made in self-help cooperatives among established farmers.

The following case indicates how community ownership might work. In Philadelphia the Reverend Leon Sullivan, pastor of that city's largest black church and a prominent civil-rights leader, convinced six thousand community residents to put up $10 a month each for 36 months (a total of $2,160,000) to purchase stock in a community-owned corporation for the purpose of constructing and operating a shopping center. Through this effort, an impoverished area gained a revitalized commercial center, a substantially increased number of jobs for community residents, and income (from operation of the shopping center), which is used to finance needed human and social services.

A more typical route to community economic development and ownership of local economic resources is the eclectic path of generating and combining relatively modest amounts of federal grant funds, foundation money, private enterprise financing, and bank loans to support a community development corporation. The term "community development corporation," or CDC, is used to identify organizations created and controlled by people living in low-income areas for the purposes of planning, financing, owning, and operating firms that will provide employment, income, and a better life for the residents of these areas. There are almost 750 community development corporations across the country, with approximately 50 receiving funds from the Federal Community Economic Development program.

Here are some examples of economic development and community ownership which have emerged through the route described above. The Central Coast Counties Development Corporation, operating in rural California over the past three years, has parlayed intensive community organizing efforts, creative planning, modest grants from the Economic Development Administration and the Office of Economic Opportunity, and local bank loans into a community-owned agricultural marketing and supply cooperative that has helped its 35 member-families (all former farm workers) raise their incomes from $3,500 to $13,000 a year. On the Navajo Reservation in Arizona and New

Mexico, six communities have established thriving consumers' cooperative food stores and credit unions. The sources of funding for these community ventures were small foundation and OEO grants and loans from the Bureau of Indian Affairs and Farmers Home Administration. All of the six ventures have banded together to form a community development corporation that will coordinate the provision of technical services and the initiation of new ventures.

There are many advantages to be gained from community based economic development; two seem critical here. First, the problem of capital flight no longer exists when residents own and control the major economic institutions in their community. It is absurd to imagine residents taking their capital out of community-owned credit unions, banks, cooperatives, and other firms and investing it in someone else's community, leaving their own without an economic base. Second, unlike an absentee corporate owner, a community has every reason to divert some of the income from successful local enterprises and invest it in needed social programs and services, such as child care, low-income housing, meals to seniors, and parks. These programs improve the livability and social character of the community to the benefit of all. Community based economic development, then, serves at least two essential purposes and is rooted concretely in the collective wishes and needs of local residents.

A final example, from a lumber-based rural community in Oregon, shows how community-based development can also be used to implement broader community goals, such as the use of appropriate technology and labor-intensive (rather than capital-intensive) modes of production. The small rural town of Oakridge, Oregon, suffered severe economic problems when the town's major employer, a mill operating in nearby Westfir, shut down. Unemployment rose to 24 percent and residents became quite desperate. Several local people worked hard to convince the community that an economic development corporation might ameliorate their problems through a program of community owned and controlled economic development. The development corporation was formed with the hard-earned blessing of the city council, and a broad-based Board of Directors was elected. The "Upper Willamette Economic Development Corporation" (UWEDC), as it was called, applied for funding from the Economic Development Administration (EDA) to purchase and develop an industrial park and to initiate a community revolving-loan fund in order to capitalize locally owned businesses. With EDA funding, the plans are to lease sites in the industrial park to community-owned businesses, which will emphasize the use of local resources such as hardwoods in the manufacture of hot tubs. Site development is also underway for a worker-owned firm which will precut, assemble, and package all the materials needed for the purchaser to build a solar-heated, self-help house. These firms will be locally owned, employ Oakridge residents, use resources abundantly available in the surrounding area, and manufacture products of appropriate technology. The community destruction that comes in the wake of a mill closure is no longer a threat to Oakridge.

These stories of community revitalization and economic health are meant to illustrate the potential that exists for successful community ownership and control of the local economy. Such strategies, however, are not always successful, just as in the case of worker ownership. Like worker-owned firms, community-development corporations are heavily dependent on federal and private sector sources of capital to purchase firms and cover initial operating expenses. Community development corporations that pursue federal dollars must appease various local, state, and federal agencies in meeting their guidelines. After meetings, negotiation, and proposal-writing, they find themselves in competition with hundreds of other CDC's for limited government financing and grants. Typically the most established CDC's (with 3 to 5 years of operation) and the most successful (showing the highest rates of return on capital investment) or influential are the ones that receive federal funding and/or private-sector loans.

Structurally, the government requirement that capital must be managed to insure the highest rate of return forces CDC's into very "capitalistlike" behavior, such as hiring business managers at $40,000 annual salaries to invest in fast-food chains and other high-profit service industries instead of investing in manufacturing, housing construction and other areas of high community need. In addition, it is not unheard of for a federally funded CDC to operate nonunion shops in order to reduce costs and thus increase profits. In summary, government- and private-sector financing can easily subvert the best intentions of those organizations attempting to respond to community need.

One promising new alternative to the compromising reliance on federal- and private-sector capital is the use of union pension funds as investment capital for community economic development. On the Eastern seaboard, for example, a coalition of union leaders and progressive activists have united to invest pension funds in CDC's, cooperative housing organizations, and employee-owned and managed firms. These investments replace investments in blue-chip stocks, which largely go to increase further the accumulation of capital in the hands of monopoly capitalists.

One additional problem with community economic development must be mentioned. Some community organizations have maintained a balance between economic development and organizing activities without sacrificing community interests and accountability. However, the pursuit of business success and profit-making can seduce community organizations into neglecting their original objectives. Successful CDCs seem to require tight control by a small group of leaders, continuity and longevity of membership, and a stable climate. Money managers and city bureaucrats become nervous when decisions are made in broad-based public meetings rather than in the restricted meetings of "respectable" community and business leaders or a small group of CDC managers and officers. Furthermore, the success of a CDC requires placating local government bureaucrats and participating in consensus-style planning meetings with suave commercial money managers. In other words, a partnership of government, private business and lending institutions, and the community is characteristic of successful CDCs. This circumstance is contradictory to the tactics of demand-negotiation and confrontation, historically pursued in successful community organizing efforts in search of greater power for low-income people and neighborhoods.

However, no single model of a CDC exists. Like other community organizations, CDCs vary in objectives, strategies, style, and leadership. While we have pointed to some of their problems, we still view community economic development and community ownership to be important in the larger move toward economic democracy.

We have noted earlier that public ownership is not a strategy that is practical at this time. Still, its unique features throw into sharp relief the limits of the other two alternatives. Several advantages of public ownership are identified in a description of the British Columbia experience:

> [Government purchase] has the primary advantage of breaking the nexus with private capital . . . in legal and financial terms as well as in the minds of the workers and, at the same time, bringing self-determination down to the shop floor level. The community stabilization features are actually stronger than those of worker-ownership, since a large political entity—municipality, county, or state—assumes responsibility for its success. The broadening of the responsibility has the effect of raising in the political arena the question of economic stability in people's lives, making it a *social* rather than personal or local community responsibility. [Pacific Northwest Research Center, 1978:199]

Of the three alternatives, public ownership seems most effective in shifting the responsibility for economic stability and development to new and broader political terrain. For example, under public ownership, firms would be subject to the same exposure and scrutiny as are schools, roads, parks and other public properties. (Pacific Northwest Research Center, 1978:199)

All three strategies show some common difficulties. First, access to private capital will be difficult and, if obtained, is likely to be restrictive of worker self-management. Second, access to public funds for use as purchasing capital will greatly depend on achieving democratic control of state, county and municipal governments. Finally, under present political circumstances it will be difficult, if not structurally impossible, to attain rational and democratic coordination of all levels of the economy. Thus, even worker, community, or publically owned plants will have to exist within the constraints of cyclical demand, overproduction, and a host of other problems endemic to an unplanned, capitalist controlled state and economy.

It must be understood that problems and frustrations encountered in worker, community, and public ownership of the means of production do not arise out of some immutable "facts" of human nature. The work and private lives to which most of us are now accustomed variously involve rigid status hierarchies, impotence, exploitation, and dependence. Such structures quite obviously give rise to concomitant coping and compensatory behaviors. In sum, any strategies for change cannot be too idealistic and must deal with human beings as they are now. The evidence from more egalitarian societies, such as the People's Republic of China, should give us hope and confidence that new roles and personal relationships will evolve within a structure of everyday life that integrates community, work, and management and promotes feelings of autonomy, self-reliance, and dignity.

Taxes without unfair burdens. Our founding fathers rebelled against England in part because they were being forced to live under an unfair system of taxation. As a means to change the rules of the game and eliminate social inequities, a new tax program is no less important in building economic democracy. We need to abolish taxation that provides hidden subsidies for big business and allows concentration of capital in the hands of a few powerful people. A new tax system can be designed to encourage the development of domestic industry without giving special advantages to large corporations. The basic features of such a system are detailed below.

"Economies of scale" need to be eliminated from the tax structure so that large firms become uneconomical to run in the absence of unfair subsidies. The assets of such firms then drop to a level commensurate with their unsubsidized value, making it possible for workers or communities to purchase them and run them democratically. Another purpose of the envisioned tax program is to discourage capital flight and yet make it possible to maximize freedom of choice over how company revenues are allocated. To this end we expect that everyone will pay a fair share of taxes and that the tax system itself will reinforce democratically determined goals.

What specific features differentiate an equitable system of taxation from the one we presently have? Let us begin by pointing to the need to eliminate burdensome and discriminatory taxes on individuals. First, and foremost, we suggest that there be no personal income tax and none of its accompanying annoyances; we suggest that there be no loss of time filling out complicated income-tax forms every year, no scrambling to find questionable deductions, and no uncertainty over whether or not the forms are correctly done. Family budgeting is thus made easier as well, because the calculation of expected income does not depend on haphazard guesses about the size of the yearly tax bill. There are no limits to the use of income, which can be saved or spent precisely as the individual chooses.

Second, there is no place in such a system for a general sales tax, because such a tax robs people with relatively less wealth of purchasing power needed to acquire basic necessities. A selective sales tax, however, might be placed on ingestible items found to be a calculated risk to health, such as liquor, cigarettes, food additives, sleeping pills, etc. Ideally, whether such items are taxed or banned altogether should be decided by the public through direct referenda. Under economic democracy it is entirely reasonable to expect companies to be responsible for testing the effects of their own products and providing correct, technical information for use by the public in making purchasing judgments. A firm's failure to provide adequate testing of new products or correct information about them would warrant a fine contingent upon the number of products already sold.

Under our proposed plan the selective sales tax does not include luxury items because this deprives people of the right to decide for themselves what is a need and what is a luxury. Although it is easy to agree that all people need food, clothing, and shelter, it is not easy to agree within a certain range of possibilities which kinds of food, clothing, and shelter are needed and which are extravagant. Since great concentrations of wealth would not exist under a system of economic democracy, luxury markets would likely disappear; and food production and manufacturing would center around the needs of the broad masses of people.

A third feature of the new tax system is the absence of a tax on residential property, as long as it is located within a specified area where public services can be conveniently provided. The boundaries of public service areas, roughly coinciding with the past boundaries of urban centers, can be determined by the public, which decides by voting how to make trade-offs between efficiency in providing services and overcrowding. Residences can be permitted outside the service area, but they are taxed for services provided. Under such a system of incentives, not many people would choose to reside outside of service areas unless they were able to pay property tax on their residences with income generated from productive activity such as farming.

If individuals are not required to pay taxes on income, most consumer purchases, and most residential property, where would tax revenues come from? Generally, the major source of tax revenues should come from the same productive human labor that creates private capital. It is only logical that society as a whole, as well as its private firms, share in the benefits of the wealth produced by its workers. All firms, whether consisting of individuals or groups, will be required to pay a profit tax on net earnings and a volume tax on gross sales. Both taxes are based on a fixed percentage, which is the same for all firms regardless of size or net earnings.

The simple imposition of a volume tax will serve to discourage the concentration of capital in the hands of a few large firms and insure that there is no financial advantage to be gained from bigness per se. Larger firms must show the same per-unit returns to cost as smaller firms in order to operate successfully. As a consequence, conglomerates would likely break up into many smaller firms because subsidiary firms, formerly serving as tax write-offs to improve the profit picture of the parent firm, will add to taxes on gross sales without adding to and perhaps even subtracting from net earnings. The breakup of conglomerates and the subsequent reduced market value of the subsidiaries would create further opportunities for alternative ownership and more efficient management by workers.

Given the structure of the proposed system, the expansion and consolidation of smaller firms—that is, purchasing the assets of another firm within the United States—might still occur, but only in those instances where per-unit returns to cost can be increased in the total operation. Expansion or consolidation in a few instances could prove to be of advantage to firms seeking to increase self-sufficiency by adding a related component enterprise, such as manufacturing spare parts. Expansion or consolidation that places unrelated enterprises under the heading of the same firm, however, would rarely occur, because under the proposed democratic structure it does not enhance self-sufficiency and causes inevitable management problems.

Among the most offensive features of the present tax laws are those that provide strong incentives to invest in other countries. We suggest several changes in this regard. A firm should not be allowed to deduct overseas costs from its net earnings. Any such costs, such as those for assembly of parts using cheap labor, must be paid out of net earnings; and net earnings from foreign investments themselves will be subject to a profits tax in addition to whatever foreign taxes are required. In other words, there should be no foreign tax credits. A lack of tax incentive to invest overseas combined with worker or ownership means that American workers would get most of the benefit from American investment dollars.

The proposed profits tax, which is levied against net income, counts workers' wages as a part of net income. If this tax were based on residual income, discounting workers' wages, all of a company's earnings could be allocated as wages, thus leaving no profits to be taxed. In other words, by including workers' wages in net income, the amount of tax collected does not depend on the amount of workers' wages.

In order to encourage use of company earnings for the collective benefit of workers, we suggest that a percentage of net earnings up to a specified limit be deducted for such humanizing purposes as building recreation facilities, providing on-site day care for infants and small children, establishing first-aid and safety education programs, granting work sabbatical and travel opportunities, encouraging worker education and training, and allowing maternity and paternity leaves and time off for serving in public office.

Now that we have proposed new mechanisms for levying and collecting taxes, we can turn to suggestions for their disbursement. To begin with, each level of government—city (service area), county, state, and federal—should receive its share of the volume tax and the profits tax. To enhance democracy, voters at each level will decide by referenda the exact percentage of tax to be assessed at that level. The percentages on which the taxes are based should be uniformly applied to all firms, the only variation in actual percentage of tax paid being based on deductions for company benefits from the profit tax. Under this system the public prosperity of the city, county, state, and nation would be a direct function of the combined success of its productive firms and of a democratically determined allocation from the private to the public sector. When an optimum degree of free enterprise, as measured against the need for public services, is decided democratically, it is likely that those who now monopolize the private sector will no longer be able to siphon funds away from the public and have their actions concealed by a complicated tax system.

While we suggest that residential property not be taxed, there are sound arguments for taxing business property. A tax on business property ensures that land and buildings are not held and kept out of use at no cost to the owners. Further, paying tax on property that is not generating income is a losing proposition and acts as an incentive for owners to sell the property to others who can use it productively. Within cities or service areas and the surrounding dependent countryside, voters could determine the amount of the tax on local business property and decide how revenues are to be allocated in acquiring property for park space and the construction and renovation of public lands and buildings. Voters at the state and national levels could determine the amount of tax on property used by farming, logging, and mining industries and decide how revenues are to be allocated for purposes similar to those above.

Finally, we come to proposals for protecting the environment through provisions in the structure of taxation. We propose a set of natural-resource taxes. A pollution tax, for example, might be designed to make it unequivocally uneconomical for a business to keep operating while putting harmful pollutants into the land, air, and water. Similarly, a renewable-use tax would make it impossible for a lumber company to cut trees without preventing soil erosion and providing for an equal measure of reforestation. An extraction tax could force mining companies to return mined-out areas to original condition immediately after use. Finally, we suggest a nonrenewable-use tax to be placed on firms that produce and consume such depletable and scarce materials as oil, natural gas, coal, phosphate fertilizers, various metals, etc. Such a tax would make it more economical to rely on renewable energy resources, such as solar, wind, and geothermal power, rather than oil, gas, or coal. It would also make it more economical to recycle metals used in manufacturing automobiles, containers, appliances, etc., than to extract additional raw materials.

Since it is not possible to base natural resource taxes on a simple, uniform percentage for all industries and firms, it does not seem advisable to have voters directly decide the amount of this tax. Instead, representatives could be elected to regulatory agencies at the state and national level to give expert attention to necessary variations in assessments. The members of regulatory agencies should be prohibited from having any involvement—either past, present, or future—with regulated industries. Needless to say, all information concerning the finances of the regulated industries and the effects of natural-resource taxes must be a matter of publc record. Perhaps the revenues collected from natural resource taxes could be used to repair existing environmental damage (such as to "fill up that goddamn hole!" as miner Ramon Vasquéz suggested for Bisbee's huge aboveground pit). Another appropriate use would be to develop improved means of recycling along with more efficient means of using renewable resources.

Fiscal responsibility. The proposed system is one in which individuals are free of burdensome taxes and firms are taxed on the basis of the wealth they produce and their ecological efficiency, without penalizing them for increased productivity. This proposal involves no limits placed on free enterprise, with the exception of democratically determined allocations from the private to the public sector.

Little has been said, however, about the composition of the public sector as opposed to the private sector and what, if any, changes are warranted there.

We have argued earlier that private ownership of productive firms (or, free enterprise) has always been a strongly held ideal in American life. Thus we do not think it realistic or desirable to propose nationalization of all private industry and state control of the economy, at this time. Political dictatorships can produce the same hierarchical structure, with accompanying lack of autonomy and creativity for workers, as economic monopolization presently does. What is proposed here is more, not less, democracy. With a transition to the structures of ownership and taxation described earlier, many smaller firms now engaged in producing goods and services in the private sector would stay there. The most worrisome and destructive aspects of American capitalism would be gone.

However, there are good reasons for chartering banks and insurance companies, both of which handle money and do not produce goods or services, in the public sector. We envision such a program as a critical first step in any attempt to gain democratic control over the flow of capital. Public ownership of banks and insurance companies would mean that funds belonging to the public and handled on behalf of the public are used in the public interest. All banks and insurance companies, regardless of where they are chartered, should be required to lend a certain portion of their funds within the cities, counties, and states where they are located. The practice of "redlining," or refusing to reinvest in poor areas from which investment funds were taken in the first place, is thus largely ruled out. Presidents of publically owned banks and insurance companies could be elected at large and held accountable on the public record for their loan policies. As part and parcel of the transition to economic democracy, many low-interest loans with some risk attached could be made to workers and communities to enable them to purchase existing firms or start new ones. Publicly owned banks would be in a position to allocate more resources to development projects of high public priority, in such areas as agriculture, energy, and transportation.

Bank and insurance-company revenues will likely remain substantial even with the proposed changes. Why not turn the revenues over to government at all levels? The exact proportion allocated to city, county, state, and national programs could be determined by the national electorate in order to keep the allocations uniform for the country as a whole. Conceivably, revenues from the handling of money could be used to reduce reliance upon taxes levied directly against firms and to increase government services, as desired by the people. Eventually, all banks and insurance companies could be made public and most government revenues might be derived from this source. The initial goal, however, is to stimulate the economy by offering favorable terms on loans to increase the number and strength of worker and community-owned firms. Once this phase is completed, higher rates of interest can be obtained, and loans can be made more secure in order to bring an increase in revenues.

It seems to us that, unlike workers in private business, employees of banks and insurance companies must not have the right to be owners. In this case, an allowance for retirement is added to compensate for public employees inability to purchase shares in private businesses. Wages might be tied to an index of personal income, calculated on the basis of average personal income in the city, county, state, or nation for persons of different ages and experience in the private sector.

We think there is a role in such a system for consumer credit unions, which may now serve an expanded role as "consumer banks." A consumer bank might, for example, lend money to consumer cooperatives for the purpose of contracting with developers to build housing projects. Emphasis in loan policy could be placed on renovation of old housing that is structurally sound and located close to public services. The construction of new housing that makes efficient use of space and materials should also be encouraged. In all cases, we propose that consumer banks make loans directly to cooperatives rather than to development firms. The advantage to this procedure is that consumers can more closely control the design of the projects to ensure that their own special needs are met. Consumer banks might be allowed to handle individual savings and checking accounts and small personal loans in addition to home mortgages, but they would not compete with government banks in dealing with private firms. There is, in this proposed system of banking institutions, a clear division function in which publicly owned banks handle the capital of private firms and consumer banks deal with personal income and consumer affairs. Since the proposed consumer banks can make loans only to individuals and consumer cooperatives, there is no question of diverting the personal income intended for the benefit of individuals and consumers into the hands of private firms. The funds of private firms are likewise protected from going into the hands of consumers.

Many obvious roles can be played by cooperatives in a system of economic democracy. Food cooperatives, for example, can negotiate contracts directly with farmers for the purpose of supplying members with inexpensive products at the retail level. We can see them providing cold storage and assuming at least a few processing functions, such as debulking and packaging. Other minor processing functions are feasible as cooperatives grow stronger. Food cooperatives are of advantage not only to consumers, who are able to buy food at inexpensive prices, but also to farmers, who are able to obtain a better price by circumventing costly processors and middlemen. Direct marketing allows small producers to become successful and reinforces the move away from monopolistic control by large farms and food conglomerates. The return of direct marketing, started in the mid-1970s by a few small-scale farmers in California, could fully blossom as a result of the proposals made above. The inequities and disadvantages of scale felt by family farm operators in California suggest that a few more cautions against the resurgence of agribusiness would be necessary. For example, the advantage of receiving lower prices for buying in bulk should be confined to consumer cooperatives and individual consumers. That is, we would make it illegal to discriminate against small producers by giving discounts to large producers for buying supplies in large quantities. In this way, retailers will not be allowed to undersell competitors because they receive discounts on large purchases.

Another area of operation for consumer cooperatives is that of energy for home use. Such cooperatives presently exist in many rural areas; they would be strengthened and given preference in bidding for energy from inexpensive sources. Competition to produce inexpensive energy from solar, wind, and geothermal sources could be encouraged through passage of a new patent law. Under the law that we propose, inventors, whether private firms or individuals, will receive only a modest remuneration based on a percentage, say one to two percent, of the returns from the sale of products that make use of the invention. In addition, there could be an upper limit, adjusted according to the amount of time and money invested in the invention, placed on total rewards. This restriction allows incentive, but at the same time it encourages the use of inventions by those who can benefit from them. The present patent laws encourage the sale of inventions to monopoly capitalists, who hold them off the market. It is to their advantage to behave in this essentially unsocial way because they can limit competition while continuing to invest in technologies that bring greater profits despite being less efficient. We think the development of energy-efficient machinery suitable for the needs of small-scale farmers and small-farm partnerships would proceed at a rapid rate under such a new law.

Consumer cooperatives might also be formed for purposes of providing transportation, clothing, health care, recreation, entertainment, etc. Many already exist throughout the United States at the present time. Since these topics are not as directly related to a basic transition to economic democracy, they will not be discussed here.

In the context of economic democracy, fiscal responsibility means something more than balancing the federal budget so that as little private capital as possible needs to be borrowed by the state and as much private capital as possible can be borrowed by monopoly capitalists. What it means is to allow private firms and individuals the right to have their money handled and used in their interest without being siphoned off clandestinely to increase the profits of monopoly capitalists. It also means that private firms have the right to see their capital used for the benefit of the private economy without being diverted for consumer projects. The decisions made to allocate a certain proportion of company earnings to capital expenditures and a certain proportion to wages have integrity because the distinction between different uses for private capital and personal income are quite consistently upheld by the institutions that handle money. To have banking and insurance money used in accord with social goals and to maintain an equitable separation between producer and consumer sectors is to have fiscal responsibility.

A Strategy for Change

Some features of economic democracy have now been described and interrelated. By refusing to accept an undemocratic economy as immutable, organic reality, we have discovered that the possibilities for constructive social change are many. The features of a truly democratic economy need to be consistent only with each other and not with any features that now exist. Nonetheless, the possibilities are real in the sense that they could exist sometime in the future given an appropriate strategy for change.

Although some precedents for change now exist, such as a state-owned bank in North Dakota, a state-owned insurance company in Wisconsin, and a smattering of worker-owned companies, the move toward economic democracy has not gathered much strength. One way of getting at the problem of how to move more forcefully in this direction is to ask, what now prevents Americans from having a more democratic economy? The answer, which emerges from previous chapters, is that people are handicapped by the dependent roles they are forced to accept as a necessary means of protecting their interests against the abuses of monopoly capitalists. Relationships of dependency exist between workers and owners, between recipients of the social services and the borrowers of private capital, and between consumers and producers. In each instance, monopoly capitalists are expected to redistribute a fair share of the wealth to which people are entitled but do not control. The prerogative of monopoly capitalists to exercise authority over workers, government financial policy, and consumer markets is rarely, if ever, challenged. Concessions that workers, citizens, and consumers receive are the result of stresses that threaten social disruptions or otherwise are in the interests of monopoly capitalists to give; they do not come through a process of democratic decision-making in which everyone participates. People thus have been bought off, and if they act out of line, they are rapped on the knuckles and reminded of their vulnerable status.

If the handicap of dependent status is to be altered, preoccupation with the guarantee of material concessions and the fear of disciplining must be overcome. The restoration of democracy to our political institutions and its extension to our economy require that strong adversarial relationships be cultivated where ones of dependence now exist. In the struggle between adversaries the issue of democratic control over economic and political institutions and the integrity of the communities would be at stake instead of, or perhaps in addition to, a set of material concessions.

Let us stress that the primary prerequisite for a fundamental challenge to capitalist domination of the economy and the state can only be delivered through a progressive and strong working class party. In the United States today, there is no sign of the emergence of such a party; but we believe that it can be expedited by organizational and political activities in the following arenas. First, workers can begin (or continue) making their unions more democratic by requiring their own and others' attendance at and participation in meetings. They can form radical caucuses to challenge business unionism and to promote class conscious leadership in unions. Two immediate demands would be: (1) To equalize or at least reduce the differential in pay among union officials, shop stewards, and workers, and (2) to require that persons in positions of authority within the union rotate back to the rank and file after a limited time in office. After these objectives are accomplished, collective bargaining, strikes, and work stoppages can be used to increase leverage for the right of workers to sit on the board of directors, the right to participate in the decisions of management, and the ultimate right to transfer ownership of the company to the workers, the community, or the public at large.

The critical role that a radical caucus can play within an established union is demonstrated by the work of the Right to Strike Committee within the United Mine Workers in the winter/spring strike of 1977–78. Without the committee the union would not have struck as long as it did, and in all probability it would have lost more at the bargaining table because of a lack of militance exhibited by union leadership. It was the committee that educated, mobilized, and represented the rank and file, both to the coal operators and to the union leadership.

However, these strategies are currently available only to a minority of American workers, for only one-fourth of them are represented by a union. If current trends continue, an even smaller proportion of the American work force will be unionized in the future. Unless unrepresented workers organize together to assert their political and economic rights, their pay, job security, benefits, and other working conditions will be virtually dictated by management.

A second type of action people can pursue is to build strong community and neighborhood organizations, capable of responding to and acting on local needs. Issues such as livability, low-income housing, parks, safer streets, employment opportunities, and the policy options of local government can be advocated by these residents' organizations. Once established, such organizations may acquire the resources to pursue community economic development activities, such as the formation of a community development corporation that can then purchase or build low-income housing and provide employment through its enterprises. Of course, the capacity to move in this direction will be limited by their access to capital.

Third, activists can use the electoral arena for both political education and progressive reform. Unfortunately, the party system in the United States is not like that in Europe or Canada, where coalitions, of necessity, are made on the basis of both philosophical principles and pragmatic concerns, rather than expediency, power brokering, and ideological homogeneity. The European media, especially newspapers, reflect ideological diversity, which derives from a much wider spectrum of political parties.

Studies have shown that the average European citizen is better informed than the average American on both domestic and international issues and more receptive to socialist alternatives as well. (*Wilamette Valley Observer*, 9 February 1979 : 11). Although lack of diversity in the U.S. electoral arena has not made it very attractive to activists, we still feel that it has untapped possibilities.

In America, political education and progressive reforms can be accomplished through ballot initiatives, support of progressive candidates, reform legislation, single-issue lobbying, and political action committees. One key strategy in the electoral arena should be the use of the ballot initiative to transform the appointed agencies of the state into elected bodies. As we have pointed out earlier, the actual work of the state is carried out in appointed bodies and bureaucracies over which people have no control. The state is defined here as the military, judiciary, appointive agencies, and government bureaucracies. As distinguished from the state, the government is comprised of elected officials in the legislative and executive branches. If democratization of appointed bodies, bureaucracies and official positions of the state is combined with the demands of grassroots political organizations for accountability of government officials to their constituencies, we can bring about a decline in the influence of monied special interests.

Initiatives also can be used to place a moratorium on nuclear power plant construction, form Peoples' Utility Districts (PUDs), require stringent land use planning, change tax laws in the directions suggested earlier, and provide funding for alternative transportation systems. Another potentially important ballot initiative is one that allows for a "no" vote in elections, in lieu of voting for unacceptable candidates. Unfortunately, we have learned that such initiative and referendum action can also be abused by capitalists; for example, witness California's Measure 13, which limits property taxes for apartment owners and real-estate interests under the guise of popular tax reform.

Support of progressive candidates for political office is another important avenue of change through reform. With such leadership, legislation dealing with early-warning systems for plant closures, and job preservation and community stabilization measures, etc., can be passed. Some states (such as Ohio) and local jurisdictions are already enacting legislation requiring large employers to give advance notice to local and state governments that they are closing down or leaving the area. In some cases, such firms are charged a special tax to obtain funds to offset the social costs of economic disruption. Another progressive measure passed by Congress in 1977 is the Community Re-investment Act, antiredlining legislation that provides leverage for community groups over FDIC-regulated lending institutions to force the extension of credit to low and moderate income people, housing cooperatives, and home rehabilitation programs. It also provides for bilingual loan officers and budget counseling. The potential impact of such programs should not be underestimated, for they directly constrain the movement and flight of capital.

Two immediate issues that also might be affected by political action concern the enforcement of land reclamation laws and reordering of economic incentives for farmers to reward energy-efficient productivity and environmental stewardship. Such changes would not only encourage many part-time farmers to increase their effort in farming but also would lead to the establishment of more small farms by persons with limited capital. A resurgence of small business and industry in rural areas would naturally follow from an increase in the number of small-scale farmers.[1]

Fourth, support of environmental, public interest, and peace and justice movements is pivotal in curbing the domination by monopoly capitalists. Such support can be provided by participation in civil disobedience, lawsuits, mass demonstrations and protests, public education campaigns, and fund-raising efforts. There are many recent examples of success in such efforts. For instance, nuclear-power plant building has been hindered, the draft stopped, U.S. troops withdrawn from Vietnam, and food products successfully boycotted (such as Gallo wines, table grapes, and J.P. Stevens and Nestlé products), all through direct citizen activism and protest.

Finally, support for, participation in, and promotion of consumer and producer cooperatives is important in developing a cooperative spirit and a measure of self-sufficiency. Experience in cooperatives can provide good education in democratic decision-making and social responsibility. Widespread participation in locally owned and controlled cooperatives can also withhold demand from the products of large corporations, with adverse effects for monopoly capitalists.

In sum, power can be exercised by workers as union or radical caucus members; by citizens as activists, as voters protesting through the electoral process, and as members of strong neighborhood and community organizations; and by consumers through collective action and support of cooperatives.

The strategy for change as outlined here is not meant to be an end in itself. Adversary relationships are necessary primarily as a means of promoting democracy and providing people with experience in the exercise of power. In a system where economic democracy already exists adversary relationships will tend to disappear because decisions are made democratically. This, of course, does not mean that issues will not be hotly debated, or that everyone will be completely happy with every decision that is made. Controversy will exist just as it does now. The difference will be in the fact that people are satisfied with their degree of participation, with the clarity of alternatives presented to them, and with the integrity maintained in carrying out decisions that cannot be undermined by the behind-the-scenes manipulation of monopoly capitalists.

The economic obsolescence of workers and small producers in America has been accompanied by the dramatic weakening of democracy. Our fate has been allowed to fall into the hands of irresponsible capitalist monopolies that not only act as social dinosaurs in abusing our biological environment but also deny many workers and small producers the right to be productive and earn a living. As we are led further in this direction and the hardships become more apparent, the nature of the problem will be better understood. There is hope if increased awareness gives us the vision and the will to change. Our work and study over the last several years give us every reason to have that hope.

Notes

1. The term "economic democracy" was made popular in Tom Hayden's 1976 U.S. Senate race from California. The term has been used fairly widely since then to refer to ownership and management by workers. Here it is used broadly to refer to reforms not only in the work place but also in democratic control of the state, the tax structure, and banking system.

2. A 1977 study at the University of California, Berkeley, entitled *Economic Effects of Excess Land Sales in the Westland Water District*, indicates that a considerable amount of economic activity could occur spontaneously as a result of a shift toward farming on a smaller scale.

Appendix: Summary of Sampling

Location	Description of Sample	Number in Sample	Incomplete Cases Not Included in Total Number	Percent of Response[a] Rate	Sample Selection	Type of Interview
Oregon	1) Workers laid off from three mills	70	2	NA[b]	Stratified	Direct questionnaire
	2) Currently unemployed mill workers	12	0	NA	Stratified	Open ended; multiple visits
Arizona	3) Miners registering as unemployed	629	8	100	Total	Employment Office Forms; attached questionnaire
	4) Currently unemployed miners	12	0	NA	Stratified	Open ended; multiple visits
Hawaii	5) Adult Filipinos in Maunaloa community	144	2	73	Total	Direct questionnaire
	6) Former pineapple workers	37	0	NA	Stratified	Open ended; multiple visits
	7) Pineapple workers returned to the Philippines	6	0	38	Total	Open ended
California	8) Small farm operators in Colusa County	39	0	NA	Stratified	Direct questionnaire, open ended
	9) 16.5 percent sample of owners of agricultural land in Colusa County	138	0	30	Random	Mail survey
Washington	10) Local shopkeepers in Lincoln County	43	0	44	Total	Direct questionnaire, open ended
	11) Follow-up on same shopkeepers in Lincoln County	39	0	91	Total	Open ended
	12) Former shopkeepers no longer living in Lincoln County	6	0	NA	Stratified	Open ended

[a] Explanations of response rates and sampling bias are included in the chapters.
[b] Not applicable.

Bibliography

Chapter 1

Barnet, Richard J., and Ronald E. Müller. 1974 *Global Reach: The Power of Multinational Corporations*. New York: Simon and Schuster.

Braverman, Harry. 1974. *Labor and Monopoly Capital*. New York: Monthly Review Press.

Caudill, Harry. 1963. *Night Comes to the Cumberlands*. Boston: Little, Brown.

Frundt, Henry John. 1975. *American Agribusiness and U.S. Foreign Agricultural Policy*. Ph.D. Dissertation, Rutgers University.

Gordon, David M. 1972. *Theories of Poverty and Underemployment*. Lexington, Mass.: D. C. Heath.

Henry, Jules. 1963. *Culture Against Man*. New York: Random House.

Kahn, Kathy. 1973. *Hillbilly Women*. New York: Doubleday.

Kapp, William K. 1971. *The Social Costs of Private Enterprise*. New York: Schocken Books.

Katz, David M. 1978. "Finance Capital and Corporate Control," in *The Capitalist System: A Radical Analysis of American Society*, 2d ed., Richard C. Edwards, Michael Reich, and Thomas E. Weisskopf, eds. Englewood Cliffs, N.J.: Prentice Hall. Pp. 147–58.

Mandel, Ernest. 1976. "Capitalism and Regional Disparities," in *Southwest Economy and Society* 1:41–47.

O'Connor, James. 1973. *The Fiscal Crisis of the State*. New York: St. Martin's Press.

————1976. "Theories of Productive and Unproductive Labor." *Politics and Society*. (Spring).

Padfield, Harland, I. (In press) "The Expendable Rural Community and the Denial of Powerlessness," in *The Dying Community*, Arthur Gallaher, Jr., and Harland I. Padfield, eds. Albuquerque: University of New Mexico Press.

————, and John A. Young. 1977. "Institutional Processing of Human Resources: A Theory of Social Marginalization," in *Rural Poverty and the Policy Crisis*, Robert O. Coppedge and Carlton G. Davis, eds, Ames, Ia.: Iowa State University Press, Pp. 129–48.

Sennett, Richard, and Jonathan Cobb. 1972. *The Hidden Injuries of Class*. New York: Random House.

Skolnick, Jerome H., and Elliott Currie. 1976. *Crisis in American Institutions*, 3d ed. Boston: Little, Brown.

Young, John A., and Joe B. Stevens. 1978. "Job Rationing, Human Capital and Normative Behavior: An Example from Oregon's Wood Products Industry." *Human Organization* 37:1:29–37. (Spring).

Chapter 2

Boas, Ralph P. 1971. "The Loyal Legion of Loggers and Lumbermen," *Atlantic Monthly*, p. 226. (February).

Bureau of Business Research. Oregon Economic Statistics. 1977. Eugene: University of Oregon.

Bureau of Corporations, U.S. Department of Commerce and Labor. 1913. *The Lumber Industry*, part 1, Washington, D.C.

Business Executives' Research Committee. 1954. "The Forest Products Industry of Oregon." A Report, sponsored by Lewis and Clark College and Reed College, Portland, Oregon.

Fuqua, Gary L. 1966. "The Oregon Forest Products Industry." Oregon Department of Commerce, Division of Planning and Development.

Gedney, D. R., D. D. Oswald, and R. D. Fight. 1975. *Two Projections of Timber Supply in the Pacific Coast States*. Resource Bulletin PNW–60, Pacific Northwest Forest and Range Experiment Station, U.S. Forest Service.

Holbrook, Steward H. 1961. *Yankee Loggers: A Recollection of Woodsmen, Cooks and River Drivers*, New York: International Paper Company.

Kornbluh, Joyce L. 1964. *Rebel Voices: An I.W.W. Anthology*. Ann Arbor: The University of Michigan Press.

LeMaster, Dennis C. 1977. "Mergers Among the Largest Forest Products Firms, 1950–1970." Washington State University, College of Agriculture Research. (August).

Lembcke, Jerry. 1976. "Capital and Labor in the Pacific Northwest Forest Products Industry." *Humboldt J. of Soc. Rel.* 3:2:8–16 ff. (Spring/Summer).

Mbogho, Archie W. 1965. "Sawmilling in Lane County, Oregon: A Geographical Examination of its Development." Master's thesis, University of Oregon.

Mead, Walter J. 1966. *Competition and Oligopsony in the Douglas Fir Lumber Industry*. Los Angeles: University of California Press.

Meany, Edmond S. 1935. "The History of the Lumber Industry in the Northwest to 1917." Ph. D. dissertation, Harvard University.

Pacific Northwest Research Center, Northwest Bulletin, Nos. 3, 8, 9, 10. 1976. Eugene: P.O. Box 3708.

Scott, Ralph D. 1973. "Technological Change in the British Columbia Forest Products Industry," in *People, Productivity and Technological Change*. Proceedings of the 1973 Conference of the Industrial Relations Management Association of British Columbia, February, 1973, W. T. Stanbury and Mark Thompson, eds. Versatile Publications.

Sherman, Dorothy M. 1934. "A Brief History of the Lumber Industry in the Fir Belt of Oregon." Master's thesis, University of Oregon.

Stevens, Joe B. 1976. "The Oregon Wood Products Labor Force: Job Rationing and Worker Adaptations in a Declining Industry." A Report to the U.S. Forest Service.

Tyler, Robert L. 1967. *Rebels of the Woods: The I.W.W. in the Pacific Northwest*. Eugene: University of Oregon Books.

Wall, Brian W. 1973. *Employment Implications of Projected Timber Output in the Douglas-Fir Region, 1970–2000*. Research Note PNW–211, Pacific Northwest Forest and Range Experiment Station, U.S. Forest Service.

Wyant, Dan. 1977. "Lumberman Warns of New 'Set-Asides.' " *Eugene Register-Guard* 23 January, Pps. 1A, 3A.

Young, John A., and Joe B. Stevens. 1978. "Job Rationing, Human Capital and Normative Behavior: An example from Oregon's Wood Products Industry." *Human Organization* 37:1:29-37 (Spring).

Chapter 3

Ayer, Harry, Edwin Carpenter, Dana Deeds, and William Martin. 1975. "The Beginnings of Social Marginalization: An Arizona Example." WRDC Discussion Paper No. 6. (May).

Chaplin, Ralph. 1948. *Wobbly: The Rough and Tumble Story of an American Radical*. Chicago: The Unitersity of Chicago Press. 435 pp.

————, and Bruce LeRoy. 1968. "Why I Wrote Solidarity Forever." *The American West* 5:1 (January), 18–27 ff.

Conlin, Joseph R. 1970. "The Case of the Very-American Militants." *The American West* 3:2 (March), 4–10 ff.

Gedicks, Al. 1973. *Kennecott Copper Corporation and Mining Development in Wisconsin*. Madison, Wis.: Community Action on Latin America.

Kornbluh, Joyce L. 1964. *Rebel Voices: An I.W.W Anthology*. Ann Arbor: The University of Michigan Press. 419 pp.

Martin, William, Dana Deeds, Edwin Carpenter, Harry Ayer, Louise Arthur, and Russell Gum. 1976. "Reduction in Force in a Single Company Town: Who is Selected and How do they Adapt?." WRDC Discussion Paper No. 8. (April).

Mayhall, Pamela D. 1972. "Bisbee's Response to Civil Disorder: A Matter of Circumstances." 9:3 (May), *The American West* 22–31.

Reinmuth, James. 1974. *Applied Regression and Discriminant Analysis*. Eugene. College of Business, University of Oregon.

Renshaw, Patrick. 1967. *The Wobblies*. New York: Doubleday. 312 pp.

Chapter 4

Anderson, Robert N. 1973. Blaine Bradshaw, and W. G. Marders. "Molokai: Present and Future." Departmental Paper 17, Hawaii Agricultural Experiment Station, College of Tropical Agriculture, University of Hawaii. (November).
————, and Rebecca Y. Pestano. 1974. "Some Observations on the Socio-economic Impacts of Industrial Withdrawal from a Rural Community." WRDC Discussion Paper No. 2, Oregon State University, Corvallis. (November).
Baxa, Artemio C. 1973. *A Report on Filipino Immigration and Social Challenges in Maui County.* Pacific Urban Studies and Planning Program of the University of Hawaii. (15 March).
Choy, Brian J. J. 1973. *The Future of Plantation Communities in Hawaii: Kahuku Town, Oahu.* M. A. thesis, University of Hawaii. (August).
Clifford, Sister Mary Dorita. 1967. "The Hawaiian Sugar Planter Association and Filipino Exclusion", in Josefa Saniel, ed., *The Filipino Exclusion Movement: 1927–1935.* Quezan City. University of the Philippines, Institute of Asian Studies, Pp. 11–29.
Gray, Francine du Plessix. 1972. *Hawaii: The Sugar-Coated Fortress.* New York. Random House.
Eggan, Fred. "Philippine Social Structure." Transcript of a series of lectures presented to the first group of Peace Corps Volunteers for the Philippines at Pennsylvania State University. No date, probably about 1961. 48 pp.
Elder, Nell B. 1956. *Pineapple in Hawaii.* Department of Public Instruction, Territory of Hawaii.
Forman, Sheila. 1976. *The Social-Psychological Context of Planning in Response to Industrial Withdrawal: A Case Study of Filipino Plantation Town in Hawaii.* Ph.D dissertation, University of Hawaii, Honolulu. (December).
Garside, Jayne G. 1972. "Kahuku in Transition—the Plight of the Filipino." Unpublished paper, Church College of Hawaii, Laie.
Lasker, Bruno. 1931. *Filipino Immigration.* Chicago: The University of Chicago Press.
Lind, Andrew W. 1969. *Hawaii: The Last of the Magic Isles.* Published for the Institute of Race Relations, London. New York: Oxford University Press.
Mintz, Sidney W. 1953–54. "The Folk-Urban Continuum and the Rural Proletarian Community." *Amer. J. of Soc.* 59:136–143.
Moncado, Hilario Camino. n.d. *America, the Philippines and the Orient.* New York: Fleming H. Revell.
Norbeck, Edward. 1959. *Pineapple Town.* Berkeley: University of California Press.
Peterson, John M. 1970. "Technology and Community in Two Plantation Environments," in Henry T. Lewis, ed., *Molokai Studies.* Honolulu: University of Hawaii.
Thompson, David. 1942. "The Filipino Federation of America, Incorporated: A Study in the Natural History of a Social Institution." Unpublished paper, University of Hawaii.
White, Henry A. 1957. *James B. Dole, Industrial Pioneer of the Pacific; Founder of Hawaii's Pineapple Industry.* New York: Newcomer Society.
Wright, Theon. 1972. *The Disenchanged Isles: The Story of the Second Revolution in Hawaii.* New York: The Dial Press.

Chapter 5

Breimeyer, Harold F. 1965. *Individual Freedom and the Economic Organization of Agriculture.* Urbana: University of Illinois Press.
Burlingame, Burt B., Philip S. Parsons, and A. Doyle Reed. 1972. "Technology and Scale." Agricultural Extension, University of California, Major Economic Issues, Publication MA 36–4. (February).
Fellmeth, Robert C. 1973. *Politics of Land: Ralph Nader's Study Group Report on Land Use in California.* New York: Grossman Publishers.
Ford, Arthur M. 1973. *Political Economics of Rural Poverty in the South.* Cambridge, Mass.: Ballinger.
Fujimoto, Isao, and Martin Zone. 1976. "Sources of Inequities in Rural America: Implications for Rural Community Development and Research." Community Development Research Series, Department of Applied Behavioral Sciences, University of California, Davis.

Green, Sheldon R. 1976. "Corporate Accountability and the Family Farm," in Richard Merrill, ed., *Radical Agriculture*. San Francisco: Harper and Row.

Hightower, Jim. 1972. *Hard Tomatoes, Hard Times*. Agribusiness Accountability Project, Washington, D. C.

———. 1975. *Eat Your Heart Out: How Food Profiteers Victimize the Consumer*. New York: Random House.

Goldschmidt, Walter. 1978. *As You Sow: Three Studies in the Social Consequences of Agribusiness*. Montclair: N.J.: Allanheld, Osmun.

Kravitz, Linda. 1974. *Who's Minding the Co-op? A Report on Farmer Control of Farmer Cooperatives*. Agribusiness Accountability Project, Washington, D.C.

London, Joan, and Henry Anderson. 1970. *So Shall Ye Reap: The Story of Cesar Chavez and the Farm Workers Movement*. New York: Thomas Y. Crowell.

Madden, J. Patrick. 1973. "Economies of Size in Farming; Theory, Analytical Procedures, and a Review of Selected Studies." Agricultural Economic Report No. 107, Economic Research Service, U.S. Department of Agriculture. (January).

McGowan, Joseph A. 1961. *History of the Sacramento Valley*. Vol. 1. New York: Lewis Historical Publishing.

———. 1961. *History of the Sacramento Valley*. Vol. 2. New York: Lewis Historical Publishing.

Moles, Jerry A. 1976. "Who Tills the Soil? Mexican-American Farm Workers Replace the Small Farmer in California: An Example from Colusa County." Western Rural Development Center Discussion Paper No. 7. (March).

Moles, Jerry A., Jeanette L. Blomberg, Thomas F. Love, and Judith A. Thompson. 1975. "Family Operated Farms in Colusa County, California: A Preliminary Research Report." Western Rural Development Center Discussion Paper No. 5. (April).

Nikolitch, Radoji. 1969. "Family-Operated Farms: Their Compatibility with Technological Advance." *Amer. J. of Agr. Ec.* 51:530–45.

Perelman, Michael, 1976. "Efficiency in Agriculture; the Economics of Energy," in Richard Merrill, ed., *Radical Agriculture*, San Francisco: Harper and Row.

Perelman, Michael. 1977. *Farming for Profit in a Hungry World: Capital and The Crisis in Agriculture*. Montclair: N.J.: Allanheld, Osmun.

Raup, Philip. 1971 and 1972. "Some Issues Raised by the Expansion of Corporate Farming." Statement before the Subcommittee on Monopoly of the Select Committee on Small Business, United States Senate, Ninety-second Congress, in *Role of Giant Corporations*, Part 3A, 23 November and 1 December 1971; 1 and 2 March 1972.

Raup, Philip M. 1973. "Corporate Farming in the United States," *J. of Ec. Hist.* 33:1:274–90. (March).

Reed, A. Doyle and L. A. Horel. 1975. "An Analysis of Almond Production Costs in California." Davis, University of California Agricultural Extension Service, Publication 75-LE 12231.

Sosnick, Stephen H. 1973. "Agricultural Labor in California." Unpublished Paper, Department of Agricultural Economics, University of California, Davis. (August).

The Family Farm in California. 1977. Report of the Small Farm Viability Project, Submitted to the State of California, November 1977. Available through the Employment Development Department, Sacramento.

Thompson, Judith. 1975. "The Contribution of Women to Small Farm Operations." Unpublished Paper, Department of Anthropology, University of California, Davis.

Zwerdling, Daniel. 1976. "The Food Monopolies," in Jerome H. Skolnick, and Elliot Cavie, eds., *Crisis in American Institutions*. Boston: Little Brown. Pp. 43–50. (Reprinted from *The Progressive*, 1974).

Chapter 6

Barkley, Paul W., and Joanne Buteau. 1974. "The Economics of Rural Businessmen; A Case Study in Lincoln County, Washington." Western Rural Development Center Discussion Paper No. 3, Oregon State University, Corvallis. November.

Braverman, Harry. 1974. *Labor and Monopoly Capital*. New York: Monthly Review Press.

1970 Census Data Book. 1972. State of Washington Volume 1: Population and Housing Characteristics, Office of Program Planning and Fiscal Management. (March).

"Davenport, Washington, A Standard Community Industrial Survey." Washington State Department of Commerce and Economic Development. (September 1975).

Goldschmidt, Walter R. 1946. *Small Business and the Community: A Study in Central Valley of California on Effects of Scale of Farm Operations*. Report of the Special Committee to Study Problems of American Small business, United States Senate, Seventy-ninth Congress, 23 December 1946. Reprinted in Goldschmidt, *As You Sow: Three Studies in the Social Consequences of Agribusiness*. Montclair, N.J.: Allanheld, Osmun, 1977.

"History of Lincoln County," in *An Illustrated History of the Big Bend Country, Embracing Lincoln, Douglas, Adams and Franklin Counties, State of Washington*. 1904. Spokane: Western Historical Publishing. Pp. 65–214.

Yoder, Fred R. 1942. "Pioneer Social Adaptation in Lincoln County, Washington, 1875–90," in *Research Studies of the State College of Washington* 10:3:179–97. (September).

Yoder, Fred R. 1941. "Status and Trends of the Rural Church in Lincoln County," in *Research Studies of the State College of Washington* 9:2:83–99. (June).

Chapter 7

Barnes, Peter, ed. 1975. *The People's Land: A Reader on Land Reform in the United States*. Emmaus, Pa.: Rodale Press.

Belden, Joe, and Gregg Forte. 1976. *Toward a National Food Policy*. Exploratory Project for Economic Alternatives, Washington, D.C.

Bernstein, Paul. 1977. "Worker-Owned Plywood Firms Steadily Outperform Industry." *World of Work Report* 2:5:55–57. (May).

———. 1974. "Run Your Own Business, Worker-Owned Firms." *Working Papers for a New Society* 2:2:24–34. (Summer).

Callenbach, Ernest. 1975. *Ecotopia*. Berkeley: Banyan Tree Books.

Clark, Olivia, Jerry Lembcke, and Bob Marotto, Jr. 1978. "Essays on the Social Relations of Work and Labor," A special issue of the *Insurgent Sociologist* 8:2 & 3. (Fall).

Dickson, David. 1974. *The Politics of Alternative Technology*. New York: Universe Books.

Dollars and Sense. 1978. "Asbestos Mine Gets New Management." Pp. 6–8. (May-June).

Edwards, Richard C., Michael Reich, and Thomas E. Weisskopf. 1978. *The Capitalist System: A Radical Analysis of American Society*. 2d ed. Englewood Cliffs: N.J.: Prentice-Hall.

The Family Farm in California. 1977. Report of the Small Farm Viability Project, Submitted to the State of California, November 1977, Available through the Employment Development Department, Sacramento.

Jenkins, David. 1973. *Job Power: Blue and White Collar Democracy*. Garden City, N.Y.: Doubleday.

Lappé, Frances Moore, and Joseph Collins. 1977. *Food First: Beyond the Myth of Scarcity*. Boston: Houghton Mifflin.

Le Guin, Ursula K. 1974. *The Dispossessed*. New York: Avon Books.

Lembcke, Jerry. 1977 "Workplace Democracy: A Canadian Experiment." *The Progressive*, pp. 29–32. (July).

Lenin, V. I. 1974. *State and Revolution*. New York: International Publishers.

Merrill, Richard, ed. 1976. *Radical Agriculture*. New York: Harper and Row.

Pacific Northwest Research Center. 1978. *Report on Timber*, Eugene, Oregon.

Rifkin, Jeremy, and Randy Barber. 1978. *The North Will Rise Again*, Boston: Beacon Press.

Roberts, Dick. 1975. *Capitalism in Crisis*. New York: Pathfinder Press.

Schaaf, Michael. 1977. *Cooperatives at the Crossroads: The Potential for a Major New Economic and Social Role*. Exploratory Project for Economic Alternatives, Washington, D.C.

Schumacher, E. F. 1973. *Small is Beautiful: Economics as if People Mattered*. New York: Harper and Row.

Working Papers for a New Society. Journal focussing on experiments in workplace democracy, worker ownership, and community organizing (all issues).

Zwerdling, Daniel. 1978. *Democracy at Work: A Guide to Workplace Ownership, Participation and Self-Management Experiments in the United States and Europe*. Available from Association for Self-Management, 1414 Spring Road, N.W., Washington, D.C. 20010.

Taken together, the following bibliographies represent a near-exhaustive list of all available materials on plant closures, worker and community ownership in America and elsewhere, and cooperatives:

Behn, Bill. "Resources on Employee and Community Ownership: U.S., Canada, and Great Britain." June 1978. 9 pp. "Resources" include articles, journals, organizations, individuals, books, and films. Available from Bill Behn, Center for Economic Studies, 457 Kingsley Avenue, Palo Alto, California 94301.
———. "Bibliography on Plant Closures." July 1976, 4 pp. Available from Bill Behn, Center for Economic Studies, 457 Kingsley Avenue, Palo Alto, California 94301.
Schenkel, Walter. "A Selective Bibliography and Guide on Producer Democracy." October 1977. 17 pp. Available from Walter Schenkel, 2526–½ 37th Street, Sacramento, California 95817.

Index

ABOUT THE AUTHORS

Dr. Young is an assistant professor in the Department of Anthropology and a research associate in the Agricultural Experiment Station at Oregon State University. He received his BA at Macalester, master's degrees from Stanford and the University of Hawaii, and his PhD at Stanford. He has also taught at San Diego State University, done field work in Hong Kong, and was a research associate at the Western Rural Development Center at Oregon State. His articles have appeared in *Human Organization, Reviews in Anthropology, The Western Canadian Journal of Anthropology, Anthropology Newsletter,* and the *Journal of Research and Development in Education.*

Dr. Newton's B.S. from Oregon State University and M.S. from the University of Oregon were followed by a PhD from the University of Oregon in economics, with a doctoral field in political sociology. She was a post-doctoral fellow at Stanford University, has taught at the University of Oregon and Oregon State, directed several research projects, and contributed to *Economic Inquiry, Human Organization* and *Insurgent Sociologist.* Her current research is on the timber industry's use of insecticides in Oregon's forests; her work as an economic analyst and in political organizing contributed first-hand knowledge of the strategies and tactics the authors suggest in this book.